British Caribbean Veterans
Serving Queen and Country

This book recognises and celebrates the contribution made by Caribbean men and women to the Armed Forces and therefore to the Crown and to the country. While it gives some historical and other context, it focuses especially on the stories of 30 plus men and women who served in the United Kingdom after the 1960s.

These brave men and women were either born in the Caribbean, coming from several different Islands, or were born in the UK to Caribbean parents. They are British and are proud of the service they have provided to their country, the United Kingdom.

They are representative of several thousands more people like them who continued proudly, to join up and enter the Army, Royal Navy and the Royal Air Force. They did what was demanded of them in whichever arena here or abroad, on behalf of the Queen and the country.

More of these British Caribbeans are currently in the Armed Forces giving their service to the King and the country.

British Caribbean Veterans

Serving Queen and Country

Rose Johnson

Remb Voices

© First published in the United Kingdom, 2023 by Remb Voices
All rights reserved
© Rose Johnson 2023

The right of Rose Johnson to be identified as the author of this work has been asserted in accordance with Section 77 of the
Copyright, Designs and Patents Act 1988.
No part of this book may be reproduced in any form or by any means, electronic or mechanical, including photocopying, recording, or any information storage retrieval system nor be otherwise circulated in any form of binding or cover other than that in which it is published and without a similar condition being imposed on the subsequent purchaser without prior permission from the author or editor.

ISBN - 978-1-8381841-8-6

The views expressed in these life stories are those of 32 brave British Caribbean men and women in conversations and family reports, authentically represented. They sit alongside information about the service of pioneering Caribbean veterans who went before them over hundreds of years and of general information about the three main branches of the British Armed Forces.

A catalogue record is available for this book is available from the British Library.
ISBN (PB) 9781838184186
ISBN (HB) 9781838184179
ISBN (9781838184193)

Acknowledgements

I would like to thank my husband Ken for his never ending encouragement and support. Thanks too to my sister-in-law Juliet for her unerring attention to detail, to Clive Malcolm for his patience and advice and to Derek Haldek whose design ideas are always welcome.

Particular thanks go to Gill Shaw (https://www.gillshaw.co.uk) for her photographic brilliance and generosity with respect to the front cover and some of the photographs, to Andrew Reid a Caribbean entrepreneur and to my son Gareth from Standalone Productions. Without their support and sponsorship, it would have been a greater challenge to get this book into print. I am privileged to know that they understand the partnership it needs to allow me as a self-published author, to share widely, the experiences of these British Caribbeans.

Massive and deep felt appreciation to my 'Platoon' of British Caribbean Veterans from the Army, Royal Navy and Royal Air Force, whose openness and honesty in the sharing of their stories were humbling and often emotionally difficult to hear. You had even more to share, but hopefully, these summaries represent you as well as possible. You have left me so thankful that you contributed all that you have in service to us.

To all of the other British Caribbean men and women who served in the British Armed Forces, whether in the past or are serving currently. I want to show gratitude for what you have done on behalf of all of us, under the banner of whichever branch of the Armed Services you have served. I recognise some of the real challenges you have faced in carving out a career for yourselves, navigating within and around racist or other *'Banter'*, setbacks and *'Push downs'* to achieve promotion and continue to *'get the job done'*. I salute you for your resilience and persistence.

There are more stories out there. The pioneering Elders of the Caribbean community are reducing in number each year. I hope we get the opportunity to hear more of their voices before it is too late.

We are more than a few jewelled pebbles
in the Caribbean Sea.
We are the pulsing history of hearts, minds
and mouths, full of beautiful words.

For my sons, Gareth, Justin and Huw and my grandsons, Kyle, Nathan, Reuben and Dylan, all of whom have given me much joy. They are the next generation of young men who can carry these and other stories of their heritage forward - and share them so they are not forgotten. It is not a burden. It is a gift of a rich and powerful history, well worth carrying.

Contents

Preface

1.	A History of Service	3
	Caribbean Unity	3
	Serving Britain	4
	History of Caribbean Service to the UK and its Colonies	6
	The British West India Regiment	6
2.	Caribbeans Serving in WWI	10
	Clifford Alfred Anthony Gulley	10
	Cyril Lionel Robert James	11
	Marcus Bailey	11
	Walter Tull	11
	Herbert Morris	11
3.	Caribbeans Serving in WWII	14
	Philip Ulric Cross	15
	Cyril Ewart Lionel Grant	15
	Norma Best	15
	Arthur Wint	16
	Prince Albert Jacob (aka "Jake")	16
	Ena Collymore-Woodstock	17
	Peter Brown	18
4.	Caribbean Veterans in the Present Day	20
	Squadron WO Winston A Alleyne	22
5.	Organisations Providing Support to Caribbean Veterans	24
	Caribbean Recruits to the British Armed Forces 1960-1990	24
	Options for Change	28
	The British Armed Forces	29
6.	A View of the Armed Forces Now	30
	Percentage of Armed Forces' Officers from Ethnic Minorities (Not including white minorities) by Service Over Time	31
	Number of Veterans in the UK as of February 2023	31
7.	The Army	32

Recruitment to the Army		33
Basic Training		34
Army Sports		35
Other Sporting Activities		36
Team Building in the Army		36
Rest and Recuperation in the Army		37
Meeting Others Like Us!		39
Promotions up the Ranks		39
Colonel Andy Allen MBE		41
Achieving the Queen's Commission and NCO Ranks		48
The Royal Army Medical Corps		49
Lieutenant Colonel Patricia Gibson, MBE		51
Captain Wayne Douglas		62
Lieutenant Colonel Michael Lawrence		70
Regimental Sergeant Major Owen Bernard JP		83
Regimental Sergeant Major Roger Dussard		91
Many More Years of Service		103
Staff Sergeant Burthlan (BJ) Webb		104
Staff Sergeant Elaine Osborne		114
Gunner Frank Beswick		119
Lance Corporal Sandra Martin		126
Lance Corporal Sydney Marshall		131
Corporal Lincoln Beswick, MBE		137
Corporal Donovan Bascombe		149
Corporal John Mortley		155
Lance Corporal Ray Petrie		160
Corporal Zac Robinson		169
Corporal Margery Fraser		176
8.	The Royal Navy	183
	Rest and Recuperation in the Royal Navy	185
	Sport in the Royal Navy	186
	Able Seaman Wayne Green	187

	Team Building in the Royal Navy	193
	Basic Training in the Royal Navy	193
	Recruitment in the Royal Navy	194
	Promotion up the Naval Ranks	194
	Women Serving in the Royal Navy	196
	Writer Logistician Nicole Atwell-Mansingh	197
	Caribbean Royal Navy Veterans	202
	Lieutenant Commander Lionel Winston, MBE	203
	Chief Petty Officer Fred Coke	214
9.	The Royal Air Force	218
	Rest and Recuperation in the RAF	220
	Sport in the RAF	221
	Sergeant Roy Hunte (The Healer)	222
	Team Building in the RAF	232
	Basic Training in the RAF	232
	Flight Lieutenant Wayne Howell	235
	Warrant Officer Donal Campbell	245
	Corporal Keith Crichlow	254
	Sergeant Malcolm Smith	261
	Sergeant Noel Brathwaite	269
	Senior Aircraftman Tony Brown	279
	Promotion of Women in the RAF	288
10.	Conflicts, Peacekeeping and Armed Support	289
	Northern Ireland "Troubles"	289
	The Falklands War	290
	Other Conflicts and Peacekeeping Activities	290
11.	Tours of Germany	293
12.	Some Key Regiments where British Caribbeans Served	294

	Lance Corporal Annette Erskine (nee Johns)	295
13.	Promotions Across the Armed Forces	300
14.	Medals and Awards	302
15.	Family Support in the Armed Forces	304
16.	Arrangements for Transition to Civilian Life Pension Arrangements	305 305
17.	The Armed Forces Covenant	306
18.	Post Traumatic Stress Disorder (PTSD)	309
19.	Charities Supporting Veterans	310
	Homelessness Amongst Veterans	312
20.	Current Recruitment of Caribbeans to the Armed Forces	313
	Sergeant Nicollette Skyers Corporal Nekesha Thompson	315 319
21.	The Term 'West Indian'	329
	The Term 'Windrush Generation'	329
22.	Ongoing Risks for Caribbean Veterans	331
	Serving in the British Armed Forces and Application for British Citizenship	331
23.	Recognition and Honouring	332
	About the Author	335

PREFACE

I am committed to collecting stories of the lives and contributions to Britain, of people from the Caribbean. So many of the pioneers who travelled from those islands during the 1950s, 1960s and 1970s and beyond, have sadly, either passed on or are in the later years of their lives. We need their experiences captured before it is too late. It is vital that they get the chance to speak for themselves rather than have people outside their community interpreting their lives for them through 'Othering' or via the use of narratives these Caribbeans do not recognise. The children, grandchildren and great grandchildren of these British Caribbeans need to know about the rich and powerful foundations from which they come. We need to celebrate Caribbean voices all day long.

My interest in this particular group of British Caribbeans was peaked when I was watching the Remembrance Day Parades and Service. It was a moving, memorable and strangely calm moment. I noticed however, that there seemed to be relatively few ethnic minorities represented. I was aware that Caribbean people had served in the British Armed Forces. My own family, including cousins and two of my brothers had provided years of service. As I reflected on that special day and was reminded of all those days in the years since the last world war, I began to wonder about all those older men and women who played a full part in the defence and protection of all of us in the United Kingdom. I wanted to know more about their history, hence this book. The book does not pretend to cover everything. It is not a complete record of every British Caribbean who has served. There are thousands more stories to be told, but these loyal, courageous people whose military journeys are represented here, I hope symbolise the rest.

The stories sit alongside some simple descriptions of the branches of the Armed Forces within which these worthy Caribbean service people served. These are all retired military men and women who are quiet in their loyalty, loud in their contribution. We must do more to acknowledge their efforts on our behalf. In 2018, the then Secretary of State when introducing the Defence's new Diversity and Inclusion Strategy 2018-2030 –'A Force for Inclusion' said that it was *"absolutely right that our Armed Forces and Civil Service should reflect the society that it exists to defend"*. Five years on, even with the introduction in April 2023, of an impressive and new 'Army Race Action Plan: Enabling Equality of Opportunity for All', we can see that there is still quite some way to go. Nevertheless, it is a positive move, which we must recognise and be optimistic about.

I want therefore, to make these 'invisible' people more visible and ensure that what is written here about the 30 plus veterans, form a part of a larger historical bank to which people of all backgrounds can come, to withdraw and to invest and be enriched by what they read and hear.

Rose Johnson

1. A History of Service

This book presents the stories of 32 British Caribbean men and women who have, collectively, contributed over 600 years of military service to the British Armed Forces.

They are but a few of the hundreds, thousands even, who served many years after the Windrush ship docked at Tilbury, Essex, in June 1948. They had no idea they would be labelled the Windrush Generation if they were born in, or entered the UK during the 24-year period (1948-1972), since that well–publicised arrival at Tilbury Docks. It is of course, a myth that these communities of people only arrived here in 1948, on a ship. Caribbeans have been here for hundreds of years.

These generous-hearted people were ignorant of this 'Windrush Generation' label and of the scandal that would be attached to elements of the government's hostile environment policy, which was being enforced around them. They had just toiled and sweated in their various disciplined military environments to uphold their Regiments and ranks in defence of their birth or adopted country; the United Kingdom.

They fought, saluted and acted in complete accord with national expectations under the 'Colours' (Flags) of the Army, Navy and Air Force. They marched alongside their comrades and officers, with full allegiance to the Nation and their Sovereign Queen.

This loyalty, commitment and shared sense of military purpose from these Island peoples is significant, but is nothing new in the British context.

Caribbean Unity

The Caribbean region is a diverse area that includes more than 25 countries and territories, as well as a number of island groups and dependencies. Some of the larger countries in the Caribbean include Cuba, the Dominican Republic, Haiti, Jamaica, and Trinidad and Tobago. Other countries and territories in the Caribbean include Barbados, the Bahamas, Antigua and Barbuda, Grenada, Dominica, St Kitts, St. Lucia, Guyana and St. Vincent and the Grenadines, among others.

Many individuals of Caribbean background in the UK have roots in more than one Caribbean country or territory, and the region has a rich cultural heritage that encompasses a range of languages, religions, and traditions.

All the personnel interviewed for this book were clear that once they joined up, they were united as a Caribbean group and would not be seen as individual Islanders. They knew their separate island roots but banded together beautifully, as one black group, ready to meet and socialise wherever they were in the world, whether Army or Air Force or where possible, with their naval Caribbean personnel.

Serving Britain

Caribbean people have always served Britain and the Crown with loyalty, skill and determination, joining up for service in the British Army, the Royal Air Force and the Royal Navy.

This fact becomes evident when considering the immense sacrifices made by the hundreds and thousands who had already given their lives and limbs in both of the major wars in the early and mid-20th century. Around 10,000 left their families in the Caribbean to join the British Armed Forces, often taking important roles behind the scenes to contribute to the defeat of the Nazis.

Even this 20th century, historical contribution does not adequately reflect the magnitude of military service already given to the UK by these noble peoples of the Caribbean.

Caribbean men and later women fought for and provided Armed Service to several kings and queens of Britain for nearly 300 years: from as early as 1795 under George III, onwards to Queen Victoria and more recently to George VI and to his daughter, Queen Elizabeth II and now to King Charles III.

Their service goes mostly unacknowledged. Only recently have we seen comments in the media and a very small number of books being written referencing, usually in short chapters, these forgotten Veterans of the Caribbean. It is really shameful at best and scandalous in its worst expression.

Encompassing almost 300 years of history, it is vital to tell the story of the recruitment and role of West Indian servicemen and women in the British Armed Forces. It is important to know more about the experiences of these British soldiers and officers of the Caribbean and their combined service in various military campaigns across the ages, but certainly beyond 1790. Their service goes far back into history with the earliest formal service being in the late eighteenth century. More of this historical fact, later.

During World War II, the Caribbean colonies provided more Air Force and significant numbers of Army volunteers than anywhere else in the British Empire. These men volunteered to help the Empire and set off in their hundreds to join the common effort alongside their white colleagues.

Despite their eagerness to support the Mother Country, they were not always welcomed with open arms. Indeed, their skills were sometimes undermined and they were often put in more minor roles, ferrying the injured from the battlefields or digging the trenches. When called to arms, however, they fought with great tenacity and courage, with many making the ultimate sacrifice. A few were rewarded with the lesser significant medals and cited in reports back to headquarters.

In the Second World War, a number of the womenfolk of the West Indies also joined the war effort, as part of the Women's Royal Army Corps or Women's Royal Voluntary Services or as radar operators. Mrs Ena Collymore-Woodstock, OBE OD, a Jamaican woman who on 10 September, 2023 celebrated her 106th birthday in her home in Barbados, is an example of Caribbean women's service, going back to WWII.

She served in the Auxiliary Territorial Services (ATS) and then the Anti-Aircraft Service as a radar operator during the war, providing crucial support to the servicemen during military operations. She is the oldest surviving British Army Veteran.

More of the men took on roles in the Royal Air Force; flight aircraft men providing air support to help the fight against the German U-Boats which attempted to terrify the British and other forces. Their defensive efforts in aiding British and Allied ships played a critical role in the overall success of Britain and its allies during the war.

There were as mentioned, more Air Force volunteers from the Caribbean colonies than from anywhere else in the British Empire. One such volunteer was another Jamaican, Flight Sergeant Peter Brown, who found his own way to England to join the RAF, at the age of 17, to fight in World War II.

Other men and some women also served in Army battalions, with a number serving in the Royal Navy, the Merchant Navy and within those industries engaged in making equipment and providing supplies for the forces and overall war effort. They served in both World Wars and subsequent conflicts. These men were not conscripts, but volunteered, helping the British Empire, of whom they were a part. They set off in their hundreds to join the common effort alongside their white colleagues. They drove ambulances, helped in munitions factories and were nurses helping injured soldiers and civilians in various military and general hospitals.

In WWII, the Caribbean colonies continued to provide more Army and Air Force volunteers. These men and women showed remarkable loyalty and an unwavering sense of duty to the UK. They were prepared to give their lives for the Empire they were a part of. There was a strong feeling amongst these Caribbeans that the people the British were fighting against, were also their enemies. Some served in the Infantry, and others flew planes, taking materials to and from various places across Europe, supporting the military logistics. Whichever role they took on, the men fought with great tenacity and courage.

The Caribbeans were present throughout the First and Second World Wars and have since continued to have a presence in the British Forces right up to today.

The men and women cited in this book have origins, which cover several Islands of the Caribbean – Barbados, Dominica, Guyana, Jamaica, St Vincent and Trinidad. They have collectively provided over 500 years of military service to the United Kingdom.   They have done this with enthusiasm, loyalty and skilled, unwavering commitment.

Who knows about their bravery? Only a few in the society in which these people live their lives and continue with civilian service across their communities. They are, however, representative of thousands of others who remain anonymous, unacknowledged, and scarcely celebrated. Nonetheless, they remain proud of their contribution to the Queen and to the country they were either born in, or have lived in for most of their lives; the UK. They are the forgotten Veterans. These ex-service personnel are very much a part of what has become the newly labelled Windrush Generation. They are now in their fifth, sixth or seventh decade. They are the Elders in the Caribbean community and deserving of being honoured and recognised. They too, served. There were others who went before them hundreds of years ago and whose contributions we also need to know more about.

History of Caribbean Service to the United Kingdom and its Colonies

Men and, later, women of the Caribbean have a long tradition of providing service in the British Armed Forces, starting in the 18th century with the British West India Regiment.

The British West India Regiment

The tradition of men and women of the Caribbean providing service in the British Armed Forces dates back over 250 years to the late 18th century when the West India Regiment was founded in response to the Napoleonic war with France. The Regiment took recruits from Britain, some other European countries, and various colonies of the West Indies. It was created to defend the British colonial islands of the Caribbean and was primarily made up of black soldiers. The idea of black soldiers in combat situations was not new, but previously, they were only used in emergencies and were typically unarmed. The British observed the effectiveness of black soldiers in various slave uprisings, which led to a change of mindset. It became clear that these men could be very effective in conflict situations supporting the white, mainstream battalions. The West India Regiment (WIR) was a unit of the British Army composed mostly of soldiers recruited from the British colonies in the Caribbean. The Regiment was formed in 1795 and played an important role in many British military campaigns during the 19th and early 20th centuries.

Initially, the West India Regiment (WIR) was raised to protect British interests in the Caribbean and provide a military force familiar with the local terrain and climate. The Regiment was first deployed to Haiti, where it fought against French troops during the Haitian Revolution. Later, the BWIR served in other conflicts in the Caribbean and South America, including the Venezuelan War of Independence and the First Carlist War (Spanish Civil War: 1833-1839) in Spain.

The early recruits to the British West India Regiment (BWIR) in the 18th and 19th centuries were primarily men from the British colonies in the Caribbean, such as Jamaica, Barbados, Trinidad, and other islands. These men were typically of African descent, though there were also recruits from other ethnic groups, including some Europeans.

Many of the early recruits to the BWIR were former slaves or free people of colour who saw military service as a way to gain economic and social mobility. Others were recruited by force or coercion, as colonial authorities sought to meet the quota of soldiers required by the British government in their desire to protect the territories they were acquiring in the West Indies, especially.

When you consider those first pioneering men of the eighteenth century, it is possible to catch a scent of the thousands of those chained and packed sardine-like in the bowels of ships crossing the oceans from their African homelands. The dusty smells and rich lives on the grasslands and forests must have seemed so distant and out of reach. There was no going back. At least in the Army of other black people, they could exchange, often in their home languages, stories, songs and memories of the families from which they had been stolen.

Such was their life, complete with uniforms and food each day, and they would often be able to take their wives and children with them. Their children, especially the boys, would attend a type of school where they, in turn, would be taught drills and other military skills, readying them to join the adults, and replenishing the stock of soldiers when they were old enough. Life in the BWIR was often difficult and dangerous. The soldiers were required to undergo rigorous training and were expected to be disciplined and obedient. They were often sent to remote and hostile areas where they had to endure extreme heat, disease, and poor living conditions.

The soldiers of the BWIR were also subject to racism and discrimination, both within the military and in society at large. Despite these challenges, many soldiers in the BWIR were fiercely loyal to the British Empire and were proud of their service to the Crown. Outside of military life, the early recruits to the WIR often faced limited opportunities for education or advancement. Many were employed as labourers or worked in other low-paying jobs. However, the military service offered by the WIR provided some opportunities for career advancement and social status, particularly for those who distinguished themselves through bravery or exceptional service. These hardy men knew they would have to be tough to survive. They perfected the skills they needed to use muskets, which had to be kept in tip-top condition, ready for defensive action during the various conflicts.

Some older soldiers had already experienced war during the American War of Independence. They were conscripted to fight. Once the war was over, a number of them were pulled into the newly created WIR. Others were returned to plantation life. Those who were recruited to the WIR were, unusually, given status equal to the rest of the British white soldiers. However, none of them achieved ranks above Sergeant. Many lost their lives defending British interests in the Caribbean colonies. They were also sent to places like Ghana and Belize, where Britain wanted to strengthen their presence and reap the benefits to be gained from those countries.

The West India Regiment (BWIR) uniforms varied over time but generally consisted of a distinctive blue and white uniform with unique features that set it apart from other British Army Regiments. The uniforms were designed to be practical and comfortable for soldiers serving in the tropical climate of the Caribbean. The design and colour of the uniforms were influenced by the views of Queen Victoria and therefore had a distinctive look that reflected the unique history and heritage of the Regiment.

For the men in the Regiment, there was no going back to their original homelands. At least in the Army of other black people, they could work together with the clear knowledge that they all shared a common history and culture, which would help them in times of stress and challenge in their military endeavours.

The 1st Battalion of the new British West Indies Regiment (BWIR) was formed in 1915. It consisted of Caribbean men already in various units of the Army and some of the officers from the long-established WIR. It was necessary to draft other Caribbean men into this new Regiment, due to losses incurred during WWI. Therefore, another ten battalions were formed. Thousands of posters were printed and displayed throughout the islands of the Caribbean, to attract young men to join up. Some of the wording of these posters included emotive words to inspire and persuade the men, often with direct appeal, such as *"His Most Gracious Majesty King George call on the men of his Empire, men of every class, creed and colour, to come forward to fight so the Empire can be saved and the foe well defeated."* Altogether, 15,600 brave men answered the call and served in the BWIR, with two-thirds coming from Jamaica.

The BWIR served in several theatres of war, including the Middle East and Africa. The Regiment's soldiers fought with distinction, earning numerous medals and commendations for their bravery and service in WWI. They were awarded 81 medals and many were mentioned in dispatches for their courage and action in that brutal war. According to the records at the Imperial War Museum, by the end of the First World War, 185 men from the BWIR had been killed in action, 1,071 had died of sickness and 697 were wounded. Despite their courage and sacrifices, the soldiers of the BWIR faced discrimination and segregation within the British Army. When they arrived for training, they were met with extreme hostility. White men refused to salute black officers, and black officers were often barred from the officers' clubs and quarters. They were paid less than their white counterparts and were often assigned menial tasks rather than combat duties. Their treatment was, sadly, overlooked or condoned by those in more senior positions. It was a measure of these young men's resilience, commitment and loyalty to the Empire that they still *"did their bit for the country and the King"*.

Overall therefore, the British West India Regiment (BWIR) played an important role, over many years, in the defence and security of the British colonies in the Caribbean and in WWI and WWII.

Britain still wished to retain a smaller WIR force, but it would now only take volunteers. Those who fought in the two major World Wars were mostly volunteers from the West Indies. However, the people who led the Regiments continued to be White British non-commissioned officers (NCOs) and commissioned officers. Black soldiers would be promoted, but again, not usually beyond the rank of Sergeant. After some of the Caribbean islands achieved independence in the 20th century, the role of the BWIR diminished, and new Armed Forces were developed to take its place. The BWIR was disbanded in 1927.

Many of the soldiers who had served in the BWIR were incorporated into their respective countries' new national Armed Forces, providing valuable experience and expertise to the new military organisations. However, some former BWIR soldiers also faced challenges in transitioning to civilian life, as they had limited opportunities for education or training outside of military service.

Today, the legacy of the British West India Regiment is only partly remembered and celebrated in the Caribbean and the United Kingdom. Its soldiers were not officially recognised for their contributions to the war effort until many years later. The Regiment's soldiers should be honoured more for their service and sacrifice. Their story should be a reminder of the important role that people of African descent have played in the history of the British Empire. One organisation trying to raise the profile of this important Regiment and to provide information, education and honouring of its members is the Community Interest Company (CIC), British West India Regiments Heritage Trust. This Trust organises talks and events, including visits to parts of Northern France, where many BWIR soldiers lost their lives in the major world conflicts.

2.   Caribbeans Serving in WWI

During World War I, the soldiers of the British West Indies Regiment (BWIR) as well as volunteers who travelled directly to the UK to join up, provided a range of services to the British Army, both on the front lines and behind the scenes. As the war progressed, some soldiers from the BWIR were assigned to combat roles and saw action in France, Belgium, and Italy. They fought in some of the bloodiest battles of the war, including the Battle of the Somme and the Battle of Passchendaele. Many soldiers from the BWIR were assigned to support roles, such as carrying ammunition and supplies, digging trenches, and building fortifications. They were also responsible for maintaining equipment and providing medical care to wounded soldiers.

Black soldiers from the BWIR were often used as labourers, performing a range of tasks such as loading and unloading supplies, digging latrines, and building railways. They were also used as stevedores, working in ports to unload ships. The BWIR soldiers were also employed in pioneer work, which involved constructing roads and digging trenches, often in dangerous and challenging conditions. Soldiers from the BWIR also performed various camp duties, such as cooking, cleaning, and maintaining camp facilities. Some soldiers were involved in recruitment efforts, encouraging others to join the British Army. They also participated in propaganda campaigns to boost morale and promote the war effort.

The soldiers from the BWIR responded to the call to support Britain and provided valuable service to the British Army during World War I, both on the front lines and behind the scenes. They played an important role in the war effort and helped to pave the way for greater opportunities and equality for black soldiers in the British Army later on. Other young men from the West Indies joined the war effort while they were living in various parts of the world. For example, some West Indian men who were living in Canada joined the Canadian Expeditionary Force and fought alongside Canadian soldiers in France. There were also instances of young men from the West Indies lying about their age in order to join the war effort. Here are some examples:

Clifford Alfred Anthony Gulley

At the age of 16, but pretending to be 19, Clifford travelled from Kingston, Jamaica, to England to join the other 15,600 men of the British West India Regiment who fought for Britain in WWI. This young black teenager fought with courage and commitment for his Mother Country. Although he spoke little about those harrowing experiences later in his life back in Jamaica, it was clear that those experiences sat uneasily with him. This was despite heading up a new family and becoming a successful businessman.

Cyril Lionel Robert James

Cyril Lionel Robert James was a Trinidadian writer and activist, who joined the British Merchant Navy at the age of 16 by lying about his age.

Marcus Bailey

Marcus Bailey came from the Mercantile Marine in Barbados to join the crew of the Royal Navy on HMS Chester in 1916. He was an Able Seaman who worked mainly as a cook, but also had assignments with ammunition supply, damage control and casualty clearance. Bailey served on the HMS Chester during one of the bloodiest naval battles, the Battle of Jutland, on 31 May 1916.

Two of Bailey's children, James and Lilian, went on to serve Britain's Armed Forces during WWII.

Walter Tull

Walter Tull was one of the first black professional footballers and, later on, the first black officer - Second Lieutenant - to lead white troops into battle in the British Army. Tull had played for Northampton Town. Tull was of mixed race, with a Barbadian father, Daniel, who emigrated in 1876 to the UK when he was a 20-year-old. Daniel married an English woman, Alice. Sadly, Alice died when Walter was seven years old, and he and his brother, Edward, were put into care, eventually being fostered by a white family.

Tull served in the Middle East and France during World War I, became an officer despite suffering racist abuse, and was mentioned in despatches for his bravery in the face of significant danger. He was later recommended for a Military Cross, which he sadly never received.

Tull died in action in Northern France on 25 March 1918. His recognition has been a long time coming. Evidently, Tull's bravery and leadership in the face of discrimination have made him a symbol of hope and inspiration for many. Unfortunately, until fairly recently, his heroism has not been recognised or acknowledged publicly. However, Tull has been recognised on a first-class postage stamp released by the Royal Mail. This special stamp was distributed in September 2018 to mark the 100th anniversary of the end of WWI.

Herbert Morris

This Jamaican teenager is worthy of being represented for the service he provided, having travelled from Jamaica on his own at the age of 16, to join the war effort. Herbert became a Private in the 6th Battalion of the British West Indies Regiment and fought in that dreadful conflict on behalf of the King and Britain.

During that brutal war, Herbert's job was to stack shells. He suffered immense trauma on the front line, and told the court martial that he could not take the noise of the shell and the gunfire and the doctor did not give him anything to help. He was executed - shot at Dawn - for desertion on 20 September, 1917, at the age of 17.

His name is on one of the 346 posts representing those who were executed in WWI. They are remembered in the 'Shot at Dawn' memorial garden located in the National Memorial Arboretum. There is a particular wreath laying ceremony held there each September, to remember young Herbert.

Many of those who know of this young man's story and service have felt moved to write about him, some to share their feelings about him in poetry. Two such people are Mrs Joan Greagory-Bortosh and Ms Jenny R Turner who wrote the following poem - '7429 Private Herbert Morris' for The National Caribbean Monument Charity as part of their efforts to install a lasting memorial in the National Memorial Arboretum.

Herbert received a pardon in 2006, when it was accepted that he was one of the many victims of the war and did not deserve to be executed. It is very likely that this young man may have been suffering from post-traumatic stress disorder at the time.

Many young men from the West Indies were motivated by a sense of duty, patriotism, and a desire to prove their worth and gain greater opportunities for themselves and their homelands. Herbert was an example of that huge desire to help the Motherland.

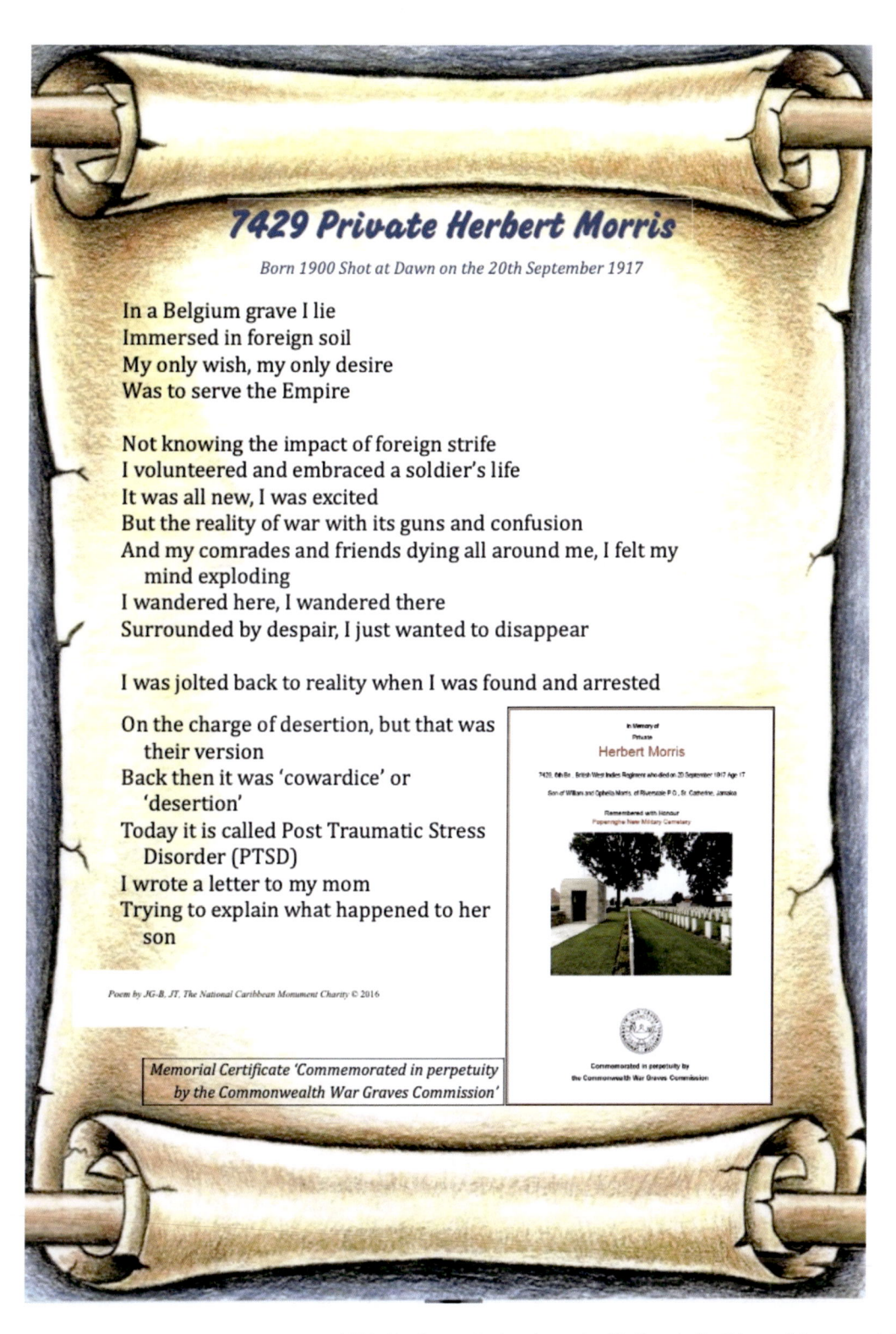

7429 Private Herbert Morris

Born 1900 Shot at Dawn on the 20th September 1917

In a Belgium grave I lie
Immersed in foreign soil
My only wish, my only desire
Was to serve the Empire

Not knowing the impact of foreign strife
I volunteered and embraced a soldier's life
It was all new, I was excited
But the reality of war with its guns and confusion
And my comrades and friends dying all around me, I felt my mind exploding
I wandered here, I wandered there
Surrounded by despair, I just wanted to disappear

I was jolted back to reality when I was found and arrested

On the charge of desertion, but that was their version
Back then it was 'cowardice' or 'desertion'
Today it is called Post Traumatic Stress Disorder (PTSD)
I wrote a letter to my mom
Trying to explain what happened to her son

Poem by JG-B, JT, The National Caribbean Monument Charity © 2016

Memorial Certificate 'Commemorated in perpetuity by the Commonwealth War Graves Commission'

With kind permission from the National Caribbean Monument Charity

3. Caribbeans Serving in WWII

During World War II, the Caribbean once again made a significant contribution to the war effort. Men and women from the Caribbean served in various capacities, both at home and abroad.

Caribbean men served in the British Armed Forces and played a crucial role in the war effort. The RAF's No. 139 (Jamaica) Squadron, for example, was made up entirely of Caribbean personnel. Caribbean men also served in the Army and the Royal Navy, and many saw action in the Mediterranean, Africa, and Asia.

Caribbean men also served in the Merchant Navy, undertaking a vital role in providing essential supplies to Britain and its allies during the war. Many worked as seamen; some were involved in dangerous convoys, transporting goods and supplies across the Atlantic.

Caribbean men and women made invaluable contributions to wartime production in various ways. They worked in factories, producing everything from ammunition and clothing to aircraft parts and engines. They worked on farms, producing food to feed the population and the troops.

The women played a significant role in nursing and medical care during the war. The Jamaica Nurses' Association, for example, sent nurses to Britain to work in military hospitals. Caribbean women also worked in hospitals and clinics in the Caribbean, providing care to wounded soldiers and civilians.

Some men and women were involved in intelligence work during the war. For example, a group of Jamaican women worked as wireless operators for the British government, intercepting German messages and providing valuable intelligence to the Allies.

One of the most significant contributions made by women was their participation in the war effort as part of the British Armed Forces. Many Caribbean women volunteered for the Women's Royal Naval Service (WRNS), the Auxiliary Territorial Service (ATS), and the Women's Auxiliary Air Force (WAAF), working in a range of roles, including clerical work, driving, cooking, and communications.

Additionally, Caribbean women in the UK contributed vital support to the war effort through their work in the Women's Voluntary Service (WVS). The WVS provided support for civilians affected by the war. They assisted with tasks such as distributing food, clothing, and other essential supplies, as well as helping to find accommodation for people displaced by the conflict.

Despite their contributions, Caribbean women faced discrimination and prejudice in the UK during this time. Nevertheless, their contributions to the war effort were crucial, and they helped to pave the way for greater racial and gender equality in the country.

Overall, the contribution of Caribbeans to World War II was significant, and both men and women played a crucial role in the war effort. Despite facing discrimination and prejudice, they proved their worth and helped to secure victory for the Allies. There are many other examples of Caribbean men and women who provided outstanding service during World War II. Here are a few notable examples:

Philip Ulric Cross

Philip Ulric Cross was a Trinidadian who served in the Royal Air Force during World War II. He became one of the highest-ranking officers - Squadron Leader - in the RAF and received several medals for his service, including the Distinguished Service Order. He was a member of the elite Pathfinder Force and flew 80 missions over Germany and occupied Europe.

He later had a distinguished career both in the UK and back in his home country of Trinidad, and later in Ghana, Cameroon and Tanzania. He served as High Commissioner for Trinidad and Tobago in the UK and as Ambassador to both Germany and France.

Cyril Ewart Lionel Grant

Cyril Ewart Lionel Grant was a Guyanese actor, writer, and poet who served as a commissioned officer in the Royal Air Force. He became a Flight Lieutenant with 103 Squadron, mainly flying Lancaster Bombers during World War II. Unfortunately, after being shot down over the Netherlands, he was imprisoned by the Germans for two years, being liberated in 1945. After the war, he became a barrister and a successful actor and musician in the UK.

Norma Best

Norma Best was from British Honduras, but trained in Jamaica before joining the Auxiliary Territorial Service (ATS) during World War II. Her father had already served in WWI, in Egypt and encouraged her to support the war effort in the new war. She arrived in Scotland in 1944 and, following further training in Guildford, served in office-based roles in Preston, Derby and London. Norma was keen to adopt the wartime spirit. In 1946, she went on to do a degree at Durham University and then to become a primary school teacher. She was not allowed to stay in the UK, however, being forced to return to British Honduras. She was persistent in pursuing her teaching career and, in the 1950s, returned to the UK to continue this.

I met her towards the end of her career, the early years of mine, in the London Borough of Brent, where she and I were headteachers. She had a huge amount to give to others and had journeyed far to support and serve in her short military career.

Arthur Wint MD OD MBE

Arthur Wint OD MBE was born in Jamaica and was an 800m runner who won many accolades in his teens, including winning a gold medal in the Pan American Games in Panama in 1938. In 1942, he and his brothers, Lloyd and Douglas, joined the war effort. He was awarded his RAF 'wings' in 1944 and became a Spitfire pilot. When he left the RAF in 1947, he trained as a doctor at St Bartholomew's Hospital. He continued to train as an athlete and took part in the Olympic Games in London in 1948, winning Jamaica's first Olympic gold medal in the 400 metres and a silver medal in the 800m.

He went on to be a part of the 4x400 metres relay team in the world record-setting race in Helsinki in 1952. That was also the year he graduated as a doctor. He was awarded an MBE by the Queen in 1954, the Jamaican Order of Distinction (OD) in 1973, and received the Careeras Foundation's Certificate of Merit for his work in Sports Medicine in 1982. Wint served as Jamaica's High Commissioner in London and was Ambassador to Denmark for a period of four years.

Prince Albert Jacob (aka "Jake")

This quite special 98-year-old Trinidadian and RAF Veteran from WWII, recently received his medals, after waiting 70 years for them. He was a Sergeant in the RAF during the War and was also a talented sportsman.

It was a neighbour who heard about his story and learning that he had never received his RAF and Service medals, took the time to help with the application for them to be sent to Sergeant Jacob. On opening the package, 'Jake' was heard to say, *"It's about bl...y time!"*.

Jake was one of the 6,000 men who were recruited from the British colonies in 1940. This large number of people was significant given the fact that the Caribbean population at the time was only around three million. Jake travelled to the UK at the age of 17 and a half to serve with the Royal Air Force in WWII. He saw it as his duty to help defend Britain in its time of need. And he did. He was also a talented sportsman, representing the RAF and GB internationally. He is amongst the reducing number of veterans from WWII.

This sprightly nonagenarian is in great health and has celebrated 75 years of marriage with his amazing wife who he met when he was serving at the RAF base near Warrington.

Meeting him at a commemorative event for Herbert Morris held at the National Memorial Arboretum in September 2023, was a great privilege. He has some stories to tell, which he does with wry humour. His sharp intellect is evident in the rich descriptions of his experiences gained from a life well-lived.

Ena Collymore-Woodstock OBE OD

This amazing Veteran is a Jamaican (now aged 106 and living in Barbados) who served in the Auxiliary Territorial Service (ATS) at the outbreak of WWII, before joining the Anti-Aircraft Service as a radar operator in Belgium. After the war, she served as a War Office Clerk before starting her law studies. She became Jamaica's first woman Court Clerk Crown Solicitor and Resident Magistrate. Mrs Collymore-Woodstock is currently the oldest known surviving female British Army Veteran. She was a part of a group of women whose contributions were crucial to the war effort. These women played a vital role in identifying and tracking enemy aircraft, allowing the British military to mount effective counterattacks against the enemy.

She was awarded an OBE and an Order of Distinction for her services.

The Jamaica Defence Force continues to recognise and honour this talented centenarian, with visits and mentions in their various online message boards as she celebrates each birthday.

Peter Brown

Peter Brown was born in Jamaica in 1926 and made his way to England at the age of 17 to enlist in the RAF Volunteer Reserve in September 1943. He was then trained as a wireless operator and gunner and took part in missions in Tripoli, Palestine, Egypt and Malta. He continued his service to the end of WWII and beyond, finally leaving the RAF in 1950, still at a young age; 24.

Sadly, he died alone and unacknowledged at the age of 96 in a flat in Maida Vale, Westminster, in December 2022. He was one of the RAF's last black WWII Veterans.

It is a sad indictment of the lack of knowledge and recognition of these brave men that Flight Sergeant Brown's war service remained unknown until after his death. A number of people were so concerned that his passing would also go unmarked that there was a lot of publicity, including within his homeland of Jamaica, to find any relatives and friends who could give him a *"good, honourable, send-off"*. Several high-profile people also began to get involved, from prime ministers, the Jamaican High Commissioner, and MPs, to the Lord Mayor of Westminster and an RAF spokesperson.

In a report published in the Guardian online on 22 March 2023, the Lord Mayor of Westminster said, *"Mr Brown was one of the many servicemen and women who volunteered from the West Indies and across the former colonies to fight for the UK and the world at a time of its greatest need. We owe him – and the many others like him – a huge debt of gratitude. His obvious modesty meant that we did not know of his actions until after his passing."*

The RAF said, *"Flight Sergeant Brown is an example of the selfless contribution of all Commonwealth personnel who have served throughout the RAF's history. We should never forget their sacrifices which have defended our freedom and kept us safe."*

On 29 March 2023, Flight Sergeant Peter Brown's funeral should have taken place at Mortlake Crematorium with honour guards in attendance from Caribbean ex-service personnel from the Armed Forces. Huge numbers of Veterans had planned to turn out in recognition of a man who had contributed so much in service to this country.

Given the new publicity and the expectation of nearly 1,500 mourners, the funeral had to be rescheduled to the 25 May to a newer, bigger venue, the RAF Central, 600-place Church, St Clement Danes, in the centre of London. Applications to attend this funeral were avidly pursued and not only by ex-servicemen and women.

Flight Sergeant Brown's funeral was a well-attended event. It was a privilege to be a part of it. Hundreds of black and other Veterans and well-wishers attended to show respect, affirm and acknowledge his contribution, and honour this man.

Some senior RAF personnel, including Air Chief Marshall Sir Mike Wigston, Chief of the Air Staff, attended, and the Reverend Michael King, son of the Windrush Founder, Sam King, was also in attendance.

Comments from some of the lead contributors at the service included:

Peter embraced the journey at 17 to protect the country. He was willing to put his life on the line on behalf of the Queen, defended our way of life, and sacrificed himself to protect our freedom, and he was immensely proud of what he did for our country. He should be acknowledged as a hero of our nation. He was dedicated to the Queen and the country; he was born in the same year as the Queen – she in April, he in August.

Maurillia Simpson, a black female Veteran who sang a solo at the service, remarked, *"It is good to see other Veterans who look like me."*

Flight Sergeant Brown and the other honourable servicemen and women are a few examples of the many Caribbeans who made significant contributions to the Allied war effort during World War II and have been forgotten. It is possible that there are Caribbean ex-servicemen and women from World War II who are still alive today, but it is difficult to be certain without more specific information being available. There are still gaps in the information about these individuals, despite the existence of the Armed Services Covenant, which all local authorities across the United Kingdom have signed.

There is some indication that perhaps following the huge publicity surrounding Flight Sergeant Brown's case, there will be more articles appearing in publications. For example, the Royal British Legion, in April 2023, has a number of stories of famous black people in its online platform, as well as examples of men and women who served in both World Wars of the 20th century. Still more needs to be done to provide important information about their service and that of the thousands following them, during the major wars and in the major conflicts and defensive support events, in the decades since.

It is especially important to consider the laudable statements included within the Armed Services Covenant and then to advocate and ensure that the words lead to positive, meaningful actions for the Veterans, both black and white. There is a useful Latin phrase used by my eldest brother's school, Holmwood, in Jamaica, that should indeed be *'facta non verba'*. By applying that statement to all those who have served and are serving, it would be the true honouring and appreciation of the service given to the country by these Caribbean Veterans.

4. Caribbean Veterans in the Present Day

The Caribbean is home to many different countries and islands, and each has its own set of Veterans who served in World War II and wars and conflicts since then. However, it is unlikely that these islands have continued to monitor or keep records of the men and women of Caribbean origin who have served in the British Armed Forces since 1945 until the present day.

Recording the different ethnic origins of these military personnel appears to be difficult enough within the UK, where the data appears incomplete in relation to the different black and ethnic minorities. This data is being collated as a whole and does not show the exact heritage of the different black minorities.   The UK Armed Forces Biannual Diversity Statistics, show that as of 1 April 2023, ethnic minorities (excluding white minorities) personnel accounted for 10.1 per cent of the UK Regular Forces (14,240 personnel) . This was out of a total number for the British Armed Forces of 142,560 personnel. Around half of that total number(77,540) are in the Army.

There have been some efforts in recent years to document the experiences of Caribbean Veterans from World War II. Organisations such as the Caribbean Veterans Association have been established to support and honour these individuals. However, given that World War II ended almost 80 years ago, it is likely that the number of surviving Veterans is relatively small.

Historically, the contributions of black and minority ethnic (BME) soldiers and Veterans have often been overlooked or marginalised in official commemorations and narratives of World War II and other conflicts since then. However, in recent years, there has been small but slowly growing recognition of the sacrifices and contributions made by BME soldiers, including those from the Caribbean.

For example, in 2018, a ceremony was held at the Cenotaph in London to mark the 100th anniversary of the end of World War I, which included a tribute to Caribbean soldiers who fought in that war. Additionally, in 2020, a wreath-laying ceremony was held at the Cenotaph to mark the 75th anniversary of Victory in Europe Day, and included the participation of representatives from the Caribbean High Commissions. It was, however, marked by the absence of a few of the surviving Caribbean Veterans.

The Falklands War ended just over 40 years ago, and there were various events organised in 2022 to mark this. Caribbean servicemen, such as Owen Bernard, RSM, were involved. He and a minority of others did participate in formal speeches and activities. The recognition of their efforts in and around this conflict, still however, needs wider publicity.

While more work needs to be done to ensure that the contributions of Caribbean Veterans are fully acknowledged and celebrated, more should be done towards true recognition of their valiant efforts within the major wars, as well as within the wars and conflicts of the latter part of the 20th century and the 21st century. These men and women Veterans saw service during the conflicts and peacekeeping activities carried out in the second half of the 20th century and beyond. The men gave their all in Aden, Cyprus, Belize, the Congo, Sierra Leone, the Falklands, Bosnia, Kosova, Northern Ireland, both Gulf wars, Afghanistan and Iraq, to name just a few.

My cousin, Private Radley Edward Ashman Beswick (seen here) and my brother Corporal Lincoln Beswick served with the British Army in Aden, Libya and Cyprus as young but loyal men, but were often scarred by what they saw. Three other family members also served in the Royal Air Force. Their service was exemplary and contributed to the overall, positive and effective peacekeeping efforts of the British Armed Forces.

There were many other Caribbeans who also served and who sadly, have now passed away. Another example of someone in this group is Squadron Warrant Officer Winston A Alleyne.

Squadron Warrant Officer Winston A Alleyne

The story of Winston Alleyne was published in the RAF Association's 'Air Mail Magazine' on 6 October, 2021. Winston travelled from Barbados in 1958. His mother had named him after well-known British politician, Winston Churchill.

When he got to England, Winston found it to be a less than welcoming place for a young black man.

This six feet, six inches tall young 17-year-old arrived in the UK alone, carrying a single suitcase. With employment a priority, Winston soon found himself in the cotton mills of Oldham; a very different culture and environment to what he had been used to.

It was not until an RAF recruitment poster caught his eye that his life begun to change. Leaving the cotton mill behind, Winston enlisted as an RAF Regiment Gunner at Catterick on 31 July 1961. He had a very successful military career. He provided expertise in his military postings in the UK and abroad. Some of his tours included countries such as Germany and Cyprus. He was also posted to countries in the Middle and Far East.

Winston achieved several promotions up the ranks. In August 1985, his hard work and record of outstanding competence was recognised and he was promoted to Warrant Officer at RAF West Raynham. He was the first black man in the history of the RAF to reach that position. Winston went on to achieve even more in his military career.

Warrant Officer Winston Alleyne completed 35 years of service to the country and for this, he should be acknowledged and applauded.

During his career he was also fortunate to meet a range of people, including Her Late Majesty, Queen Elizabeth II.

After a second career involved in supporting people with complex needs, Winston Alleyne passed away in 2020. On learning of his death, Air Commodore Scott Miller – Commandant General RAF Regiment – noted that Winston was simply *"an RAF Regiment legend."*

His daughter, Sara-Eden Ludwell, remembers that Winston would always say, *"Never have a job. Have a career"*. Her father certainly lived those words.

5. Organisations Providing Support to Caribbean Veterans

The West Indian Association of Service Personnel (WASP) is an organisation established in the UK in 1990 to provide support and advocacy for Caribbean Veterans and their families. WASP was founded by a group of Caribbean Veterans who felt that the contributions of black and minority ethnic (BME) soldiers were not being properly recognised or celebrated. The organisation aims to promote awareness and appreciation of the sacrifices made by BME service personnel across the British Armed Forces Services. WASP is also committed to providing support for Veterans and their families.

In addition to WASP, there are other organisations in the UK that work to support and honour BME Veterans, including the African and Caribbean War Memorial and the Black Cultural Archives. Another important charitable organisation is The National Caribbean Monument Charity (TNCMC) which has been in existence since November 2016. Its aim is *"to install and instil a lasting cultural and educational legacy for present and future generations, in the National Memorial Arboretum (NMA) in Staffordshire"*.

These and the few other organisations which exist, are working to ensure that the contributions of BME soldiers and other Veterans are fully acknowledged and celebrated, and that their stories are properly represented in official narratives of British military history.

It is possible to find, though thinly spread, publicly available written records reflecting these modern-day Veterans' service to the late Queen, the King and the United Kingdom. Where these writings exist, they are usually found in short chapters in magazines and books, rather than in books solely dedicated to their stories and service to Britain.

Caribbean Recruits to the British Armed Forces 1960 - 1990

Throughout the 30-year period between 1960 and the 1990s, the main reason for recruiting Caribbean nationals was a shortage of British-born, Caucasian individuals interested in joining the Armed Forces. The British government actively recruited individuals from Commonwealth countries to fill the gaps in the military. Other Caribbeans who were either born in the UK or arrived here as young children and teenagers, to join their parents, also joined up.

Many joined the British Armed Forces during the 1970s, especially after the end of colonial rule in the region. The recruits were initially treated differently from their British counterparts. Some faced significant challenges once they joined. For example, they were often in the lowest ranks, given the most menial tasks, and subjected to racial abuse and discrimination from fellow soldiers and superiors alike. They were not given the same opportunities for training or promotion.

Additionally, there were cases where recruits complained about being unfairly punished or even court-martialled for relatively minor infractions while their white counterparts received more lenient treatment. This led to a sense of injustice and alienation among some Caribbean servicemen.

In a report (Hansard HC Deb 14 March 1991 vol 187 cc1260-74) of a speech by Diane Abbott, MP, Member for Hackney North and Stoke Newington, she said

"For years during the 1960s, there was a very strict quota limiting the number of black recruits. At the beginning of the 1960s it was 2 per cent, and towards the end it was 4 per cent. Throughout the 1960s, there were some Regiments that would not accept any black recruits. That was revealed in a War Office memorandum that was published in newspapers during that decade. The Regiments that would officially accept no black recruits include the Household Cavalry, the foot guards, the Highland Regiments, the Lowland Regiments, the Royal Military police, the intelligence corps and the physical training corps. There was an official quota, and black people were officially excluded from certain Regiments. During the 1960s, 1970s and 1980s, many individuals from the Caribbean joined the British Armed Forces. These individuals were mostly from former British colonies in the Caribbean, including Jamaica, Trinidad and Tobago, Guyana, St Vincent, Barbados, Dominica and Grenada."

She went on to say, *"When applicants were monitored in 1987, MOD figures showed that black people comprised only 1.6 per cent. of the applicants when black people of the particular age range applying to join the armed services constituted 5.7 per cent. of the population. There is a much lower application rate among young black men and women. Worse, there is a much lower success rate. There is a perception, which no one has been able to prove one way or the other, that once black people get into the armed services, their chances of promotion are not good. In that regard, I want to quote Scotty Muir, an ex-bugler. He left the armed services because he was disillusioned. He said: "I feel strongly about people not getting promoted because of their colour. You can go to Northern Ireland and get killed. You can do just about everything else, but you can't get promoted."*

She spoke of the exclusion of black soldiers from certain Regiments and that the then heir to the throne, Prince Charles had queried the absence of any black guardsmen. She even mentioned a quote that she found in The Daily Telegraph, from an anonymous, white guardsman who had said *"It doesn't look right; you don't know where the bearskin ends and the face begins."*

It appears from the Hansard record of Diane Abbott's speech, that until 1968, young black men were officially kept out of the Household Cavalry, the foot guards and the Highland and Lowland brigades. Diane Abbott referenced Guardsman Richard Stokes, who was one of the first black men, if not the first, to enter the Guards. He was only 17-years of age when he joined that top Regiment. His entry to that group was widely published in the newspapers at the time, with pictures of him smiling and his family looking on proudly.

Sadly and unsurprisingly to some of the black Veterans who were interviewed for this book, young Richard left the Guards less than three years later. He had been subjected to sustained humiliation, racist taunts and threats of violence. It is obvious that many black people will be suspicious therefore of the recruiting processes, even to this day. Undoubtedly, things are changing however. The recruiting adverts do show a more diverse profile. Nevertheless, the reality of the history of the recent past remain strong in people's minds.

Overall, while not all Caribbean recruits to the British Armed Forces experienced serious mistreatment, discrimination and prejudice were certainly issues that many had to contend with. Some of these differences in treatment would include so-called 'Banter'; others were outright, loudly expressed and direct racist abuse. An example of the 'Banter' included being called 'Snowy', an unwarranted nickname, which was offensive to those black recruits, who grew to realise quite what it really meant.

The treatment of Caribbean recruits in the British Armed Forces began to change in the 1980s, with the implementation of various policies and initiatives aimed at promoting equality and reducing discrimination. It is fair to say, however, that massive change was not experienced quickly by recruits and by the more experienced black men and women who served at that time.

A pivotal milestone that brought about significant changes was the enactment of the Race Relations Act in 1976. The landmark legislation made it illegal to discriminate against someone based on their race or ethnicity. This legislation provided a framework for addressing instances of discrimination within the Armed Forces and other institutions.

The British military also began to take steps to recruit and retain more people from ethnic minority backgrounds, including Caribbean recruits. This involved increasing community outreach efforts, providing more support for recruits during training, and promoting diversity within the ranks. The Army set up an equalities group and recruited a small number of senior black men and women as advisors, and to promote its work. One such person was Lieutenant Colonel Pat Gibson, who later received an MBE for her work in the area of the Army's Ethnic Minority Recruitment. Another was Major Wayne Douglas, who became an Ethnic Minority Liaison Officer (EMLO) with the Army. In the Royal Navy, Lieutenant Commander Lionel Winston, received an MBE from the Queen for his work in raising awareness of naval opportunities when he worked as the Navy's Ethnic Minority Liaison Officer (EMLO).

In addition, and more generally, the military began to take the issue of racial discrimination and harassment more seriously and implemented policies to prevent and address such incidents. For example, soldiers found guilty of racist behaviour could face disciplinary action, including discharge from the military.

While discrimination and mistreatment did not disappear entirely in the 1980s, the British Armed Forces began to take a more proactive approach to addressing these issues and promoting equality among all members of the military.

The improvements in the treatment of Caribbean recruits in the British Armed Forces that began in the 1980s generally continued into the 1990s. Nevertheless, there were still some challenges and setbacks.

One major event in the 1990s that affected Caribbean recruits was the Gulf War, which took place in 1990-1991. Many soldiers from diverse backgrounds, including Caribbean recruits, were deployed to the Gulf War, and some experienced discrimination and racism from their fellow soldiers.

However, in the aftermath of the Gulf War, the British military began to take a more proactive approach to promoting diversity and equality. This included efforts to increase the representation of ethnic minorities in senior leadership positions and establishing formal policies to prevent and address discrimination and harassment. In 1997, the Labour government introduced the Race Relations Amendment Act, which extended the protections against discrimination in the Race Relations Act of 1976 and required public institutions, including the military, to promote equality and diversity actively.

Overall, while there were still instances of discrimination and mistreatment of Caribbean recruits in the 1990s, the British military continued to make some progress in promoting equality and reducing discrimination during this time.

Data is available on the number of Caribbean young men and women who were born in the UK or emigrated to the UK as youngsters and then joined the Armed Forces as young recruits.

According to a report by the Ministry of Defence (MOD), between 1962 and 1984, over 20,000 Commonwealth citizens were recruited to the British Armed Forces. Of these, a significant proportion were from the Caribbean, particularly during the 1960s and 1970s.

In more recent years, there has been a decline in the number of recruits from the Caribbean and other Commonwealth countries. In 2019, the MOD reported that approximately 4,500 Commonwealth citizens were serving in the British Armed Forces, making up around 5% of the total Armed Forces' personnel. However, the MOD does not provide detailed breakdowns of the demographic characteristics of these personnel, including their ethnicity or country of origin.

Some organisations and charities collect data and provide support to Veterans and serving personnel from the Caribbean and other ethnic minority backgrounds. For example, the Black Cultural Archives in London has collected oral histories and other materials from Caribbean Veterans, and the African and Caribbean War Memorial Trust aims to raise awareness of the contributions made by soldiers from the African and Caribbean communities.

It is, nonetheless, difficult to provide an exact figure for the number of Caribbean heritage men and women who served in the British Army between 1960 and 2000, as data was not consistently collected on the ethnicity of military personnel during this period. However, we can provide some estimates based on available information.

In the 1970s, the British Army was estimated to have around 4,000 soldiers of Caribbean heritage out of a total strength of around 160,000. In the 1980s, this number had increased to about 6,000, but in the 1990s, it was estimated to be approximately 5,000.

The Royal Navy, like the British Army, recruited Commonwealth citizens, including those from the Caribbean, during this period. According to the MOD report, the British Armed Forces recruited over 20,000 Commonwealth citizens between 1962 and 1984. Even so, the report does not provide a breakdown of how many of these recruits were in the Royal Navy.

The Royal Navy has made, in more recent years, efforts to increase diversity and promote inclusivity. In 2021, the Royal Navy reported that around 3 per cent of its personnel were from a black, Asian or minority ethnic (BAME) background, although this figure does not specifically identify those of Caribbean heritage. The Royal Navy also reports that it has various initiatives and support networks in place to promote diversity and inclusivity among its personnel.

The RAF, like the other branches of the British Armed Forces, recruited Commonwealth citizens, including those from the Caribbean, during this period.

In recent years, the RAF has also made efforts to increase diversity and promote inclusivity. In 2021, the RAF reported that around 5 per cent of its personnel were from a black, Asian or minority ethnic (BAME) background, although this figure does not specifically identify those of Caribbean heritage. The RAF also has various initiatives and support networks in place to promote diversity and inclusivity among its personnel.

Options for Change

Options for Change was a major defence review conducted by the British government in 1990. Its objective was to reduce the size of the UK Armed Forces and make them more flexible and better suited to the changing political landscape in Europe following the end of the Cold War. The review resulted in significant changes to the structure and size of the Armed Forces.

One of the critical outcomes of Options for Change was a reduction in the total number of personnel across all branches of the Armed Forces. The review proposed a reduction of 25 per cent in the size of the Armed Forces, which equated to a reduction of around 57,000 personnel over a four-year period.

The cuts affected all branches of the Armed Forces, but the British Army was particularly affected, with a reduction of around 35,000 personnel, representing a 28 per cent reduction in total strength. A number of the interviewees for this book were affected by this policy change. In a few cases, they took the opportunity to leave the forces to start new careers outside the military or take early retirement.

The British Army was restructured as a result of Options for Change, with the number of regular infantry battalions reduced from 55 to 40. The Royal Air Force also saw a significant reduction in the number of aircraft and personnel, while the Royal

Navy was reduced in size and decommissioned several of its ships. The review also led to significant changes in the role of the UK Armed Forces, with a greater focus on peacekeeping and humanitarian missions.

The implementation of Options for Change was not without controversy. Many critics argued that the scale of the cuts would leave the UK ill-equipped to respond to potential threats and that the reduction in personnel would place an undue burden on those who remained in service. However, the changes brought about by Options for Change were seen as necessary by the government of the time, given the changing political landscape in Europe and the need to reduce defence spending in light of the end of the Cold War.

The British Armed Forces

The overall purpose of the British Armed Forces is to protect the United Kingdom and its interests, both at home and abroad. This includes defending the country against external threats, supporting international peace and security efforts, and providing humanitarian aid and disaster relief. Caribbean men and women have been very much a part of these efforts.

The British Armed Forces comprises three main branches: the Royal Navy, the British Army, and the Royal Air Force. The size of the Armed Forces varies depending on several factors, including budgetary constraints and operational needs. As of 2021, the British Armed Forces had approximately 150,000 active personnel, with additional reserve and auxiliary forces bringing the total number to around 200,000.

The size of the British Armed Forces has changed significantly. In 1960, the British Armed Forces were considerably larger than today. At the beginning of the decade, the total number of active personnel was around 340,000, with an additional 240,000 reserves. By the end of the decade, the active personnel had dropped to about 290,000, with an additional 175,000 reserves.

In contrast, by 2000, the total number of active personnel in the British Armed Forces had fallen to around 205,000, with an additional 185,000 reserves. This decrease in numbers was partly due to changes in military strategy and technological advancements, which allowed for more efficient and effective use of resources. Additionally, budgetary constraints and changing political priorities also played a role in the reduction of the Armed during this period.

6. A View of the Armed Forces Now

The Army has the largest proportion of ethnic minorities (excluding white minorities) intake despite having a significant decrease in Commonwealth hires due to COVID-19 restrictions on travel to the UK and therefore, their ability to join the Armed Forces.

As of 1 April 2022, 6 per cent of the Future Reserves 2020 (2,120 personnel), or the former Territorial Army (TA) declared an ethnic minority (excluding white minorities) ethnicity. For both the UK Regular Forces and the Future Reserves 2020, the Army and Army Reserve represent the largest parts of the UK Armed Forces and have the greatest proportion of ethnic minorities (excluding white minorities) personnel, accounting for approximately 77.5 per cent of all ethnic minorities (excluding white minorities) personnel overall.

According to the Ministry of Defence in its report of 3 October 2013 in the House of Commons Library, the transformation of the reservist forces would enable the Armed to fulfil all of its military tasks with a reduced Regular force and greater reliance on Reservists: The Reserves have become even more important in defence of the country.

Ethnic minority personnel are an important part of the regular and reserve forces. Ethnic minorities (excluding white minorities) personnel accounted for 9.6 per cent of the UK Regular Forces (14,110 personnel) on 1 April 2022. It has now increased by 0.3 per cent and as of 1 April, 2023, is 14,240.

On 1 April 2022, ethnic minorities (excluding white minorities) personnel represented:

- 2.8 per cent of officers and 11.2 per cent of other ranks in the UK Regular Forces.

- 4.5 per cent of officers and 6.4 per cent of other ranks in the Future Reserves 2020.

Over time, however, from 2012 - 2018, the percentage of officers in the Armed Forces, by ethnicity, remained largely flat, with only imperceptible change in the Royal Navy over the period. The Army and the Royal Air Force show no change over that period.

Percentage of Armed Forces' Officers from Ethnic Minorities (not including white minorities), by Service over time

Ethnicity	Apr-12	Oct-12	Apr-13	Oct-13	Apr-14	Oct-14	Apr-15	Oct-15	Apr-16	Oct-16	Apr-17	Oct-17	Apr-18	Oct-18
	%	%	%	%	%	%	%	%	%	%	%	%	%	%
All Services	2.4	2.4	2.4	2.4	2.4	2.3	2.3	2.4	2.4	2.4	2.4	2.4	2.4	2.5
Army	2.8	2.7	2.7	2.7	2.7	2.7	2.7	2.7	2.8	2.8	2.9	2.9	2.9	2.8
Royal Air Force	2.3	2.3	2.3	2.3	2.3	2.3	2.2	2.1	2.2	2.2	2.1	2.0	2.2	2.3
Royal Navy/ Royal Marines	1.8	1.8	1.8	1.8	1.8	1.8	1.8	1.9	1.8	1.8	1.9	1.9	1.9	2.0

Number of Veterans in the UK as of February 2023

According to the Office for National Statistics (ONS), there are 1.85 million Veterans in England and Wales as of 3 February 2023. A total of 251,400 are women, and 1,601,705 are men. One in 100 (1.0 per cent or 19,315 people) Veterans identified themself within the Black, Black British, Black Welsh, Caribbean or other Black minority.

7. The Army

The British Army is the land-based branch of the British Armed Forces, responsible for conducting ground operations and providing support to other branches of the military. The Army is composed of Regular soldiers, who serve full-time, and Reserve soldiers, who serve part-time. As of 2021, the Army had around 82,000 Regular soldiers and 30,000 Reserve soldiers.

It is organised into a number of different Regiments and corps, each with its own unique history, traditions, and specialisations. These Regiments and corps are made up of battalions or units, which are further divided into companies, platoons, and sections. The structure of a Regiment is designed to foster a sense of camaraderie and identity among its members, and to provide continuity and stability over time.

In addition to infantry and cavalry Regiments, the British Army also includes several specialised corps, such as the Royal Engineers, the Royal Signals and the Army Medical Services. These corps provide essential support functions, such as engineering, communication, and medical care, to enable the Army to conduct operations effectively.

The British Army has a hierarchical system of ranks that includes both commissioned and non-commissioned officers (NCOs).

There are two categories of ranked officers: non-commissioned and commissioned. Commissioned officers are individuals who hold a commission from the monarch. They are responsible for commanding troops and making strategic decisions.

Commissioned officers include:
- Second Lieutenant
- Lieutenant
- Captain
- Major
- Lieutenant Colonel
- Colonel
- Brigadier
- Major General
- Lieutenant General
- General

Non-commissioned officers are enlisted soldiers promoted to leadership positions based on experience and ability. They are responsible for leading and training soldiers and ensuring discipline and order within their units.

Non-commissioned officers (NCOs) include:
- Lance Corporal
- Corporal
- Sergeant
- Staff Sergeant

- Warrant Officer Class 2
- Warrant Officer Class 1

The rank of Private is the lowest rank in the British Army and is held by newly enlisted soldiers.

The progression of rank for a soldier typically starts with Private, followed by Lance Corporal, Corporal, and Sergeant. Staff Sergeants, Warrant Officer Class 2 and Warrant Officer Class 1 are considered senior NCOs, and hold significant leadership positions within their units.

The ranks of the British Army differ slightly from those of other Commonwealth nations, although they share many similarities.

The British Army offers a wide range of specialisms, also known as trades or job roles, to its recruits. These specialisms are divided into four main categories: combat, engineering, logistics, HR, finance and support.

Combat specialisms include infantry soldiers, armoured crew members, and artillery soldiers trained in combat techniques, weaponry, and tactics. They are responsible for engaging with the enemy and carrying out missions in often hostile environments.

Engineering specialisms include roles such as engineer, electrician, and plumber, responsible for designing, building, and maintaining the Army's infrastructure and equipment. They also play a vital role in ensuring the Army's operational readiness.

Logistics specialisms include roles such as driver, supply chain specialist, and chef, who are responsible for providing the Army with the supplies, equipment, and resources it needs to carry out its missions effectively.

HR, finance, and support specialisms include roles such as human resources, finance, and IT specialists, responsible for managing the Army's administrative functions and ensuring the smooth running of those functions.

In addition to these main categories, the British Army also offers a range of specialist roles, such as intelligence, medical, and military police, which require additional training and qualifications.

Recruitment to the Army

When recruiting new male and female soldiers, the British Army looks for key characteristics and attributes. These include:

1. Physical fitness: The Army requires recruits to meet certain physical fitness standards, as soldiers must be able to handle the physical demands of military training and operations.
2. Mental resilience: The Army looks for recruits who are mentally resilient, with the ability to remain calm under pressure and to adapt to changing situations.

3. Teamwork and leadership: The Army values recruits with good teamwork and leadership skills, as soldiers need to work effectively with others and take charge when required.
4. Discipline and commitment: The Army places a high value on discipline and commitment, as soldiers are expected to follow orders and to be dedicated to their duties.
5. Problem-solving skills: Soldiers must be able to think on their feet and solve problems quickly and effectively, often under difficult and challenging circumstances.
6. Cultural awareness: The Army values recruits who are culturally aware and sensitive to different cultures and backgrounds, as soldiers may be deployed in various countries and contexts.
7. Integrity and trustworthiness: The Army places a high value on integrity and trustworthiness, as soldiers must be honest, trustworthy, and reliable.

The recruitment process for the British Army has changed significantly over the years. In the 1960s, the Army relied heavily on conscription, which meant that while young men initially volunteered to join, they were then required to serve in the military for a set period. The recruitment process was largely focused on identifying and screening potential conscripts rather than actively recruiting volunteers.

Today, the British Army is an all-volunteer force, and the recruitment process is much more focused on attracting and selecting suitable candidates. The process typically involves a range of assessments and tests, including medical checks, physical fitness tests, aptitude tests, and interviews.

The Army has also become more diverse in its recruitment practices, with a greater focus on attracting women and individuals from diverse backgrounds. The Army reports that it actively promotes itself as an inclusive employer and has implemented various measures to encourage greater diversity and inclusion within its ranks. It is, however, important to note that there has been little shift in the overall numbers of black and ethnic minorities achieving higher ranks both as non-commissioned and of those achieving commissions to the most senior ranks.

Overall, the recruitment process has evolved significantly since the 1960s, reflecting changes in the nature of military service and broader societal shifts. Today, the Army seeks to attract and select individuals with a range of skills, attributes, and backgrounds to create a diverse and effective fighting force. However, in reality, there needs to be greater action taken to increase the numbers of ethnic minorities in higher and, therefore, more influential leadership roles.

Basic Training

Basic training in the British Army is designed to provide new recruits with the necessary skills and knowledge to become effective soldiers. The training received by all soldiers, including those of Caribbean heritage, is physically and mentally demanding. It covers a wide range of topics, including military tactics, physical fitness, and discipline. Some of the key elements of basic training in the British Army include:

Physical training: Physical fitness is a crucial element of basic training, and soldiers undergo intensive physical training to develop strength, endurance, and agility. This includes several activities, such as running, obstacle courses, and strength training.

Weapons training: Soldiers learn to handle and fire an array of weapons, including rifles, machine guns, and grenades. They are trained in safety procedures, marksmanship, and weapons maintenance.

Military tactics: Soldiers are taught military tactics, such as how to navigate in different terrain, how to conduct reconnaissance, and how to set up defensive positions. They also learn to operate as part of a team and communicate effectively with their fellow soldiers.

Fieldcraft: Soldiers are taught essential fieldcraft skills, such as how to set up camps, build shelters, and forage for food and water in the wild.

First aid: Soldiers learn basic first aid skills, such as how to treat wounds, fractures, and other injuries.

Discipline and ethos: Soldiers are instilled with the Army's core values, including loyalty, courage, respect, integrity, selfless commitment, and discipline. They learn to follow orders and to work as part of a team.

Overall, basic training in the British Army has been designed to be challenging and rigorous to produce physically fit, mentally resilient soldiers skilled in diverse military tasks. All the Caribbean recruits interviewed, largely enjoyed the challenges offered within their basic training and most excelled in each of the required activities.

Army Sports

The British Army offered then, as now, a broad range of sporting activities to its soldiers to promote fitness, teamwork, and healthy competition. It is seen as a key element of strengthening the team, developing camaraderie and increasing 'dependability on each other, of the unit or battalion and the force as a whole.

The Army organises intra-level, inter-force and combined forces competitions. Additionally, Army personnel had and have the opportunity to represent the national teams or at individual levels. This involvement was supported and encouraged by senior officers. The athletes representing the Army had targeted training and support given to ensure good health and high-level fitness and participation in national and even Olympic competitions.

A number of the men whose service is cited in this book are good examples of national and Olympic representation and even medal successes. Caribbean soldiers usually excelled in the sports in which they participated. Indeed, they were often the only persons of colour in teams and competitions.

Other Sporting Activities

Some of the most popular sporting activities, which Caribbean soldiers had access to and were encouraged to participate in, included:

Football: Football is a popular sport in the British Army, with regular tournaments and matches held at all levels.

Rugby: Rugby is another popular team sport in the British Army. Some of the teams competed with a few Caribbean soldiers involved at various levels - unit and combined.

Boxing: Boxing is a highly respected sport in the Army with a long tradition of producing talented fighters. Soldiers could train and compete in boxing at all levels, from novice to elite. A number of Caribbean soldiers represented the Army and, in fact, the country in this sport.

Athletics: The Army has a strong tradition in athletics, with soldiers competing in a range of track and field events at national and international levels. Many Caribbean soldiers participated in these activities, often excelling and representing their Regiment and the Army in various competitions.

Swimming: The Army offered swimming facilities and competitions, with soldiers able to compete in a range of distances and strokes.

Shooting: Shooting is a highly regarded sport in the Army, with soldiers training and competing in various disciplines, including pistol, rifle, and shotgun shooting.

Adventure sports: The Army also offered a range of adventure sports, such as mountaineering, and skiing, which allow soldiers to challenge themselves both physically and mentally

Overall, the British Army recognised the importance of sport in promoting fitness, teamwork, and mental well-being. It offered a broad range of sporting activities to its soldiers. Caribbean soldiers generally took advantage of these opportunities and gained many benefits, including, in several cases, national and sometimes international recognition from them.

Team Building in the Army

Apart from sporting activities, the British Army emphasised team-building activities promoting cohesion, trust, and effective communication among its soldiers. Some of the team-building activities offered to soldiers included:

Obstacle courses: Obstacle courses are a classic team-building activity in the Army. Soldiers work together to overcome physical challenges and obstacles, promoting teamwork and problem-solving skills. This activity was often used to test soldiers' fitness and build their skills, especially in the event of conflict and the need to rescue of their colleagues.

Field exercises: Field exercises involve soldiers working together to complete military training scenarios, often involving mock combat or simulated situations. These exercises required soldiers to communicate effectively and work together to achieve a common goal.

Leadership development programmes: The Army offered various leadership development programmes, which provided soldiers with opportunities to develop their leadership skills and practise leading others in challenging situations. These programmes were especially utilised in the more senior NCO roles and were key to the development of those commissioned officers whose responsibilities were critical to the success expected of their Battalions and Corps.

Adventure training: Adventure training activities, such as hiking, rock climbing, and kayaking, required soldiers to work together and support each other in physically and mentally challenging environments.

Sports: As mentioned earlier, sports were also an important team-building activity in the Army. Soldiers participated in various sports, both individually and as part of teams, to promote teamwork, communication, and healthy competition.

Overall, the British Army recognised the importance of team-building activities in promoting cohesion, trust, and effective communication among its soldiers. Caribbean soldiers participated fully and often excelled in these activities, which were designed to develop soldiers' skills and promote a strong sense of camaraderie and teamwork within each unit.

Rest and Recuperation (R&R) in the Army

The British Army provided a range of rest and recuperation (R&R) opportunities for soldiers during their service. These were designed to allow soldiers to take a break from their duties and recharge, both physically and mentally. For many Caribbean soldiers, these short breaks allowed them to learn more about the culture, food and people of various foreign countries. They travelled more than they had ever been able to.

Military life broadened their horizons, exposing them to some wonderful cultural and social activities, which made their lives all the richer for it.

One of the main R&R opportunities available to soldiers was 'Leave'. Soldiers were entitled to a certain amount of leave each year, depending on their rank and length of service. This would be taken as either regular leave, which is typically two weeks long, or longer periods of special leave, which were granted for various reasons, such as personal or family circumstances. Caribbean soldiers took full advantage of this and were able to travel back to see family from time to time to refresh themselves in their roots and birth culture.

In addition to leave, Caribbean soldiers also accessed a range of activities and facilities designed to help them relax and unwind. These could include recreational facilities, such as on the sports fields and gyms, as well as social activities, such as organised events and clubs. There were many parties and gatherings in which Caribbean men and women soldiers organised or participated. Where these took place in or near to the postings, especially in Germany, they were well attended and thoroughly enjoyed by everyone.

The Caribbean men and women publicised these events near and far, especially to their other Caribbean friends or newly formed friendship groups of other Caribbean military service people. They made sure that the latest music, 'Yard' food and just great conversations and sharing of jokes and reminiscences about their shared histories filled the air.

Soldiers who had been on operational tours were also often eligible for specific R&R programmes. These could include opportunities to travel home or to a designated R&R location for a period of rest and recuperation. Many Caribbean Veterans took these opportunities to travel to places relatively near to the countries to which they had been posted to explore new cultures and build their knowledge of these interesting, very different countries. They all spoke highly of these opportunities, which were both welcomed and enjoyed in full. They realised that their time in the military allowed them to be exposed to very different cultures and people whom they would otherwise have struggled to see and experience.

Based on the comments gathered from the interviews with the Veterans, these little external views experienced in other countries and of different cultures were appreciated even when they were stared at because of their 'differences'. The opportunities supported their broader education and helped their physical and mental well-being.

Meeting Others like Us!

In relation to the Caribbean soldiers, the rest and recuperation periods also allowed them to return home to see their family and friends, and connect with other black soldiers as well.

There was a small minority of black men from other Regiments and contingents of black soldiers from the USA, Belgium or France in the main. For the first time, the black soldiers serving in the British Army could see that there were other black servicemen who looked like them. For many Brits, it was an amazing and wonderful time. They could meet and greet, dance, drink and more with *"people who looked like us!"*

In addition, there was an obvious welcome for many of the men, mainly from local women living, for example, in the areas around their German barracks. For others, sadly, the racism was direct and, sometimes, even viciously obscene. It was at those times that the fact that there were more (though still small in number) of them as black people, they could defend themselves robustly, and survive.

Some men reported that they occasionally deployed such robust defence to protect themselves from other British soldiers who used to go "N....r hunting". Extraordinarily, this happened more than a few times. Sometimes, black soldiers were accused of using extreme force and were disciplined, whereas those doing this obscene 'hunting' went unpunished. The unfairness of this response in the 1970s began to feel normalised, with black soldiers just shrugging and accepting they just had to proffer a strong defence of themselves and their black 'brothers'. For some, it was a brutal time, with its attached brutal truths.

Promotion up the Ranks

Over the years, the British Army has implemented various diversity and inclusion initiatives to increase the representation of individuals from diverse backgrounds in its ranks, including those of Caribbean heritage. This was not always the case. There have always been some black soldiers within the Army. These have been very much in the minority, with, in many cases, only a handful of black recruits going through each year, with few achieving promotions beyond that of Sergeant. Most remained at the Lance Corporal or Corporal ranks. This was especially the case before the 1980s.

Evidence suggests that more individuals of Caribbean heritage have achieved higher ranks in the British Army over the last two decades. However, it remains a fact that the percentage of personnel in the higher ranks remains relatively low.

In recent years, the British Army has made efforts to increase diversity and representation in its ranks, including those of Caribbean heritage. According to a report published by the UK Ministry of Defence in 2021, as of April 2020, there were 280 Black, Asian, and Minority Ethnic (BAME) personnel holding the rank of officer in the British Army. This represents an increase of 45 per cent since 2015. While the report does not provide specific data on the representation of individuals of Caribbean heritage, it suggests that there has been marginal progress in increasing diversity and representation of non-white personnel in the Army's higher ranks.

There are positive signs from the Army through their recently published Race Action Plan and the appointment of a 'Champion' at the highest rank of General, that they are taking their responsibilities very seriously and want to achieve more measurable changes and be more inclusive. That is significant progress which should be noted and encouraged.

There are individual success stories of soldiers of Caribbean heritage men and women achieving some of the higher ranks in the British Army. For example, Colonel (Retired) Andy Allen, MBE provided lengthy service and in 2008, achieved, as the first black person then to do so, one of the highest ranks in the Army. An exceptional achievement for this now retired Caribbean man.

Colonel Andy Allen MBE

Andy's parents were born in Jamaica and came to England as part of the Windrush generation. He is the youngest of four siblings. Apart from his eldest brother who was born in Jamaica, Andy, his sister and other brother were born in North London.

Well documented, the Windrush generation faced incredible challenges on arrival in the UK and Andy's parents were no exception. As Andy says, *"They hoped for a better way of life and there was a sense of improving yourself; this was an opportunity of a lifetime."*

The Windrush generation were the entrepreneurs of their peer group in Jamaica. With a zest for life, they were incredibly brave, adventurous and hardworking. However, there was disappointment on arrival in UK due mainly to open racism and social inequalities. Moreover, the streets of London were not *"…..'paved with gold', as they'd been told in Jamaica (through the story book Dick Whittington and His Cat) and there was the realisation that actually, it was flipping cold!"*

Family circumstances meant a move to South London, where he will always be eternally grateful to a very close Jamaican family who played an influential role in shaping Andy and his sibling at an early age. Andy was curious about everything around him. He attended the local primary school and gained entry into a Grammar school. Although bright, at secondary school he was not the ideal scholar. Rebellious and often the class prankster, he much preferred the distractions of London life.

Strangely he was drawn to a local Army Cadet unit and found that he was actually quite good at it. His enjoyment of all the Cadet and leadership activities this youth organisation offered, developed in him a keen interest in joining the Regular Army as an Officer. Such an aspiration was very rare and unconventional for a black youth in the 1970s. But Andy was never one to follow the crowd, plus this potential career was quite different from that expected of him by his family. His eldest brother was a trained carpenter, his sister was training to be a nurse. Later on in life, Andy found out she had aspirations to join the Royal Navy as a nurse. His other brother was the first in the family to go to university. They were a hardworking family, but Andy wanted a bit more for himself.

"What really inspired me about being an Army Officer was the opportunity to be different and embark on a career that was alien to my family." He had great ambitions for himself, even then. *"I wanted a life of full of adventures that a young Black Londoner could only dream of."*

With his sights set on making something of his life, he needed a drastic change. So Andy took the bold decision to leave school for South London College to refocus and reset his academic ambitions to join the Army as an officer. His Plan B was to become a teacher. The 1981 Brixton riots also had a profound impact on Andy as they brought to the surface the many inequalities and injustices that still existed in the UK and that education was a route out. Andy left South London College with eight 'O' Levels and three 'A' Levels. These were sufficient qualifications for Army officer training and to read for an In-Service degree, in Engineering, if selected.

With no military family links and an officer corps that oozed elitism and the privileged class at that time, getting into the Royal Military Academy Sandhurst (where army officers are trained) was not going to be easy for this young brash Black South Londoner. However, Andy saw no limitations for himself. He stood out as an Army Cadet so he felt confident to proceed with his application. He was initially interviewed in Whitehall, London for officer suitability.

Andy undertook the relevant tests and with his sights clear about where he wanted to be, he was determined that he was not going to start his military career as a private soldier. He knew he was different and wanted to start his career as an officer. After all, he was eminently qualified, given the entry requirements at the time were just five 'O' Levels (of which mathematics and English were mandatory).

As expected, it was not all plain sailing to get to Sandhurst. His first attempt at the Army Officers Selection Board (AOSB) - a three-day assessment centre - was not good. He failed. Andy still remembers a line in the letter which read *"....we do not believe a second attempt at AOSB will be more successful...."* This was a punishing blow to Andy. Moreover, to some in his family, this was clear evidence that the Army did not want a black officer.

Fortunately, Andy wanted to join the Royal Electrical and Mechanical Engineers (REME), a relatively young forward-thinking technical arm of the Army, formed in 1942. The REME recruiting Captain spotted the raw talent in Andy and took him under his wing (they are still friends to this day). It was this Captain who recommended to Andy a three-month Potential Officers' (PO) course which concluded with those that 'survived' the course being able to take AOSB. However, there was a catch. To undertake the course, Andy would have to join the Army as a Private. If he passed AOSB at the end of the course he would go to Sandhurst. If he failed, he could leave the Army or continue to serve as a soldier – a route Andy was still vehemently against. Undeterred he signed up and attended the PO course.

Unsurprisingly of the 14 young men that started the PO course, Andy was the only person of colour. For Andy, this was to be the first of many such occasions throughout his career. Andy passed the course, attended AOSB and thankfully received a more favourable letter. He was off to Sandhurst! Of the 14 that started the PO course, nine finished and only three passed AOSB.

And so, this aspirational young man got his wish and he began his officer training at the top army training establishment of Sandhurst. He was 21 years old – a similar age to that at which many of his Caribbean Island forefathers left their homelands to seek their fortune.

Andy remembers those first days at Sandhurst very well. Here he was, in his sharp, officer cadet uniform, firmly and through merit, in the Royal Military Academy at Sandhurst.

He was in a platoon of 30 Officer Cadets and there were six platoons in his intake; 180 cadets in total. There were many cadets from overseas (princes, sons of dignitaries, specially selected), but Andy was the only British person of colour. Such a position would often cause confusion for cadets not in Andy's platoon and for instructors as well. He was more often than not mistaken as an overseas cadet, a 'floppy' and it was not a term of endearment. This both frustrated and annoyed Andy but he had no other option but to put up with it. It certainly would not be the case today.

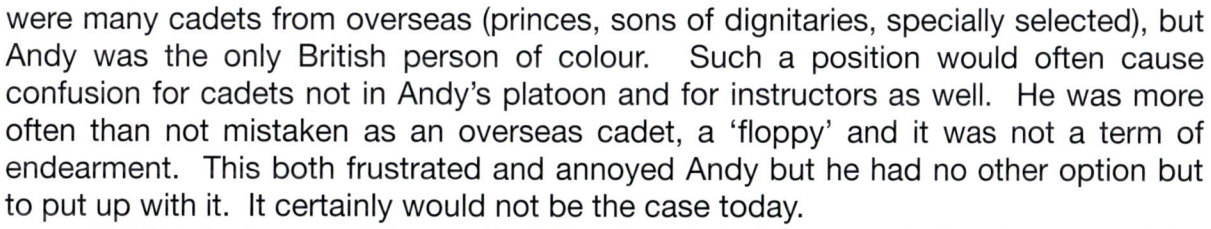

Whilst Andy was doing well at Sandhurst, being promoted to be part of the Cadet Government, he was always worried about 'the system' finding an excuse to get rid of him. Fortunately, the academic and leadership skill set required to be an officer came naturally to Andy and he did not want to ruffle any feathers or provide an opportunity for an early departure. He worked hard and played hard, a theme which continued throughout his 31-year military service.

Andy was successfully commissioned into REME – his first choice. During his REME Young Officers' training course, he won 'Best Young REME Officer' of his intake. Andy was so proud of this achievement. With a career spent defying the saying *"if you can't see it, you can't be it"*, it was another first.

"One of my secret career challenges was to be the first Black British born Regular Army Colonel, and when I was promoted to Colonel in 2008, it

was the realisation of so much that I had dreamt of. I was so very proud. At every rank, I stretched myself more."

Being promoted in 2008 as the first Black Colonel also called into sharp focus a poignant reality. Whilst there had been not many Black officers in the Army, why had it taken so long for one to reach such a high rank? That said, since Andy left the Army in 2015 the Army has had two Black Brigadiers and one is still serving. However, to date the Army has still not had a Black General. As an officer, apart from a couple of occasions, racism towards Andy was never overt, which certainly would not have been the case if he had joined as a soldier in the 1980s where mental and physical racism was a daily occurrence. Andy believes it was more insidious and hidden in the officer corps.

Andy's 31 years in the Army reads like a *Roy of the Rovers* bumper edition. What follows is just a snippet from his collection of scrapbooks containing many memoirs of his career.

As a professional engineer, who specialised in helicopters and guided weapons, Andy is a Chartered Engineer and Fellow of the Royal Aeronautical Society. Within a year of passing out of Sandhurst, he studied for his first degree, a BEng, at the Royal Military College of Science (RMCS), which was the military university. As a Major he obtained a Cranfield University MSc in Guided Weapons and as a Lieutenant Colonel he was selected to attend the Advanced Command and Staff Course and obtained a Kings College MA. All three degrees were full time and paid for by the Ministry of Defence (MoD). He also studied for an Open University MBA but dropped out after passing the Diploma due to a poor work/life balance.

In 1999 Andy had the honour of being awarded an MBE by HM The Queen. This was in recognition of his work on Anti-Tank Guided Weapons.

He served in many different locations both in the UK and abroad, including Germany, Croatia, Hong Kong, Iraq and Afghanistan. He held many key appointments, each with a considerable degree of responsibility. In Hong Kong he was Captain Officer Commanding an engineering Light Aid Detachment of helicopters (some of which were also in Brunei).

Whilst serving as an Acting Major in HQ Allied Command Europe Rapid Reaction Corps, he deployed to HQ United Nations Protection Force in Zagreb Croatia. In one of his postings to Germany (he completed three tours to Germany), he was Major Officer Commanding an engineering Workshop of helicopters.

Andy returned to Sandhurst as a Company Commander (Major) to train Officer Cadets and the irony was not lost on him. Occasionally he would escape the Sandhurst intensity to find solace in the Academy Chapel and spend time reflecting about those who had made the ultimate sacrifice and his career. As a Lieutenant Colonel he was the Commanding Officer of an Officer Training Corps unit and at the same rank, he was deployed to Iraq as Deputy Chief of the Iraqi Security Forces, training and preparing Iraqi security personnel for when they took governance of Iraq.

As Colonel Assistant Director Operational Support and Chief Aircraft Engineer to the Joint Helicopter Command, he deployed to Afghanistan as part of Operation Herrick, the UK forces contribution in support of the UN-authorised NATO led International Security Assistance mission and as part of the US led Operation, Enduring Freedom.

As Chief Air Engineer and Assistant Director Operational Support in the Joint Helicopter Command, Andy would routinely visit different Army, Royal Navy and Royal Air Force aviation sites. This was to ensure that all the appropriate personnel were in place, that the engineering standards were being maintained and that all logistics were operationally efficient and effective.

Andy also loved sport and adventure training. He boxed for Sandhurst and RMCS, and whilst at RMCS, he organised and led an adventure training expedition to Jamaica. Some of his sporting achievements include free fall-parachuting, qualifying as a Sub Aqua Dive Leader, bob sleighing for the REME and qualifying as a ski instructor. Rugby was his main sport though, playing for REME and the British Army of the Rhine, captaining British Forces Far East, and gaining international rugby honours playing for Hong Kong. Andy was also Chairman of the Army Masters rugby team and became Director of Senior Army Rugby – winning the International Defence Rugby Cup and attending the 2011 Rugby World Cup in New Zealand in this role.

Andy has a great family life, for which he is very thankful. He is married to his childhood sweetheart, Linda.

They have known each other since they were just 16, and whilst Linda sacrificed her accountancy career due to the nomadic lifestyle Andy's service demanded, she has recently gained her accountancy qualifications and is now a Finance Manager.

Andy is very proud of her as he is too of their two high-achieving children, Cassie and Alexander who have both attended University gaining First Class Honours' degrees. Education remains the fundamental pillar to success in the Allen household.

In his spare time, Andy is on the Royal Aeronautical Society Board of Trustees and a Non-Executive Director of Defence UK. He is assisting the Royal British Legion and British West India Regiment's Heritage Trust with regard to Windrush/Caribbean veterans and is a Windsor Leadership Trust Alumni. His love of rugby has not waned; he is President of the Jamaica UK Rugby Union Academy.

As he reflects on his career, Andy recalls that in the early stages he was more concerned about being from a working-class background in a space which seemed to be full of those from more privileged environments and schools (but in reality this was not the case). He was less concerned about being in the minority, as a black man. Class overwhelmed race in the officer context, in his mind. However, this did not mean that his experience as a black officer was absent of racism. *"Of course, there was overt racism"*. He expresses relief that things have changed. *"Thankfully, there is some really good work being done by the Army to understand its challenges and they are beginning to do more to support their multi-cultural community."*

There are now officers and soldiers who are Black Asian and Minority Ethnic community Champions. There is a recognised and thriving Army Multicultural Community Network and the current most senior Black Brigadier is of Caribbean heritage. Andy remains hopeful that one day the Army will have its first Black Major General.

Andy now works in the defence industry. He has been with the same company since he resigned from the Army in 2015 for a second career and is currently Head of Land Domain, UK Sales & Business Development.

For Andy the transition to civilian life was very easy. His experiences, education and seven years in the Defence Equipment and Support organisation, dealing closely with civil servants and industry on a daily basis, made stepping out of uniform into a suit a natural progression – he was ready for the next challenge.

Looking back to that time just before he set off for Sandhurst, Andy would love to look his 18-year-old self in the eyes and say to that earnest young man, *"Dare to dream and work hard, play hard. Your limitations are only bounded by your own imagination, self-confidence and what others may think of you – take delight in proving them wrong. I had a fantastic time in the Army, which has underscored a second career in business – I would do it all over again"*.

Colonel Andy Allen is a man of strength and stature. He has provided loyal, committed and exemplary service in his 31 years of service to the late Queen and to his country, the United Kingdom. He has indeed, demonstrated that in seeking to be the best, he evidenced in the manner in which he carried out his military service, that he was *"the best"*. He deserves our thanks and appreciation for everything he has done for all of us.

Achieving the Queen's Commission and NCO Ranks

Since the time that Colonel Andy Allen was promoted in 2008, and for the very first time in the near 400 years of Caribbeans serving in the Armed Forces, we now have the first ever Black British Caribbean Brigadier in the British Army. He is serving currently, Brigadier Karl Harris. He is a man of stature and vision, having being part of the development of an army BAME Committee, now the Army Multicultural Network (AMCN). Having met this impressive man, it was to hear him tell a hall of important, mixed service people and others, including a few civilians that *"We all need to lead well, follow well, and be the change we want to be."*

There are many remarkable British Caribbean soldiers. In relation to a few examples of others who were promoted up the ranks to progress into being commissioned, we can list three such - Lieutenant Colonel Pat Gibson, MBE, Lieutenant Colonel Michael Lawrence and Captain Wayne Douglas. All three of them as their stories will confirm, provided outstanding service to the Crown and country.

There are also more currently serving personnel, whose talents are being identified and who are being promoted, thankfully. All of these examples represent some change, albeit slow ones, in the promotion of members of the British Caribbean military community.

With the development of the Army Champion, we look forward to great changes beyond these notable achievers who cracked and even broke through the glass ceilings over the past three decades. The new vigour and apparent determination expressed by the Army should finally result in increased and fair representation of people, including British Caribbeans, at all ranks of the organisation.

In relation to the group of Veterans interviewed for this book, the outstanding promotion successes, included a few at the highest NCO rank of Warrant Officer (WO), also known as Regimental Sergeant Major (RSM).

The RSM is the most senior non-commissioned officer (NCO) of a British Army unit and is responsible for maintaining standards of discipline, conduct and drill. They act as an advisor to the Commanding Officer and are responsible for the welfare and professional development of the soldiers under their command. RSMs typically have long and distinguished military careers and are selected for the role based on their experience, leadership ability, and exceptional performance.

Here are a few examples of Caribbean men and women who achieved this high rank:

Warrant Officer (Regimental Sergeant Major, RSM) Owen Bernard is an individual of Caribbean heritage who achieved a high rank in the British Army. Bernard was born in Jamaica and joined the British Army in 1962. He served in British-based conflicts in Belize, Cyprus and the Falklands War and was promoted to Warrant Officer Class 1 in 1985, becoming one of the first black Warrant Officer Class 1 in the British Army. He was awarded the Queen's Gallantry Medal in 1983 for his actions during the Falklands War. Bernard retired from the British Army in 1993 after 30 years of service.

Warrant Officer (Regimental Sergeant Major) Burthlan Westpal (BJ) Webb, hailed from Jamaica, rose to the highest NCO rank of RSM. He served over 17 years in the Army.

Warrant Officer (Regimental Sergeant Major) Roger Dussard, another Jamaican served 24 years in the Army, contributing in several roles and arenas within the UK and across the world.

Warrant Officer (Regimental Sergeant Major) Rip Wilson served at the same time as Owen Bernard and later obtained a Commission to become a Captain.
This is an impressive achievement for these people of colour. From the changes being observed in very recent years, there will be more names to add to this short but remarkable list of Caribbean heritage men and women.

Overall, while specific data on the precise representation of individuals of Caribbean heritage in the British Army's higher ranks may be limited, there is evidence to suggest that some progress has been made in increasing diversity and representation in the military in recent years, since the label, Windrush Generation was created for those living here between 1948-1972 (born here or abroad from the Caribbean).

The Royal Army Medical Corps

The Royal Army Medical Corps (RAMC) is a specialist corps in the British Army that provides medical services to all Army personnel and their families. The RAMC also has responsibility for providing health care to the British Armed Forces at home and abroad, including during operational deployments. Established in 1898, it has its headquarters at Millbank in London. It is headed by a Major-General who holds the appointment of Surgeon-General.

Members of the RAMC are responsible for providing medical support on operations and training exercises, as well as delivering healthcare within military establishments around the world. They can be deployed on both land and sea missions, with duties ranging from front-line battlefield medicine to humanitarian aid work.

Medics play a crucial role in the British Army. Their role involves:
- Providing medical care and support to soldiers in the field and the garrison.
- Receiving training in an extensive range of medical skills, from basic first aid to advanced trauma care.

- Being deployed in combat zones, working closely with infantry units and other combat arms to provide medical support during operations.
- Providing medical care and being responsible for training soldiers in basic first aid and other medical skills, ensuring that all soldiers have a basic level of medical knowledge.

The RAMC played a critical role in the various conflicts between 1965 and 1990. During this period, RAMC personnel served on the front lines of many operations, including the Falklands War (1982), The Gulf War (1991) and Northern Ireland during The Troubles (1965-1998).

As well as providing medical care to military personnel injured in combat, they provided essential support services such as evacuation, triage and treatment of casualties, laboratory testing, logistics support, medical intelligence gathering, and preventive medicine services such as immunisations and health education programmes. In addition, they conducted research into new treatments for battlefield injuries with an emphasis on trauma-related illnesses.

RAMC medics typically hold qualifications such as a diploma or degree in nursing, paramedic science, midwifery or other relevant medical fields. They are also trained in the application of battlefield first aid techniques and basic life support skills. In addition to these qualifications, RAMC medics must be competent in areas such as triage, diagnosis and treatment of injuries and illnesses, patient transportation, and providing psychological support to patients.

The stories which follow, provide some insight into the military journeys of highly trained Caribbean soldiers who provided vital medical support as Medics or Nurses and also carried significant leadership responsibilities in the Army.

Lieutenant Colonel Patricia Gibson, MBE

Pat Gibson was born in the UK to parents, Coral and Denis, who migrated from Barbados in the 1950s. Her parents provided post-war support to rebuild the country, taking on employment, working on the buses and within hospitals.

Pat is one of six children. It was a tough life for her parents, but they met those challenges, working hard and providing for their growing family.

The family moved to Kent in the late 1960s. Pat completed her primary schooling in the County, in a school in which initially, there were no other black children.

Pat's earliest memories is of always wanting to be a nurse. There was something which attracted her to helping others, wanting to get them better. She knew somehow, even then, that she would pursue this type of career.

When Pat left secondary school, she went on to do her "O" levels and a pre-nursing course in Orpington College. This was followed by her starting her training as a nurse.

While she was at Orpington College, one of her colleagues had told her about nursing in the Army, something she had no knowledge about. Her friend persuaded her to go to the Careers' Office in Blackheath. There, she met Sergeant Pat Smith, a recruiter, who asked her if she wanted to take the tests with her friend. Obviously, she said no as she could not see herself being shouted at, marching everywhere and generally being restricted from a lot of things. However, Sergeant Smith said she might as well take the test as she had nothing to lose. So, Pat took the main tests along with some other tests.

At the end of the day, they said her tests results were good and she could join and do her student nurse training in the Army. There were conditions to the offer however. She would have to pass her 5 'O' Levels. Unfortunately, she failed her physics and chemistry. She was not too upset, as by then, she had secured a student nurse place at Orpington Hospital, not too far from home. She informed Sergeant Smith, who told her she could always come back once she had qualified.

In 1976, Pat started her nurse training. She started as a student nurse. Unfortunately, she failed her intermediates. She took them again, as well as the pupil nurse paper, both of which she passed. She had obtained a State Enrolled Nursing (SEN) qualification. She was immensely proud of that achievement. Subsequently, she went on to work in geriatrics before then getting a male surgical ward job, to broaden her experience and expertise. Pat was already showing a great degree of resilience. She persevered, showing strong evidence of someone who was not going to give up.

Pat was fortunate to have worked with a Sister in the hospital. This senior member of the nursing staff, was known for operating with the highest standards. Pat was able to learn much from that relationship and modelling. She was not completely sure that she would stay within the NHS. She remembered the conversation she had had with Sergeant Smith the Army recruiter, while she was doing her 'O' levels. A decision was being formed in her mind about her future.

Pat decided to pursue a military pathway and went back to the Careers' Office to start the application. Pat was surprised, but pleased that Sergeant Smith was still there and remembered her. Pat went along with a friend of hers and went through the application process, including completing the relevant tests.

She knew that she had failed her chemistry and physics and was not as optimistic. However, Sergeant Smith was encouraging as the Army took SEN's qualification as being relevant to her application. Pat was successful and was offered a place as an SEN in October, 1979. As she needed to give notice, she opted for the January intake.

She was really happy, and with the support of her family and armed with the experience she already had as a nurse, she joined the Queen Alexandra's Royal Army Nursing Corps (QARANC), in Jan1980.

Pat set off and to begin her basic training in Aldershot. She had been sent her Travel Warrant and was met at the station by a Sergeant and taken by bus to the Queen Alexandra Training Centre, (QATC). At the platform, she bumped into a girl, also an SEN she had worked with at Orpington Hospital previously. Both women were shocked to see each other in that strange environment, but pleased, as they each, now had an ally. Unfortunately, they were not in the same squad, but managed to see each other most days.

When she and the other new recruits walked up the hill, they were separated into groups. Each had their own room. There were 20 people in each Squad. They were issued with the prescribed grey uniform - black shoes, grey cardigans, beret, grey tights, clip on badges and three shirts. The women had to provide their own skirts. These skirts had to be dark in colour. After being measured, they were finally issued their grey skirts and service dress

Soon she was diving into the various soldiering skills she was expected to acquire. Soldier firstly, Nurse second.

There was only one other black woman recruit, but she left shortly after joining and Pat was on her own.

Pat made a number of friends during basic training, five of whom retain that lifelong friendship, despite not having been in the same squad as Pat.

She passed her basic training successfully and was soon able to move to her first posting at Louise Margaret Maternity Hospital in Aldershot. In this post, she supported the needs of the midwives, within another challenging arena within the UK. Pat was then posted to Northern Ireland (NI), a post she was really looking forward to doing. It was one of the jobs on her wish list; the other being British Military Hospital Hong Kong. Failing that, she would have liked Cyprus. Germany it was, following a year in NI.

Here, she did not see many Caribbean people like her. There was a Corporal, who was a Staff Nurse, and a couple of male Operating Department Practitioner (ODP) theatre technicians, but that was it.

Pat continued to do a good job in her Army post and secured a promotion to Lance Corporal. She saw the Matron, who awarded her the new rank in an informal ceremony. Pat could now have the chevron on the arm of her uniform. She was very pleased.

As a Lance Corporal, Pat had responsibilities which included leading and looking after others in her German posting. She held that post for just under two years, during which time, she also got married and moved into married quarters with her military partner.

Within a short number of years, Pat progressed through the ranks, achieving Corporal, Sergeant and Staff Sergeant. While she was a Sergeant, she had achieved her English National Board 115 (and Intensive care a six-month course) qualification for SEN and was back in the UK, in Woolwich, still working as an SEN Nurse.

She decided to apply to do the higher nursing qualification in order to become a State Registered Nurse (SRN). She had to go through the formal application processes and obtain the support of more senior officers (a Matron, for example).

She applied a number of times and had setbacks. She did not get it at first. Undaunted, she applied again and was still unsuccessful. She was spitting nails by this time and spoke to her Matron. Matron's words were not encouraging, as she said, *"What makes you think you're so special?"* Pat told her Matron that she knew she was better than some of the other successful applicants.

Pat was not about to give up. She knew her worth and knew that she was perfectly capable of doing an excellent job as an SRN and that the higher qualification would be beneficial to her within a promoted role. She therefore arranged to speak with the even more senior 'Big' Matron. He told Pat that he would *'look into it'*. Two months later, during a telephone call, Pat was told that she could now do the SRN conversion course. She was ecstatic. Now, she could really achieve more in the medical sphere. She knuckled down and was soon able to complete her SRN qualification and convert her ENB115 to ENB100 (for RGN aka Registered Adult Nurse) in a hospital in Portsmouth.

Pat's service record continued to build. She was being recognised by senior officers for her experience and expertise in her field. She continued to focus on her career, applying for and achieving further promotions. She finally, secured the top NCO position, as a Warrant Officer, at the age of 38. A great and well-deserved, achievement.

This Senior NCO rank was a tremendous achievement for this amazing Caribbean woman. Pat's ambitions however, were still incomplete. She wanted more. She aimed now for a Queen's Commission. Thus, she applied for and was interviewed to become a commissioned officer. She was successful. At the age of 41, Pat had become an Army Captain.

She went to Sandhurst for her officer training. Pat had previously visited Sandhurst as a newish Army nurse and recalled being awed by the Old and New College buildings and the grounds, at that time. Going back now, as a commissioned officer, with the sun shining overhead that day as she drove through the Sandhurst gates, she felt so lucky to be there. It was a wonderful feeling, which she still treasures.

Pat found this short Phase 1 Sandhurst training very enjoyable (most of the time). She was involved in specific military training, which included exercises, orienteering and other designated, leadership-type activities. New friendships were made, many of which she has maintained through the rest of her career and beyond into civilian life. In fact, she would meet some of those Sandhurst officers in other areas and conflicts, in which she and they were both involved. She has great memories of the Sandhurst Officers' Passing Out Parade, following that special experience.

While all these promotion opportunities and successes were taking place, Pat was still heavily involved in providing Army medical support in a variety of military arenas and conflicts. For example, before her commission, she was serving in Bosnia, where she celebrated her 40th birthday. She was there as part of the blue beret, UN peacekeeping force for the first of two, six-month tours. She was posted to Woolwich to the Queen Elizabeth Military Hospital, while the Gulf War was on. The hospital was a

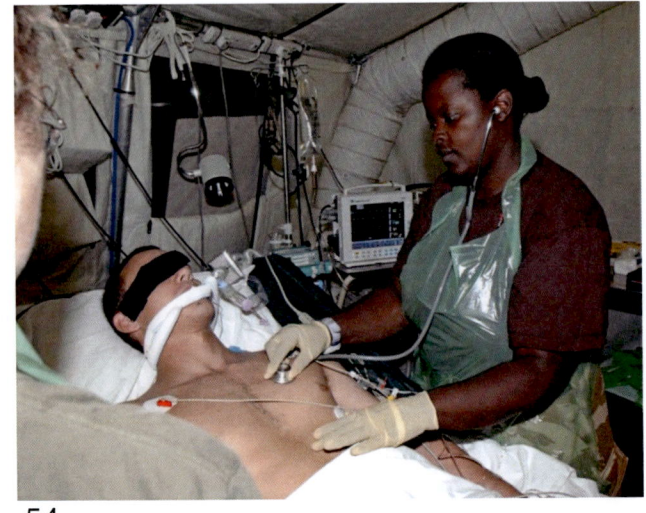

54

receiving hospital, providing close support to injured and other sick military personnel.

Despite not serving directly within the Gulf War, Pat was subject to being trained for any eventuality as a soldier, wherever she was required to go. She served in Iraq, completing two tours there and was in Afghanistan again. for two tours.

She provided service above and beyond, when called to support during the Ebola crises in Sierra Leone.

This was not a woman soldier who stood still and avoided challenges. She met them head on, serving with courage and commitment.

Pat continued to rise up the ranks. She was commissioned as a Lieutenant, Captain Major, where she was Deputy Matron at Queen Elizabeth Hospital, Portsmouth and Staff Officer 2(SO2) to The QA Chief Nurse for the Army and deployed to Afghanistan as the Lead Nurse in ITU.

She went on to become a Lieutenant Colonel, her highest position in the Army. This was a great achievement, worthy of her skill, commitment and bravery in a range of conflicts and across her leadership and management of ranking personnel who served alongside her.

Throughout her long, loyal and courageous service to this country, Pat never once shirked her duties. She never once questioned her postings at any point in her career.

She always sought *"to quickly get into"* whatever role she was required to undertake. She just settled in quickly and got on with the job.

She was in Iraq and then Afghanistan as a Major, before coming back to the UK to be a Lieutenant Colonel where she was the Senior Intensive Care Nurse. In this role, she had significant leadership responsibilities for the whole nursing team, including for their deployment.

At this time and at the age of 55, she had already completed 33 years in the Army and had achieved a huge amount in her various roles and in her promoted ranks. She had navigated successfully, a range of challenging situations and environments. These ranged from foreign conflicts to medical support in a distressing, acute Pandemic environment. In between, she returned to UK Bases in locations such as Catterick, Woolwich and Aldershot.

Towards the end of her time in the Army, Pat considered *'Where to next?'* within the military sphere. She was interested in influencing the recruitment process, especially within the Ethnic Minority Recruitment Team (EMRT). She even managed to speak with the Colonel at a Cocktail Party to put her case forward. The post within the EMRT had gone to someone else.

Luckily for her, the person who had been appointed to the Ethnic Minority Team had to leave, and as luck would have it, the Colonel that she had hosted at the cocktail party, remembered her and asked if she was still interested. She was and thus took the post.

It was her work within this team, which attracted great exposure for her and admiration for the things she was achieving within that role. So much so, that in 2003, she was awarded an MBE by the Queen, specifically for her work in this area.

Pat was posted to Portsmouth as Deputy Matron and had gone on to become the SO2 to the Director of Nursing. The Director of Nursing was a massively important strategic post, the highest and most significant in the QARANC.

By this time, Pat had been awarded eleven medals for her military service. She made the decision to retire from the Army having completed more than three decades of service.

She was not finished yet, however. She went on to serve another seven years in the Army Reserves. She used her experience to support the Regulars, validating teams who had been preparing for the different conflicts, making sure they understood their roles. She ensured that following her experience of working with Ebola, she could make sure the medics had good awareness of that dreadful disease and could be better prepared as a result. It was during her role as Senior Nursing Officer and following her return to the UK, that Pat was award her 12th Medal for her work during the Ebola crisis. A great recognition for the stunning, critical contribution she had made as part of the collective efforts to improve conditions and treatment of this awful illness.

As a reservist, Pat was involved in a range of different things. These activities and events, she accepted gladly, offering her experience and expertise, as required.

Some of these activities included participating in NATO exercises and speaking at international events. and being the SO1 Med for the University Officer Training Corps. In this role, she was responsible with her team, for ensuring approximately, 2500 required medicals were carried out across the country for everyone prior to them joining. She has had a great time meeting a variety of personnel and visiting a host of different countries.

In 2020, Pat moved fully into civilian life. She has continued to work as a nurse. During the COVID Pandemic, she was very active, realising why she had trained in nursing and affirming in her mind, the value of that profession to the patients and to society more broadly. She knew very well why her skills were critical and needed by so many people at that time.

She looks back on her lengthy military career within the QARANC and is clear that she had made a good contribution throughout. She also took time to participate in the various Regimental, social events and to be part of the range of team building activities, held by the Army. She remains glad that as a 20-year-old, she had made the decision to join up. In her view, it was a good move, despite occasionally feeling that she had *"made her bed and had to get on and lie in it"*.

Pat continues to have a 'presence' in events related to the military, attending events such as those held at the Arboretum. She is particularly supportive of those events organised to commemorate the part played by Nurses in the various conflicts.

She is often recognised for what she has done, especially within the Ethnic Minority Recruitment Team. She and the other black and Asian males and females in the Team had the opportunity to tell their stories to schools and gatekeepers about why they joined and what they have achieved since joining the military.

She would advise young Caribbean people to join, to *"go for it!"* The biggest bit of advice she would give to them is that the initial training is only for a short time. They can do so many things, including getting a trade, which would be a good grounding for their future.

It is her firm view, that a career in the military can set you up for life. She certainly benefited from her time in the Army. She did so many things, including meeting her husband, who was also serving in the military when they met.

She has travelled extensively and has also had several short moments (fortnights) of rest and recuperation. This is despite the stresses and challenges of the various conflicts in which she was involved.

Pat enjoys her life. She feels grateful for so much, but especially for her family and also her friends, many of whom she has known for decades.

She treasures these relationships.

There have been times when she has met people 'outside' who seem to have a preconceived idea about a black person being in the Army, especially being ones in the higher ranks.

She has been asked if she was an actor or was she in the Jamaican Defence Force. She has been abused and had paint thrown at her car when her team were at a recruiting fair. She feels a little sad about these sorts of views.

Equally, she has had had people come and tell her how proud they are to see women of colour in the Army. She loves the fact that there are increasing numbers of minorities who are being recognised in a range of other careers, and businesses more generally. She wants to see more of this recognition also, for those who have served and are still serving in the military. *"There is not enough recognition and acknowledgement of their service".*

Lieutenant Colonel Patricia Gibson MBE, is a strong, powerful and positive woman. She has achieved a great deal in her long, exemplary and effective service to the country, achieving significant promotions through the ranks. This is a woman who should be applauded and lauded for this service to her country and to the Crown.

Photo by Gill Shaw

Captain Wayne Douglas

Wayne was born in Bristol to Caribbean parents who journeyed separately from their Island homes in 1954 and 1955 and met and married in London. Wayne's parents moved their family first to Dulwich and then to Bristol and Rugby, before going back to live in London, where Wayne grew up.

Wayne was the second of three children - all boys - and was educated in primary and secondary schools in the Stockwell area of London.

Once Wayne was 16 and armed with his 'O' levels, he attended a local college, where he studied electronics for the next two years. He went on to do various jobs, including that of a mechanic, before deciding at the age of 20, to join the Royal Army Medical Corp.

He did his physical test in Sutton Coldfield and passed with flying colours. He went through basic training and again, passed successfully before moving on to the army medical career, which he pursued throughout his time in the military.

When he started in October 1982, Wayne went through a 16-week, Basic training programme, before his Passing out Parade in February 1983. He felt very proud of his achievements and was very happy that his Father and his Partner and a friend, were there to see his success.

A military career was almost inevitable for this young man. He had joined the Sea Cadets and the Army Cadets at the age of 13 and was familiar with much of the elements of basic training before he actually *"took the Queen's shilling"*.

Basic training was therefore reasonably easy for Wayne. When he arrived in Ash Vale to start his career, he was put into a 12-man room. He found himself one of only two black people in his whole intake. Each intake consisted of 48 people. By the end of training there were only 32 on parade.

He remembers clearly being in awe of WO2 Herbie Providence, who was the Squadron Sergeant Major.

WO Providence was one of the very few black men to hold this senior NCO position at the time. Viewing a black man in this lofty position, when you are a mere very junior Private would have been a huge thing for Wayne. It would certainly have been a formative issue for enabling Private Douglas to see the more senior ranks as being possible for him in the future.

Once Basic training was over, Wayne moved on to his clinical training. He spent one month at Woolwich Military Hospital (now Queen Elizabeth Hospital), before going on to Colchester to train with 19 Field Ambulance until October 1983.

Wayne was then posted to the Cambridge Military Hospital in Aldershot for the start of his Operating Theatre Technician Class 3 course for six months.

Wayne became an Operating Theatre Technician, also known as an Operating Department Practitioner (ODP), assisting the Anaesthetist in the theatre. He was also the secondary scrub who assisted the Surgeon.

Wayne was posted to Munster, Germany for a year to undertake his Class 2 training. He failed the Class 2 exams and had to redo it in North Catterick Yorkshire. Sadly, he failed this again, after he had been informed that he had passed initially to be then told that he had failed. He put in a complaint and requested feedback. Having done this, he was removed from the role and sent back to a Field Unit in Colchester. This was a reduction in status and pay. It is not difficult to imagine his disappointment and sense of injustice. Nevertheless, he went back to work in the Field Unit in Colchester where he was constantly sent on military medical exercises all around the world.

Rather oddly, despite his reduced situation, but because his academic qualifications were higher than other soldiers, he was moved to the training wing to help in the training of other soldiers. At this point, he decided to apply to do 20 hours of surgery training with the NHS. Completion of this training would make him a qualified ODP. However, the head of the School of Military ODPs would not authorise the time off from work for the training to be completed.

That September, Wayne was sent on to the Unit Pre-Junior Management Training Course which took place across Okehampton and Dartmoor.

On completion of the course, he was then promoted to the rank of Lance Corporal. His strength of character and resilience in the face of challenges, served him well. Six months later, he went to Keogh Barracks, Ashvale to do his Class 1 Combat Medical Course. He passed out in 1985.

An opportunity came up for a six-month posting to Belize. In this posting, Wayne would be providing general practice support, running a small medical centre. Wayne's role was to provide medical support and medical packs for other soldiers going on exercise. His role was to make sure these men kept as healthy as possible.

Wayne loved the idea of being in a country where he would for a change, be a part of the majority as most of the inhabitants were also black. By this time, Wayne had become a Corporal. While in Belize, a position on the Junior Management Course became available. However, this would require him to return to the UK to do a course which would help his promotion chances; but he was not allowed to return. After the Belize placement came to an end, Wayne returned to Colchester where discussions took place with his seniors about not being allowed to participate in the course he had initially been encouraged to attend. He was placed on the next available course. However, by then, this had caused Wayne a loss of six months' seniority towards promotion.

With the Junior Management Course now completed, Wayne requested pay of a higher rank as he was running his Section, which was a Sergeant's job. However, this was not to be, as he was given a quick posting still as a Corporal, to a military hospital in the UK. This new posting did not make any sense, so Wayne addressed the issue with the chain of command at the hospital. He was told he would have to wait two weeks for feedback about his complaint. Wayne considered whether it was time to leave the Army altogether but two weeks later he was informed he was to be promoted and posted in seven months' time. Wayne was posted one week before a major incident occurred in the region.

He was posted to Berengaria, Limassol, Cyprus to the Married Families' Medical Centre. There was a very positive aspect to Wayne's life prior to this posting; he got married. This meant that he and his family would now be living in a 3-bedroom married quarter on arrival in Cyprus. Wayne had achieved the rank of Sergeant, and was the Group Practice Manager, a post he held for the next three years. His role involved running the Medical Centre which had a range of services, pre- and post-natal care, dentistry and a pharmacy. There was a variety of staff working at the Medical Centre; a mixture of locals, expats and dependant Registered General Nurses RGNs).

Gulf War I in the Kuwait-Iraq border started and all medical assets in Cyprus were deployed either to the desert, or to the low care transit medical facility in Akrotiri. The build-up and the conflict were over within 6 months (Aug 90-Jan 91). Wayne thought long and hard about what he would do next in terms of his military career. He returned to the UK for another training course which was a requirement for a posting to the Medical Support Troop in Hereford. However, on return to Cyprus, a Posting Order had already arrived, informing him of a posting to 1 Armoured Field Ambulance Hohne, West Germany in March '93, for three years.

Wayne was posted to 1 Armoured Field Ambulance, which provides close medical support to the Army's Armoured Battle Group training exercises in Canada. Wayne was sent on exercise as part of a medical treatment section consisting of 16 Medics and a doctor in four armoured vehicles to Canada then on to Bosnia for six months. This was as part of the United Nations' Peacekeeping efforts. He also strengthened his skills further by undertaking a weapons' training instructors' course.

It was now 1994 and Wayne's daughter was 10 years old. Wayne and his wife decided that their daughter needed to return to the UK to be educated. Thus, they organised for her to attend a boarding school in London. It was another two years before Wayne and his family would be posted back to Aldershot in the UK.

Wayne was posted to Aldershot in 1996 and stayed in Aldershot for the next four years. Whilst there, by 1997, he obtained the rank of Staff Sergeant and was sent on deployments to the Congo and to Kosovo for six months. He became Acting Warrant Officer for a six-month attachment to the training team in the British Army Training Unit in Suffield (BATUS), Canada.

On return to Aldershot, the Army decided to move the airborne brigade units to Colchester. After six months in Colchester, Wayne was promoted to WO2, (Squadron Sergeant Major, SSM). This was a tremendous achievement. Wayne had become the top-ranking officer, like the one he had first seen when he met SSM Herbie Providence when he was a recruit all those years ago. Where would he go next? Wayne still had ambitions to fulfil.

Wayne was promoted and posted to 254 Field Ambulance in Cambridge which is a reservist unit. There he was employed as the Regimental Quartermaster (RQM) responsible for the receipt and demand of stores and material. He would be commuting from Cambridge as his family was then living in North London. After two years in Cambridge, Wayne was posted to 256 Field Hospital in London in the same role. Wayne then applied for a Commission in the Royal Army Medical Corps as a Medical Support Officer.

However, it was now 2003, Wayne had completed 22 years' service in the Army and the unit was preparing to deploy to the desert. The build-up and deployments for Gulf War II had started. However, Wayne felt that he had done enough conflict support and realised that his last day of service would be in the desert, which he did not want to do.

He spoke to a colleague about his options. This colleague was an Army representative with the Ethnic Minorities Recruitment Team (EMRT) which led the Army's diversity campaign. This colleague was on long service and worked in the community. That line of work seemed interesting to Wayne. So, in September, 2003, Wayne was posted to London District as the Ethnic Minorities Liaison Officer (EMLO) London.

Over time, he was supported by Staff Sergeant Burns, Royal Artillery (RA) and Sergeant Lin, Royal Electrical Mechanical Engineers (REME). The Team's job was to organise events in the various ethnic minority communities in the London area in order to dispel the negative narrative about a career in the Army.

Alongside this, Wayne continued to address his promotion prospects and decided to apply for a Commission, again. His ambition was not dampened by some of his previous experiences. The first time he applied for a Commission, he was unsuccessful. He was in 13th place. The first 12 people succeeded, so before making his second application, he decided to do a practice interview, by applying for a role as the recruiting and retention officer back at 256 Field Hospital. However, after attending the Interview Panel, Wayne was offered the role. He had to make a decision to either take the job, or wait for the regular Medical Support Offices Commissioning Board. Wayne decided to take the Job. Thus, this competent, highly motivated, and skilled soldier, was rewarded. He had succeeded and received his Queen's Commission. He was so very proud.

He was given a start date and a date for his Late Entry Officers' Course (LEOC) which is the start of his officer training with other late entry newly Commissioned Officers. This would take place in the prestigious environment of Sandhurst.

Sandhurst was an experience for Wayne, very different from everything else he has been exposed to in other previous training. Fortunately, for Wayne, his Syndicate Directing Officer was in the RA and he had worked with Wayne's older brother. Getting that support made the whole experience much more fulfilling and effective for Wayne. There was only one other black man on the LEOC at Sandhurst, when Wayne started his course. That person is now a Colonel in the Rifles.

After receiving his Commission, Wayne became a Medical Support Officer at 256 Field Hospital with the following roles: Recruitment and Retention Officer and Unit Welfare Officer. The main focus of his team was end-to-end recruitment of clinical doctors, nurses and allied health professionals from the NHS into the Army Medical Services.

Wayne has been awarded several medals for his service. He was given the General Service Medal 62 and Clasp, the Gulf Medal 90-91, a UN Medal (unprofor)1994, NATO Medal and Clasp, Kosovo Volunteer Reserve Service Medal and Clasp.

He also has the Army's Long Service Good Conduct Award and Clasp, and the Golden, Diamond and Platinum Jubilee Medals.

Wayne has deployed into various different countries as part of the military medical support effort in order to deliver forward surgical support within a combat support hospital. He has served in various conflict zones around the world. He was also a key part of the UK's support efforts during COVID. He was the Unit Welfare Officer for deployments to Afghanistan, the Ebola support in Sierra Leone and troop deployment to Mali. He was also proud to support each of the Queen's Jubilee events.

Wayne took a pragmatic view of his career at this time. He enjoyed being a Captain. He knew the Captain's rank allowed him sufficient freedoms to do well and support other colleagues effectively; and it included a good pension! The one regret he has, was that he did not seek the opportunity to apply for a Grade 2 Staff Job and thus to become a Major after completing the Intermediate Staff and Command Course, in 2016. He certainly had the skills and he had passed the relevant course and received good reports. Otherwise, he is proud of his long service and the contributions he has made to the army, to the Queen and to the country.

Captain Wayne Douglas provided 40 years of service to this country. He joined at 20-years-old and 40 years on, he has now retired to civilian life. This is an extraordinary man, whose service to the UK was exemplary, as a ranking soldier and a Commissioned Officer.

Wayne belongs to a family, several of whom have contributed many years of service to the British Armed Forces. His brother Trevor, and his cousin Lester, and Lester's sons, have also served.

The loyalty and service of these brave men is truly remarkable.

Wayne feels it is a privilege to be amongst this group of soldiers, who are also loved and loving members of his family.

He knows he made a good move to take up a military career. He would encourage others to consider it also. It would be especially useful to them, he believes, when a young person wants to achieve particular things in life. He believes they could do this within the framework offered by military life. For example, Wayne was able to complete Level 7 in Leadership in Management to achieve an Open University, BSc degree in Social Policy, and various other qualifications funded by the government. In his view however, there is a two-tier system: one for those Caribbeans born here, the other for those Caribbeans born abroad. His advice to each group would be different.

He remains proud of his service. He contributed much within the different environments in which he served. He made some good friends, many of whom he remains in contact with. They often reminisce and smile about the 'old days' and how much they have changed since those youthful times.

Indeed, Wayne and one of his friends were reminding themselves recently that they have celebrated as much as 80 years of service between them.

68

In civilian life, Wayne continues to provide support to various organisations and causes. He is especially concerned to ensure that people take seriously, the contents of the Armed Services Covenant and thus he has attended several locations to discuss the Covenant's significance and secure 'buy in' and signatures.

There is no doubt in this remarkable soldier, Captain Wayne Douglas' mind, that despite his long and distinguished career, he understands that
"Deployment and service life is not fully understood nor acknowledged generally in a society we have spent our working life defending".
That is a great shame.

He has done much on our behalf and we must not forget. We must unquestionably, recognise and acknowledge this service.

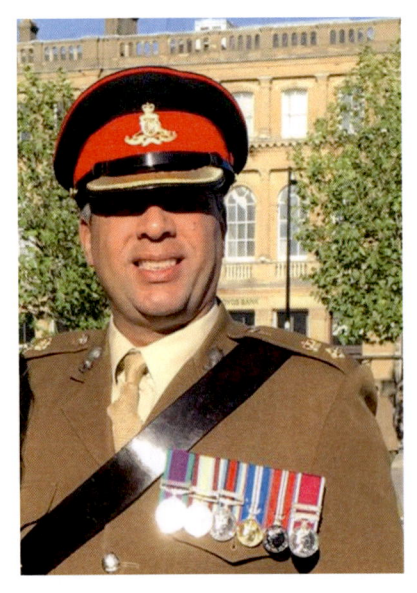

Lieutenant Colonel Michael Lawrence

Michael is mixed-race. His mother, white English, his father, black Caribbean who came to England in the 1950's as part of the Windrush generation and worked his entire life on the London Underground until his death in 1982.

"I now consider myself mixed-race – not black, not white, rather a perfect fusion of the two and blessed to be of dual-heritage. This was not always the case. In general society, I am viewed as black as anything not white, simply considered black. I've been called a black bast**d many times in my life but never a white one."

Michael was born in Hammersmith hospital in West London in 1962. He has two brothers, Tyrone and Ricardo and a sister, Amanda. Unfortunately, as a family, they were not particularly close. Michael describes his father's temperament and their environment being such that that created an atmosphere which would spiral them in different directions, apart from each other with reconciliation only being attempted in recent years.

The family were constantly moving. During Michael's younger years, they would slowly move across London from the west to the east which included Notting Hill, then not the trendy postcode it is today. The family moved on to Islington, the first place which Michael had any real memories of. They lived in a block of flats called Kempton House just down the road from Hoxton Market. It was while they were living there that Michael realised that not being white made them different. He started noticing how people would look at them and at his Mum, disapprovingly and judgementally. He recalls how his brother Tyrone, whilst walking to his primary school one morning, was shot in the back with an air rifle from one of the neighbouring balconies. The pellet had gone through his jacket and shirt and embedded itself in his back. He had to go to hospital to have it removed. This would be the first time his brother was shot, but not the last. The next time would be years later, but with live ammunition in far more dire circumstances. The police, although unable to find the culprit, believed the attack to be racially motivated. It was at that very moment that Michael registered somewhere in his young mind that there was a fundamental difference between him and his siblings and white people. It was when the word 'racism' became real and a part of his life.

Michael's dad was not prone to displays of affection. He cannot recollect any intimate moments he spent with him. *"I can't even remember a single cuddle or kiss on the forehead...nothing. That doesn't mean there weren't any, just none that I remember."* Michael does however, remember his father's temper. *"We all lived in perpetual fear of him. For us kids, his discipline weapon of choice was his belt. The very sight of it being unbuckled from his waist would strike dread into your very soul. The kiss of the belt was excruciating. And he was generous with it."*

Michael's Mum and dad's relationship was a rocky one and their marriage ended when Michael was ten years old. Michael describes the feeling of being abandoned by his father and then being taken to Ilford Police Station by his mother as the family had nowhere to go. The family ended up sleeping in the police station waiting room that night. They were homeless. The next time Michael would see his dad very briefly, was when he was working in his first job with the Post Office when he was 16-years-old. Fortunately for the family, a woman from the local council came to the police station and they were found emergency accommodation in a hostel in Ilford itself. They were allocated a room that measured about 9ft x 7ft and contained two single beds. Michael's Mum and his sister Amanda shared a bed. Elder brother Tyrone, of course had the other and Michael and his other brother, Ricky slept between the beds on the floor. The other two bedrooms in the house also had families living in them. The bathroom and kitchen were shared areas between everyone in the house, with use of those areas determined by allocated time slots.

Michael's Mum was a strong, beautiful woman who did everything she could for her children. Michael will always be grateful for all that she did for him, especially as it was tough for her as a single parent, to manage a home for him and his siblings.

At school, Michael was the only mixed-race person in his year. There were a couple of black kids but they kept to themselves. Michael especially remembers brothers, Michael and Charlie. In school, Michael messed around far too much and that coupled with the constant name-calling and abuse he got from the other pupils meant that *"the only subject I excelled at was truancy"*. His mother's pleas to the Headmaster, for him to help to stop others from bullying Michael, fell on deaf ears. The sense of dominion some felt they had the right to hold over others was suffocating. Little did Michael know that this was just the warm up act for what was to come when he would later join the Army.

As they got older, both of Michael's brothers would join the Army and both were posted to units in Germany. Life at home was depressing. Michael felt that he needed to get away. He needed to change the environment he was in, not only because of the overt racism he faced but also because he could feel the tendrils of criminality starting to get a grip of him. He was carrying out minor petty crimes that seemed to be quickly escalating. *"This was not the real me. I wanted no part of it. I really need to get away, anywhere."*

There was a number of reasons that drove Michael to joining the Army other than not wanting to become a fully-fledged criminal. They arrived in a perfect storm, a storm no one could have predicted or even believed possible.

The first 'wave', as Michael labels it, is of this impossible storm when, at home alone one day, Michael received a phone call from someone identifying themselves as a member of the Ministry of Defence asking if his mother or father were home. *"No"*, he responded. *"My dad doesn't live with us and mum is at work."*

This individual went on to explain that it was *"a shame your mother is not home"* and that Michael should *"pass on a message to her immediately on her return from work"*.

"The message was that my older brother, who was serving on a Northern Ireland tour of duty, had been shot whilst on guard duty." *"Don't worry"*, the stranger from the MoD said, *"He's in hospital and still alive"*. Nothing was said about his injuries.

"I can't remember anything else he said. My heart was beating out of my chest. I felt my legs buckle a little and I could feel the blood rushing up into my face. I hung up the phone."

When Michael's mum arrived home, he didn't know what to do. *"It was the single worst experience of my life."* As she put her key in the door, I was behind it holding it closed. She was asking what was wrong. Why was I holding the door closed. Through the door, I just blurted out what had happened to Tyrone. I felt powerless, unable to provide mum with any level of comfort as she fell to her knees sobbing."*

This was a desperate time for Michael's mother especially, but deeply scary for the rest of the family. Michael's brother would recover and the incident involving him was later reported in the local paper. He went on to serve a further five years before leaving the Army.

The second 'wave' was when Michael was approached by two men in his local pub, the Angel in Ilford. Michael had seen them about and they were known to be shady characters. They offered Michael a huge amount of money to do something seriously criminal. It was more money than Michael had ever seen in his life. The clearing of a few items from Woolworth's shelves and the odd low-level petty 'stuff' in the dead of night was up to that point, the sum total of Michael's complete criminal repertoire. This new demand from these shady characters was a few levels up the scale. Fortunately, Michael declined the offer. He decided he had to get away from his area. His life was spiralling way out of control. He therefore made the life-changing decision to join the Army. He was 17 years-old and already had a lifetime of challenging experiences. He needed a different, hopefully better and more positive experiences in his life.

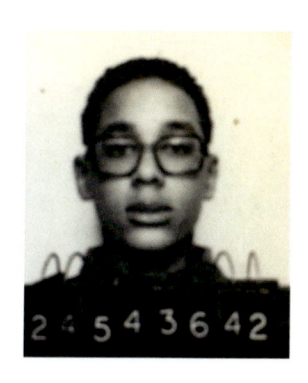

Within the Army, different regiments and battalions have different names for ranks. The common rank titles that most are aware of is 'Private' being the lowest rank and 'Corporal' being someone with two stripes. In the Royal Artillery, a Private is called a 'Gunner' and a Corporal is called a 'Bombardier'. This young man, just beyond his mid-teenage years learned the power that even a junior NCO could wield over a new recruit. Michael faced not only one, but two men who wielded their power ruthlessly, viciously and without apology, within Michael's first weeks in the Army. The continual mistreatment of this young teenager was appalling. Where were those senior staff who had responsibility for monitoring the behaviours of junior officers, towards those supposedly *"in their care"*? Times have changed, fortunately, but the story of Michael's early experience of the Army is shocking and probably, 'telling' of those times.

The Bombardier sitting at his desk in front of Michael brandishing said paper was *O'Cobb*. *O'Cobb* was one of two Troop Bombardiers. He had a pug-ish face and short stocky firm build. His nose was slightly bulbous and his head always had a red hue about it. Michael recalls that it was as if his blood pressure was permanently high or he enjoyed a few drinks too many now and then. The other Bombardier standing behind Michael and to his left was *Swan*. *Swan* was lean and tall, the type of person who would never have to watch what he was eating, always cut a fine suit and could have been a natural distance runner. Although both the same rank, *O'Cobb* was the one who called the shots. He was the boss and dictated activities and events. *Swan* was the side-kick, the Robin to *O'Cobb*'s Batman, except they did not have the same values as those fictional characters.

"No, Bombardier, I won't, Bombardier", Michael shouted. He was stood upright at attention with his heels together. It was painful to maintain the position but Michael so wanted to appear defiant, to show that his mind was stronger than his body. *"Tears rolled down my cheeks but I would not sign the paper."*

"Sign the paper Lawrence" said O'Cobb with a smug look on his face. *"Sign the paper and you can be home within 24 hours, surely that's what you want isn't it Lawrence"*.

Michael could feel *Swan*'s eyes boring into the side of his head, his intense and intimidating stare willing Michael to comply. *"No Bombardier, I won't sign Bombardier"*, Michael shouted again. He was finding it more difficult to hold his erect position. Feeling his body sagging, Michael redoubled his efforts to reach his full height. His body was racked with pain and he did not think he could use his right arm for anything at that moment.

It was 1979 and Michael was in 17th Training Regiment, Royal Artillery, also known as the Depot Regiment, in Woolwich, London. His allocated training Battery was 159 Colenso Battery which consisted of a number of Troops. Within Colenso Battery there were only two people of colour; Dennis and Michael. Dennis was from the Midlands and was of Jamaican heritage. There was something about him that drew people to him. He had a certain charisma, people wanted to be around him. He was a good-looking man with very clear, sharp eyes and good teeth, which together gave him a striking appearance. He was also heavily muscled. His body looked like it had been sculpted from ebony, every sinew defined, every movement of his body accompanied by the rippling of muscles. He was also extremely physically fit. Michael has very vivid memories of these times. Michael, in contrast, was in his own view, nothing anyone wanted to be. His father was from Barbados and his mother was white English, from London.

Michael refers to himself now as 'mixed race' or 'a person of colour', but back then the least offensive term was 'half-caste' but more commonly N….r, C…n or W..g. *"Don't misunderstand me, people referred to Dennis by those names also…just not to his face, whereas everyone was very comfortable addressing me directly in that way. I was pudgy and short for my age and short-sighted so wore thick rimmed glasses. I was everything people despised at that time and they were going to let me know how much."*

The Troops rarely came together as a Battery less for drill practice and for the final Pass Out parade, so Michael was unaware of how Dennis was being treated or the ordeals he was facing. *"I just got the impression he was fairing far better than me. I was just extremely focussed on my own predicament and how and if, I would get to the end of basic training."*

Michael attended secondary school in Dagenham, East London. He was the only mixed-race person in his year. *"The blacks wanted nothing to do with me but would leave me alone, the whites would prey upon me and the same was true of my time in basic training, Dennis and I knew of each other (in the future we would become great friends, a friendship that endures to this day)."* However, they were in different Troops and their paths rarely crossed so Michael was on his own.

O'Cobb had made it clear from day one that he didn't want "a N….r" in his Troop. *Swan* was less concerned but followed *O'Cobb*'s lead like the good and faithful lapdog that he was. It started out as verbal abuse, with *O'Cobb* regularly addressing Michael as C…n, W..g or N…r. This was not done in a covert manner, not under his breath. It was the late 1970's and those words were universally acceptable. They would be used to address Michael in any and all circumstances for all to hear. Indeed, being shouted across parade squares was not uncommon. *"To be honest the name calling barely phased me. This had been a constant in my life up until this point and was the norm for those times."*

Very early on in his time in the Army, *O'Cobb* had called Michael into his office and presented him with a paper document. At that time, individuals had the option to sign up for different time periods of service, the minimum being three years, which came into force on the first day of attendance at basic or, if under 18, on one's 18th birthday. *O'Cobb* explained to Michael that as a 17-year-old, all he had to do to be able to leave within 24 hours was to sign the formal document that would immediately terminate his service. It was this document which he presented to Michael.

"That's what you want. The Army is no place for people like you", he said. O'Cobb posed the question many times trying to increase the menace in his voice on each occasion. Michael continued to refuse to sign the document. O'Cobb became increasingly angry at Michael's response. He decided to up the ante. The first time it happened, he and *Swan* entered the ten-man room Michael shared with his fellow recruits. As expected, everyone in the room immediately stood to attention at the bottom of their beds as was customary when any one of rank entered their room.

"Everybody out", O'Cobb bellowed. *"Out now"*. They moved as one almost in a panic for the door.

"Not you Lawrence, stay where the f...k you are." Michael quickly checked himself and resumed the position of attention.

"In my office, on my desk is a piece of paper, you know what it is. I want it signed and you gone", O'Cobb said looking Michael in the eye after everyone had left and Swan had closed the door. Michael started to answer in the negative but O'Cobb cut him off quickly saying, *"I know you're going to refuse so we're going to give you a little incentive"*.

With that both he and Swan set upon Michael, pushing him down onto the bed, twisting his arm up his back and throwing in a few body punches for good measure.

"The pain was excruciating and I feared they would break my arm. It was further up my back than it had ever been. I cried out in pain. Tears were already falling from my eyes but the pressure continued."

After what felt like ages but was probably only a few minutes, they let Michael go but not before O'Cobb, with his lips close to Michael's ear, through clenched teeth mouthed that when Michael had stopped *"crying like a little girl"*, he was to report to his office and *"sign the f....ng paper"*.

As Michael's fellow roommates filtered back in, O'Cobb and Swan having left, he could see the clear confusion on their faces. What had gone on, why was Michael in obvious discomfort and why did Michael look like he had been crying? Everyone was used to overt racism and to physical beatings, but up until now they had not witnessed someone…even someone like Michael…being singled out by the Directing Staff for a beating.

"B......cks to this, I said to myself. Verbal abuse was one thing and I wasn't unaccustomed to getting into fights but this was something else. These people are the actual f.......g Directing Staff. I can't fight back. Beatings would need to be tolerated with no retaliation."

"Sign the paper! Bloody right I'll sign the paper, I didn't sign up for this sh..t. I'll march right in there, sign the paper and I'll be back at Mum's within hours."

"No, Bombardier, I won't, Bombardier", Michael shouted. The short few steps between his bunk room to the Directing Staff's office allowed Michael to quickly weigh up his options. He felt that he didn't have any. He couldn't go home now. His family had been surprised and shocked with Michael's decision to join the Army. He had

joined the Army to get away from home and particularly the deprived and increasingly dangerous environment he came from. To go home now would prove them all right. He would fail as they had all predicted. Michael realised and accepted that it was going to be a rough three months.

The beatings which followed Michael's refusal to sign the early release document would become a regular occurrence. The surprising but positive consequence of this was that Michael's roommates began to feel genuine sympathy for him. They even dropped their heads and left the room a little too slowly for *O'Cobb* and *Swan*'s liking in what was perceived to be a show of solidarity with Michael. From that point on, Michael's roommates never verbally abused him again. *"It was nine down, thousands and thousands to go"*, said Michael.

Michael showed a mental toughness, which for a young man still in his teens was remarkable. It was something he should never have had to tolerate, to be subjected to and which amounted to a form of torture. He had however, to get through basic training and would have to suffer in silence. He would then need to go on and endure the three-years that he had signed up for. Three years of that sort of vile treatment, which included at one stage having a half-brick thrown in his face by one of the Directing Staff from another Troop - completely unprovoked.

Little did Michael know then and neither could he have ever imagined, that he would definitely get through all of it. Further, he would not only succeed despite these disgusting odds and pass out. He would move onwards successfully past even his initial trade training and on to great success in his chosen career. For this amazingly resilient young man, it was the start of a military career that would span over 37 years. An impossible thing for him to consider during those dangerous first months and years.

England, particularly London over the period when Michael's father arrived from Barbados in the mid 1950s, was struggling to come to terms with the influx of black people from the Caribbean and the interracial partnerships that were starting to form. White women that spent their time with black men were deemed promiscuous with little regard or respect for themselves. Some faced rejection from their families and disgrace in the eyes of white society especially if they had given birth to a 'mongrel' child. Michael's parents had four children. His Mum had a tough time, being married to a black man.

"I remember as a seven or eight-year-old, my mother, holding my hand, lowering her gaze as we walked down the street – not in shame or with embarrassment but simply to avoid eye contact with disapproving white people. It was common place for people to share their obvious disgust at someone with a brown child by screwing up their faces whilst stepping to one side as if distancing themselves from a super contagious disease or voicing their feelings relatively politely such as "you should be ashamed of yourself" through to a less polite "N....r meat". My mother was a strong woman who knew her own mind and wouldn't bow to any such sentiment."

His first year in the Army would be *"fundamental in shaping me for what was to come and the type of person I am today"*. Michael describes the early period of Army life where, as a minority individual, he and others like him were easy prey for bigots and bullies. It was soon evident that strength and safety lay in alliances with *"others that are like you or who have a common enemy"*. Up to this point, Michael had never had any real interaction with black people. It came as a great surprise to him that he was *"taken in"* by the black community of soldiers in his barracks in Germany. He was not just taken in but protected, nurtured and given the space they created for him to grow as an individual. In particular, Michael Bridgeman and Cas McGhie would be instrumental in his development. These two men were in different ways, like both father and big brother figures for him. Another, David (Shocker) McKenzie became Michael's best friend, or as Michael says, *"He was my 'Number one Spa'"*. All three men were best friends and mentors for Michael and their friendship endures to this very day. Sadly, his friend Cas lost his battle with cancer a few years ago. It was an extremely difficult and emotional time for Michael and his other friends. The relationships which Michael had with these men, taught him what it meant to be accepted, valued, even loved – such was the closeness of their bonds.

In that first year in the military, Michael describes an incident which in any person's view, is so extraordinary that it is almost unimaginable. *"I was subjected to an ordeal that reverberated through my very soul at the time. Its deep and profound effects have stayed with me throughout my life."*

"The year was 1980 and I was on my first ever field exercise, Exercise CRUSADER, in Germany. I was part of a three-man crew and with another crew (two vehicles, six people). We had finished completing a Nuclear, Biological and Chemical (NBC) serial whereby we had to don an NBC suit which was lined with charcoal which blocked the ingress of any chemicals through the suit and respirators more commonly referred to as gas masks. One of the other crew members was called Jock. He was a known racist and felt it was his duty to ensure everyone knew this. During a lull in activities, I was sat, still in my NBC suit as it was cold and it provided an extra layer of warmth. I was chatting to a colleague, Chalky, when Jock appeared with a jerry can of petrol and proceeded to pour it over my outstretched legs. I was completely caught off guard and started to question just what the hell he was doing when he lit a match and set me on fire."

"I was desperately trying to 'slap' out the flames as they licked across my legs. This only resulted in burning my hands. Despite my abject panic, I had the presence of mind not to stand up. I knew that this would make things far worse and provide the flames with the ability to climb up my body and on to my face. Chalky, thinking very fast, started to drag the earth under us across my legs. I grabbed some earth too and we managed to effectively suffocate the flames. It was all over in seconds but felt like a lifetime. I was saved from more serious injury by the NBC suit I was wearing. The charcoal layer provided a barrier to the naked flame to my legs. The result was like having extreme sunburn. My legs were red raw and completely hairless."

Michael pauses and quietly comments that while there are no evident physical scars which can be seen, *"the mental ones would accompany me throughout my adult life, indeed, cause me to wake in the night on a regular basis"*. This was clearly a vicious assault but it appears that the miscreant, Jock, was not disciplined in any way. The Senior NCO present *"simply gave Jock a bollocking and that was the end of the matter"*. Michael's protests were met with ambivalence and a lack of interest and it was he who ended up receiving a bigger bollocking than Jock for *"going on about it"*.

From that moment on, Michael avoided this vile racist man especially given the fact that he had set him on fire.

He was to meet this Jock person two years later however, in the Falklands, while they were both on operational tour. He recalls making that lengthy flight with his colleagues in 1982, still a Gunner. *"I would at last stand up to him, without fear and with supreme confidence in my ability to defend myself."* Michael had been through so much by this time and was only 20 years old. He could now take care of himself.

By the end of Michael's first year in the Army, his transformation was complete. He was no longer a 'White Boy', someone who was neither white nor black. He had become a Black Soldier. All his friends were black. White people were seen by him to be a constant threat and where possible, to be avoided. Michael really wanted to be black. He worried about this. Many of his friends had either come across from the Caribbean or had been born in the UK but had strong ties with the Islands from which their parents came. He felt a little 'inadequate' especially as he was only half black.

The exception to Michael's view about white people was that of the Germans. Michael had got on with them brilliantly and was never racially abused by them, *"at least not to my face"*, he says. Michael liked the German people a great deal and felt some form of affinity with them. He decided very early on, within the first few months of being in Germany that he would learn their language. *"I did this with decisive intent and would achieve a level or near-fluency that very few British soldiers would enjoy."*

Throughout his military career, Michael undertook operational tours in the Falkland Islands, Northern Ireland, Iraq and Afghanistan. He would on occasion, as seen in this picture, be with his good friends, David (Shocker)

McKenzie, Michael Bridgeman and Cas McGhie. Through exercises, secondments and military related travel, Michael would visit over 30 countries worldwide.

Michael achieved several promotions during his military career. He went through each rank, accepting the new titles and responsibilities with pride. He was a hard worker, taking nothing for granted, always doing his best and a little more where he felt it was required. He was being noticed by his superiors. He studied intently and acquired a number of technical and academic skills, which aligned well with his increasingly high ranks. When he was promoted to the highest NCO rank of RSM, he took particular pleasure in ensuring that he treated his subordinates fairly. At no time would he sanction mistreatments and discriminatory behaviours from the middle-ranking soldiers he led. He was totally committed to being a different, and better leader and manager of people than some of the extremely poor examples of leadership he had personally experienced in previous positions in the Army.

Michael recalls that every time he achieved a promotion, up to and including Major, he would hear mention that *"...he was only promoted because of his colour..."*, or *"..positive discrimination..."*. The only time he did not hear this said was on his final promotion to Lieutenant Colonel. Within the Royal Artillery, from the time he joined in 1979 to the present day (over 42 years), Michael was only the third non-white person that has successfully progressed from the rank of Private soldier to Lieutenant Colonel. This is especially significant given the fact that the Royal Artillery is one of the largest Corps in the Army.

"The irony is that I achieved this because of my colour but not for the reasons they said. My experiences, good and bad, have shaped me into the adult and person I am today. I am someone who works hard, seeks challenges and always sticks up for those considered different (anyone not white, straight and male) and who are unable to stick up for themselves. I see the best in everyone until they prove me different. I choose not to belittle individuals. My mantra is 'No idea is above scrutiny, but no individual is below dignity'. Someone famous said it, I don't really care who."

Despite the difficulties he experienced in the early period of being in the Army, Michael firmly believes that the most acceptance, inclusion and camaraderie he has experienced was during his Army service. This might appear to be quite a contradiction because of all of those people who had caused him so much harm and heartache. Fortunately, they were in the minority and were feeble-minded ignorant bigots whose actions had, he believes, a disproportional effect upon him, mainly in the early part of his career. Michael is so glad that some of the kindest, most understanding, compassionate and non-racist people he knows is as a result of his Army service.

Michael remains a generous man. Few people would allow this view, given the extraordinary, evil behaviours of some of the people this special man had to contend with in his life. He has made some solid, amazing friends throughout his life. Sadly, he has also lost several, who remain strong in his memory, never to be forgotten. They had meaning for him and their value remain in his heart.

"I have shared the same spoon, toothbrush, sleeping bag, secrets and aspirations with these people, many black but the vast majority white and I have a deep and profound love for them. We have shared experiences that only being involved in wars and on operational tours can expose someone to."

While Michael accepts that racism and discrimination persists, he does see change all around him. *"I'm buoyed up by my everyday experiences, particularly those in my life following me leaving the Army at age 55."*

Michael is very satisfied with his life. It is clear that he greatly appreciates the love and care of his wife Amanda and his son Dominic.

He continues to meet with his former army pals, to reminisce and reconnect with the fun, laughter and camaraderie of trusted, authentic friends.

Before leaving the Army, Michael secured a role as a Civil Servant in a Government Department. He was able to get this position due to his military service and the qualifications he had gained during that service.

Eighteen months after taking up that post, he was headhunted by his current employer. Michael now works as a Business Executive for a British-based European Defence company. His background as a missile system operator, instructor, leader and policy maker spanning over 37 years had made him a targeted choice for his current job.

"The attitude and behaviour of those around me is refreshing and welcome. I feel valued and appreciated I have a voice and opinions that are heard and acted upon. I do not feel any racial tension. I do not feel that I am being judged by the colour of my skin or that it defines me in any way."

That is not to say that Michael had found everything in his workplace satisfactory. He was disappointed to find a lack of representation among the higher echelons of management and even at the middle management level. He therefore decided to become a Co-Founder of an employee resource group that champions ethnic diversity within the company. He has received overwhelming support from across the business areas and particularly from senior management, including from the UK MD. Since then, Michael has seen visible change within his company. *"There are non-white faces among the directors and when I look across the working floorplate, I see incredible and increased diversity."*

Michael has also made some good friends in his current employment and enjoys the collaborative work he is engaged in with them.

He keeps as fit as he can. Sporting achievements have included representing the Royal Artillery and/or Army in Squash, Basketball, Polo, Table tennis and Alpine skiing.

Lieutenant Colonel Michael Lawrence is a remarkable person. He has overcome immense challenges in his life, both as a young child and as a young adult. He has somehow, managed to take a positive and personal diversion, digging himself out of a channel of early criminality, to become the strong, thoughtful and caring man of stature he undoubtedly is today. Very few people would have had the inner resilience to do what he has been able to do.

Michael has survived, grown, progressed and achieved a huge degree of excellence so far, over his lifetime. Without people like Michael having 'our backs' in times of war or in relation to undertaking his peacekeeping duties on our behalf, this country would not, could not have done as well as it has done over the years. If he could have the opportunity to go back and speak to his 17-year-old self, he would look that young man in the eyes and say,

"Girder yourself for what is to come. Do not falter as you strive to be more than you currently are. Aim high and weather the consequences. You're in for the long-haul. Just try to be a better person than the one the day before. Back yourself and don't allow shadows to overwhelm you. You are Michael, never forget that."

In his life beyond the Army, this British Caribbean, mixed-race man remains connected to some of the existing military networks, including the Army Multi-cultural Community Network (AMCN). Michael is a regular contributor and keynote speaker on a number of civilian and military webinars, podcasts and events. He continues to do much to increase and enhance the position of others where he can and is an active champion and advocate for those who suffer inequities. There is evidence of his success in these areas. He is a man who should be acknowledged for all that he has done. He is worthy of our appreciation.

Regimental Sergeant Major (RSM) Owen Bernard JP

Owen Bernard left his home country at the age of 13 to journey to the United Kingdom to join his family in Battersea, London.

When Owen first attended the local school, Tennyson Secondary Boys' School in Battersea, he completed a test. Following review of his results, he remembers the headmistress telling his Aunt, who had accompanied him, that he scored so highly in those tests that he needed to go to a better school than the one he was heading to. Other memories of his UK school days, include receiving a book, 'Men and Machines' as a prize for achieving second place in his very first term at the school.

Despite the successes he achieved academically, in school, Owen found the environment in his new country to be dull, drab even. It was in this backdrop that Owen would soon see the Army as an exciting organisation to join.

When he was 18, he confirmed this view and joined up. He went to the selection centre in Corsham. Again, Owen was subject to a variety of tests to consider where best he would fit in the Army. He ended up in the Royal Medical Corp and was sent off to Ashvale, Aldershot to begin his basic training. Basic training was a tough but enjoyable experience for young Owen. Most people feared the drill and 'square bashing', but Owen did not. He found the training activities, pleasant, exciting even. In training, Owen was not the biggest person in the group and everything was tough for him and for all the other new recruits. He remembers a taxi driver once remarking to him as he was returning to camp one day, 'What is it about you? You don't look too depressed!' Owen's response is reflective of how he managed and made the best of his time then and throughout his career; *'Well, I'm not in jail.'*

Some of his new friends were suffering throughout the weeks of initial training. However, Owen completed the training and ended up being awarded the prize for the best all 'round recruit for his group. He still retains the Cup, which has pride of place, on display in his home.

After training, Owen was posted to Bergen Hohne, Germany. This area of Germany was internationally known because of the desperately gruesome, genocide events which took place in the Belsen Concentration Camp nearby.
Owen continued to develop his medical skills and experience in his German posting.

In these early years of military life, Owen saw distressing events, including the loss of some of his close friends, including Errol Leroy Gordon, whom he lost in a traumatic conflict. He knew at the time, that Errol had a one-year-old son, who Owen would love to hear about. He heard recently that the British Legion has honoured his friend Errol and his Regiment on a plaque, donated by ex-members of 4th Regiment, Royal Artillery. This plaque is displayed at the National Memorial Arboretum, Staffordshire. The events around the loss of his friends, still cause Owen pain and distress. He will never forget Errol and the other brave young men. His friends.

Owen served as part of United Nations peacekeeping efforts in the conflict between Greece and Turkey in Cyprus, in the Buffer Zone. He served also in Belize for six months and in Hong Kong for two years. He went all over the world - to Singapore, Malaysia, Denmark, Holland, Egypt, to name just a few locations.

Owen progressed up the ranks, becoming Lance Corporal and then Corporal. He served in the Falklands, in the relatively brief, but bloody conflict between Britain and Argentina. In that war, he served with 16 Ambulance. He was a Sergeant at that time. He subsequently served with 48 Gurkhas Infantry Brigade, part of the Gurkhas Field Ambulance. Owen was the Group Practice Manager of the New Territories Group Practice (NTGP). On the way to the Falklands, he sailed on the ship, 'Queen Elizabeth 2' (QE2), and returned after the war, on 'SS Uganda'.

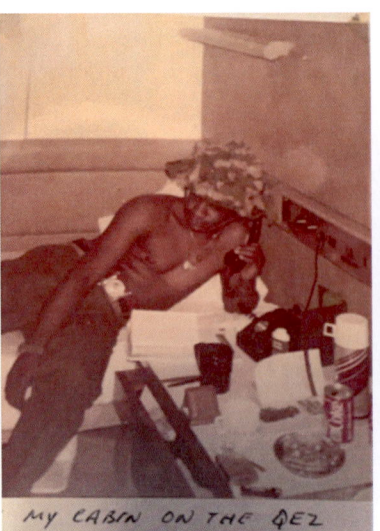

ME AND THE BOYS IN A BOMB SHELTER SAN CARLOS BAY FALKLAND 82

Owen pauses as he considers how his time in the Army was not always pleasant. These memories still disturbs him. There were several moments of challenge, trauma even, for him. He was subjected to racism, both subtle and overt - blatant. During that time in the Army, there were no obvious structures in place to deal with those issues, or so it seemed to Owen.

As the years went on, when he served with three different Units, he found the treatment by some of his senior officers, to be discriminatory, bad even. This awful treatment was widespread, *"all over"* recalls, Owen. He describes a period, when he was first promoted to Sergeant. He recalls a particular RSM, who made his life an absolute misery. Owen was one of five newly promoted sergeants and he should have been over the moon at this achievement. It was however, the worst time of Owen's career in the Army. He still smarts at the awfulness of it. The particular RSM was not someone who believed in guidance or indeed motivation of his Sergeants. This time in the Army is one that Owen recalls, as "scarring" for him. He still wishes he could have retaliated somehow, but that was not something that would be countenanced then, or even now. It felt impossible to complain. There were no procedures; no support to call on.

After serving 20 years in the Army, Owen's talents were recognised and he was promoted to Warrant Officer, Class 1 of 220 Field Ambulance, achieving the top NCO rank of Regimental Sergeant Major. This was the highest rank for a non-commissioned officer. Owen was justly, very proud of his achievements. He was especially struck by the fact that he was taking over, as RSM, from his old friend, Rip Wilson, who had himself achieved the same high rank of RSM.

Wilson later went on to receive a commission from the Queen and then to achieve the rank of Captain in the Army. These two men made history. Here were two black Regimental Sergeant Majors in the British Army - inconceivable at the time. Most black men in the military did not get promoted beyond the rank of sergeant, at that time. Their achievements were momentous, incredible and unusual. In fact, Rip Wilson was one of the few black men at that time, to move up into the commissioned group. These men were pioneers. While they were unusual at that time, it is nowadays, still a slow growth area for black men and women in terms of percentage increase in promotion to the upper ranks of the Armed Forces. They are still a rare breed.

Before Owen left the Army, he took great pleasure at being on a Going Away Parade, organised for Lieutenant Colonel Robin Short, who also became Director General of the Royal Army Medical Corps (RAMC). Owen recalls Robin Short presenting him with his Long Service Medal then. When Owen speaks about Lt. Col. Robin Short, it is with warmth and gratitude. This very senior officer, Owen describes as *"An officer and a gentleman; a very caring man, who was an inspiration to me. He had a massive impact on my life"*.

Owen remembers the lows of his career, but will always be thankful that the positives outweigh them. He remains full of admiration for such an officer and believes Robin Short to have been the best commanding officer ever. *"It was a real privilege to have known him."*

Owen was always keen to be involved in sporting activities, in keeping fit. He enjoyed running and hiking, especially. He took up long-distance running, often doing Marathons in places such as Hong Kong, Berlin, London, Hamburg and Frankfurt.

Owen continued his academic interest throughout his time in the Army. His enthusiasm for study was something he had started not only in school, but also continued at Brixton College where he studied after leaving school.

He had ambitions of becoming a dentist and while this was not pursued, he worked hard to build his skills and expertise in other aspects of the medical field. He qualified as a Podiatrist, a qualification he carried into civilian life. He did his qualifications, while carrying out his military duties. Alongside this, he was supporting his colleagues in various arenas, in a number of conflicts and countries where the Army provided defensive and peacekeeping support.

Owen is a man of character, high skill and commitment and his 'worth' would not be suppressed. He was good at his job and was recognised in achieving promotion up the ranks, despite the discrimination and poor treatment he was exposed to over the long years in his chosen career. He held true to an inner strength and bloody-minded resilience; innate characteristics. This served him well in his work and in the way he modelled exemplary behaviours in the treatment of the men he led, as an RSM. He feels that the prior, poor experience to which he was exposed, made him do better in his senior role as the substantive RSM. It was about *"Being kind. Service above self"*.

It was while Owen was an RSM of 220 Field Ambulance, that for the first time in a hundred years, he in his senior NCO role, was proud to welcome females into the Territorial Army (TA). There were 20 women in that first group.

As Owen reflects on his own military career, he was keen to pay tribute to a person of colour currently serving in the British Armed Forces. He speaks admiringly of Brigadier Karl Harris, CBE, Founder and Chair of the Black, Asian Military Ethnic Network (BAMA) for the past six years, and member of the British Army's Multicultural Network. Owen believes that it is when black people like Harris, are seen in some of the highest ranks of the Armed Forces, that real progress can begin to be observed in achieving higher ranking promotions for people of colour.

Brigadier Harris can be heard in a 'You Tube' discussion, organised by the Royal British Legion, with another senior black officer, retired Colonel Andy Allen, MBE. Allen provides another example of someone who managed to achieve one of the higher ranking positions in the British Armed Services. It was in 2008, that Allen became the first ever black person to be appointed to the rank of Colonel. In this video, Harris and Allen share parts of their military stories, including some comment about the contributions from men and women Veterans of the Windrush Generation.

It was in his position as Regimental Sergeant Major, that Owen would provide supportive advice and make sure he motivated and inspired his men, rather than demean them. Other colleagues who have been interviewed, refer to Owen as an inspiring person, who always encouraged and supported them to reach higher and do more, to achieve the successes he believed they were capable of. He was a progressive, innovative leader, perfect for a modern Army. It is a measure of this remarkable man that these were unsolicited comments were made by people he led, or had met later and beyond his career in the British Armed Forces.

Owen met and married his wife in Germany and went on, during his Hong Kong tour, to have two children, Kimberley and Steven, of whom he is very proud. He would never swap his life for any other, or for anything. He believes in *"giving back"* to young people, even funding their schooling when he can.

Owen has no doubts about the long-lasting effects of war, on people serving in the Armed Forces. At the time he served, there was no general understanding about, or acceptance of post traumatic stress disorder (PTSD). *"In 1982, PTSD, he says, was not taken seriously or even discussed. We suffered in silence."*

He feels some level of dissatisfaction that his and other Caribbean men's and women's service is hardly recognised in Britain. Owen was asked to speak at the Falklands War's 40th commemorations.

In his speech that day, he made it clear that

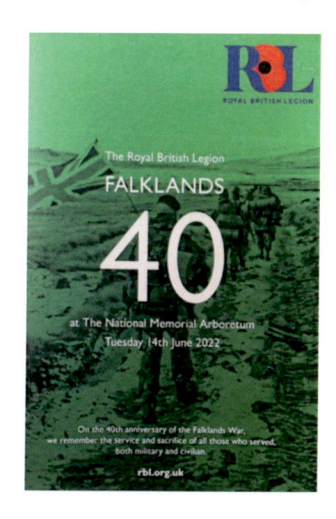

"At the time of the Falklands War, I was a British soldier, trained and paid to do a job, which I did! Unless you are challenged, you will never know what you are capable of doing. I have no regrets!"

Nevertheless, despite having had the privilege of being a part of the commemorations, he continues to feel that little is being done to reference *"our"* contributions generally, in and for the country. He is disappointed by this.

Looking back, he would have loved the chance to say to his 18-year-old young self, *"Just stop thinking negatively. Pursue your career with focus."* He knows that he has had a successful career and that his success has certainly continued beyond that lengthy military career. He would be happy to encourage young men to consider a career in the military. He believes that they would experience a level of positive discipline and help, to *"drive out of you, that hidden talent and provoke the best in you"*. In his view, these young people could achieve a huge amount if they looked beyond the shouting and think that the short term behaviours by others *"is not a death sentence"*. If they did this, he believes, they could be very successful, gaining skills which they could take out into the wider world afterwards. He truly feels that, that is what he did.

In 1993 when he left the Army, Owen continued to contribute to the medical field. In the three years before he left, he was already making preparations for life beyond. He had considered the idea of a commission in the Jamaica Defence Force, but that was not to be. He had met the President of the Diabetes Association in 1990. Following a detailed conversation with the President, Owen was motivated to enter that part of medicine, as a Podiatrist, with a strong interest also in providing education, advice and treatment.

After Owen left the Army, he became the Executive Director of the Diabetes Association of Jamaica in 1993. This Association is part of the International Diabetes Federation (IDA), which has its headquarters in Brussels. As a result of his appointment, Owen was required to travel across the world, from Abu Dhabi to South Africa, representing Jamaica in this field. Owen is very clear that the foundation which his career in the Army gave him, was at the heart of why as a civilian, he would prove to be good in his new role.

Soon after being appointed, in 1994, Owen was involved in his first big international conference, in Japan. That particular experience linked him to the World Health Organisation, with whom he was able to lead the development of a national diabetes education strategy for Jamaica. The Diabetes Care programme, which the WHO asked him to present and be an advocate for, led to him being a vital part of training in that area, across the Caribbean. As a result of all this exposure, Owen became the author of the 'Footcare Assistant', Level 1 Programme, which is being used across the Caribbean and in some parts of Africa. The programme is sponsored by the Pan American Health Organisation (PAHO), a regional group of the World Health Organisation (WHO).

Owen lives a very productive and enjoyable post-military, professional and personal life. He has an active medical practice, is president of various associations and is fully involved in clubs and societies across the island. He looks back on his long military career with some pride in his achievement and contribution to the British Army. There is very little that he would change and much that he recalls positively. He has always prided himself on developing mentorship and has always tried to inspire others where he can. He *"walks it"*.

Regimental Sergeant Major Owen Bernard served Britain, with honour, loyalty and in the clear knowledge that he did a good job for the country and for Her Late Majesty, The Queen. This is a man of courage, strength and immense skill, who is a valued son of the Caribbean and a member of the Windrush Generation. His service should be recognised, acknowledged and appreciated for all he has done on behalf of all of us.

Regimental Sergeant Major (RSM) Roger Dussard

RSM Roger Dussard gave 24 years of military service to the Queen and to the country, in order to ensure that our freedoms are protected.

He was born in New Cross Hospital in Wolverhampton. His father had come to England, from St Ann, Jamaica in the late 1950s. His uncle was already here and was part of the group already engaged in rebuilding the country after the war. Roger's uncle did not stay in the UK very long however, but continued his journey on to America, where they too needed support after WWII had ended.

Roger's father, Lascelle, stayed in the UK for three years, before returning to his homeland. There, he met and married a lovely woman who had caught his attention. This newly joined couple were very much in love and decided to go back to the UK, to Wolverhampton to make a life together. It was here that Roger and his four siblings were born.

Mr Dussard Senior, arrived in the UK as a Jamaican-trained construction worker specialising in Painting and Decorating. Initially, he went to work within the many foundries located in the Black Country. Eventually, he took up jobs as a builder for various Midland Construction firms.

At first, the family lived in the more deprived area of Wolverhampton called Whitmore Reans. They were in the minority in the area. Despite the support of some lovely white people around them, they experienced a fair amount of racism.

The family, with hard work and determination, were able to move out to a better part of Wolverhampton, where they were the only black family there at the time. That too had its challenges, but they settled down and got on with their lives.

Roger and his brother and sisters were able to attend local schools. His school was an excellent one. Roger was a bright boy, who made much of all the opportunities provided to him there.

Roger had great opportunities to engage in sports, to go on visits to interesting places and to take field trips and go on school cruises. He was a top shot putter, setting the shot put record for the longest throw in the District Championships. Roger still holds the school shot put record to this day. He played cricket for the Wolverhampton Town as it was then called, and was also a good 400 metre sprinter.

His school had great connections in the community and beyond, including being able to offer some of its students, work experience on HMS Dryad, in Portsmouth. Roger loved this work experience, so much so, that it sowed the seeds for his later career in the military.

92

Around the age of 15, he and two of his pals, Steve and Lee, decided to join the Army. To prepare for this, they would run around the neighbourhood delivering newspapers. The idea was to carry their heavy bags and other bags and build the weight-carrying runs into a fitness regime. They would therefore be well able to meet the demands of Army training, in advance of joining up.

These earnest young boys were so serious about their ambitious plans, that they volunteered to increase the paper rounds and also increase their weekly earnings whilst they were at it. Roger recalls that they moved from weekly earnings of £2.75 to a whopping £5.00.

Soon, the boys were ready to apply for their new careers. All three went to the Wolverhampton Careers' Office and took their tests and underwent the relevant interviews. When the boys completed their tests at the Careers' Office, the results were shared with them. Two of them got in, Roger and Lee. Talking about this time in his life and the memories of those close childhood friendships, brought back a level of sadness, which was evident in Roger's eyes. Sadly, one of his childhood friends was to lose his life sometime later in a tragic accident. Roger still remembers his good friend's loss with deep sadness.

Roger did very well indeed in the Army recruitment tests. He was offered a range of options. He was pretty good at biology and there were areas within that particular subject which he had particular interest in. He decided that he would choose the Royal Army Medical Corp (RAMC).

Roger's parents were not very happy about his decision. They would have preferred to have Roger stay in school and complete his education in the normal way. Nevertheless, they accepted their son's decision and supported him.

The RAMC was one of the four branches of the Army Medical Services (AMS). Once his decision was made to join the RAMC, Roger was sent to Sutton Coldfield to undergo a physical test. When he got through this, he was then subjected to the full medical. This hurdle was overcome and he could finally swear allegiance to the Queen and take her shilling. This was done formally, back in Wolverhampton. He was now fully signed up and 'belonged' to the British Army.

Throughout the recruitment process, from decision to join and the various levels of testing, all the officers he met had a very courteous pleasant attitude to the potential recruits. Once those recruits succeeded and actually put their mark on paper, Roger saw their tone changing. There was now a much sharper tone to their voices. They were letting these young men get a flavour of that which was to come; keying them in to what they should expect.

Roger was sent information about the next steps: where to go, when he had to be there and what to take with him. He was also sent a Rail Warrant for his travel. This 16-year-old young man was beside himself with excitement.

After a good home haircut and packing of a new suitcase, Roger said goodbye to his four siblings and his mother. His father took him in his precious blue Morris Minor (which he still has), to Wolverhampton Train Station. Roger was apprehensive, but really could not wait to start his new career. He set off to Wokingham to the

Princess Marina College in Arborfield. This was the Junior Leader and Apprenticeship College. Roger was sent there because he had had one of the highest possible test results that would allow him to carry out Junior Leader Training. This was training for those that the Army believed had the aptitude to make the future Junior and Senior Non-Commissioned Officers of the British Army.

It was an amazing experience for this bright young man. To be involved in a Junior Leader training course at such a young age was quite special. This leadership course would, if he succeeded, be of particular benefit to Roger in the latter parts of his career.

When Roger got to Wokingham Station, he was met by a Drill Sergeant and taken in a white coach, with the other 49 new recruits to a staging area. Orders were barked at them all, as they were grouped, sent to collect uniforms and to get their sharp, short haircuts.

Roger was put into a dormitory with three other young lads. The boys were grouped, thoughtfully it seemed, with people from a similar area. The idea was that the new recruits would feel a little more comfortable, if they heard accents similar to their own.

Roger was at the college for a year, being involved in intense training. Even though Roger had joined as a Royal Army Medical Corp soldier, there was hardly any actual medical subjects then. It was more focused on academic classes, including geopolitics and learning German as well as an even greater focus on Military Tactics and Physical fitness. Roger learned alongside people from different walks of life. He found the Scots interesting, but was more comfortable being with other 'Brummies'. He is still in touch with one of the friends he made then, Michael Cotgreave.

Throughout his time at the Princess Marina College, Roger's sharp intelligence, application and emerging leadership skills were being noticed by those in charge. He was the only black person in the College and he was achieving top results academically. He described himself as then being academically strong, but 'only middling' when it came to the physical areas of the work.

Roger passed out successfully.

He went on to do his Special to Arms training in the Keogh Barracks, in Surrey. It was at Keogh that he started his 14-week medical training. This training was followed by exams, which led him to becoming a Class 3 Medic (a Combat Medical Technician).

Roger was now fully trained and thus able to join one of the Field Units. His first posting was to 16 Field Ambulance, RAMC in Bulford, Wiltshire.

Roger's first assignment was within a Medical Dressing station where daily routine involved sorting and checking medical equipment and supporting various units within the Brigade.

He was in the 16 Field Ambulance Regiment for the next four and a half years. However, after less than one year working in the Dressing Station, he volunteered for a part of the Regiment which specialised in Artic Warfare. He did the test and became the youngest person to be accepted. He was then deployed to Bomoen, Norway to

Getting back to army basics

Young medics Michael Brannagan and Roger Dussard today showed a superior officer what they had learned on their basic training course.

The two Wolverhampton 17-year-olds are spending a week in the army careers office in Queen Street telling would-be recruits about army life.

Michael (left), of Vicarage Road, and Roger, of Warstones Drive, Warstones, have just completed their year's basic training with the Royal Army Medical Corps near Reading.

They are pictured giving first aid to Warrant Officer Ken Richardson, who is in charge of recruiting at the Queen Street office.

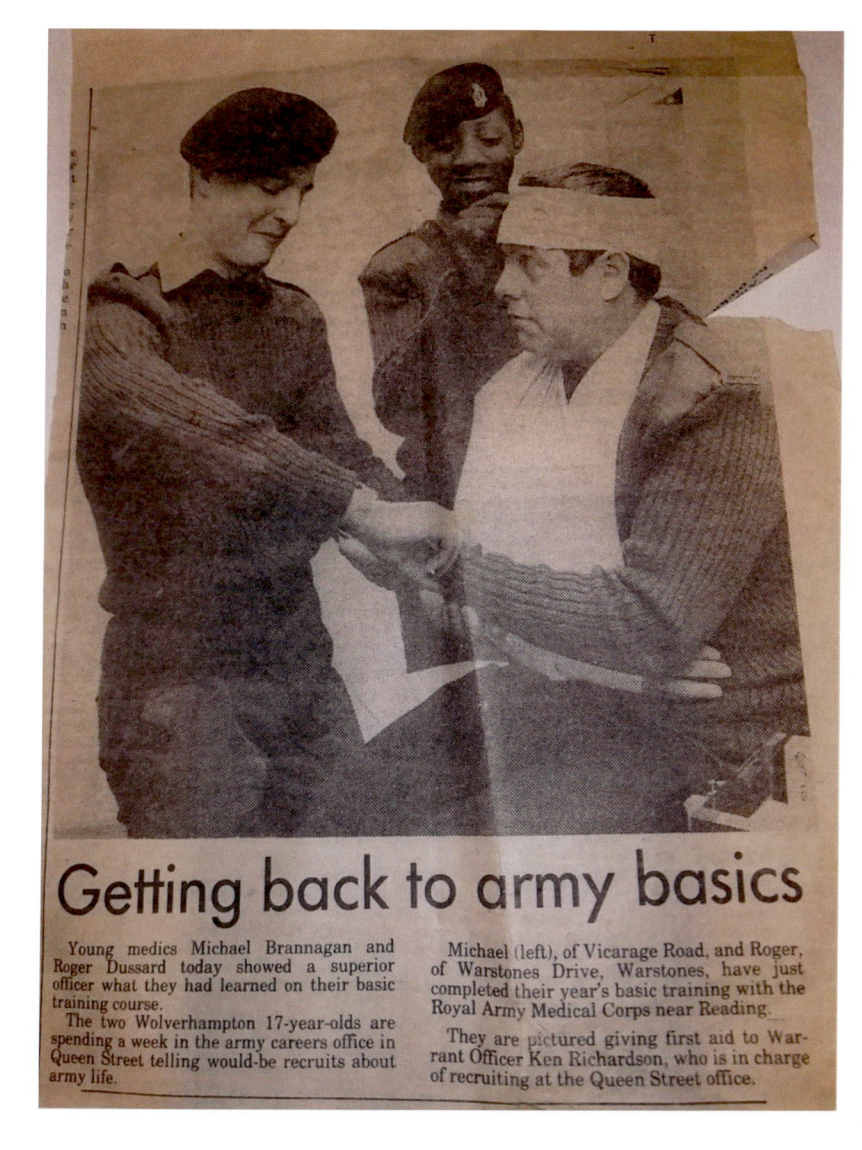

be with the Royal Army, Ordinance Corp (RAOC). It was an incredible experience for Roger. Of the group of 80 men who started the feared Arctic Warfare Course, only eight passed. Roger was one of them and the only person from the Royal Army Medical Corps to have done so. In fact, he was signed out as the best - exceptional even. Originally, when he had been selected for the AMF(L) troop, he was told that he *"Won't last two minutes."* So much for that comment. He had proven otherwise, not just lasting, but succeeding well.

Following the success of that training and accomplishment, Roger was embedded in the medical section of the Medics supporting Artic Warfare. A very positive report from this work led to him achieving his Lance Corporal stripe.

Roger was with this Unit for four and a half years, ending up as a military ski instructor responsible for training new recruits in the intricacies of operating in the Arctic. This was a very arduous role, involving some tough training. *"You had to be driven and have good administrative skills."*

By the age of 21, Roger had become a Corporal. He was probably one of the youngest to achieve that level of promotion in 16 Field Ambulance. He had already completed his Class 2, six-week training and exams in-house and passed them successfully. He was then able to move on to Class 1 at the Keogh Barracks in late 1988, allowing him to work independently. All of this had confirmed him as someone who could move into a Corporal position, which he did. As a full Corporal, Roger went back to Norway and was in charge of 10 men in various locations. He also set up a medical centre, with a team, and with prescribing capabilities in the remote environments in which he was operating.

Unfortunately for Roger, the powers that be decided that a new posting was in order, removing Cpl Dussard from his role in support to a new one in UK forces supporting the geographically remote areas of Europe. Just before this posting, Roger decided that he wanted to be a Paras. He was deployed as part of a United Nations tour to Cyprus and to the Gulf War in the early 1990s. He was a part of a medical support team working out in the Oil Fires Operation. He was also actively involved as a Bomb Disposal Medic. In this post, he was really tested as a Medic. He saw some horrific injuries, often caused by IEDs. This was challenging time for him, operating in a terrifyingly intense arena of war.

In terms of rest and recuperation opportunities, Roger was able to take leave to go home. He visited Bahrain as part of his rest and recuperation whilst on operations in the Gulf. On return to the UK, he was sent back to 16 Field Ambulance for a brief period before he was posted to the Depot Parachute Regiment and Airborne Forces in Aldershot as a P (Pegasus) Company Medic. There he obtained 'Wings', having passed the arduous P Company selection on his second attempt. He was to do three years of service with the Depot before being posted back to 23rd Parachute Field Ambulance (23 PFA) under the control of 5th Airborne Brigade. On return to 23 PFA, the unit was hurriedly preparing to deploy on a United Nations deployment to Rwanda.

He regrets somewhat, that he missed the opportunity to be deployed to Rwanda, when the violent struggles were taking place there in 1993. He was forced to stay behind as *"the Rear Party required specialisms"*, like those he possessed. He was able however, to go to Germany and to Poland where he was able to carry out parachuting descents from various aircraft, attaining both his German and Polish wings to add to the British and US wings he had obtained earlier. This was a man who would not "stand still" in his ambition to gain further skills and contribute even more in his wok in the military.

By 1995, Roger had been promoted to the rank of Sergeant. As a Medical Sergeant within a Section, he supported Brigade Units as required. He was also responsible for Induction. This often involved getting men ready for P Company selection. This preparation was especially important as it soon transpired that there was an increased number of Medics getting through this tough selection process. Roger had been through this selection process before and was well placed to document it and help others to achieve success. His work in this area, led to a 40% increase in the numbers of Medics passing the selection, unheard of before then.

Roger made good progress through the ranks. He was involved heavily in carrying out induction for the Regiment and was promoted to Staff Sergeant. On this promotion, he was posted to 144 Parachute Medical Squadron (V) in the role of Senior Permanent Staff Instructor to a Territorial Army Unit in London. This role saw him responsible for all training and equipment care for four sub-units - London, Glasgow, Cardiff and Nottingham. These were big responsibilities, with Roger experiencing huge shifts in the critical roles he was expected to undertake. He proved himself up to the tasks required of him.

During this period with the Territorial Army, Roger remained on the Spearhead Lead Element for the British Army. This led to him being deployed into Sierra Leone to participate in necessary rescue missions. This work took place in an intensive, fast-moving environment, living in tough conditions. Roger was up to the challenges, working with others to carry out the required tasks. He recalls being in his garden having a barbecue, when he received the call to move quickly to respond to the Army's call. He was responsible for up to 40 men, all of whom worked efficiently and effectively to complete the mission.

Following his work in Africa, Roger was redeployed back to London to take up his position as the Senior Permanent Staff Instructor (SPSI). However, he was pre-selected for promotion to Warrant Officer Class 2 and returned to the regular element of 16 Close Support Medical Regiment. Here, he took up position as Squadron Sergeant Major to 23rd Parachute Medical Squadron, a manoeuvre medical Squadron. Roger was still only around 33 years of age at that time.

This young man was not only showing outstanding ambition within his military career, but seemed to do so in preparing for a future outside the Army. He had the foresight to start building a property portfolio, by buying one of his first houses in a popular tourist area in his parents' homeland of Jamaica. That part of his personal interest would lead him to expand his house purchasing to other parts of the world, including in his base home in the UK.

Roger demonstrated fine leadership skills in his man-management and in many areas of military life. He was a handling Instructor on helicopters, an Equipment Manager, ski instructor and of course, a Paratrooper.

He was involved in various operations in different contexts, including Afghanistan, Kosovo, and Iraq. He had been involved in building Camp Bastion in Helmand Province. He saw first-hand, the warfare in the second Gulf War, where he had to *'dig in'*. They were crazy times. Madness. Being in the centre of activities, with responsibility for protecting these areas. These six-month tours, tested him mentally and physically.

During these intense, crazy periods, Roger still had time to be identified for his undoubted skills as a soldier, a Medic and a leader.

He was promoted to Regimental Sergeant Major (WO1), taking a lead role within his Regiment. He had, however, to return to another six-month deployment, this time to Al-ʻAmārah. This appointment sat within a real hotbed of indirect and direct fire attacks, mortars, 107 Chinese rockets and missiles.

Over this six-month tour, Roger faced over 70 indirect fire attacks. He took up position as the Air Operations Warrant Officer for Task Force Maysan. The job was a difficult but vital role, which allowed the Task Force to move people and equipment throughout the theatre of operations. In his view, Maysan was *"one of the most complex Provinces ever"*.

During this role and during an operation involving thousands of troops, Roger was involved in a helicopter crash. A Sea King helicopter had lost control and crashed to the ground. Roger directed the initial casualty evacuation and was able to alert the Task Force commander to the situation. For his actions, he was awarded the Joint Commanders' Commendation and received a Citation from the Queen.

Throughout his military career, Roger took great pleasure and comfort from the camaraderie amongst the men in the Regiment within which he served. It was a big thing for him and saw him through some tough times of conflict in the different locations in which he gave service. The power of that camaraderie cannot be underestimated.

He knows that austerity and being tested are not bad things. This is in relation, he says, *"to truly understanding how little you really need to survive and even thrive"*. He has been through very challenging times and has been able to get through them.

Alongside the challenge of his key military tasks, Roger also had some happy times, enjoying several social events with friends and colleagues.
He appreciated those times as he could wind down and have fun.

**OFFICERS, WARRANT OFFICERS
AND SENIOR NON-COMMISSIONED OFFICERS
23 PARACHUTE FIELD AMBULANCE**

December 1995

Roger expressed great appreciation for the support he received from the Privates (known in the Army as 'Toms') he was in charge of. He believes that he was effective in his leadership of them. His men understood what was being demanded of them and played their part in *"getting the job done"*.

This is a man who knows what a good leader has to do to get the best out of his team. His organisation and people management skills are evident and have made a positive difference to his work in the Army. He has transferred many of these skills into his civilian life. None of these skills and qualities will allow him to forget however, about the loss of some of the good men with whom he has served. This haunts him still. *"They'll never come back. There's only bone left."*

Roger was involved in several conflicts over the last 20 years of his career. He has seen much to disturb him as well as a lot of positives to be proud of.

He retained his RSM role for three years, before being encouraged to move to a Commission. He was being particularly encouraged towards this by Colonel Abby DuBaree, a senior officer who saw in Roger, someone who could go much, much further as a leader, a soldier and a man. Abby DuBaree was the first RAMC officer whom Roger had met. DuBaree was then a Lieutenant when Roger first joined the Army. DuBaree was the first officer to speak to Roger's parents on an Roger's Open Day for the Junior Leaders' Depot. DuBaree was instrumental in putting Roger's parents' minds at rest because he was also brown-skinned and had come through the ranks, having been born in Mauritius. In addition, DuBaree had also joined the RAMC. Abby DuBaree was always in the background, watching Roger's progress in his career and giving him sound advice. Col DuBaree believed that Roger would show exemplary performance in more influential, higher ranks. Roger remains appreciative of the support and advice he was given by this exceptional soldier and man. However, in relation to seeking further promotion within the commissioned ranks, Roger decided not to pursue this advice; a decision he continues to have mixed feelings about.

As Roger progressed through his 24th year in the Army, it became clear to him that he needed to get on with other aspects of his life, ones he could pursue outside, in civilian life. He was now 40 years old.

In the background of his career, he had continued to acquire other properties and so he began preparing to leave the Army. He feels disappointed in the lack of sufficient support from the Army system or of other systems outside it, for those military personnel who have left the services. *'They are abandoned. I have even known of people who have killed themselves.'* Sadly, this is a tragic view being expressed by the majority of Veterans who were interviewed.

There is broad acceptance, that around one in ten Veterans will suffer from a mental health issue, often depression. Those personnel who have been deployed into the many conflicts which we have seen over the past 20 plus years, would often have been in a combat role. The effect upon these men, including on their ability to show empathy to family or friends, or more generally, should not be underestimated.

The first year out for Roger, was *"weird"*. He went to Jamaica to visit his mother and father and spent a full year there. He then returned to the UK, but found people around him rude and disrespectful, generally. It was tough for this senior Army Warrant Officer. He had joined the Army at the young age of 16 and had spent his formative years growing into adulthood within a disciplined organisation in which everyone understood the rules, roles and ranks. Civilian life was radically different.

Roger decided to get on with managing his property business and to take up various projects outside it. He became the Operations Security Manager for the London Olympic Games and the Commonwealth Games. He worked for an Oil Refinery as its Operational Manager.

He also had a fascinating and enjoyable job, working for three years as the Assistant Military Medical Adviser on a film set.

RSM Roger Dussard looks back over his life in the Army and has few regrets. He wished he had pushed himself a little more. He is conscious that if he had taken up commission, he could have made a positive impact to the marginalised personnel coming through the ranks. There is a lot he values about being in the Army. He would have continued to respect others, but he would have put himself *"out there"* more.

While, in his view, there is a little more known nowadays about the contribution of Caribbean Veterans to the Armed Services, it is still not enough. He clearly remembers that bright, enthusiastic 16-year-old Roger and would, as his adult self, look him in the eyes and say,
"The man from Wolverhampton done good! He's put himself out there. He's embraced things. Done it my way!"

And so he has; successfully.

Many More Years of Service

Thousands more men and women of Caribbean heritage provided significant service to Queen Elizabeth II and the country throughout the monarch's reign. All of them did so with commitment, skill and loyalty. A disproportionate number of them continued to serve despite their quite extraordinary tolerance, survival and resilience in the face of mistreatment, discrimination and depressed or no opportunity for promotion. The following stories of several others of these brave Army Veterans are merely representative of many, many more ex-service men and women who live quietly, anonymously, among us.

Staff Sergeant Burthlan (BJ) Webb

BJ left St Thomas, Jamaica when he was four years old. His father was already in the UK and then sent for him and his mother.

The family settled in Ipswich, Suffolk. After a move out to the suburbs, BJ entered the local primary school as the only black child. At that time, they were also the only black family in the neighbourhood.

BJ loved sports and represented his high school in most of its sports teams. His favourite subjects were physics and technical studies. He was top of the class in these subjects. Even then, he was being told that he would make a good engineer. At the age of 13, BJ joined the Army Cadets.

The Army Cadets is a youth organisation in the United Kingdom that provides military-themed training, adventure and community activities to young people aged between 12 to 18 years old. It is one of several cadet organisations in the UK that also includes Sea Cadets, Air Cadets and the Combined Cadet Force.

The Army Cadets' organisation is sponsored and supported by the British Army, but it is an independent organisation that operates under the guidance of the Ministry of Defence. The organisation is run by adult volunteers who are typically former military personnel, reservists, or civilian instructors with relevant skills and experience.

When BJ was growing up, the Army Cadets was quite popular in most cities in the UK, providing opportunities for young teenagers to learn new skills and use their spare time well. It had similar effects on young lives, as entering the Cubs or Scouts did. The Cadets tried to inspire young people to develop self-confidence, leadership skills, and a sense of responsibility. The training was designed to promote teamwork, discipline, and physical fitness while instilling values such as respect, loyalty, and integrity.

BJ really enjoyed the activities the Cadets were engaged in, including all the military and adventurous training and of course, the marching and drills, which he was very good at. It was a good source of discipline for young BJ. He embraced all it had to offer and often excelled in the various activities which were organised.

As a Cadet, BJ participated in a variety of training activities, including drill and ceremonial, weapons' training, fieldcraft, navigation, first aid, and adventurous training. He was also able to take part in competitions and events such as the Duke of Edinburgh's Award scheme, shooting competitions, and expeditions. BJ's Cadets Group also visited a regular Army unit, in Germany. BJ thoroughly enjoyed his time as a Cadet. So much so, that at the age of 16, he decided to join the Army.

Rather interestingly, he found out recently, from his 100-year-old aunt, that his great uncle had also joined the British Army at the age of 16, to fight in the first World War. BJ feels a deep sense of pride about this. He often wonders what that young man must have experienced as part of that bloody conflict. He is aware of other Caribbean men who joined up during WWI, but had not known of his own family connection to that war effort.

BJ joined the Army as an Apprentice technician, going to an Army Apprentice College, where he excelled. BJ remembers clearly, those first days and weeks in the Army. Just like the other new recruits, he was given a uniform, a suitcase and a kit bag of equipment and marched off to the barbers. His Platoon Corporal, made a *"song and dance about him"*, because as an ex-Army cadet, he knew much about drill, map reading and weapons' handling, and was therefore challenged a lot; so much so that everyone soon knew his name. He was often 'volunteered' to demonstrate something, or to march the Platoon back from a PT session.

When BJ first joined up, he was one of only two black boys at the college, the other guy left soon after, and other than one black civilian who worked in the cookhouse, there was no other black person on camp. But as BJ had grown up in the suburbs of Ipswich this was nothing new or even relevant.

BJ was determined to be known for the *"right reasons"*. His motto was that *"Oil always rises to the top"*, and he tried to live up to that. His hard work and high standards were rewarded by being the first of his intake to be promoted and also being awarded the Burma Shield for 'Outstanding Excellence'. Promotions continued during the next two terms and he rose to become the senior apprentice in the college. This apprentice experience was, extremely useful to him as he progressed into 'regular man service' in the Royal Electrical and Mechanical Engineers (REME) at the age of 18 years.

The Royal Electrical and Mechanical Engineers (REME) is a Corps of the British Army responsible for the maintenance and repair of the Army's equipment and vehicles. The Corps was formed in 1942 during World War II, and its role has since expanded to include a wide range of technical and engineering support for the Army.

The REME is made up of officers and soldiers with technical and engineering backgrounds. It maintains a wide range of equipment including wheeled vehicles of all sizes, armoured vehicles, tanks, helicopters, missiles, lasers and night vision equipment and many types of radar and communications equipment. The REME also provides support to the Army's medical and logistics services.

The REME's responsibilities also include providing technical advice and support and training to allied military forces, and also to humanitarian and peacekeeping missions.

The REME is organised into several specialist trades, including vehicle mechanics, electronics technicians, weapon technicians, and avionics technicians. Soldiers in the REME receive extensive technical training and ongoing professional development to ensure that they have the skills and knowledge needed to maintain and repair the Army's equipment and vehicles. Overall, the REME plays a critical role in supporting the operational effectiveness of the British Army by ensuring that its equipment and vehicles are maintained and repaired to the highest standards, allowing soldiers to carry out their duties effectively and safely.

In the REME, BJ started at the rank of Craftsman, the REME equivalent of Private. He then qualified as a REME electrician upon completing Trade training at the School of Electrical and Mechanical Engineering and also the School of Electronic Engineering.

His sporting prowess made him many friends and allowed him greater acceptance amongst his peers, his soldier comrades and with the senior officers with whom he came into contact.

BJ's main sport was Rugby, but he was active in pursuing a broad range of sporting and team-building activities.

He was also good at football, athletics, boxing and skiing and represented his units at both junior and senior levels.

He also participated in rock climbing, mountaineering, sailing and flying gliders. He recalls not being prepared for the 20 degrees Celsius freezing cold weather of Norway.

He did however, enjoy more, the warmer climes of Cyprus, Brunei, Hong Kong and Belize.
For him, the Belize experience was especially interesting as it was the first time he had served in an environment where the local populous was also black.

BJ as with others, were involved in active service as required. All of these soldiers had to ensure their fitness levels were high and their preparedness and responsiveness, sharp.

After completing his technical training, BJ was posted to Germany, where he married his first wife; a relationship which, sadly did not work out. He was however, happily a father to his lovely older daughter and was gifted to become the father of four more wonderful children, including a set of twins.

He met a number of people with whom he became friends. One such person, was a fellow Jamaican, Owen Bernard, one of the first black person to become a Regimental Sergeant Major in the British Army. He maintains an abiding friendship of immense trust with Owen, up to this day.

BJ went from one Regiment to another, which is the usual progression in the REME. He noticed that the treatment of some other black men within some of these Regiments was different to that meted out to white colleagues. One such memory revolves around a Sergeant, who was a South African and was for a short while, BJ's boss. This Sergeant found it hard to accept that BJ had been promoted to Corporal and always tried to give him the most menial and demeaning jobs (which BJ would then surreptitiously pass on down to the Lance Corporal). This man clearly wanted to reinforce his greater seniority and power over the black man.

BJ was keen to achieve the rank of Sergeant, mainly as he recalls with a smile, so that he would not have to do guard duty out in the cold and wet.

Every Regiment and Corps had pride in its history and traditions. REME was no different in that regard. BJ was proud to be a part of REME. He met a number of people from different military regions, including some from the Jamaican Defence Force (JDF). He was pleased to see that the JDF men he met as part of joint training, seemed to hold the British soldiers in high esteem. They saw their efficiency in deployment and skills honed through rigorous practice and robust discipline. He was proud to be viewed as part of this group.

At the age of 25, BJ qualified for, and attended the REME Artificer Course. He had left his previous unit as a Corporal, but started the course as a Sergeant. He took part in a one-off conversion course. It was to qualify Electricians and Aircraft Technicians to become Instrument Technicians. Once the conversion course had been completed successfully, the qualification allowed the men to go straight on to a 1st class upgrade course. This next course was a very good technical qualification, enabling the men to move even further, to the Artificer Instrument Technician Course and leave, as a Staff Sergeant.

BJ was completely focused on committing himself to this career pathway, achieving highly in all of the technical areas. These are not easily completed studies and examinations. Failure was not in his view, an option. He worked and studied hard, alongside completing his other duties as a Senior NCO.

Being a REME Artificer, is a powerful, technical role in the Army, influencing and supporting the commissioned officers, as well as leading and motivating the men in the ranks below. It was an exciting time, full of responsibilities, which BJ met competently and with pride.

Altogether, BJ had by now, served in the Army for 17 years; two as an apprentice and 15 years of Adult Service. He had achieved the rank of Staff Sergeant. He had taken advantage of opportunities given to him to travel and experience fascinating sights and cultures of different countries. He was also able to obtain further training and skills, including those related to leadership in these senior positions.

It was also a time when the Army had decided, under 'Options for Change', to allow numbers of its soldiers to leave the service.

Options for Change was the document setting out the government's policy for restructuring the British Armed Forces, in 1990. The policy reflected the country's reduced security needs, following the fall of the Berlin Wall in 1989, and then the collapse of the Soviet Union, over the next two years.

As reported in Hansard (HC Deb 25 July 1990 vol 177 cc468-86), the then Secretary of State for Defence, Tom King, who held the position from 1989 until 1992, serving under Prime Minister Margaret Thatcher and later John Major, told Parliament that

"We envisage in broad terms by the mid-1990s a Regular Army of about 120,000, Royal Navy/Royal Marines of about 60,000 and a Royal Air Force of about 75,000. On that basis, the overall reduction in regular service manpower would be about 18 per cent."

In Tom King's view, it appeared that the role of NATO within a Cold War was no longer needed, or not in quite the same way, including in relation to numbers of military personnel to defend the Western Front. The British Parliament decided, following the Statement set out by the Defence Secretary, that this new security environment would no longer need the larger numbers for its new peacetime operations from thence forwards. It was time therefore, to facilitate the reduction in numbers of members of the British Armed Forces. At that time, some people did feel that the decision was financially driven, rather than being truly based on continuing military need.

It was fairly soon after this decision was made, that the events around Saddam Hussein and Iraq, came to a head. In any case, and based on the government decision of 1990, the British Army was cut by over a hundred thousand of its soldiers, with other cuts being made to the Navy and to the Air Force. It was, altogether, and as described by Tom King, earlier, a significant cut of around nearly 20% to the total British Armed Forces.

BJ and a large number of other personnel from the three military organisations, took advantage of Options for Change. They were given a healthy one-off payment and allowed to start receiving their military pensions immediately.

BJ made good use of his unexpected payment to buy a house. He was now financially secure.

Civilian life was all a huge change for BJ. He had been used to many years of Army life. Adapting to 'civvy street' would therefore, be enormously challenging for him.

In his last years of military service, he had undertaken further education and study and obtained a Teacher's Certificate, which allowed him to work as an instructor at the School of Electronic Engineering. He had become used to living in the Sergeant's Mess, and had Army people always around him with the culture, banter and close supports in which he had been immersed. Now pushed out into civilian life, it all hit him really hard. The sudden change was a huge struggle for him. He moved to London and was able to visit his parents, see his brother and get some support through that familial connection.

In BJ's Regular Army Certificate of Service (the red Service Book), his military conduct is described as *"Exemplary"*. He is confirmed as someone with the ability to organise and manage, being a high calibre Technician with a wide variety of skill and experience. Undoubtedly, these comments were very helpful to him in any of the recruitment pathways in which he was involved.

He had had a successful Army career of 17 years and 126 days and was in receipt of a number of awards, including active service medals and also the Long Service and Good Conduct medal. Going forward, he was in a great place to garner more success in his new civilian life.

Once BJ left, as part of the Options programme, that was it; no more support came from the Army, only the quarterly newsletters. He had to get on with his new life, 'outside'. When he first came out, he spent two months in Jamaica before then getting a job with the IBM Corporation, as a Senior Engineer.

IBM Corporation, is a multinational technology and consulting company with headquartered in the USA. It was founded in 1911 as the Computing-Tabulating-Recording (CTR) Company. It was renamed as 'International Business Machines' (IBM), in 1924. IBM had a significant presence in the United Kingdom, with offices and facilities located throughout the country. It produces and sells computer hardware, middleware, and software, as well as providing consulting services in areas ranging from mainframe computers to nanotechnology.

Working in IBM was a fantastic position for BJ. He was awarded quick promotion. He became the manager of a new engineering support team for major IBM clients in the City of London. This senior role enabled him to put a team together. His previous senior positions in the Army had really prepared him well for his new role in civilian, business life. He could lead and motivate, recognise talent and identify and reward others in the teams he led. He had been given the honour of leading and training others in the military and these skills translated well into his new career. He was able to develop systems with his team, each of whom were individually and collectively, praised for their efforts.

BJ is a man who is passionate to learn about the history of the community from which he has come. He recalls reading about those Caribbean men who had served in the Second World War and had been sent back to their various islands when war ended. He reflects on their situation. Those men were not even allowed to participate fully in the Victory in Europe (VE) celebrations.

While these soldiers had fought for Britain during the war, they faced discrimination and racism upon their return to the UK. After the war, many Caribbean soldiers were sent back to their home countries and were not allowed to settle in the UK. This was despite the fact that they had contributed to the war effort and had made significant sacrifices for Britain. The discriminatory policies and attitudes towards Caribbean soldiers therefore continued even after the war had ended. Clearly not all Caribbean soldiers were treated in this way. Some were able to participate in the VE Day celebrations. However, the fact that many were not allowed to do so, highlights in BJ's view, the discrimination and racism that existed within British society at the time.

BJ is further reminded of an earlier case; that of the SS Verdala. SS Verdala was a troop transport ship that carried several contingents of West Indian soldiers to Britain. However, its most infamous crossing was when it carried the Third Jamaican Contingent.

SS Verdala left Jamaica on the 6th March 1916, carrying 1,140 volunteers. It was forced to divert from its planned course across the Atlantic in order to avoid enemy submarines. It headed northwards to Nova Scotia. It was here, that due to a combination of a blizzard, a lack of appropriate winter clothing and a lack of heating on board, that over 600 members of the contingent developed hypothermia and frostbite. This resulted in over 100 of them having to have limbs amputated in Halifax, Nova Scotia. There were reports about this incident in the 'Daily Gleaner', at the time. Five men died, due to the extreme cold.

Thereafter, the event came to be known as The Halifax Incident. There was no compensation for the victims or their families, and there was a sense of people not caring about their suffering and loss. This in BJ's view, IS symbolic of a continuing lack of acknowledgement about the service that he, and hundreds, thousands even, have given to Britain, in service to the Queen and the country, over a very long time.

BJ cares passionately about these matters, especially in relation to all of us, including the Armed Services, taking the time to learn from them.

He describes another example of the indignity of men who were involved in particular events in Taranto, Italy, in November 1918. It was during this incident that the soldiers of the British West India Regiment had not only carried out arduous physical tasks, such as loading and unloading ships, but they were also made to perform demeaning tasks like building and cleaning toilets for white soldiers. This was made worse with the discovery that white soldiers were being given a pay rise, while black soldiers were not. The black soldiers complained and sought justice, but some were then imprisoned and even shot.

Although these blights were in the past, BJ believes that they need to be acknowledged as having happened. They were reflective of previous injustices, discrimination and racism, which *"should cause pause for thought and lead to changed actions"* in the treatment of today's British Caribbean service men and women.

"There does not seem to be much appreciation."' He uses a bit of Army slang to say, *"It grits my sh..t, to know this about their view of our service."* He believes that this lack of recognition is made even worse by the manner in which the Windrush Scandal happened in 2017 and continues, seemingly, to draw contempt and inaction from each Home Secretary that has been appointed over more than a decade.

It is not just in the Armed Forces that there is little acknowledgement of Caribbean peoples' contributions to the UK. BJ believes that it is even at local levels where this minority have lived and helped the areas to improve, that there has been a failure to notice, to appreciate them. He feels that there are probably several areas around the country where this has happened.

It might be interesting to consider areas such as Brixton, Notting Hill and Kensal Rise in London and perhaps parts of Bristol, where communities settled. These areas have now been reclaimed it seems, through gentrification, by white professionals. The black people who made their lives there, when it seemed 'too poor', have now been edged out. They can no longer afford the high prices being demanded for these, previously discarded houses in newly upscaled, often renamed areas. It appears, for example, that much of Kensal Rise is now known as Kensal Heights.

The Caribbeans came from the West Indies and were united in their effort to rebuild the UK, alongside what they considered to be their fellow Britons. BJ believes it to be shameful to have their contributions go unrecognised; very largely unappreciated. It is, hopefully, a part of history that is now beginning to be acknowledged and addressed.

Over the past five years especially, small but significant efforts are being made to recognise and honour the contributions of Caribbean soldiers to the war efforts of the past. More needs to be done about that, but also to recognising that these Caribbean men and women did continue to serve in the post WWII period and are serving currently.

Nonetheless, BJ is fulsome in his pride in his Army service. Although he continued to be very successful in his civilian careers, with reflection, he does have some regret that he left the military when he did. He feels that he should, maybe, have served a bit longer.

Looking back, especially as he had already been recommended for further promotion, he believes he would have progressed even further upwards in the ranks of the Army.

"If I left school tomorrow, I would do the same again; join up. My military career helped me in life in many ways. It gave me confidence and self-discipline. It allowed me to develop a range of skills including how to manage people effectively and positively. I made some good friends, and learnt what it was like to be part of a supportive team. It was all worthwhile."

Staff Sergeant Elaine Osborne (aka 'Ossie')

Elaine came up to England at the age of 11, from Jamaica to join her parents. Elaine's parents were already in the UK for 8 years, leaving Elaine with her older brother and her uncle.

Many Caribbean people were driven to be a part of the rebuilding of what they saw as their mother country and sacrificed family life, often leaving their young children to be cared for by relatives back home. They felt that it would be easier to start a new life and make a new life for their children who they would send for later on, when things were more settled and affordable.

Elaine grew up in the London Borough of Harrow, an outer borough of the Capital.

Following school, which she left at 15, Elaine worked as a Clerk in an insurance company. While she was in this post, she attended night school to train in shorthand and typing. Elaine's father taught her to drive, and she succeeded in passing her test. Her Dad was a strict teacher and she was proud to meet his expectation that she would be successful in getting her license, which she did. Elaine was also keen to gain other skills and really would have liked to develop some expertise in computing.

She lived in a home which was very much about discipline and love. Elaine wanted more freedom. The Army seemed to offer her the chance to gain that freedom and to develop her IT skills. So, she decided to apply for a career within it.

Off Elaine went and made her application. She was asked to attend for interview in the office at Scotland Yard, where she went through the tests and had her medical. When she passed her various tests and the medical, she was then given two choices - clerk or store woman. She thought that a clerk career seemed most appropriate for her.

Elaine went to Guildford to do her basic training for six weeks. She remembers very clearly being sent a Travel Warrant for her journey into her new career. Her parents took her in the car to Waterloo Station, where she would travel by train to Guildford Station.

When she arrived at Guildford, she and the other recruits who came that day, were met by a non-commissioned officer and driver, and taken to Guildford Barracks.

Elaine was put into a dormitory with seven other women. She was sent to be kitted out, into a white shirt, tie, suit jacket, skirt and a great coat. It was a green kit, which she loved. The women had to provide their own 'American Tan' coloured tights.

Basic training was a challenge. The women did 'square bashing', marching, drilling and personal care. They also had to make sure that the group in each dormitory, kept it clean and tidy and successfully got through each check by their senior officer.

During the period of basic training, Elaine was fully engaged with the process. She did however, feel a loss of identity, that each person was on a conveyor. Recruits were told to do things and they had to do it quickly and well. Elaine believed it to be programming really. Recruits had to book in, book out and literally jump to it when they were given their orders. She had weekends off and could apply to go home.

She made friends in that first few months in the Army, some of whom have remained friends right to the current day. Around 20 women still meet up for regular reunions. In fact, they had a reunion at the Union Jack Club recently and Elaine describes it as a 'blast'.

Following basic training, Elaine decided that she would move into the clerk area of work. She had been a part of only four black women in the group of 300 women at the time. She did very well indeed and was awarded the Best Recruit label. She was delighted to be called out by a very senior officer in the Great Hall in Guildford. She was over the moon to be identified.

Full of confidence therefore, Elaine went on to Blackdown Barracks to train as a Clerk. She did however, move quickly to another trade and ended up as a Storewoman in Bicester. She worked as a Storewoman for around a year before moving to another very interesting posting in Wiltshire.

The Wiltshire posting would last for two years, focusing especially on service within the Intelligence Corp. During that posting, Elaine made friends with a girl, with whom she remains friends to this day. Strangely, but happily, they found themselves living in the same borough, after Army life. This was a happy coincidence for these two women, as they have been able to meet regularly and share memories from their time in the military.

Elaine soon became a Lance Corporal. She went on to take up another posting to the Garrison in Rheindahlen, in West Germany where she then became a full Corporal. She served in West Germany for around four years.

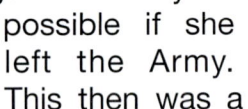

While in her Rheindahlen post, Elaine gravitated towards other British service people, but she also met American and Dutch soldiers. There was little connection with the locals who seemed more interested in the black, male soldiers. Despite all of this however, Elaine had great fun, socially during this posting. She also had the opportunity to do skiing, which she loved.

Elaine served in the regular Army for six years, completing the period she had initially signed on for. She was considering the next stage of her life, including wanting to have a family, a house and all the things a 'normal' civilian life entailed. She believed that these things would only be possible if she left the Army. This then was a firm decision for her and so she terminated her military service and went home.

She lived with her parents and got a Data Entry Clerk job for the local authority.

Life was good. Elaine soon realised however, that she really should have stayed in the Army longer. She missed it. She missed the discipline, the opportunity to meet a wide range of people.

Therefore, a few months after leaving, she joined the Territorial Army, 31 Signal Regiment - 4 7 Squadron, Harrow. She did this TA work, part-time, carrying out drills and other exercises, including travelling abroad.

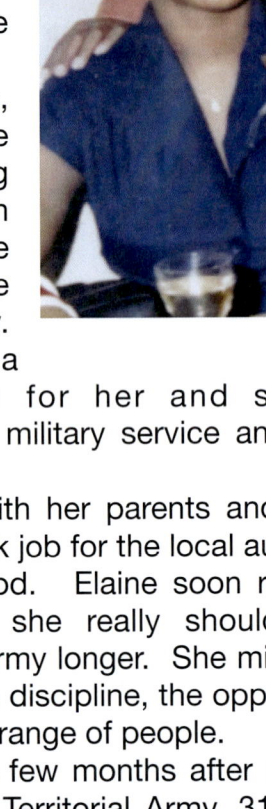

Elaine thoroughly enjoyed this work, which she felt fulfilled her expectation of a balanced life, which included continuation of military service to the country. Elaine served in the TA for 17 years, becoming a Staff Sergeant.

Elaine reflects on the totality of her military service, over the 23 years. She believes that the service, which she and many other Caribbeans gave and continue to give, is not sufficiently acknowledged, or known about. In her view, Veterans who have left the Army, receive no benefits, and are left to their own devices, with little or no support for their mental health.

She believes that the government does not recognise Veterans, but especially not those of Caribbean heritage. An example of this relates to the pension she receives.

Elaine feels strongly that the Army pension benefit, which she had worked for falls short of her expectations and is unfair. She contributed to it when she was in the Army. She believes that now when she needs it to help her with her living as a retiree and pensioner, it is not there to provide that critical support. Despite several requests to the 'powers that be', her pension has still not been reviewed and uplifted to reflect her length of service. A number of Veterans who served in the British Army around the same time as Elaine, are aggrieved by the perceived disparity in their pension rights. The amount they receive is paltry and leaves them in a poorer position than they believe is deserved.

Despite all of this, Elaine is still proud of her military service. She wished that she had received better advice when she joined at 18. At that young age, she wanted someone who had her best interests at heart, who could direct her about her career choices. If she had, she believes, she could have done even better.

Her advice to other Caribbean young people considering a military career, is clear. If they are good academically, they should think about pursuing a career in the Army, as an officer. *"Go for a commission"*, she advises. It would save them university fees, while ensuring that they achieve degree-level qualifications, travel and obtain a range of skills, including leadership and management of people. There is every profession in the Army, and they would have options.

Elaine is pragmatic however, and realises that a military life is not for everyone. But still, Elaine's advice to them is to

"Pursue your goals, if not in the Army, find and join a large company that will give you benefits, high level training and nowadays, a good pension."

She knows what she is talking about. Those views are deeply held and are based firmly on her personal and military experience. Elaine continues to work for various charitable organisations and travels to support needy groups in a number of countries, working in a voluntary capacity.

She spends quality time with her family, who are very precious to her. Elaine enjoys her life. She can often be seen parading in support of fallen comrades, whose service she feels should be respected and honoured. She is a force to be reckoned with. She is wise, with valuable views and experiences.

Elaine is well thought of by everyone who knows her and with those she meets.

She is a woman whose service to the country should be acknowledged, remembered and honoured.

Photo by Gill Shaw

Gunner Frank Beswick

Frank, was born in Jamaica in the Parish of St. Elizabeth, in the early 1950s. He came to London when he was almost 13 years of age. He joined his parents Enid and Charles, who had left for the UK some years before to contribute to the rebuilding efforts in which the UK was engaged. He was pleased to be reunited with them and with his siblings, whom he missed greatly.

Frank went to school in North West London until he was 15. Those two years of English education felt very strange to him. He felt dislocated because of the lack of discipline as he saw it, in the classrooms. He was also uncomfortable with the strangeness of the life he encountered in his new country.

In school, the teachers did not appear to really know how to properly assess his intellectual and academic strengths and establish his 'place' in the different year group and subject sets. As he reflects on this, Frank believes that it was an absence of care from the professionals at that time.

His parents had grown up in an island country where teachers were revered and what they said and did, was considered to be absolute 'gospel'. They believed that the English teaching staff in this 'Mother Country', could do no wrong with their children. In their mind, they left their sons and daughters in the safekeeping of the school and thus, surely, they were being given the best teaching and the best nurturing to succeed. Sadly, this *"old time"* trust and confidence in the British school system, would prove to be misplaced, not only for Frank, but it appears was the case for many hundreds of young people who had been brought to the UK in the 1960s and 1970s. Therefore, in the short time Frank was in that North West London school, he was put in lower groups and left to his own devices, floundering. The school *"was not quite right for me"*, so for those two years, he just coasted along until he could leave. School had not been a happy time for him, for this newly arrived young man.

During the time that Frank attended his comprehensive school in London, there were increased numbers of students who were new Caribbean immigrants. This was due to the post-World War II wave of immigration from the Caribbean, which brought many West Indian families to the UK seeking better economic opportunities and helping to rebuild many areas in the UK. As a result, many Caribbean children ended up attending either secondary modern or the new comprehensive schools that were being established at the time.

Comprehensive schools were a new type of secondary school in the UK, designed to provide a broad education for students of all abilities and backgrounds. However, during the early years of comprehensive education, there were still many challenges to be faced, particularly in the areas of discipline and academic assessment. For students like Frank who were new to the UK, these challenges were even more pronounced, as they had to adjust to a new culture and new educational system. Many of these students struggled to find their place in the school system and were not always given the support they needed to succeed.

Frank had to think about what he wanted to do with his life. He had left school after two years, with no qualifications at all. He went on to become a trainee in Lewis and Lewis construction company in Park Royal in London. He didn't enjoy that construction job. After a very short time in his trainee position, he spotted what seemed at the time, to be an opportunity to use his brain in the financial world. He saw an advert for a job in a finance house in London. He applied and was very fortunate to get this new job as a Trainee Broker. This placement was in a stockbrokers' firm in the City of London. The company he joined, saw great potential in him. They could see his intelligence, his sharp problem-solving. In their view, he could clearly go far in Killick and Hayley, a stable, thriving City firm.

Although full of enthusiasm at first to join this company and to learn about stocks and shares at that middle teen years, he soon became bored. The work seemed to have more than its fair share of monotony, which to a teenager, seemed relentless. He was also a little fed up at home. He really got himself into a bit of a spiral of indecision about his life.

Looking back now, from his more mature years, he realises that as an immature youth of nearly 17, he needed more support and direction at that time. He remembers not wanting to talk to anyone about this chaotic, rudderless time in his youth. He was from a good home, but he was not settled. He had not seen his older siblings for years, nor had he, his parents. Living with them now in his new, strange country, he did not know how to open up about his fears and potential life choices. It was a tough time for this young man. He felt that his new London life at that time, was restrictive in the home environment he was in and with the larger numbers he now lived with. It was far removed from the rural setting he had come from; the animals and freedom he had had in acres of farmland, away from other houses and towns.

He truly felt adrift from his family and his adopted country. It was not long into his second job, after falling asleep on the train and missing his stop, that he decided that city work was not for him. He really did not have the best advice at that time.

However, when he heard about the Army, the excitement that the Army seemed to offer was to his mind, too good to miss. It would take him away from the daily commute and what he experienced, as the relentless drudgery of his daily life. With hindsight, he feels he should have stayed with the stockbroking company. and the stockbroker vacancy which had previously drawn him in and which would have led him towards a richer, more secure future. However, it was not to be.

Given the fact that Frank had only been in the United Kingdom for a very short period of time and he had not lived with his parents for the previous four years, he had to get to know them all over again. He didn't really feel very comfortable to be in a crowded house in a very strange place: this England that he had been brought to by his parents. The draw of the Army was more about getting away, rather than a deep desire to serve at that time. It was his escape.

The Army interview was at Marble Arch, a place he had never visited. There was a test to see what level he was at educationally, including in English and mathematics. There was also a medical. He got through all of the tests, easily. There was only a tiny medical concern about his slight flat-footedness. He felt lucky to get through the tests and yes, he could now start his service with the Army. He felt really excited. At that time and with the exhuburence of youth and a lack of maturity, Frank at the age of 17 and a half, did not really understand what his decision to join the Army meant. He was just looking forward to this new life and was glad to get away from home.

He set off to start his basic training. He didn't know what to expect. He remembers being put into a dormitory with others, none of whom were black. All the new recruits were given some basic information about hygiene, clothes washing, bed tidying, polishing shoes, ironing and sock tidying. Everything had to be perfect and the dorm was inspected thoroughly each day. Even the bathrooms and other communal areas were subject to inspection, so all of those in the dorm had to work together to make sure they were not penalised. The discipline level was extremely high and the expectation was that they had to work as a team, so no one would let the group down. It all felt pretty tough at the time and sometimes even unfair, but Frank feels that it was worthwhile. Each person became very independent in their personal care, something about which their parents would be proud.

During basic training, these young men learned how to march and salute appropriately. They were exposed to numerous drills which they had to learn to perfect quickly. Within weeks, everyone got the hang of it. Frank made friends in those first weeks. He remembers Kenny, Sidebottom and Geordie especially, men who trained and served with him throughout. There was a high level of banter which was new to Frank, but he learned to manage his responses and survive. His main focus was always on doing his best and better where he could. He felt that he had to prove himself especially initially, until things settled - he hoped.

Frank completed his basic training successfully and had his Passing Out Parade on the Garrison Square at Woolwich. He remembers the massive parade ground at the passing out. He was in full uniform, every part of his uniform ironed and sharp, buttons shining and boots you could use as a mirror. He was puffed with pride in his achievement.

While he was at Woolwich, a very senior army officer from the Commandos, decided to take the whole group of new recruits on a physical test to assess their suitability to join the 29 Commando unit. Frank excelled in the activities he faced, and passed with flying colours. Having completed these early but arduous tests, he was then sent on to The Citadel at Plymouth, where he was able to pursue the first stage training towards becoming a member of the elite Commando unit. He was one of only two black men in his year. The two black men tried to support and encourage each other. They knew that all eyes were on them, even within the context of all of their comrades working for the benefit of the Team. However, he really enjoyed the continuous challenges he faced. It was not easy, but he got through and moved up to the second stage of training with the Royal Marines in Devon.

This second stage had more stringent challenges to overcome. He faced them head on. He was always being praised for his commitment and for completing successfully, the arduous physical activities required of the group of tough men, with whom he trained.

He felt desperately sad to see that the other black person who had struggled through the tests, became defeated at the very last stage on the long and last challenge before Green Beret success. The last challenge was a 30-mile run, with full kit, within a set time. Frank tried to do everything he could to carry this soldier in his last battle, but failed. He was especially upset as his friend and only other black person in his Battery, just could not get through that last testing exercise. Frank still remembers this with great sadness. Despite his regret for his 'mate', Frank was able to gain that often elusive, but amazing if you succeeded, Green Beret. There were three other black men from another Battery who also achieved their Green Berets at that time. Frank is immensely proud of his achievement, and he was not yet 19-years-old! As a Commando, Frank felt a huge sense of achievement. It was especially so as very few people succeeded in completing the arduous training and getting a Green Beret. But mostly, it was the beret, the Green Beret sat over his new haircut, which just finished his outfit perfectly - and everyone was there to see him. Well, that is what he thought, how he felt then. He just felt a great sense of achievement, especially knowing how few of them actually got through the training, or indeed got to train as a Commando in the first place. He was bursting with pride. He still smiles at this memory - one of the best memories of his time in the Army.

Frank is a British citizen by both birth and heritage. He had two grandfathers and a great-grandfather who were white British men. In 1962, when he was aged ten, Jamaica became independent. He was then given a Jamaican passport in preparation for travel to the UK. Using this passport to come to the UK as a teenager to be with his family, he therefore went into the army as a Jamaican whose right of abode in the United Kingdom was stamped into his passport. He had indefinite leave to remain (ILR) in the UK, but in reality, his citizenship was clear. Despite what was alleged in the Windrush generation scandal which later emerged, he was also indisputably British.

When he joined the Army, Frank took the Queen's shilling and he also swore an oath of allegiance to the Queen and to the Realm.   He was happy to do this as he knew that he was both Jamaican and British. He was perfectly at ease with the idea of service to the Queen and to Britain, as a soldier.

He had pursued his training in the full knowledge that Army life would be important; it would matter in the society to which he was now a part. It was a key job in the safety and security of the country. He therefore accepted all the rules and regulations and moved along into the different military training pathways.   He immersed himself fully into Army life. He was good at the different tasks and activities presented to him. He was also commended for the strength of his hard work and the successes he achieved. He had also become a Paratrooper, passing the relevant tests and tasks required to be a part of that also elite, group.

The soldiers who passed into the Green Beret group, now Commandos, were then allocated to 145 Battery, within 29 Command Light Regiment, Royal Artillery. They continued with normal routines over the next year as well as serving where necessary, in designated conflicts. As a Commando Regiment, 29 Commando is a specialist unit that is trained to operate in a variety of challenging environments, including mountainous terrain, jungle, and desert environments. The Regiment is also trained in amphibious operations, allowing it to operate in conjunction with the Royal Navy and Royal Marines.

Within the Regiment, 145 Battery is responsible for providing close support artillery fire for 3 Commando Brigade, which is part of the Royal Marines. This involves providing indirect fire support using a range of artillery systems, including 105mm Light Guns and 81mm Mortars.   The Battery also operates a range of supporting vehicles, including Land Rovers and Pinzgauers, which are used to transport personnel and equipment in challenging terrain. In addition to its primary role of providing artillery support to 3 Commando Brigade, 145 Battery is also trained to operate independently as a quick reaction force. This involves being able to deploy rapidly to a range of environments and to provide direct and indirect fire support as required. The Battery is also trained in reconnaissance and surveillance techniques, allowing it to operate effectively in complex and rapidly changing situations.

Overall therefore, 145 Battery is highly skilled and versatile, with a wide range of capabilities that make it well suited to a variety of challenging operational environments. Frank was also trained as a Paratrooper. This more elite group of soldiers were classed as the Winter Warfare group and thus were required to participate as appropriate, in a number of survival type situations. Part of their skills training included enjoyable activities such as skiing, rock climbing, parachuting and so on. Frank does however, remember yearning for warmer climates at that time, especially when he heard people discussing their time in places such as Singapore!

Frank thoroughly enjoyed his time in the Army. Some of the best experiences he had were those involving training and even the assault courses, though tough, were fun. He believes he may still hold the record for doing one of the assault courses in the fastest time!

Unfortunately, Frank saw some bullying in the time he was in the Army, some racist incidences too. These were difficult both to process and to manage, but as a minority black soldier, it was something he grew to *"accept as the way it was for us"*.

Frank served in various tours and in places in the UK and abroad, as required. He was able to learn how to look after ammunition, carry out patrols, guard civic buildings and do everything he could to avoid death in situations in which he was being, or could be, fired upon.

He has no regrets about the service he provided to the country; to his adopted land. He did however, have to make a decision about whether to continue this service soon after his qualification and service in various conflicts. His family was important to him. It was a key relationship with his fiancee, which caused him to reflect on the next stage of sign-up to the Army. It became increasingly clear that there may be some serious issues in his relationship if he continued with his career. He was quite conflicted, but finally made a decision to leave after nearly four years service.

After completing an ex-services' course on construction repair, Frank prepared for his transition out of the Army by gaining a qualification through a Government training programme. He went on to join the internationally renowned Wimpey Laboratory. It was while he was working with Wimpey that he achieved his City and Guilds qualification in construction and mechanical engineering. Frank went on to spend nearly two decades working for Wimpey.

He conducted site investigations on onshore and offshore projects across the world, including in locations such as Nigeria, Saudi Arabia, Bahrain, Singapore, Sudan, Kenya, Qatar, and the North Sea. Sometimes, he was located in particular countries for years at a time in order to complete major construction projects. Some of his work also included conducting the important site investigations before the Severn Bridge was built. He always looks up with pride, as he travels over the Severn Bridge, remembering the part he played in its building. Frank is immensely proud of his engineering work with the Wimpey company.

He believes that his training and career with the Army helped him manage himself effectively, in a range of different situations and among the different cultures to which he was exposed. At first, when he left the discipline and security of Army, life felt very strange, and Frank remembers feeling a little lost, unsure, and insecure. He missed the Army. Sometimes, life outside did not feel *'quite right.'* It took some time to adjust to civilian life. It was not until he had started at Wimpey that he began to settle. After the first few years, things stabilised.

Frank got married two years after leaving the Army, and three years later, he had the first of his two children.

Frank does not regret his time in the Army. In fact, he wishes he had stayed longer, as there had been opportunities to do so. He had been doing well and he believes that the discipline offered by a military life and the acquisition of skills and qualifications that go alongside the service, are definitely worthwhile.

In his view, little is known about the contribution and service of men and women like himself who took that shilling and swore an oath to the Queen, often at a very early age. This feeling is often reinforced when he sees events that include white ex-servicemen and women parading along streets and around monuments, including at the Cenotaph each year, few black Veterans among them. Following his time in the Army and subsequent careers, such as with Wimpey and other organisations, Frank looks back over his life and achievements with pride. The Army part of his life was very meaningful for him. He had stood ready to be a part of anything demanded of him in defence of the Realm. He does however, want to be recognised and acknowledged for this military service.

Frank is a part of a family which has provided many years of military service. His brother and two of his cousins served in the British Armed Service. His eldest brother was also in the Jamaica Defence Force Youth, when he was a secondary school student in Jamaica.

Frank tries to keep in contact with other ex-servicemen. He attends various clubs and events which are organised by Veterans' charities. He continues to show respect to those who have passed away and have been ignored by the communities in which they lived, after their loyalty and commitment to the Monarch and their bravery and service to the country. The honouring of them he feels, is crucial to them believing that their efforts are valued, their contributions mattered.

"It is especially galling", he says, "to hear refrains coming mainly from Caucasians that 'My dad/brother/uncle/ grandfather served this country!'", suggesting it seems, that they were the only ones who did.

As other members of his family served in the Armed Forces, on behalf of this country Frank wants everyone to know, to acknowledge, that *"I did my bit. I too, served."*

Lance Corporal (LCpl) Sandra Martin

Sandra was 11-years-old when she left her homeland of Jamaica in the late 1960s to join her parents in London. She attended school outside of her locality as her parents were not confident about the calibre of education she would receive. When Sandra left school, she went on to college to further her education.

While at college, Sandra decided that she wanted to join the Royal Navy. She had wanted to be a Radar Operator and she felt that the Royal Navy was ideal for her to achieve her goal. However, when she attended the interview in Central London (Southampton Row), she did the required tests, but was not told of her true results from them. Instead, she was told that her mathematics was good, but her English was less, and she could only be offered a position as a cook.

Sandra knew that of the two subjects, it was her English that was good. She had achieved her GCE 'O' Level in that topic. The comments from the Royal Navy interviews seemed a bit of a red flag, so she decided that a naval career was not for her. The next option was the Army.

Sandra applied to join the Women's Royal Army Corp (WRAC) based in Guildford and was successful, following the usual interview and testing process.

"All of us females did our six-week Basic Training in Guildford before we were posted to our relevant Army Camps to do our Trade Training."

The Women's Royal Army Corps (WRAC) was formed in 1949. It absorbed the remaining female troops of the war time Auxiliary Territorial Service (ATS) after the war. With the creation of the WRAC, it was the first time that women were subject to all sections of the Army Act. The Corps eventually included all women serving in the Army except medical and veterinary orderlies, chaplains and nurses. It was common for women of the WRAC to serve with other Army Regiments on long-term attachments, such as with the Royal Corps of Signals, but retaining their WRAC cap badge. This opened up more and more roles to women.

The Royal Army Ordinance Corps (RAOC) was the body charged with the supply and repair of weapons, ammunition and equipment to the British Army. Sandra joined the RAOC as a Clerk, doing her training in Guildford. During her six-week training, she went through all the necessary, tough and challenging soldiering activities.

Sandra started in the Army with a big Afro, which was not permitted. She had, therefore, to cane row her hair and pull it all back to comply with the Army's regulation and expectation of smartness. Sandra was from a very strict Caribbean household, so she had already experienced the type of discipline that other new recruits had not. She was amazed by how much the other women seemed to struggle with basic things, such as washing, ironing, and cleaning. She could not believe it. She remembers that before she set off to do her Basic Training, her parents, especially her mother reminded her, that *"You're going to be with 'white' people, so you have to live up to their expectations!"* The reality was further from the truth and rather different, in Sandra's view. They were having to live up to her standards. She was already trained in these matters. This was so in relation to having good table manners, especially coming from the family she had left behind. Soon she was seen as very smart throughout this early training and in fact, all the way through her military career. Sandra comments, *"How little we valued ourselves then. The pressure of colonialism and the low expectations from others and even of ourselves. These were the messages we were being given, which in turn reinforced our being marginalised".*

Sandra believed then and during her eight years of service, that she and the other black women with whom she would build lifelong relationship, would try to always be the best, wherever they were in the world. She was fortunate to travel to different locations, including to Holland. The memory of that period in her life, still fresh in her mind, Sandra then recalls, *"However, we could go out at night, which was great!"* Sandra was not as aware as she would become later in life, of the racial overtones and explicit nature of some of the direct comments directed her way. She talks about *"Being blind to everything during Basic Training"*. "Perhaps, she said, *it was a way of survival."* Sandra was one of only two black women in her Basic Training. She recalls that even the tights the black women had to wear were those more suited, in colour to the white women recruits. The other black woman told the senior officer that *"It doesn't match my skin colour"*. That led to a Corporal giving her and Sandra, permission to go out and buy tights with shades more appropriate to their skin tones. Her comrade"s example of speaking out showed Sandra that she too, could speak up.

Having completed, successfully, her Basic Training she proudly marched out in the 'Passing Out Parade'. Her parents were present to witness this event.

Sandra left Guildford after the six weeks of Basic Training and went on to do her 'Trade-Training' in Deepcut, Surrey. This Phase 2 training focused on developing her secretarial skills and lasted for 12 weeks. After completing Trade Training, she was posted to Germany at her request. Not many soldiers got their first choice. Sandra recognised that she was one of the lucky ones.

Sandra is still disturbed by the level of racist abuse she was subjected to mainly from men. She recalls a particular time when, as a very young soldier, she was on exercise in some caves. There were a couple of officers who were in charge and were sitting down reading a magazine. One of them called out to her and summoned her to where they were busy looking at a Playboy magazine. She was soon to discover that this magazine had pictures of naked women, including a black woman, in the centre spread with their private parts exposed. This officer showed her the picture and called out, *"That's you!"*.

Sandra remembers, vividly, feeling insecure and vulnerable at that time. She was traumatised not only by what she had been exposed to in the images, but by the vile comments of this officer who was in charge of the group. Sandra had never seen anything like the magazine's contents, in her life. The fact that this male officer felt that he could do this brought home to her, her lack of power.

This was not the only incident to which she was subjected. In those instances, the abuse of a senior officer was directed towards her as a black person. It was clearly racist and sexist. When they made the comments, she was told that they were *"joking"*. In the past she had been called, *"Jungle Bunny"*, had loud comments of *"Have you had a Chimp?"*, directed to her by a few male soldiers talking about their service in Belize. There were no organisational protections in place, so *"you had to learn how to protect yourself"*. As a black female soldier, she therefore had to *"suck up the racist and other sexist banter"*. When she tried to argue back, she was told, *"You can't take a joke"*.

There were several occasions when Sandra's hair would be touched quickly, without her permission, and comments such as *"Your hair is nice and spongy"*, were made. She was outraged at all of this personal intrusion, which those people seemed to think was ok. However, she said she managed, most of the time, to ignore the behaviour as she realised that in some cases, it was based on ignorance.

Sandra found herself being tongue-tied and nervous in those early months and years of military life. She had to toughen up. She realised that she then had to take the racist abusers on and respond in kind to reduce the level of abuse she was getting. To an extent, this seemed to work.

Once Sandra had completed her Trade Training and worked as a Clerk in Germany, she transferred from the Royal Army Ordinance Corp to the Royal Signals and retrained in Catterick. It was while she was in the Royal Signals that she was promoted to the rank of Lance Corporal. This allowed her to do different things, including telecommunications, telephonist work, and more. She did her training in the

North Yorkshire. She remembers a particular Commanding Officer, a Major, who spoke to her, commenting, *"You are a Jack of all trades, but perhaps a master of none!"* This was something that would resonate with Sandra when she heard that her promotion was turned down. This news came at a time when others, who she had trained, were being promoted above her. These women went on and up past Sandra. She found it demoralising. It was clear to Sandra that *"They really don't look at you as being one of them"*. This was despite being liked for her *"bubbly character"* and being given the nickname of *"Smiler"*.

Sandra was in Blackdown Barracks when she heard that she would be despatched abroad. She was posted to Germany. She was on a Base where there were American soldiers. Sandra had never seen so many handsome black men in one place. It was a marvel to her. She had a great time in Germany. Outside her work context, she was able to make friends and build a good social life, including enjoying lots of dancing in the many nightclubs, which were available locally.

Throughout her career, Sandra was able to participate in numerous Army exercises, working with others as a team. She sailed, did canoeing, hiking, climbing, lived in the wild, and engaged in survival activities. She participated in winter events in the Alps, learned to cook survival rations, ski and participate in the adrenalin-inducing activity of parachuting from helicopters. It was generally very exciting. She learned a huge amount and in the various locations, in which she served, gained hugely, from the variety of military experiences in which she was involved.

As she reflects on her military career, there is one area she still finds upsetting. It relates to her promotion opportunities. Sandra had achieved excellent results in her Trade Training, and as a Private, later obtained her B1 qualification alongside two other black women. A B1 level was considered good enough to study at a level that would enable a soldier to move on towards promotion to the rank of Sergeant. This promotion was seemingly unavailable to Sandra and the other two black women at that time.

However, Sandra persevered and was posted to Aldershot during the Falklands War. In Aldershot, as a Lance Corporal, she supervised the Telephone Exchange. After 12 months she was posted to Salisbury and continued there as a Telephone Supervisor. It was during this posting that she was offered the opportunity to participate in the Army Display Team with the Royal Signals, for six months. It was at this stage of her Army career that Sandra decided to leave the Army. She handed in her notice.

Sandra thoroughly enjoyed the Display Team tour and met some *"really great soldiers who had her back"*. Unfortunately, she also met others she considered undesirable to become her friends.

After her six months tour travelling with the Army Display Team across the South East, South West and the West country, Sandra returned to Salisbury and then shortly afterwards went to Catterick to complete her Resettlement Course. She was ready to take on new ventures in 'civvy street'. She felt that the Army would not be able to meet her academic and vocational goals. When she shared her news with her friends, many of them gave her six months before she would be *"running back to the Army"*. Sandra stated that she had no intention of running back, and their comments were, *"We'll wait and see!"*

Sandra smiled as she said, *"I guess they are still waiting"*. Lance Corporal Sandra Martin believes that the Army enriched her life. She had gained some valuable skills and learned a lot about people. She was able to live with strangers and developed friendships that would last a lifetime. *"In the Army we became a family and yes, the Army has shaped the way I think, based on some of my experiences both negative and positive. I learnt how to turn the negatives into positives. I felt that I was always in the role whereby I had to teach others that were ignorant to race, culture, etc. due to the environment in which they grew up."*

Sandra served her country well. She demonstrates a loyalty and commitment to the Army, despite some of the challenges she faced. She showed great resilience throughout and that provided her with the strength to manage her work and career to good effect.

"In the WRAC, our motto, was 'Gentle in Manner and Resolute in Deed.' I would like to believe that is how I have tried to live my life."

Sandra continues to grow in her life as a civilian, tending to her academic and intellectual skills, which she has in abundance. Her military life as a soldier, provided a foundation upon which to build. This legacy has enabled her to progress powerfully in her civilian environment.

Lance Corporal Sydney Marshall

Sydney was born in Guyana, previously known as British Guiana until its independence in 1966. He was the eldest of six children and came to the UK in the mid 1960s.

Before he came to the UK, Sydney had taught for three years. He also worked for the Bauxite Company and was a part-time volunteer with the Guyanese Forces.

Soon after volunteering, he was called up to work in the Force full-time. He was part of the Island's military efforts to keep the peace in Guyana when conflict broke out between the local Black and Indian communities.

Whilst Guyana was a multi-ethnic country, it was split down ethnic lines in political, social and economic terms. For around two years, especially between 1962 and 1964, there was a series of political and social upheavals in the country. The situation deteriorated seriously in 1963, almost sliding into Civil War. It even led to the loss of hundreds of lives within the relatively small Guyanese population of 700,000 at the time. It was a scary time for all Guyanese people, but Sydney and his colleagues showed huge commitment to securing peace in the country.

It was while he was serving in the Guyanese Force, that Sydney heard that the British were seeking recruits to relocate to the UK to join the Armed Forces. He applied and was successful in obtaining a place. He therefore made preparations to leave his home country and start his journey to his new career in the UK military. He was now aged 24, still a young man.

Sydney came over on "a propeller plane" - one of the early BOAC ones operating in those days. He travelled with 14 of the 15 young men who were selected. One person, although selected, had decided not to join up. Sydney met another 17 others, thus becoming a group of 30 black Caribbean men, off to serve in the British Army.

131

The first place Sydney saw in the UK, was Ireland, where his "propeller plane" landed.

This was an exciting time and Sydney, though apprehensive about what he would find in this new country, was confident also. He was already armed with the knowledge of his previous military work, and alongside other Guyanese men like himself, was filled with enthusiasm for the new stage of his life in the UK.

Soon after their arrival, three members of the Guyanese group applied for a Commission. They were unsuccessful, initially. Later, one of the men achieved his commission and rose to the rank of Captain in another Regiment.

At first, Sydney was placed in the Devonshire and Dorset (usually just known as the Devon and Dorsets) Regiment. The motto of the Devon and Dorsets was "Temper Fidelis" (Always Faithful). The Devon and Dorsets was formed in 1958 by the amalgamation of two County Regiments. It was later to be merged, in 2007, into The Rifles. Sydney served in this Regiment for nearly four years.

When Sydney landed in Ireland on that January morning, having stopped to refuel in the Bahamas and in Portugal, he was very excited to be in a different country. Everything was strange, so very different from his warm, Caribbean country. There would be much to learn, to become accustomed to - weather, people, military organisation.

At that time and because he had already served for a few years in the Guyanese Army, Sydney had no real intention of continuing within a military career for the rest of his life. He really wanted to further his academic studies, but understood that because Guyana did not have a university at the time and secondary education had to be paid for, it would mean that he would have to look elsewhere, for other options to develop himself. He felt that being in the British Army and living in the UK, would allow for more of those development opportunities.

He had been encouraged by a friend from home, who had been with him in the Volunteer Force to apply for the new military opportunity abroad. He had little time to decide, so quickly forged ahead with the application. He did a test. He was one of 50 others who also applied. They only wanted 15 people and he was fortunate to be a part of the successful group.

In those first few days of Sydney's arrival in Holyrood, Ireland, he found the weather bleak: cold, misty and wet. Those first impressions did not change much over the following months of training and acclimatisation. However, Sydney stuck it out. He was not ready to abandon his extended military career in this new place.

While he and the other Guyanese men were in Ireland, there were serious fights with others in the Army. It seemed that the other soldiers did not like these black men who had joined them. Sydney and the other Caribbean men had to really assert themselves as a group, to survive. Throughout all of this deeply unpleasant time, these black men did not have any problems with the Irish. It was some of their own, white colleagues who seemed determined to make their lives a misery. The Guyanese soldiers decided they had to draw closer and support each other even more. In fact, this support was then extended to any other person of colour who was being picked on, bullied or subject to racist and physical abuse.

He recalls an incident in which an *"Indian guy was hit by someone when he was asleep"*. The group decided to adopt the *"You hit one, you're hitting all"*, way of operating. In this way, they could be strong, defend themselves and survive any onslaught. There was however, some comeback from the Commanding Officer of the time. The CO came in the next day and said to the group, *"There'll be no black magic in this camp. You shouldn't take the law into your own hands"*.

The group decided however, to assume the "Jumbie lash" of their homeland. In Guyanese Creole, a 'Jumbie' is the generic name given to all malevolent entities. That is, these men wanted to make sure they were always ready to defend themselves from ambush by "bad people". Jumbie lash would be their response not only to the hitting incident, but to anything nasty from the other colleagues, all of whom were white. They just let it be known around the camp. They were having none of it.

Sydney did his three-month basic training in Exeter, before returning to Ireland. It was here that the bus he was on was hijacked. The five Guyanese men who were on the bus were told to get off as *"We have no argument with you lot"*. Fortunately, the other soldiers were unharmed and were able to get back to camp safely.

During his time in Ireland, Sydney was promoted to the rank of Lance Corporal. He could type and he was sent straight into the Battalion headquarters, where he became a Grade 2 Clerk. He went to C Company as a Clerk and it was here that he met a Major, who was very supportive of him. Sydney decided not to pursue his clerking qualification to become a Grade 1 Clerk. He was already considering what course of action to take for his future life. These considerations are things he would return to, during the next few months and years of Army life.

Sydney did participate in some social events while he was stationed in Ireland. There were functions in the camp, which included local civilian girls. He was also a very keen and talented sportsman. He did the 100 and 220 races in athletics. He competed in inter-Battalion events, winning each time during his years in the Army.

Following his Trade Training and within a few months of his return to Ireland, Sydney was posted to Munster and to Osnabruck, Germany, where he stayed for the next three years.

When Sydney describes his time in Germany, again he says, he *"had no problems with the Germans"*. Unfortunately, this was not the case with his white soldier colleagues. He describes the experiences he had of some of the old white soldiers who often tried to hit him and others like him. These black men were being continually, racially insulted. They had to develop strategies for avoiding these abuses, even to retaliating and attacking the racists in return.

This was a deeply unpleasant time for Sydney. Without other black men nearby, survival might have been virtually impossible. These black men had to be on their guard, always, including with the other ranking white men. He recalls a particular Drill Sergeant who seemed to take pleasure in demeaning black soldiers. An example of this was when on an official break from duties, being told by this more senior soldier that *"All these years, this wall has been standing. It doesn't need anyone to prop it up"*. He pauses in the memory that the particular comment was made to him when he was not on duty and could therefore really be relaxed, against a wall or otherwise. Sydney remembers that these comments were not heard when the Sergeant saw white soldiers taking their breaks and *"propping up the wall"*. However, Sydney reports that this Sergeant's comment was only one of the less serious comments to which he and other black men were subjected. There were many other very serious, discriminatory, racist ones.

There were however, some very good times for Sydney, in Germany. He met some people who "knew everywhere". They drove him around to functions, including travelling 300 miles to meet some Trinidadian women, to hold a party. He remembers the five people he travelled with having to sleep in the car as the party was so noisy. He recalls travelling back and still getting to church the next day! Those times were positive and memorable for the right reasons.

Throughout his Army career, Sydney was pleased to be exposed to other countries and cultures as part of his Army life. He had already seen something of Ireland and of West Germany. He participated in exercises in France and in the Middle East, in Tripoli.

He was then transferred back to Exeter to serve his last year in the Army. He decided that along with his Guyanese military service, he had done enough. Altogether, he had now served for nearly six years. He now wanted to do other things with his life.

When Sydney was living in Guyana, he met and became engaged to a woman whom he would later marry. She came over to the UK and the couple married. His wife got a job working for the Ministry of Agriculture. Sydney's decision to curtail his military career included being able to pay the Army so that he could obtain an early release. He and his wife then went to live with his sister in her house in Wimbledon. By this time, the couple had two boys. With great determination and much hard work, they obtained a mortgage through the Greater London Council and amazingly, with their then £5 deposit, bought their first house. Sydney was delighted to have had the support and to be well-placed to continue his life and prepare for his future.

It was thus the beginning of another new stage in Sydney's life. Here he was, an Army Veteran, about to embark on a new career. He has no regrets about his Army service. He sees it as being *"All life experiences"*.

He feels that the independence he gained, the discipline he was subject to, was all positive. There were lots of thrills in the training exercises and he thoroughly enjoyed and benefited from meeting a variety of people. He believes that there is the beginning of some acknowledgement of Caribbean servicemen and women, but that has only really happened in recent years. That recognition is only small. Still, in his view, there are few black faces in the crowds on Parade, but there seems to be limitations on the numbers who are representing "Us".

As soon as Sydney left the Army, he started applying for jobs straightaway. He went on the Dole, but was immediately put off by the treatment given to those seeking employment. In Sydney's view, that treatment was pretty bad. Dole was the payment made by the government to those people who are registered as seeking employment.

Sydney managed to get a job with British Rail. However, as that involved shift work and he needed to do evening study, he did not take it. Fortunately, he was then able to get a job at the Post Office. He held this job for eight years. He also worked at the Military Hospital, on Victoria Embankment.

Sydney continued to strive, to better himself academically, attending classes five nights per week. He studied mechanical engineering, electrical engineering, civil engineering and finally ended up as a Highways and Traffic Engineer. He achieved an HNC qualification, which allowed him to apply for and obtain an engineering position with British Rail. Sydney was the only black engineer across the geographical area, from Waterloo to the Isle of Wight.

He muses about his life in the military. He believes that with hindsight, if he had his 24 -year-old young Sydney time again, he would do quite a few things differently. For a start, he would tell himself to do more research about the UK, including about the weather!

In his view, the whole of British society is different now. He would still advise young Caribbean people to join up. They should however, look carefully at the different structures that exist within the military. Doing this research, would then enable a potential recruit to consider the career pathways that would best suit them. They should look particularly, at ones that would then allow them to transition positively and profitably into civilian life.

Sydney continues to be in contact with his original Guyanese colleagues who came up on the "propeller plane". They meet up in organised reunions, but are mainly in touch via telephone. They were an important part of his military journey. They gave him support, advice and encouragement when he needed it and were key to his survival at critical times in his Army career. He appreciates their friendship.

Sydney has also continued to provide support to other Caribbean Veterans. He has done this through his work with the West Indian Association of Service Personnel, (WASP), where he is the current Chairman. He is also a member of other organisations which support Caribbean peoples.

Some of these organisations that Sydney supports were started by small groups of committed people who felt that they were not being acknowledged by the community around them. This is especially so in the case of WASP, which was started by four women and nine men. Their legacy can be seen in this valued, thriving and focused organisation.

According to the Charity Commission's website, WASP's Charitable Objects are "1. To relieve the need, hardship and distress of (A) men, women, children and other dependants from the West Indies. (B) Widows, orphans and dependants of those who have served in Her Majesty's Navy, Army, Air Force or auxiliary forces or in the Mercantile Marine during hostilities afloat or in any Red Cross organisation whilst serving with Her Majesty's Armed Forces who are necessitous financial circumstances or who are suffering from ill-health or injury.

2. To advance the education of ex-servicemen and women of the West Indies, their widows, widowers, children and dependents."

The WASP organisation is therefore firmly based within the Caribbean Veterans' community and is often the first port of call for those in need, or for those Veterans who have no-one to depend on when they or their loved ones need to be given a respectful, honourable funeral. They step up. These extraordinary men and women are often to be seen, Standards in hand and on show, at quite humble funerals of their comrades who have succumbed to death.

The work in which Sydney and others are involved is largely unknown, mostly unseen. It is however, vital in its effect and necessary in its impact on this group of often poorly-regarded, unsung heroes of the Caribbean who have contributed much to Britain.

Corporal Lincoln Beswick, MBE

Lincoln came to the UK in 1962, four weeks after Jamaica achieved independence. He joined his parents, who had answered the call from the UK to help it to continue to rebuild after the War.

His parents were, through their birthright, British. His Mother was daughter to a white Scottish man, Hugh Wallace, and his Father was the grandson of a white man, Arthur Beswick, who was born in Cheshire in 1814 and travelled to Jamaica in 1834. These were facts, which gave his family entitlement to British Citizenship.

Lincoln had stayed in Jamaica with his grandmother and his eldest brother, who was chief engineer with the Bauxite Company. Lincoln's brother, Windsor Banks who was the product of one of the top schools in Jamaica, Holmwood, was a military cadet and was already very involved with the People's National Party (PNP), one of the two major political parties in Jamaica. Lincoln would remember his brother's experiences and think later on, how some of them were to mirror much of his own.

In preparation to leave Jamaica, Lincoln had travelled to the capital, Kingston. He was there to see Princess Margaret and the lowering of the British flag followed by the raising of the brand new black, green and gold of the new Jamaican flag. Lincoln remembers that moment with great pride in Jamaica's independence.

So, it was September when Lincoln arrived in his new country to see his parents, who he had not seen for four years. It was a momentous occasion. He had missed them terribly. It was a very emotional time. He also met his sister, who was born in the UK and was already nearly two years of age. He was reunited with his brother Donald, who had arrived a few months before.

In the 1960s, Lincoln recalls seeing a few more black people, Caribbeans like him, who had settled in the Kensal Rise area. However, on his first day in that area, he encountered capitalised signs that stated, *"NO BLACKS, NO DOGS, NO IRISH"*. He asked his brother, *"What's that all about?"*. His brother just shook his head.

Lincoln's brother Donald was at the local secondary school, so Lincoln joined him there. He remembers the headteacher at the time, Mr Morris, who spoke to his parents after he had taken the tests to assess his ability and stage of education. Mr Morris was very complimentary about Lincoln's results. He told Lincoln's parents that he had excelled himself and was in advance of many of his age group. Mr Morris then recommended that Lincoln apply for and take up an apprenticeship in engineering.

Lincoln was already just over 15 years old when he came to the UK, so an apprenticeship was suitable for him when he left the school a few months later, at the age of 16. Lincoln was accepted for the apprenticeship and soon started with the Lucas Company in one of its subsidiaries, Truvox, as an electronic engineer. Truvox made electronic parts for televisions.

A year later however, Lincoln made a huge decision to change his career. He had moved from Truvox to another job with the FJ Evans' company. This company manufactured road springs for Heavy Goods Vehicles (HGV). Still a teenager, Lincoln was unsettled. He had already made the journey, thousands of miles to a new country. He wanted to see more. In fact, he decided that he wanted to see the world. He believed that military service would allow him to continue to learn a trade and still give him opportunities for travel. The Army was known for its sports and for a place in which you could continue your education in its learning hubs. Therefore, with his parents' blessing, he went off to the Careers' Office in Finchley. He took and passed the relevant tests and secured a place in the Army.

At around the same time, Lincoln also joined the Labour Party and separately, joined a Trade Union. These were organisations, he would set aside for the time he was in the Army and would return to once he had left, years later.

Lincoln set off to start his basic training with the Royal Electrical and Mechanical Engineers (REME) Corps.

The Royal Electrical and Mechanical Engineers (REME) plays a critical role in the British Army. REME is responsible for maintaining and repairing the Army's equipment, vehicles, and weapons' systems, ensuring that they remain operational and effective on the battlefield.

The importance of REME to the Army's operational effectiveness cannot be overstated. The Army relies on its equipment and weapons' systems to function correctly in order to carry out its missions successfully. Without REME's expertise in repairing and maintaining these systems, the Army would be unable to operate effectively in the field.

REME personnel are highly skilled and trained in a range of different engineering and technical disciplines. These include mechanical engineering, electronics, and vehicle maintenance. They work alongside soldiers from other units to ensure that equipment and weapons systems are kept in good working order, providing support both in the field and at bases and depots. Lincoln would be an important part of this vital part of the Army.

In addition to their role in maintaining and repairing equipment, REME also played a key role in developing new technology and weapons' systems for the Army. Overall, REME was then and is now, a critical component of the British Army.

Throughout his career, Lincoln would recognise the significance of his then emerging skills and expertise in ensuring that the Army remained effective in delivering efficient equipment in whichever arena it operated in. However, at this early stage of his new career, Lincoln could only dream of the new things he would learn, the new people he would meet and the possible new countries he would, hopefully, travel to.

He set off therefore, to Berkshire, Travel Warrant in hand, to start his exciting new career.

Lincoln's basic training took place in Arborfield, Berkshire, a place, which seemed very far from home in Kensal Rise, North West London. The training lasted for three months. In Lincoln's intake, he was the only black person. He was in a dormitory with 11 other young men. Basic training involved handling weapons, drilling, marching, washing, ironing and cleaning with others in his dormitory, to make it ready for the regular inspections they had. Lincoln got through his basic training successfully and was able to Pass Out and be ready to start the next stage, his Trade Training.

When Lincoln was unable to start his Trade Training in Hampshire, he was despatched to the British Army on the Rhine (BOAR) to 4 Armoured Workshops in Detmold, hometown of the infamous General Rommel. It was in Detmold, that Lincoln was able to begin the first part of his engineering Trade Training. He was here until he qualified a year later, in 1965. In that same year, Lincoln became a lifelong member of the REME Association.

He went back to the UK for a short time, but was then sent back to BOAR to B Squadron REME, 17/21st Lancers. Their motto, which is also embroidered on their cap badge, reads, *'Death or Glory'* and set above it, is the skulls and crossbones insignia. This was a tank Regiment based in Paderborn-Sennelager, Germany, at the time. It was formed in 1922 by the amalgamation of the 17th Lancers and the 21st Lancers. It was then further amalgamated with the 16th/15th The Queen's Royal Lancers to form the Queen's Royal Lancers in 1993.

Lincoln served in Germany for four years. He was in the Athlone Barracks in Paderborn-Sennelager at the time of the famous 1966 World Cup. He remembers that it was certainly 'war' with the locals! A memorable event.

Lincoln continued with his Army service in his posting to Libya, with the 17 21st Lancers.

He was involved in several desert activities there, important work with the Army, before being sent back to BOAR for a further two years.

He was able to build his engineering skills further, including returning to the UK to upgrade his Trade

Training to the next level.

He then returned to Libya to RAF Eladem, where he learned to navigate across the desert by sundial! Lincoln was in Libya at the time of the overthrow of King Idris by Colonel Gadaffi. The British Army had a defensive and peacekeeping role, supporting the Middle East security at the time.

Lincoln took part in desert training, living in tents, learning to navigate in the extreme environment. After all, while he was an engineer, he was first and foremost, a soldier. He and the other British soldiers, did however, have some opportunities for relaxation, and young Lance Corporal Lincoln, recalls appreciating those moments.

Another return to the UK for more Trade Training and then a further tour in Germany, this time, to 9 Squadron, Light Aid Detachment, REME. The Squadron was based within 10 Regiment, Royal Corp of Transport, in Bielefeld. Lincoln served here for two years, before going back to the UK for a catch up at Arborfield, in preparation for his next posting.

Lincoln's next posting was with 50 Command Workshops in Sham Shuipo, Hong Kong. There are special memories for Lincoln, of that time in Hong Kong. Once he landed at the RAF Base at Kai Tak, he was taken to the Barracks. He shared the Barracks with the world-famous, but fearsome, Gurkhas. These extremely highly skilled soldiers have served alongside the British Armed Forces for the past 200 years. Their motto is *"Better to die than be a coward"*. Since WWII and for the past 50 years, the soldiers of the Gurkha Brigade have loyally fought for the British all over the world. They have served especially in Hong Kong, Malaysia, Borneo, Cyprus, the Falklands, Kosovo and more recently in Iraq and Afghanistan.

Sharing the Barracks with the impressive Gurkhas, gave Lincoln a great opportunity to learn about these significant Nepalese soldiers, to hear about their traditions. He really understood how deserving they are, of their reputation. He remains full of admiration for these courageous men.

By this time, Lincoln had responsibility for all the Trades. He was second-in-command of the Transport Depot, supplying transport to each section of the Military and recovery support to all of its vehicles in Hong Kong. Other than Lincoln, there was only one other non-Chinese, the Sergeant in charge. The rest of the Section were Hong Kong soldiers.

Lincoln found Hong Kong a very interesting place to be. There were cheap hotels, massive shopping opportunities with loads of cheap goods and many nightclubs, some of which were not 'visitable', safely. There were hotels which catered for the non-Chinese.

While in Hong Kong, Lincoln was able to enjoy sailing in the Gordon Hard Sailing Club, where he sailed the Enterprise Class and also Fire Fly in the Dunhill International Sail.

He had a very good time during this tour. Lincoln and his military colleagues tended to integrate within each of their Barracks, but took advantage of much of the entertainment which surrounded their location in Hong Kong.

Lincoln was the only black person in his Hong Kong posting. He recalls a woman, a Jamaican, who had stayed in the country after the Korean War ended in the 1950s.

Lincoln's love of sailing took him into many parts of the globe, including sailing in lakes up in Canadian Province, where the 'Dambusters' famously trialled their bombs. He sailed yachts around the Baltic, for weeks and also sailed in Swedish waters. He joined the British European Sailing Club in Kessel, West Germany and even took part in international competitions. He misses sailing.

Work-wise, he was able to provide engineering support to all the major Barracks which were based in the Hong Kong. He was a part of the British Army's strategic operation on the island. In this posting, Lincoln supported the Black Watch (Royal Highland Regiment) for several months. The Black Watch was the last British military unit to leave Hong Kong in 1997, and it played a prominent role in the handover ceremony at that time.

Lincoln continued his service in that part of the world, going on prescribed Army activities in a number of locations. He flew to Guam and on to Suva and Fiji. He participated in jungle training, but his main focus was to provide technical engineering aid, from the main base. He did however, continue to enhance and strengthen his soldiering skills, foraging and building escape rafts, in case of military necessity.

When he was in Fiji, he learned to sleep on coconut matting and wear a Sulu, just as the locals did. A Sulu is a kilt-like garment, similar to a sarong, worn by men and women in Fiji since colonisation in the nineteenth century. Lincoln adopted some of the Fijian customs for months on end. The Fijians looked after him and his colleagues very well. He recalls their songs as beautiful, their uses of flowers so impressive in their welcome. Sadly, he also remembers how some of his fellow Europeans treated these kind and loving people; badly.

Apart from sailing, Lincoln did a fair bit of parachuting, caving and skiing as part of his Artic training with the Army. He played hockey, participated in some boxing and had fun with land yachting on sand on wheels as well. These activities reinforced team building and supported the development of Lincoln's leadership skills.

Throughout his Army career, Lincoln was fortunate to be involved in a range of experiences, including, he recalls, doing a recovery exercise across a minefield still potentially active, from WWII. He learned the importance of staying alive, the ability to evade and escape despite being in dangerous situations. These were life skills necessary for any soldier. Fortunately, for him, there were only relatively few opportunities where those 'escape and evade' skills had to be put into practice. He pauses with a frown, in being reminded of some of those, 'near misses', which in his and in many other soldiers' cases, were not always within a foreign environment. This is a man of courage and resilience.

Lincoln remembers some really good times in his 12 years and 327 days of military service, before joining the Reserves. These were years, which he was advised were pensionable ones. Later, when he achieved pensionable age, obtaining his Army Pension would prove to be a contentious issue for this ex-serviceman. *"An injustice"*, he believes.

Throughout his service, Lincoln enjoyed the camaraderie he had with so many of his Army pals, some of whom became good friends. Together, he and his friends would often take full advantage of the local social clubs and events It was after all, in Germany, that Lincoln moved out of his teens, into adult life. He is particularly reminded of those times in Germany - the friendships, including with a German family with whom he was able to live, off base.

He was also struck by the quality of the professionals who supported the Army's work. He was part of various sporting activities, some of which were described earlier. He remembers playing cricket, but also recalls some of the less positive elements of his career then. He remembers much of the boisterous ignorance of some of his colleagues, the regularity and commonality of racist remarks, which seemed to come too easily to some of the people with whom he worked.

Despite all of this, Lincoln really loved being in the Army. It was in his view, *"an Army of education"*. He feels that the discipline, the qualifications he gained and the opportunity to see the world, are invaluable things to him still. These things have had a lifelong influence on him, on how he matured, how he learned through the various experiences as he moved from teenage boy to the man he became. Through the quality and effectiveness of his service across a variety of arenas across the world, he was mentioned in despatches and awarded both his General Service Medal and others related to other conflicts. He served in the Middle East and in Malta where he was part of Britain's peacekeeping efforts. He also remembers clearly the conflict in Cyprus between the warring factions and the peacekeeping efforts of the British military at the time.

However, having completed a full 12 years and almost a thirteenth, he made a decision to leave the Army. He joined the long-term Reserves, in which he served for the next 15 years. Thus, this tough, brave man has given to the country almost 28 years of military service. In his Discharge Book, his final report reads very well. It describes him as providing *"exemplary service"* and that he *"displays drive and initiative in all he undertakes"*.

Lincoln's first year out was a challenge for him. He still struggles with the fact that people do not appear to treat each other kindly, or with honour. However, in his new civilian life, Lincoln went on to successfully, expand his career options, working in engineering and leadership roles, with the Pickfords' Company. He became the boss of one of Pickfords' key workshops, before being transferred to one of the companies' subsidiaries, Homespeed, again in a management position.

People seemed to recognise Lincoln's worth, his skills, commitment and dedication to doing the best he could for each organisation. He was in these positions for many years and then went on to work with British Telecommunications, especially at the time when communication systems were evolving and high technical skills were being sought. It was while he was working with BT that Lincoln was elected as a Senior Branch Member of the largest Trade Union branch of the National Communications Union (NCU). In this role, he supported over 12 years, every union event in the country. For his Union service, he was given a Gold Award in recognition of his trade unionism.

Lincoln had not forgotten his earlier interest in the field of politics. During his employment with BT, Lincoln forged his political ambition by being selected and then elected as a Councillor, in 1994. He went on to be internally elected as the local Cabinet Member for Crime Prevention and Community Safety. In this role, Lincoln showed an impressive focus on making a difference to the areas for which he had leadership responsibility and achieved an almost legendary reputation for the differences he was able to make for his Borough, in local government more generally, and on a wider scale.

He was involved in work with the voluntary sector, the police, probation, the health services, fire services and the community. He chaired community development groups and was involved in discussions at the time of the building of the new Wembley Stadium and of those related to the new Willesden Sports' Centre. He is proud of the work he did as part of developing what he still feels, *"is the best Crime Prevention Strategy, not only for Brent, but which is still relevant for London and the country"*.

When he was working in the Crime Prevention area, Lincoln was presented with an award by the Metropolitan Police Commissioner at the time.

In addition to his work in his political Ward and within his main Cabinet role, Lincoln also provided a breadth of support to several organisations and individuals. Some of this support was provided to people seeking a career in politics, encouraging young people of colour to consider Eton Public School as an option for them too. He also spent some time, and because of his own military experience, supporting the Army's Ethnic Minority Recruitment Team (ERT) to encourage more black youngsters to join up.

144

This is a man whose nature is one of service, of loyalty and of dedication. He hardly 'drew breath' in his desire to help others. He still finds it difficult to understand those people who are not determined to show these qualities, especially when they assume a public servant role. He believes that choosing a public service career, surely demands close attention to truly and honourably, giving service to others. There should be no compromise in delivering that service with integrity and commitment, each and every time, without apology or excuses. He has always done this, with a high degree of passion in the manner of his service to his community and to the country, both within and outside the military.

He remains passionate about supporting others, especially those who feel disenfranchised and are vulnerable to being ignored and *"thrown away"* by organisations or by people in society who should be serving them better.

He is clear about the role of Active Advocate and has had huge success in ensuring better service, better provision, better treatment for the poor, the disadvantaged, and vulnerable especially in his local area. He has loved being in a diverse community of people about whom he cares so much.

He has worked nationally, with the Home Office, the police and with other organisations, such as the Probation Service, all of whom should be providing essential support to those who have some needs in the Justice system, in society. He is not afraid to call out injustice, wherever he sees it, or hears about it. He realises that this sort of attitude, has not made him popular, or made him friends among those who in his view *"should know better, how to serve others".*

His service as a local politician, especially with the Probation Service, was recognised and acknowledged by the award from the Queen, of an MBE.

Lincoln has also met other members of the Royal family, including King Charles 111, when he was Prince Charles.

He has met several Ministers and Secretaries of State from government departments during his public service.

Lincoln speaks with pride about his involvement in the development of The Armed Services Covenant and also when he was asked to brief Commonwealth High Commissioners about the historical service of Caribbeans to the British Armed Services.

He stands tall in every respect, when it comes to his contribution in public life, to the many causes and important policy changes affecting local and national aspects of our society. He believes that he *"should be judged by his humanity and service to his fellow humans"*. He walks with his head held high. However, few people know about his work. It is impossible to even recognise the valued contributions of this quiet, pensioner as he strides around the community in which he lives.

He does have some regrets about his military career. He wished he had stayed longer and perhaps become more influential. That influence is also certainly what he craved in respect of the national and international security work, in which he was involved.

He knows that his Army career *"stood him in good stead"* in all the jobs he held subsequent to leaving. As he speaks about all of this he says,
"My memory is making me quite emotional. I have not been recognised for my public or military service. It has not been acknowledged or recognised. What I have done has been significant, but nobody says thank you. Even when I left political life in Brent, nothing - not a phone call, not a cup of tea in appreciation of my contribution."
Such a shame.
He is still disappointed, hurt even, by this absence from that local authority of even the most basic courtesy for his many years of contribution and service to it.

In terms of his Army career and his feelings about that, he would still recommend to Caribbean heritage young people, that they consider a military career.
"It is still there for them as an opportunity to be disciplined, to contribute to a better society. It is also a source of full employment, a place to obtain good qualifications, to be able then to go on to other professions later on."

Overall, although he takes pride in having served in the Armed Forces for several years, he feels that, *"They don't look after their service personnel, once they have left the service. They don't look after us"*. He describes what he sees around him and what he hears about. *"Many Veterans are living on the streets, dying alone and do not ask for help."*

He tries to do his part to acknowledge and honour the service, which all Veterans have given to this country. He will not forget them. He still stands outside his home, each Remembrance Day in November and gives a salute to all those who have 'fallen' in service to the Queen and country. He does this, because he cares that people know about them, that their efforts are applauded and lauded. He does this too, for those unsung heroes like him, who are quietly getting on with their lives, unappreciated by those they have defended for years in the British Armed Forces. They must not be dismissed.

Lincoln wants local authorities to review and update their Electoral Rolls so that these Veterans, including those who came from abroad to serve here, can get the help they need. He believes that these Veterans have been left behind. A few get publicity about their situations, often after their death, but most are still struggling for even the basics. He acknowledges that there are a few charities that try to help, but fundamentally, it is the near absence of help from government and military organisations that disturbs, disappoints and even angers him.

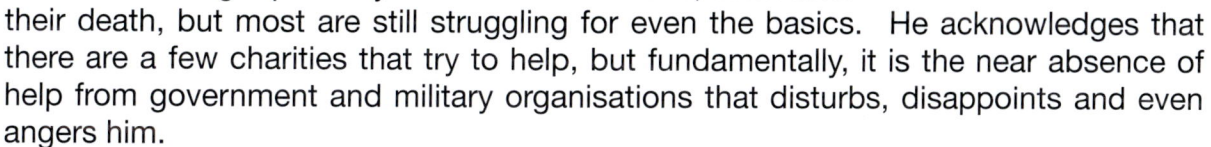

He is especially scathing about the lack of support for Veterans of colour whom he believes, have been abandoned.

"These particular Veterans are not the assets and resources of their former countries, islands", he remarks. *"They served the UK and the Queen, most of them for a substantial part of their young lives. What about fairness?"*

With respect to fairness, Lincoln feels aggrieved that after years of service in the Army, he has still not received a military pension. This is despite making several representations to officials over several years. He is now in his 70s, well into his pensionable years and still no acknowledgement through receipt of a pension, that he had served. He is still left wondering how this can possibly be fair.

Undoubtedly, Corporal Lincoln Beswick, MBE, is a man of honour. He has provided decades of service to the people of this country. He has done this through his years of military service, through his political service and in what he is still doing, in what should be his retirement.

He has not stopped serving others. He continues his support of local people, who often find it difficult to get the support and services they desperately need. His strength of character, his knowledge and skills, alongside his loyalty to the Crown and to his local community and beyond, is unquestionable. He should be recognised, acknowledged and celebrated.

Photo by Gill Shaw

Corporal Donovan Bascombe

Corporal Donovan Bascombe was born in Flat Rock in St George, Barbados. He travelled with his sister at the age of 13 to join his parents in an outer London borough.

Donovan's parents had left the two of them with family when he was three years old. They had gone ahead to be part of the post-war, rebuilding efforts, which many Caribbean people had responded to. It took his parents rather a long time to obtain suitable jobs and create a home for him, his sister and the two other children they had in the UK.

It took eight years for Donovan's parents to save enough money to buy their own house in Southall and to be able to find the funds to send for their other children whom they missed terribly.

When Donovan arrived in England, everything seemed very strange indeed; the weather, the houses around him and the school he had to attend. He also had to get used to parents he had not seen for several years and a new brother and a sister he had never met.

Those early years in his new homeland and within a different family grouping, were not especially easy for the young teenager. He got through it all however. Following the end of his Boys' School, he was able to obtain an apprenticeship with the Rank Pullen Control organisation. Donovan started his day- release to college, training, studying and working in the area of electrical engineering.

When Donovan was 18, and on his lunch break, he met someone he had known from Southall. It was a man called Bob, who was now an Army recruiter. They had quite a long chat, which led to Donovan applying to join the Army. Soon after that conversation with Bob, Donovan went to do the appropriate tests and scored very well on them, allowing him to be sent off to join up formally and start his basic training in the Royal Signals.

The Royal Corps of Signals was founded in 1920 and has been a key part of the communication elements of the Army, especially in operational arenas. They are highly trained to secure efficient and effective experts in engineering and all forms of communication. Donovan would become a part of this critical communications Corps.

Donovan was sent to Sutton Coldfield to complete his assessment and then on to Catterick. He was one of only seven other black men there. One friend he made in basic training was Tony Howard, who was a Technician. He and Tony had attended the same school in Barbados and were surprised and delighted to meet up again, as adults, during basic training. These two became lifelong friends and were also to serve together, later on, in their German posting and in the Falklands. Both men are still in touch, all these years later.

Donovan was surprised and delighted to be mentioned, after completing his basic training, in his local newspaper, 'The Southall Herald'. Clearly, his local community was very proud of his achievement. A picture from his Passing Out Parade sits proudly in his Mum's front room.

After finishing basic training, Donovan moved to 8 Signals Regiment, Catterick Garrison, to begin his next stage of training for the next 12 months. This stage of training was significant, in that he had to learn various tele-mechanical skills, battlefield telecommunications, all of which involved senior Army instructors, combat lineman work and other relevant operational work necessary to his developing expertise for the Signals.

Still, Donovan saw few other people like him. He recalls a tiny proportion of other black people in a 700 strong group in the 11 Signals Regiment. He saw a few more black men in the Queen's Regiment but, even then it was proportionally, very small in number.

Donovan was promoted to Lance Corporal. Donovan then had the opportunity to attend and complete a Detachment Commanders' course. This led to him achieving promotion to the rank of Corporal.

When he was a Corporal, Donovan was one of 30 men who were sent to Port Stanley, in the Falkland Islands, in 1984. It was that team's job to ensure that there were modern, effective digital communications in place. This was a critical job for the Army. Alongside Donovan, there were around seven other black soldiers involved in the six-month tour in the Falklands.

Donovan and his fellow Caribbeans tried to look out for each other. After all, the men considered themselves to be "*all West Indians*" not separate island peoples. They were a collective group, Caribbeans one and all.

When they served in the same place, such as in Belgium with his friend Errol (on the left), or in whichever country, they shared so much of their joint culture. They were able to come together to season and cook the food they loved and to listen to music and generally, have a great time.

Whilst in the Falklands, he and his team had to make sure they transformed the old analog telephone exchange and bring it up to date, digitalising as necessary. It was a crucial area of work, but challenging in the environment in which they found themselves. When Donovan was on that Falklands tour, it was at a time when things were still pretty risky. He and other colleagues were living in a floating complex in Stanley Harbour. He observed serious incidents, some of which included losses. These are incidents, which he will always remember. They still haunt him. Some of the devastating events, caused Donovan to do what he could to help. His efforts were such that he was mentioned in dispatches. This is a brave man, whose courage was recognised at the time, but whose scars from his involvement, continues to affect him still.

Donovan took a course to then be able to apply to become a Sergeant. As a Sergeant, he would be earning around £20,000 annually. At that time, *"that was a decent salary"*. He decided however, not to pursue this potential promotion.

During his Army service, Donovan served in a number of countries, including Germany, Belgium, Canada, the Isle of Man, the Orkneys and the Ascension Islands. He enjoyed the various opportunities he was given, to participate in team and individual activities. Some of these included skiing in Austria, canoeing, cricket and even grape picking in the Mosel Valley. He was also delighted to be involved in a charity cricket match with celebrities such as Sir Harry Secombe and England test cricketers.

He also enjoyed being on Army team building exercises. He loved the camaraderie, something which remains with him and those with whom he is still in touch. *"It is something which unites you. It is never lost"*, he says. Some of the group activities in which he was involved, included being a part of the 4-Ton Truck driving competition. He was proud to get the winner's cup.

He has no regrets whatsoever about his 12 years of military service. As a young recruit, he had a real lust for adventure. He got that in the Army.

His military service, he says, *"Moulded me to be who I am today. It built in me, a confidence, which has served me throughout my life."*

Donovan married a girl he had met in a youth club in Southall. They married at the age of 23, when he was abroad, serving on a British Army tour to Germany. They are parents to two children, of whom he is very proud.

He played cricket for the Army, even going to his homeland of Barbados to play the game. Donovan loves the game of cricket and maintains a great interest up to this day.

Before leaving the Army after 12 years service, Donovan and his wife, who also worked for the MOD, as a civilian, bought a house in Luton. Living there, meant commuting to their different jobs each day. Donovan took up a position in the School of Signals, as an instructor, teaching military personnel about fibre optics, which were new at the time. He also did a variety of digital projects for the Army both here in the UK and abroad.

Donovan went on to take part in a resettlement programme, joining Cable and Wireless and Mercury Communications on what was then a fairly good salary. As part of this work, he was able to recruit around 20 ex-Signals' colleagues, whom he knew to have the relevant expertise to complete the range of work effectively. He knew their worth and their high level of skill and was confident that these people would be committed, dependable employees.

Donovan was still on the Reserves list, when he left the Signals. In fact, he left in December 1989 and was on the list for Kuwait, Gulf War One, a matter of months later. It was an anxious time for him and his family.

In his view, it is doubtful that people, more generally, really understand the service provided by Caribbean men and women in the various branches of the armed service. *"It tends to be only your own family, or other ex-service people who know about us and appreciate what we have done."*

Looking back to the young 18-year-old Donovan, he remembers the environment around him in Southall, at that time. In those days, there was a lot of *"running around"* among the youth in the area. It was also the time of the Blair Peach incidents and the troubles around the Notting Hill Carnival.

Blair Peach was a local teacher who attended an anti-racist demonstration against the National Front, an extreme right-wing, racist organisation. He died of a head injury during that event. In the late 1970s, there were various clashes between the police and various attendees of the Notting Hill Carnival. Donovan's life was surrounded by these events.

"The Army became an alternative for many of us. It was a good decision to take yourself away from potential trouble. It gave you a career to pursue and to take back into society."

Donovan had been a member of the Young Socialists at the time. He was a politically aware young man, engaging in political discussions with like-minded people. He has maintained an interest in national politics throughout his life. His

Army experience just allowed him to gain different perspectives and dimensions to his thinking.

Corporal Bascombe has no regrets about the choices he made in relation to the military. He would advise other teenagers who may not be sure about what to do, what career to pursue, to consider the military. Joining the military, would be a very different experience for them now. He does however, believe that the discipline, control and respect for authority it gives you, alongside the skills and training you can benefit from, is worthwhile.

He cautions that these potential recruits should remember however, that *"You still need to know how to speak your mind, to the senior officers who have power and influence over your promotion prospects!"* He wished he had been given that advice early on in his career. On the other hand, Donovan provided excellent service to the British Army, to the country and to the Queen, who was head of the Armed Forces.

Corporal Donovan Bascombe is proud of his service. He is worthy of our appreciation.

Corporal John Mortley

John came to the UK in the mid-1960s, when he was 20 years old. He had already completed a four-year mechanics' apprenticeship at the famous Appleton Estate in St Elizabeth, Jamaica.

John had always wanted to be a mechanic and a soldier. He was already saying that to his family when he was only ten years old.

Whilst he was committed to his apprenticeship, he felt that he also wanted to do more with his life.

Before he left Jamaica, he reapplied to join both the police force and the army. He decided however, that travel to the UK to pursue one of these careers would suit him and help him to realise his dreams. Therefore he set off to get everything ready for a departure to this new, strange land.

When John arrived in the UK, he went to live in South East London, where he had connections. Two months later, he went to the recruitment office in Blackheath, where he was interviewed by a senior army officer, Major Blackman. He got through the interview and passed the various tests, required of him. He was delighted and was full of anticipation about finally realising one of his childhood dreams; that of being a soldier.

Using his Travel Warrant, he travelled to start his basic training with the Royal Army Service Corp (RASC). The RASC became the Royal Corp of Transport (RCT), part of the Royal Engineers.

The Royal Corps of Transport (RCT), located at the Buller Barracks in the Aldershot Garrison, was a British Army Corps which was established when the RASC was disbanded in 1965. Its main role was to manage all matters related to the transport of men and material for the Army and the wider Defence community. It too was later disbanded, 28 years later, when its trades and units were amalgamated into the Royal Logistics Corps.

John found basic training with the RASC hard, but as a volunteer, he decided to give himself to the system. He had no regrets for doing so and got on with the marching, drilling, rifle training, saluting and keeping his dormitory clean and tidy, as part of the team of new recruits. When he joined, John was the only black person in a group of 200 men in Aldershot.

He recalls taking great pride in his turnout, making sure he received no criticism regarding the state of his uniform, only praise. John was getting noticed. He remembers that after he passed out and was posted to Germany, his attention to looking smart, got him even more attention. It was a Major Ridley, he remembers, who called out to him one day. This Major had also called the Quartermaster to come and look at John, to *"Look at this soldier. Look at his uniform and tell me what you see!"* It was clear that this Major saw John as a role model for others. John's tunic fitted properly. In actual fact, he had been to a local tailor to get his jacket adjusted, so that it fitted him perfectly. From then on, John therefore, did become the model for the other soldiers, and possibly, for some of them, someone to be resented, certainly for the sharp turnout, anyway.

After basic training, John went into the Paras, 63 Squadron. He was then posted to West Germany to the Transport Unit of 14 Squadron. He stayed in Germany for around four and a half years. When John was in West Germany, it was the height of the Cold War. He was therefore, very aware of the potential for far-reaching issues related to Pandemic-type incidents which might have affected people worldwide. He and his military colleagues were very well-prepared.

It was while John was in Germany that he met and married his wife, also a Jamaican. They had four children.

John recalls volunteering for various military activities, including going to outdoor training sessions on the border between Norway and Russia. John happened to be the only volunteer at that time, but he went out every night, knowing it would be freezing. He managed to complete the exercise. He was also involved in long exercises with NATO.

When he had some 'free' time, he was quite happy to go off sailing in the Baltic, really enjoying himself. He followed Standing Orders and was thus able to avoid restrictions on his activities.

Following his time in Germany, John was posted to Bahrain first, then on to Cyprus, on United Nations duties.

John continued to be the only black person in every unit in which he served. John describes this time as one in which *"You don't know who is watching you. You are really a lump of coal in a field of snow."*

He was called *"The black skin, blue-eyed boy"*. This was because he was often the person to whom others came to sort out their diesel engines and getting them to work. John was happy enough with this label and the work which followed, because he was able to build his expertise with these engines.

John served in a number of locations, at home and abroad. He worked mostly in land situations, but also worked on ships, as an engineer.

He was promoted to corporal when he was on tour in Germany. While he was very pleased to have this promotion, he comments, wryly but with acceptance, that in those days in the military, things were different for black men. *"Black men hardly ever got commissioned at that time. They would often use the black guys in the Infantry and send them in first."* John describes the ranks of corporal and sergeant, as being the *"workhorses of the army"*. He believes these two positions, form the real backbone of an army. *"They are the men and women who do the real work and often make the most difference to the army's effectiveness."*

John took the opportunity, when he was in Bahrain, to visit other Middle Eastern countries, such as Saudi Arabia and Dubai. It was an interesting time, seeing such different cultures and traditions.

He then returned to his German posting after which, he went back to the UK as part of the Strategic Reserve Group, ready to be shipped out to wherever he was needed, including to troubled areas within the country. John would often travel in armoured vehicles where necessary, escorting journalists for example, keeping them as safe as possible in the challenging environments in which they would find themselves. The risks were severe and life threatening. Tough times.

John also worked in the Military Corrective Training Centre in Colchester, supporting the army in that area of their work. He was a skilled, highly experienced and courageous soldier, who was well regarded in all that he did.

John's personal life had become difficult and led to some stressful changes for him and his family. He had now served 12 years in the army. When he had returned to the UK to continue his service, he looked at the people around him. He felt that some of the senior people with whom he served, appeared to be less effective than those he had served with in some of his foreign postings, including in Germany. While he had thoroughly enjoyed his military career, it was time he felt, to make some changes in his life. He decided to leave the army.

John spent his first three years out in his Clacton home in the UK, doing a variety of driving jobs. He drove up and down the country, sometimes moving mobile homes around. He was a trained HGV driver and a mechanical engineer. He also worked with London Transport as a bus mechanic. By this time, he was living in Tooting, London and had saved enough to get a mortgage and buy his own house. He missed being in the army. He was still not settled in his civilian life. He decided therefore, to relocate to Trinidad. Here, he had his own business and home and was reasonably comfortable. He lived on this new Island, for the next 15 years.

John then decided to move back to Jamaica in the mid-1990s. He continues to live independently, farming as well as utilising his mechanical engineering skills in a second business on the island. His agricultural work includes cultivation of a broad range of foods, but also growing sugar cane for manufacturing sugar in two nearby factories.

He is reasonably satisfied with his Jamaican life and was pleased to take a bit of time to meet visitors. Meeting John on a recent visit to Jamaica was a great privilege. The man striding towards me, held himself proudly, covering the hot ground with ease. He looked like a person used to keeping fit, physically and mentally. Those years as a highly trained soldier could be seen in his commanding presence on that sunny St Elizabeth afternoon, in Jamaica.

John has been back in Jamaica for the past nearly three decades. He is not fully happy with civilian life - with civilians he often meets in actual fact.

"They are not like the trustworthy, dependable people I had been a part of, when I was a soldier."

He misses that life of trust and dependability. He has absolutely no regrets about having served in the army. It was there that he felt most comfortable and it is possible to hear in his voice, the shadow of yearning for that period in his life.

"They always had a solution to deal with any situation I faced; and some of those situations were very tough for me."

One of the things he struggled with however, was the lack of preparation for leaving. There was also no contact afterwards.

"Margaret Thatcher had made cuts. There was no pension when I left - after 12 years of service", he says. Sadly, this hardy Veteran and Pensioner is not alone in being disappointed about a lack of Army pension. There is a sense of shame in hearing his comments about this perceived absence of appreciation for years of military service in the British Armed Forces.

Now, nobody knows that John had been a soldier. The army had a profound effect on John. Fundamentally, he says, *"God save the Queen was how I was brought up. You were always loyal to the Queen".*

Serving in the British Army, and believing that *"Our freedom was more valuable than the pay you got"*, drove John to be the highly skilled soldier and excellent engineer he became when he was a part of this military organisation. He does not feel that his service has been sufficiently acknowledged - or in fact, known about.

He looks back at his 20 year old self and would still advise him to *"Go for it!"* He would also encourage Caribbean young people to consider a career in the Armed Forces. In his view, everyone needs to have some military experience. He believes in

National Service. He believes it would offer, *"sound discipline and an understanding of how to conduct yourself in society"*.

Clearly, his military service has had a long-lasting effect on John. His steely-eyed look as he remembers some significant events in his time in the army, yet his absolute deeply-held warmth for the work he did, is quite moving to observe.

This brave, strong Caribbean man of integrity, served the UK and the Queen with honour, skill and loyalty   He should be recognised and celebrated for his service.

Lance Corporal Ray Petrie

Ray Petrie was born in Mosside, Manchester. His father was from St Kitts and his mother was Irish. He had an older step-brother, who was six years older than him. He also had a younger brother.

Ray's father was a Merchant Seaman. At the time he served, a third of the world's merchant ships were British. Many merchant seamen came from parts of the British Empire, including from India and the West Indies. It was in 1942, during WWII, whilst he was serving in the fleet that Ray's father lost his life. His ship was torpedoed by an Italian submarine. Ray remembers to this day, the moment his father said goodbye on that last night, as he went off to rejoin his Merchant Navy ship.

Ray attended the local primary school in Mosside. When he was around 13, he passed an exam, achieving tenth place out of 2,000 children. He and his family were very proud of him as it allowed him to attend a prestigious Technical College. It was not until he went into his first class, after the exams, that the teacher, Mr Thompson told him the results.

Mr Thompson was a very influential person in Ray's life at the time. It was he who had identified Ray's talents early on and had given him extra homework to help Ray to be well prepared for the exam. Ray took full advantage of his technical college education. The College focused on teaching its students, engineering skills, which would enable them to be fit for the world of work. He joined the College at 14 and worked very hard to learn everything he could over the next two years.

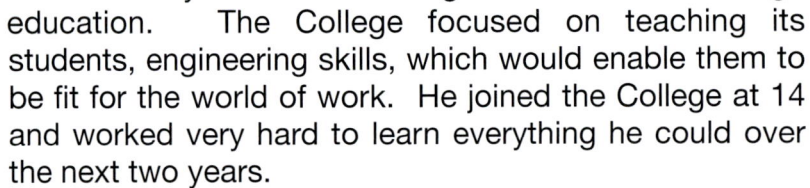

When Ray completed his studies, he left the College at the age of 16, ready to enter the job market. He made a number of applications and was successful in getting a job through a telephone interview. Ray was over the moon. He was asked to bring a pair of overalls and some refreshment and to turn up the following Monday morning.

When he got to this first job, complete with his work equipment, there was huge shock from his prospective employers, seeing this non-white young person. Ray was told that there was no longer a job for him. This obvious discriminatory and racist attitude was directed towards Ray, several times. He was really disheartened.

Eventually, when Ray was waiting outside the cinema for a film to start, the manager, came outside and spoke to him. It was a conversation, which was to change the direction of his life. The manager offered Ray a job as an apprentice projectionist. Ray would be with two other apprentices. This was a turning point for this young man. He worked as a projectionist, having completed his apprenticeship, for the next three years. Ray thoroughly enjoyed his job. He found the whole experience both exciting and fascinating, in that he was not only doing the basics of projection work, he was also involved in Trade Shows and meeting some of the stars. He recalls seeing the Platters in his cinema, which was a wonderful thing for this youngster.

It was while Ray was working as a projectionist, that he met this lovely young woman, who would later become his wife. She was also a member of staff, working as a cashier and also selling ice creams during the intervals. It was not very long before the two people decided to marry, which they did when Ray was nearly 18.

This was a time when National Service was still in operation in the UK. A letter was sent to Ray's house calling him up. He could choose to serve in any part of the Armed Service. Ray's older brother, Alec was already in the Army, serving his third year with the Manchester Regiment. Alec had told Ray all about the Army, so he chose to do his National Service with the Army, but in the Royal Signals Regiment.

When Ray was at school, he had enjoyed doing sports, especially sprinting. He also ran for the school's relay team, where his pleasure in this, could be clearly seen in a picture from that time. He was very fast, out running most of his peers. He did so well that he went on to win the Manchester Schools' 100 yards race when he was 15. He still has a great sense of pride in this particular achievement.

princess road relay team 1951
Mr Towers Keith Chadderton Ray Petrie
Mr Clough G wall and R Slingsby

It was his favoured teacher, Mr Thompson, who again, had spotted and encouraged this aspect of Ray's school life. He remembered that Mr Thompson had been in WWII and had also suffered the trauma of being a prisoner of war.

Ray travelled from Exchange Station in Manchester in October, 1959, to go to the Barracks in Catterick.

Ray was one of around 30 young men of different ages, arriving at the station near Catterick. He was the only black person. The new recruits were met by Military Police, who organised them into groups and took them by coach to Catterick. Ray had now become a soldier.

The recruits were housed in Nissan huts. They all embarked on their basic training. Ray found it rough. The men had to really focus on self-care, folding their kits precisely (9" x 9"), polishing their boots to mirror standard, cleaning, parading, marching, saluting and learning various rifle and other skills. Ray felt fortunate that he had had good information about Army expectations from his older brother. He had even practised doing the shoe polishing before he joined. He made a few friends, one of whom he kept in touch with for many years. Sadly, that friend has now passed away. Ray still misses him.

It was during this basic training that Ray's first son was born. He was able to take leave to visit his wife and baby. *"That was heavenly"*, he said.

Ray passed out six weeks later. His Mother was able to be there to see him at the Passing Out Parade. Once this was over, Ray had the chance to join the Regular Army. He took an informed view about whether to continue and complete National Service at the pay of 2 guineas per week, or go into the Regulars, with a weekly pay of 9 guineas. Given his married status and new child with others possibly to come, the pay determined his choice. It would be a big jump in pay and so he joined the Regulars.

Before he made that final decision, Ray had taken some exams, which helped him to choose which Trade would suit him best. He chose to train in the Royal Signals, as a Radio Technician. He did this training for four months, before then going on leave to see his family, whom he missed dreadfully. Unfortunately, Ray could not bring himself to return to his Regiment and so was still at home four weeks later. The Military Police came to retrieve him, taking him firstly to the Manchester Regiment Barracks, where his brother had served. His brother Alec had been at Manchester for many years. He was also a successful boxer with the army and was well known in the Barracks. That was a lucky break for young Ray. He was treated very well before being collected by the military police officers, to be returned to Catterick. He was reprimanded by a senior officer and then continued with his basic Trade training. He was very lucky.

Following completion of the basic level, Ray then went on to a Trainee Morse Code course, Trade 2 course, completing it successfully. The Morse Code role was vital to the army and they decided to despatch Ray to Germany. When Ray heard this, he absented himself again to see his growing family. By now, Ray had another child on the way. Naturally, he was then collected by the Military Police and returned to the Catterick Barracks. Four weeks later, he was on his way to the German posting, to 4 Division of the Signals Regiment. This Division was based in Herford, West Germany. Herford is a town in North Rhine-Westphalia, Germany. It is the capital of the district of Herford. This was a posting Ray would retain for the next two years. Again, Ray was the only non-white person there.

At first, he was placed on an armoured vehicle as a radio operator. Berglen followed this posting, for a further six months, doing special ops work.

Ray continued to miss his wife and children terribly. He decided to approach the Regimental Sergeant Major, to request married quarters for himself and his family. To his relief, the request was granted. His family had by then grown, with two children. They were all relocated to Berlin and Ray was able to continue his military duties.

Ray was so happy to be with his family. The quarters were only a few minutes from the local school and the yearning for the family to be with him was no longer a problem. He and his wife could settle down and strengthen their family life in a new country. Ray's family had now grown to five, the youngest being born in Berlin. A smile appears on Ray's face as he recalls being given 5 sporting medals from the Brigadier's wife, with her commenting that 'there was one for each child'.

At this time, Ray was still a radio operator, but in the new location, he was very much 'in the thick of things'. There were many Regiments in Berlin, with personnel from a wide variety of countries. Still, very few black people however. Eventually, Ray remembers there being a new, black Corporal coming to take charge of the three radio operators. Ray learned a lot from this man. This junior NCO was really good. He and the team, worked effectively, together for the next two years. Ray enjoyed his time in that post and three years later, he left Berlin and returned to Herford, to 7 Signals Regiment.

Unfortunately, there were no married quarters available in Herford, so his wife and family had to return to the UK to army accommodation in Blackpool. The children were able to attend local schools there. Ray stayed in the Herford post for a further three years, travelling back and forth to visit his family back home. Ray missed his family, who had grown in number, again, by this time.

Nevertheless, he was needed in the workplace back in Herford especially, given the communications elements of it and its importance to the efficient operation of the British Overseas Army on the Rhine (BOAR) at that time. Ray and his team had a significant role to play in that historical period, during the Cold War.

Ray had the opportunity to travel to Norway to participate in outward bound activities, including canoeing through the Fjords. That was quite incredible. He was on these exercises for six weeks. He found the Norwegians very friendly. He describes them as amazing. They took him and his colleagues into their homes and gave them food and shelter. There was a real warmth of welcome and the actual warmth in their homes made it all the better for these cold, young soldiers. Ray really enjoyed those six weeks.

Ray was then sent to Singapore - in the jungle and with an attachment to the 1 10th Gurkhas. He cannot speak highly enough of this amazing group of soldiers. In his view, they are 'beyond brave' men. Ray was also sent, again with the Gurkhas, to Borneo to support the British Army's peacekeeping efforts. He was involved in jungle training, hiking, tent survival and much more. These were critical skills for any soldier serving and surviving in those tropical conditions. It was his more technical skills and experience, for which Ray was especially known. They were rated very highly, including when he was ensuring clear and effective communication between different locations, such as Brunei, Borneo and Malaya.

Because of the distances involved, soldiers would sometimes experience problems getting their pay on time. This could mean that the normal fortnightly pay could be delayed by several weeks. The men, including Ray would head off for rest and recuperation in places such as Taiwan, where they would meet up with 'the Scousers' and have a great time drinking and generally, just chatting together. It gave everyone a break. As getting to their location was difficult by road, they would often travel by helicopter. On one occasion, Ray was due to travel on the helicopter to start his leave. However, he had to wait around for the Pay Corporal, so missed his ride. Fortunately, although he was irritated to have to delay his ride and his leave, his life was saved that day. Sadly, the helicopter was lost. There is sadness in this Veteran's eyes as he remembers this incident.

Before long, it was a further change in location, for Ray. This time, to Malaysia as an attachment to the New Zealand (NZ) Army. The NZ Army needed his technical skills. There were other people with Morse Code skills also part of his team. Ray was impressed with this army, especially as they paid their soldiers more than the British did. He was even offered a job with them, something he considered very carefully. They also seemed to have better conditions. The NZ army was the highest paid army at that time. He was certainly tempted, as were others from his Regiment; the Signals. Ray turned down the offer, however. He decided to stay with the British Army and continue to do the best job he could for them.

The second time Ray served in Herford, he met up with a Captain who had been in the same athletics team in Berlin. Both men had competed together for the army. Ray recalls that Athletics competition fondly. He also remembers vividly, running the 100 yards, 200 yards and 400 yards races. The soldiers even took part in a 3-legged race, just for fun. These events took place in the famous Olympic Stadium in Berlin. Ray remembers looking around that place, with awe. He thought about the event which had been held there, where the African American, Jessie

Owens won his race in front of the infamous Nazi leader. Ray being there now competing in the same space was special, overwhelming even.

On one particular day, the Captain from Herford, met with Ray and asked him what rank he was. At that time, Ray had the rank of Signalman. After that unusual conversation with the Captain; within a short few hours, a recommendation from that senior officer, was actioned and Ray was promoted. Ray was delighted to become Lance Corporal, to have achieved promotion. He was already being identified for his technical skills. Now, as Lance Corporal, he was the leader of three other soldiers. It was not an easy ride to be that leader however. One of the men for whom he was responsible, came up to Ray one day and said, *"I'm not taking orders from you!"* This was something that needed to be sorted out, which Ray was able to do, so that he could carry out his leadership role effectively.

Overall, Ray really enjoyed his time in the army. He loved taking part in the various military exercises, which fine-tuned his soldier skills and strengthened team building among the Unit and Battalion within which he served. It was however, after nine years, time for him to leave the army and move into the next stage of family and civilian life. Ray therefore gave in his notice and served the last weeks in the base in Germany. Whilst he was in the process of doing so, it was clear that the Corporal he was working with, did not want him to leave. Ray's decision was set. He was anticipating the reunion with his family. An intervention was necessary. This needed a senior person to make sure Ray was able to move back to England and back to his family. Fortunately, the Regimental Sergeant Major sorted everything out, and soon Ray was on his way.

Finally, Ray went back home, not to continue as Lance Corporal Petrie, but to become a civilian, 'Mr Ray Petrie of Manchester'. Civilian life was very different. It was strange. It took Ray a long time to settle into this new life.

Ray and his family first stayed with his sister-in-law and then went on to live with his Mother. The family was then able to obtain support from the local Council and were housed in Staley Bridge, near Manchester. Ray was able to get work in a Foundry, doing shot blasting. He enjoyed the work. It paid well and Ray was able to make some good friends in his new workplace.

Looking back, Ray feels proud of his time in the military. He knows that he did a good job within it, as part of the defence of the country. He had enjoyed most of his career. Before he went into the army, he used to listen to the Berlin radio stations, British Forces Network (BFN) and the American Forces Network (AFN). On one occasion, as he listened, he heard a piece about his brother Alec, who was a boxer for the Army. Alec was the only person to have beaten a senior officer in a boxing competition and Ray heard about this from listening in to AFN. It was a great feeling to hear the news. Ray was puffed with pride in the achievement of his older brother. He still has a warm feeling about that time.

He has no regrets. He feels he *"did alright"*. He believes it was the right time and right place for him. He had many opportunities, but especially the opportunity to run. He loved the fact that he could continue to do something he had a passion for, even while he was working as a soldier.

He does not feel that the service of people like him, non-white service people, have been recognised or acknowledged. Despite feeling that disappointment, he would still have chosen to join up after National Service. That is not in question. He would have advised the young man that he was, to "get his head together and do his best". He believes that is exactly what he was able to do throughout his Army career. He did have some problems settling away from his family in those first months, but he got over that and managed to organise himself to make it all work.

Ray is the father of 10 children, all of whom he is very proud of. Sadly, he has lost two of them.

He would not discourage young Caribbean people from joining the military.
"It would depend on the person. They would have to be able to take some stick. Don't take it to heart."

A few years ago, Ray was fortunate to have been invited to join the Chelsea Pensioners in London. A Chelsea Pensioner, or In-Pensioner, is someone who lives at the Royal Hospital Chelsea, a retirement home and nursing home for British Army Veterans. This home caters for 300 retired male and female (since 2009) soldiers.

The opportunity to become a Chelsea Pensioner, came about because of a conversation Ray had in Oxford, with someone collecting money for Poppy Day. That person happened to have been a Veteran like Ray, and from the same Regiment, the Royal Signals. During the conversation, the two people shared something about their lives, including the fact that Ray's wife, had died and he was now alone. The Poppy Day volunteer and ex-service woman, encouraged him to apply to become a Chelsea Pensioner. Ray thought long and hard about the idea, and decided to send off his application.

He was invited to the Barracks and went through a four-day stay to see if he would be a good fit and whether he would be able to live here. A joint decision was made and within a fortnight, Ray moved in.

The first few weeks there, were filled with learning about the culture and meeting all the other Veterans. It is a fascinating place, filled with a good variety of people, mostly men, who come from many different Regiments.

There are tremendous opportunities for Ray to attend wonderful events, such as Wimbledon, the Chelsea Flower Show and weddings, as well as meeting royalty and other VIPs.

He has even become one of the faces on the poster advertising the Royal Army Museum.

Despite these fantastic experiences, for which Ray is enormously grateful, there are some small moments which disturbs and concerns him about his new life. He has been a Chelsea In-Pensioner now for a number of years. He is the only black person there. It is not always easy for a minority to be in the minority, even in such august surroundings.   Ray is well looked after however, and appreciates that very much. He has made a few friends, with whom he will take lunch regularly. Recently, he has suffered some ill health, but is recovering well, making sure he keeps up with daily walks around the nicely kept gardens. It is very largely, a good life.

Ray has had some wonderful times over the years. He feels blessed to have had a whole athletics' team of 10 children with his first wife. She sadly passed away. Ray still remembers the happy times with the young woman he first met in the local cinema. He was fortunate to have met and partnered with a woman with whom he lived for the next 30 years after his wife passed away. Ray regrets that they were not able to get married. He continues to feel deeply sad about this. There were, unfortunately, some family tensions surrounding this matter and which were never resolved. Unfortunately, his partner of three decades, has also passed away. Ray is now left on his own. He sees some of his family and welcomes the visits he has from his lovely grandchildren and great grandchildren.

Lance Corporal Ray Petrie is a very quiet and thoughtful man. He was an excellent soldier and a loyal and committed man, in all the postings in which he served. He contributed much to the army and to the country. He continues to demonstrate a sense of loyalty and courage in the way he views the Armed Forces and its purpose. He remains forever, a military man whose place in history must be recognised and his contribution honoured.

We owe him and others like him, a debt of gratitude for what they have done.

Photo by Gill Shaw

Corporal Zac Robinson

Zac was nine years old, when he and his two siblings travelled from Jamaica, by airplane, to the UK to join his parents. This was 1964 in the cold month of February. Zac can still remember the coldness and strangeness of his new country. Zac and his family lived in the Stoke Newington area of London.

Zac attended local schools and at the age of 15, left school to undertake an apprenticeship. The apprenticeship did not last and he went on to work in the Homefare shop. It was also at this time, that Zac describes being involved in 'activities' locally and which he knew, would surely have brought him to the attention, negatively, of the local constabulary. Things had to change.

He went to the Finsbury Park Careers' Office to apply to join the Army. Zac took the various tests and underwent relevant interviews successfully and was sent off to Sutton Coldfield. Within a month of that first part of the testing process. Zac went through a medical, again successfully. He had been shown videos of different Regiments, before making his decision about where to make his commitment. He had achieved a 98% mark in his tests and therefore, had the opportunity to join some of the highly regarded Regiments, except that is, the Household Cavalry and the Royal Military Police. He remembers the sergeant saying, in respect of the two Regiments in particular, *"You can't do that because they don't take Blacks."*

It was with this statement resonating in his ear, that Zac decided that he would join the Royal Green Jackets. The Royal Green Jackets (RGJ) is one of the Army's Infantry Regiments. Zac was attracted by stories about their fast pace. The exciting information he was given about them marching at 140 paces per minute, rather than the usual 120, he found fascinating. He saw them as being better soldiers, who were better switched on than others. It was his view then and subsequently, that the Royal Green Jackets had a good sense of danger and risks. They would always be fully aware of the need to try and stay alive in any dangerous arenas in which they were placed. Their motto was Celer et Addax (*"Swift and Bold"*). He decided that he wanted to be a part of this elite group of soldiers.

Zac set off for his first day and week in Winchester. He was joined on his train journey by another new recruit, Jeff Dawes. When they arrived in Winchester, they were the only two there that first night. Nevertheless, they had to get on with it.

Zac recalls going out in the town that night, for a drink in a local pub. The two young men had an altercation with an older man, who, as it turned out, was one of the Army trainers. That event was firmly set in Zac's memory. So too were the numerous incidents of racist language used by a number of the trainers throughout his basic training. *"It was the usual nastiness - names familiar to many people"*, but Zac had not had experience of those names being directed his way, ever. Zac decided to do everything possible to get through the whole thing. And he did, successfully passing out along with his comrades, including Jeff. They were now fully a part of the RGJ.

There were very few black men in the Royal Green Jackets.

Following basic training and passing out, Zac was posted to Celle, in Germany. He hated it; this new country and language. Fortunately, he was able to go to a new posting with 3 RGJ in Shrewburyness, Southend. He enjoyed this posting, finding other black men there. Despite being the only Private there, he shared a room with four Corporals. He had to do all the cleaning, as decided by his seniors and was late to Parade on the first two days. Zac soon developed friendship with another black Private who advised him to make sure he asserted the *"equal shares"* attitude with his room mates.

Zac continued to develop and build his soldier skills in the RGJ, taking them to the highest level of preparedness expected of such an elite group. He made lifelong friends with some of the men in his Regiment and still meets up with them on Cup Final weekends to reminisce and raise a glass to the RGJ.

Zac recalls some memorable officers from that time. There was Simpson, who was a boxer. He remembers, especially, the wise words of Dave Goldsmith from basic training especially. Zac remembers himself as a very young, wild 17-year-old, coming from North London and how those words helped him to get control of himself. There was also the Platoon Sergeant, Andrew Anderson, who would still put him and others forward, even when they were being knocked back or when the system seemed stacked against them. He appreciated that attention from this man, who did not have to support him, but did so, even joining in with dominoes playing occasionally. There were of course, others who Zac remembers for very different, more negative reasons.

As part of his work in the Army, Zac was deployed to a number of locations, both in the UK and abroad. He was heavily involved in team building activities and refining his skills as a soldier. He was involved in jungle training in Singapore and went to Canada, where he learned to ski. He did scuba diving, trekking and hiking, lived in tents and got through successfully a number of survival training activities.

There were down times also. He was able to unwind, socialising, drinking and more. He bought himself a car, while he was in Berlin. He remembers the Ford car company doing discounts for serving military personnel. He took advantage of this offer and was able to collect his new car while he was in the UK. He enjoyed that car and while he was taking it on 'show', on a particular car outing, he was stopped 22 times in the space of a single night. This was a highly unusual occurrence even when you consider how many young men reported the frequency of stops by the police, to which they were subjected. Shocking. The experience of that particular night has stayed in Zac's memory, even after all these years.

Zac met his wife in the early stages of his Army career and they have celebrated 48 years together. The couple have two children - a son and a daughter.

Zac achieved promotion in his career, something he is proud of having done; *"against the odds"*, he says. To achieve promotion,, Zac did the Cadre test and got through as one of the best out of 30 men. He was promoted firstly to Lance Corporal. On the day of his promotion, he went to the Corporals' Mess, only to hear the comment, *"F....me. It's got dark in here."*

As Lance Corporal, Zac was part of the Mortars' section of the Regiment. He worked in the defensive force serving in Berlin in the late 1970s. This was a challenging time for this young man.

He has good memories of meeting other black men who were stationed there at the time. Although they were few in number, they gravitated towards each other, especially in response to the racism they experienced. He describes a particular very senior officer explaining the sound pattern of the emergency bugle call to the whole Battalion gathered one day. He told that huge number of soldiers that they were to listen to it as *"There's a N.....r on the wall."* To this day, Zac remembers this with horror at the seeming acceptance from that officer and apparently from those listening, that this language was normal and therefore okay.

The young black men had to stand to attention to hear their senior leader tell the hundreds of mostly white soldiers of the Battalion that they had to learn the rhythm by internalising those racist words. It was beyond anything they could have imagined. Zac and his new friends therefore decided to support each other, to never be seen to argue amongst themselves and to close ranks supportively. They became known as the 'Black Mafia', well before, they still believe, the phrase was adopted by others elsewhere. They cared less about what others thought. They knew that in terms of how they were being treated and the abuse which others seemed to see as acceptable, was not okay to them.

He saw some dreadful things whilst he was a serving soldier. These are things that stay with him.

There were also some wonderful times, with some great experiences, including being on public duties in the Olympic Stadium in Berlin, during the Queen's Silver Jubilee. His Regiment was also involved in a number of public duty events elsewhere. Zac was proud to see his colleagues playing their part in these public events.

After serving seven years, and with a wife who was pregnant with their first child, Zac made the decision to leave the Army. He therefore brought forward his leave, rather than completing the nine years he had originally planned. He had provided significant service in a number of challenging locations, dodging death and knowing that over time, his Regiment had lost members of the Battalion. In his view, it was now time to leave the military and start another career within civilian life.

That first year out was strange to Zac, but generally good. He enjoyed the excitement of the arrival of his new son. However, he had to find work, so he became a mechanic. His wife had just passed some important first exams which would support her towards her career in the legal profession. Things were continuing to change around him. It was while he was at a social, celebratory event, that he had a breakthrough in his thinking about his future. He decided to do a business degree. He went on to study and was successful in achieving his objective.

Following his graduation, Zac went into management of a car dealership with the Ford Company. The owner of that car dealership was ex-military. That man was another special person in Zac's life. It was thanks to his support and strength of character, that Zac was able to do his management job. He knew that this man "*had his back*"and would not tolerate other people's racist attitudes towards a manager who happened to be black. To that car dealership owner, it was about merit and competence. In his actions when others thought differently, this owner showed an intelligent awareness, which Zac continues to remember and appreciate.

Looking back to his time in the Army, Zac has no regrets at all. He made some extraordinary friends, whom he meets regularly. In his view, throughout that time in the military, it was all about never giving up, not looking back, but keeping going forward. He enjoyed learning vital skills, developing friendships and travelling to new locations. Thinking about his 17-year-old self, back then, he would still join up. It was a good decision. He does however wonder about new Caribbean heritage recruits. He says, *"It's different for them; but they are different."*

This is a man with honour and integrity. He is someone who served his adopted country with loyalty, skill and commitment.

His service deserves to be acknowledged and lauded by our society. He comments that it is only in recent years that some acknowledgement is being seen, and not from the Army. He cites two organisations, the National Windrush Museum (only in year 2 now) and the British West Indian Heritage Trust (1 year old), that are at the early stages of promoting the service which these brave men and women have provided to the nation.

More needs to be done.

Corporal Margery Fraser

Corporal Fraser was born in Wolverhampton. Her parents had come to the UK in the late 1950s.

Her father worked in the Goodyear factory in Wolverhampton. Three years later, he was joined by his wife and his 17-year-old, eldest daughter. Margery, the couple's second child was born a year later. Margery's mother had only been in the UK for a year, before Margery was born.

Margery attended local primary and secondary schools In Wolverhampton before emigrating with her parents to Jamaica, in June 1973. There, she attended the prestigious, Mount St Joseph School in Mandeville, in the Parish of Manchester.

Her three years in Jamaica, was a massive challenge to her emotionally, especially, as her mother, tragically, passed away. For young Margery, the turmoil of leaving her country of birth, to live in a country she had a fondness for, but did not know, the sad loss of her mother and the further displacement back to the UK, was a lot for her to deal with. Her schooling was not yet over, as she came back before her 16th birthday, to attend the last academic term, in a secondary school in Southampton.

Margery then went on to study at a college for the next two years, but changes to her family life continued. Her father remarried and home life was not settled for this young girl. Relationships in the home were tense and Margery was not happy. While she was at College, Margery took on part-time work in a Marks and Spencers' store, working from 7.00 to 8.30 each day, before she had to leave to start her college study at 9.00. Margery needed the money to support herself with little, but important treats and necessities.

At the age of 18, she decided to go to the Army recruiting office and join up. Margery got through all the tests and medicals and soon joined the Women's Royal Army Corps (WRAC). She swore her Oath of Allegiance to the Queen and was given the Queen's shilling. She was now fully part of the British Army.

Margery was excited and a bit apprehensive about her basic training in Guildford. Apart from the odd white people she had encountered - the milkman, the local newsagent - she had little to do with them, either in her local area or when she was abroad.

In Guildford, she was in a room with three other girls, all white. She was the only black girl among the recruits. In her room, she found that the other girls *"did not seem to know how to clean the room or themselves"*. Margery became the champion ironer for her group. Coming from the family she had, Margery was well-versed in all those self-care activities.

Basic training was, altogether, a rude awakening for her. *"They stripped you down to build you up again."* The food was also very different for her, but she decided that she had to 'suck it up' and get on with things.

She had collected her full kit, including the tights, which were clearly not the right colour for black people. She got on with the activities, which included marching, saluting, being on parade, 'bulling' shoes, ironing learning the phonetic alphabet and so on. She also learned how to budget, after collecting her wages.

There was a particular NCO, Sergeant June Raynor, who Margery remembers well. This Sergeant was a kind woman, who also gave this young recruit, her time to listen. Margery thought the world of Sergeant Gaynor; respected her. Later on in her career, Margery was to see her again, as she and the Sergeant were posted to the same location.

Margery made some friends during basic training, which lasted 12 weeks. There was strong camaraderie among all the women. *"It was all for one and one for all"*. That saying, meant something to them. *"That has made me what I am today"*, remarks Margery. She completed her basic training successfully. Her Passing Out Parade was attended by her father and step-mother and her little brother. Margery was very proud to have completed this part of her service and to have her family to see her do that.

Margery went on to have 13 postings over her 17 years of military service.

Following basic training, she was posted to HMPO in Mill Hill. She was there for six months before being despatched to Rheindalen as a Postal and Courier Operator, for a few months and then on to Dusseldorf. It was in Dusseldorf that Margery met a Commanding Officer, Colonel Len Calcutt, who offered her an Army driving job, working directly with him. Margery had hated the Post job, so this offer was a godsend to her.

She loved the job and she really liked the Colonel, who became almost like a second father to her. They had a great relationship. So much so, that despite the fact of *"Nothing going on, but there was*

talk about us!" Margery had a quiet chuckle at the memory. The Colonel was a kind-hearted man, whom Margery respected and admired.

Unfortunately, the Colonel went to another posting and his replacement was quite different in character, and in Margery's view, in his ability to manage people well. Margery became very unhappy and tried to keep doing the job. This was despite it soon becoming clear that she was expected to respond seven days a week, almost 24-hours each day. There did not seem to be sufficient thought about appropriate duty of care, including for refreshment breaks. It was a quite unpleasant time for this young soldier.

Margery went on to do more Trade Training to formally, become an Army driver. Once she had completed this, she was despatched to Latimer, to the Defence College to become a second driver to the Rear Admiral, in charge.

This was a critical time in the country as the Falklands War had begun. Over the next 18 months, Margery became a second driver to British 1 Star and 2 Star Generals. It was a very responsible position to hold. One of trust, loyalty and responsiveness in case of any issues emerging for those in her charge.

After this post was finished, Margery was sent back to Rheindalen to work with 68 Squadron, Royal Corps of Transport (RCT). Rheindalen was the German Headquarters (GHQ) for the British Army Overseas on the Rhine (BAOR). In her new post, Margery was inducted as the Brigadier's Pool Driver. Six months later she was chauffeuring senior visiting officers, the Creme de La Creme of the Army. It usually took 18 months to become one of these specialist drivers, so Margery was unusual in obtaining such a prestigious role, after only six months. Margery was surprised to get this job and only realised that she had been selected, when the Staff Sergeant Storey, called her in one day, saying, *"Go to Bay number 4 and bring the car to the front."* She could not believe it. She was, of course, delighted to be selected.

Margery was still a Private at this stage of her career. She was doing very well and getting noticed, positively. She loved doing this job. She remembers driving Sir Hugh Beech, who was visiting BOAR. He was the first 4-Star General she had driven. It was a great memory for Margery, especially as this high-ranking officer was so courteous and pleasant, in all his dealings with her.

Margery obtained promotion to a Lance Corporal, when she was in Rheindalen. She became the driver for the Director of Intelligence Security officer in Ashford. She found that posting, fascinating, as it took her to many critical places. She remembers clocking up huge mileage and having to change around three cars each year as she drove up and down the country.

By this time, Margery had already strengthened her driving skills through advanced driving courses and obtaining further qualifications, including those related to driving heavy goods vehicles and coaches.

Margery then left that posting to go to Warwickshire to become the Chief Ammo's driver. It was while she was in this job, that a particular Major advised her to think about how she could achieve further promotion. In the Major's view, promotion would not be achieved, if Margery maintained a driver's role. His advice was that she would not. Therefore, Margery decided to abandon the driving and go into Army office work. She did this and eight months later, she was promoted to the rank of Corporal.

Corporal Margery Fraser was then sent off to Episkopi, Cyprus to work in the Motor Transport office of the General Commander. Her main tasks involved catering for the needs of the Cypriot civilian workers, in the Camp. While she was doing this work, it became clear that this officer's drivers were not lasting long in their roles. Within three months of being in Cyprus, and after discovering that Margery was an experienced, advanced staff car driver, that she was soon detailed as his permanent driver. She started off as his third driver and when he discovered her experience as an advanced driver, she soon became his first driver. There seemed to be a revolving door with the others who had very short terms in that position. Margery *"just had to suck it up"* and get on with the driving job and whatever came with it.

Margery was rated highly for her skills, firstly as a soldier, but importantly, as a trusted, highly skilled driver. She drove a number of very important people. Some of these included Tom King, then Defence Secretary, the Duke of Gloucester, the King of Saudi Arabia and various other dignitaries.

Unfortunately, during her Cyprus posting, Margery did not always enjoy her work. There were some significant people management failings from one of the very senior officers, with whom she worked. This led to what she describes as an obvious block to her further promotion prospects, despite an evident and very positive recommendation being received about her. Margery resents this, still, but knows that she was powerless to do anything about it at that time. She realises, with hindsight, that perhaps even then, she might have had a chance to report this mistreatment and had it at least investigated.

Very soon, it was time for the Army to be replaced by the RAF and thus her posting and those of the particular officer and men, came to an end and Margery could move on to another location.

This time, it was to work in an intensive location with 3 Paras and then to 1 Paras. She was part of a group of 36 women whose role was to support each Regiment. They were to release the men from administrative duties, so that they could be out on the frontline.

Margery's particular job was the scheduling of transportation - cars, lorries, mini-buses, etc. - for the Regiment. The Colonel described her as the person who *"runs that Motor Transport Unit"*. She was efficient and effective in her role and was pleased that she was being noticed.

Margery loved that job. She had great comments from the senior officers and was recommended for promotion to Sergeant. Margery felt very much a part of this Regiment. The Regiment also adopted her into their group. She became part of them and when she was leaving, was awarded her own red beret and a Paras shirt as well as a bronze model. Her work with this Regiment was clearly valued and she appreciated the fact that they saw her worth. This appreciation and valuing were, in her view, a long way away from her nasty experience in Cyprus, which lasted 18 months, with the particular, very senior officer. That negative experience still resonates, negatively in her mind. She still wishes she had known how to appeal.

Despite these small, but still important misgivings, Margery served out her 17 years in the British Army. She had provided excellent service and support to her colleagues and as part of the team, wherever she went. She had gained a range of valuable skills and qualifications, many of which she could take with her into civilian life.

She is a woman, who does not drink alcohol. She never married and in her own words, was known as *"Everybody's friend, but nobody's lover."*

When she was 35 years old, she decided that she *"did not want to get old in the job"*. The policy, entitled 'Options for Change' was being implemented across the Armed Forces, giving opportunities for serving personnel to leave with a reasonable package. Margery decided to take advantage of this opportunity. She had a slight concern that if she had completed the full 22 years' service, she might even have been able to become one of the Beefeaters at the Tower of London. However, the Option for Change exit pathway, seemed too good to miss, so Margery left the Army.

Margery started working for Lynx, the parcel carriers, as a Business Development Assistant. She was responsible for any account spending between £1 - £1000. She covered the Exeter, Brighton and Southampton areas. The carrier company had a male dominated environment, which suited Margery as it was similar to the environment she had left in the Army. She also worked in the Southern Tourist Board and with Ciba Vision, which is part of the Pfizer company. When the company was locating to Germany, she decided to find work elsewhere. She was successful in obtaining a new job, working as a civil servant in the Courts' system. She has been in her current post for the past 22 years, a job she finds satisfying, especially as her support is valued by the top legal brains she supports.

She looks back on her Army career, where there were great moments, but also others, which she cannot forget. She recalls one of the events in particular. She had been the only black staff driver in Germany. She had been driving the Director General of the Household Cavalry and the Aide de Camp. These high-ranking officers were taken to the Blues and Royals' Officers' Mess.

Later in the officers' Mess, Margery was subjected to comments from two soldiers who were waiting on the officers, asking her if she knew there was *"No black in the Union Jack'* and that it was the *'Closest I've been to one of you Yetis."* Margery remembers responding to these comments, saying something like*, "I guess that being a Yeti, I know how to behave in public."* There are other comments, which were directed at her that she would rather forget.

She describes how she felt when she viewed the recent Trooping of the Colour and of seeing Remembrance events. In the Trooping of the Colour event, she observes what seemed to be around 78 soldiers on parade in each Platoon. The main Platoon receiving the colours *"did not have a single black person escorting the colours"*, she comments. *"It is difficult to even see any black officers."* She watched the very recent event, the new King's first big event and was surprised that as far as she could see, there were no black soldiers escorting the new King's colours. She decided that she would have to watch it all again, as she really could not believe it, considering we are looking at an event in 2023 and she remembers comments made in 1991 by the then Prince and heir. He had apparently expressed surprise not to see non-white faces in one of the Regiments. She acknowledges that there were of course, black soldiers to be seen in the 2023 parade, but significantly, in her view and from her observations of the event, none seen in the important escorting Squadron. She was very disappointed by this. She believes that *"There is still an undercurrent there in relation to race which is not going anywhere, anytime soon."*

Margery has no regrets about her military career. The only one perhaps, she is reminded, is that she *"allowed that Cyprus man to block me."*

Throughout her service, she has valued loyalty, the people with whom she served, punctuality and trust. These qualities have great significance to this amazing woman. *"You don't stop until the job is done."* Margery describes exactly what this means. *"A good staff car driver turns up five minutes early; an excellent staff car driver turns up on time; and a driver who doesn't want to live, turns up one minute late!"* While this last comment is not meant to be literal of course, she is uncompromising in using these expressions to confirm how critical it is to always be ready. She showed this commitment in everything she did as a soldier.

Margery does not believe that the service of Caribbean service men and women has been acknowledged. However, she does not talk much about her views on this matter.

When she looks back on her 18-year-old self, she would have advised her to *"Get her head down and wind her neck in."* She does not suffer fools gladly.

She is unsure about recommending Caribbean young people to join up. In her view, the modern Armed Forces has changed considerably. She wonders whether political correctness has changed the way soldiers are being managed and whether it has compromised the approach to discipline, for example. She feels that there may be a watering down of many things which are critical to an efficient and effective military force. So, for the enquiring and aspiring potential recruits, she comments, *"Is it worth it to join?"*

Corporal Margery Fraser is a strong, resilient woman, whose service in the Armed Forces has less to do with taking up arms to engage in battle, but more about securing safe, confidential, discrete transfers for those who are in powerful positions. She did this as part of the defence of the State. In this, she provided 17 years of exemplary service to her country.

8. The Royal Navy

The Royal Navy is the United Kingdom's naval warfare force and is one of the three main branches of the British Armed Forces. Its core purposes are to protect the UK's interests at home and abroad, to provide maritime security, and to support international peacekeeping efforts.

By preserving the safety of its territorial waters and defending its economic interests, the Royal Navy is in charge of protecting the nation's interests. The Royal Navy is also responsible for protecting the UK's overseas territories and providing support to UK citizens in times of crisis, such as natural disasters or civil unrest.

The primary responsibility of the Royal Navy is to ensure maritime security. This includes preventing and countering threats from terrorism, piracy, and illegal trafficking. The Navy also works to safeguard the flow of international trade, protecting vital sea lanes and working with partner nations to ensure a secure and stable maritime environment.

Furthermore, the Royal Navy is also committed to international peacekeeping efforts. It works with partner nations to support NATO and other global security organisations, and it provides humanitarian assistance and disaster relief in times of crisis.

Many Caribbean recruits were not always clear about what a naval career would look like, despite their desire to join. It was attractive to them in many respects and, for those who were interviewed, it gave them a taste of adventure in travel to various countries. Furthermore, it enabled them to acquire a variety of skills and expertise.

The Royal Navy is organised into several branches, each with its own specialised tasks and responsibilities. Here's a brief overview:

Surface Fleet: The Surface Fleet is responsible for the Navy's warships and includes aircraft carriers, destroyers, frigates, and amphibious assault ships.

Submarine Service: The Submarine Service is responsible for the Navy's fleet of nuclear-powered submarines.

Fleet Air Arm: The Fleet Air Arm is the branch of the Royal Navy responsible for the operation and maintenance of the Navy's aircraft, including helicopters and fighter jets.

Royal Fleet Auxiliary: The Royal Fleet Auxiliary is the civilian-manned fleet that provides logistical support to the Royal Navy, including fuel, ammunition, and supplies.

Royal Marines: The Royal Marines are the amphibious infantry of the Royal Navy and are responsible for conducting amphibious operations and providing security on board ships.

Naval Reserves: The Royal Naval Reserve is a part-time force that provides support to the Royal Navy in times of need.

In addition to these branches, the Royal Navy is also organised into several different commands, including the Fleet Command, the Maritime Command, and the Naval Personnel Command. Each command oversees specific aspects of the Navy's operations and ensure they are carried out effectively.

In the decades following the Second World War, the Navy experienced a decline in size and capability as a result of post-war demobilisation and budget cuts. In the 1960s and 1970s, the Navy focused on modernising its fleet and restructuring its organisation to better meet the demands of the Cold War.

One major change that occurred during this period was the development of the submarine-based nuclear deterrent, which led to the creation of the Submarine Service as a separate branch of the Navy. Another significant development was the introduction of aircraft carriers and the formation of the Fleet Air Arm as a distinct branch of the Navy.

In the 1980s and 1990s, the Royal Navy underwent further modernisation and restructuring, including the introduction of new warships and submarines. Its overall size was reduced, and greater emphasis was placed on joint operations with other branches of the British Armed Forces.

Today, the Royal Navy remain a highly capable and adaptable organisation with a focus on expeditionary operations, maritime security, and global engagement. Caribbean men and women form a part of these efforts.

The Royal Navy has a complex system of ranks and ratings, which reflect the levels of responsibility and authority of its personnel. Here is a brief overview of the main ranks and ratings:

Officer Ranks: The officer ranks are divided into three categories: senior officers, junior officers, and sub-lieutenants. The senior officers include admirals, vice admirals, rear admirals, and commodores. Junior officers include captains, commanders, and lieutenants. Sub-lieutenants are the most junior commissioned officers in the Navy.

Warrant Officers: Warrant officers are senior non-commissioned officers who hold a warrant from the Queen. They include the rank of warrant officer 1st class (WO1) and warrant officer 2nd class (WO2). These ranks mirror those of the Army.

Petty Officers: Petty officers are non-commissioned officers who have significant leadership responsibilities. They include the ranks of chief petty officer, petty officer 1st class, and petty officer 2nd class.

Ratings: Ratings are enlisted personnel who perform various tasks on board Navy ships. They include the ranks of leading hand, able seaman, and ordinary seaman.

In addition to these main ranks and ratings, the Royal Navy also has several specialist branches, such as the Royal Navy Medical Service, the Royal Navy Chaplaincy Service, and the Royal Navy Legal Branch. These branches have their own specific ranks and structures.

After the 1960s, the Royal Navy's system of ranks and ratings have undergone some changes. The four main changes include:

Officer Ranks: The senior officer ranks of Admiral of the Fleet and Admiral were abolished in 1995, and the rank of commodore was re-introduced as a one-star rank. The rank of sub-lieutenant was renamed as Second Lieutenant in 1975.

Warrant Officers: The rank of warrant officer class 1 (WO1) was introduced in 1973 to replace the rank of chief petty officer (special), which was introduced in 1958. The rank of warrant officer class 2 (WO2) was introduced in 1976. The WO ranks mirror those of the Army, with its two levels.

Petty Officers: The rank of chief petty officer (special) was abolished in 1973 and replaced with the rank of warrant officer class 1 (WO1). In 1973, the rank of petty officer (radio) was abolished and replaced with the rank of petty officer (communications).

Ratings: The names of some ratings have changed over time, reflecting changes in technology and job roles. For example, the rating of stoker was replaced with the rating of marine engineer in the 1980s.

Despite these changes, the overall structure of the Royal Navy's rank system has remained largely consistent, with officers, warrant officers, petty officers, and ratings all occupying distinct levels of authority and responsibility.

Rest and Recuperation (R&R) in the Royal Navy

Over the last four decades of the 20th century, some of the key developments in rest and recuperation (R&R) opportunities include:

Sailors would typically only get short periods of shore leave when the ship was in port. This would allow them to visit local towns and cities and take part in recreational activities, but the time available was often limited. Some larger ships had recreational facilities on board, such as a cinema or gym, which could provide some relief during long periods at sea.

In response to the demands of operations in the Gulf War and Balkans conflicts, where sailors and marines were often deployed for long periods in stressful and dangerous environments, sailors had more comprehensive R&R packages. They had longer periods of shore leave, recreational facilities on board ships, and access to welfare support and counselling services. The Navy also began to offer more opportunities for adventure training and sports, such as skiing, mountaineering, and sailing, as a way to help personnel unwind and build team spirit.

In general, R&R opportunities in the Royal Navy have always been somewhat limited by service demands. Nevertheless, the Navy still tried to provide its personnel with the support they needed to stay healthy and motivated during deployments.

Sport in the Royal Navy

There has been a tradition of promoting sports and fitness among its personnel. Some sporting opportunities provided by the Navy include traditional sports such as football, rugby, cricket, and boxing. There were also opportunities to participate in individual sports such as athletics, swimming, and sailing. Sports teams were organised at unit level and competed against other units and services in inter-service competitions. The Navy also offered training and facilities for physical fitness, including gymnasiums and sports fields on board ships.

In recent decades, the Navy expanded its sports opportunities to include new activities such as mountain biking, windsurfing, and triathlons. It also introduced the concept of "adventure training", which involves outdoor activities such as mountaineering, skiing, and kayaking as a way to build teamwork and leadership skills. There are similarities in their offer to that of the other branches of the Armed. In addition, the Navy has also invested more in sports facilities, with new gyms and sports halls being built on shore and on board ships. One particular talented, successful Caribbean sportsman and sailor who has taken advantage of some of these sporting opportunities is Able Seaman Wayne Green.

Able Seaman Wayne Green

Wayne Green was a talented boxer who served in the British Armed Forces.

He was born in Trinidad and came to the UK at the age of ten to join his mother who was recruited to do nursing here. Wayne had been left with his grandmother, in Trinidad, as a baby.

His mother had married and had two further children, before sending for Wayne. The family lived in Manor Park, London and Wayne attended a local primary school before moving on to a secondary school that was adjacent to the West Ham Football Club grounds. Wayne was fascinated by football and was somewhat talented in this area, leading to him obtaining an apprenticeship with the club.

Unfortunately, Wayne began mixing with the *"wrong crowd"* locally. Following a stern intervention from his stepfather, he was encouraged to visit the Navy Careers' Office, where he took and passed the relevant tests. He was then able to and join the Navy as a Boy Seaman. He continued training with West Ham FC and the club wanted him to stay with them. However, after discussion with his family, he decided to opt for a naval career.

He was sent his Travel Warrant from the Navy and off he went by train to be met in Ipswich by a Petty Officer.

He attended HMS Ganges to start his training. HMS Ganges was a land-based training establishment for the Royal Navy. Wayne found the start of the training for his new career, very exciting. When he arrived, he saw only 14 other black boys, out of the 200-strong recruits at that time. He was the only black person out of a dormitory of 20 young men.

As part of his basic training, he had numerous classes to prepare him for this part of military life. These included undertaking drills, knot-tying, marching, rifle training, swimming and endless other important military exercises to prepare him for this part of military life. The exercises were sometimes quite scary. In addition, some of the activities were very rigorous. For example, the men had to make sure they carried out their self-care effectively and pass all their Muster checks as a whole dorm. During this time, Wayne made friends, some with whom he maintained lifelong friendships.

At HMS Ganges, Wayne was also involved in 4-hourly watches and other activities, which the Able Seamen of the Royal Navy were expected to do. These tasks were routine and not especially exciting for this young man, who was only one of four black men on his first ship.

It was when the Ship got into port and sporting activities were organised, that Wayne's interest peaked. He loved being involved, especially when the men would go off to play against another country.

Boxing was one such sport which caught his attention. Wayne remembers the first ever time he became involved with boxing. He smiles at the memory.

When Wayne was on Parade on ship one day, the PT Instructor asked all of the men if any of them were interested in boxing. Everyone stepped back, except for Wayne. He found himself to be the only person left standing, and that was it. He was now a boxer for the Navy. This unexpected, 'forced', volunteering opportunity was to have a profound effect on this young man over the coming years.

Wayne continued his training and passed out as a Leading Junior Seaman. He went on the HMS Bulwark, which was an aircraft carrier. His main job then was loading the shells as a young 4 5 Gunner. HMS Bulwark was a huge ship, with hundreds of navy personnel. There were only four black people of the ship's company. Wayne describes the reality he experienced as, *"There was still racism in there".*

In his various roles on HMS Bulwark, Wayne was able to travel all over the world. Wayne served on the ship, carrying out a variety of duties. He painted, manned boats, worked in the Galley, scrubbed the decks, acted as Watchman and Lookout and undertook whatever tasks were required of him.

He was able to build up his boxing skills, with encouragement from others. A fellow sailor, but more senior to Wayne, and lifelong friend, Ray Ewing, got Wayne really interested in the sport. He and Ray often made use of the punchbag, although Ray's particular expertise was weightlifting. Nonetheless, Wayne found his forte and built his talent as a light welter weight boxer. He went on to box for the Royal Navy, including in Inter-Service Matches and Combined Services competitions.

Wayne recalls one of his early matches, against a man named Paul Kelly, who just beat him in the Championship competition. Kelly went on to win the Amateur Boxing Association championship and boxed for England. Although Wayne was beaten in that particular match, he maintained a great interest in boxing.

'79 ROYAL NAVY BOXING TEAM
All boxers ranked in the Top 5 in GB

He was being noticed by his senior officers as a talent in the area and was continually being put forward to compete for the Navy. This almost forced encouragement was, in Wayne's view, one of the reasons he did not rise up the ranks. In fact, he was kept in one of the lowest ranks - that of Able Seaman - throughout his career. It was however, the boxing which enabled him to develop good relationships with his senior officers. They seemed pleased to see Wayne become well-known outside the Navy and were keen to be seen with him at the more public matches, where there was publicity to be had.

At the age of 21, Wayne was chosen to represent England. His first international match was against Romania. In that ABA competition, three of the English competitors were black, including a boxer called Delroy Parks. Wayne recalls thinking that *"All the hard fights seemed to include the black guys!"*.

Although Wayne thoroughly enjoyed and appreciated his time in the Royal Navy, there were times during his boxing career, that he thought himself lucky to have boxing, as it meant he didn't have to go to sea!

Wayne went on to serve on HMS Intrepid for a few months, before heading back to HMS Nelson, to the boxing base there. HMS Nelson was the place where all the sailors who were boxers and who were in the different weight categories did their training.

In Wayne's first few years in the Royal Navy, he served on the Ship, Mobile, which was sent to Alabama.

The four black men on the ship could not go out with their white colleagues. In those days, black people could only be seen on the black parts of the area. It was a new and very strange experience for young Wayne. Where he was allowed to go out, it was only to be hosted by black families. These families were curious to know what it was like for Wayne, living with white people on the ship.

Despite the racial attitudes he encountered, Wayne had a great time with these families, with whom he was involved for the fortnight he spent in that racist State.

Outside of his military life, Wayne found boxing very physically demanding. He trained both with the Navy and with the England Team, where keeping himself in peak condition was vital to securing his place in the Squad. He boxed for England in several matches.

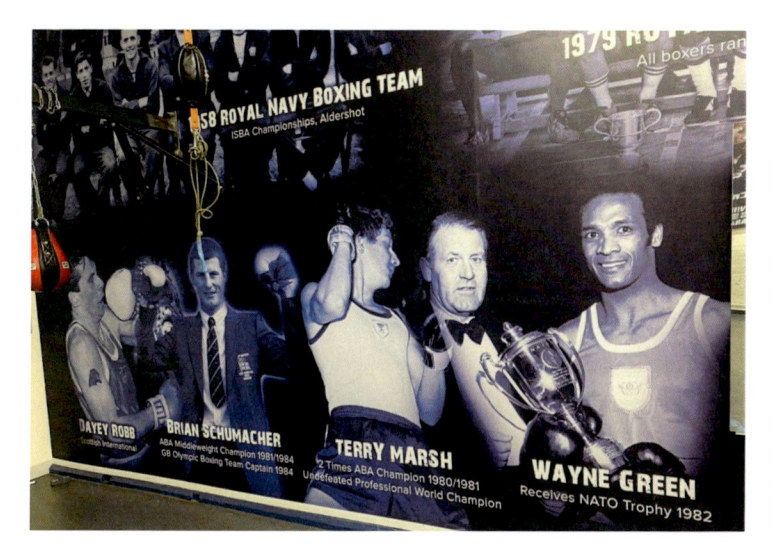

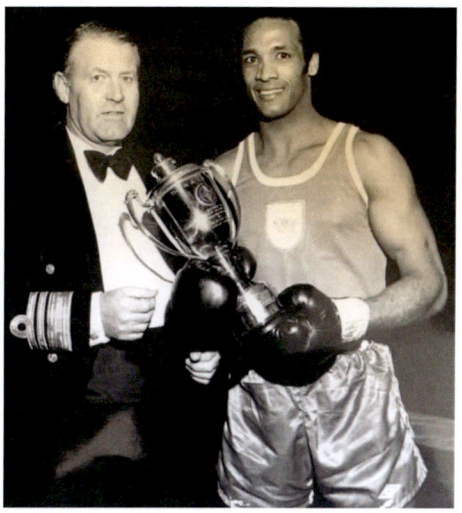

This was in the days of Chris Eubanks, who was then very well known, nationally and internationally.

Wayne decided not to become professional at this stage of his military and boxing career, because at the time, there didn't seem to be much money in it. He was however, feted by many and enjoyed the exposure and entry into interesting events and nightclubs that the boxing successes had allowed. It was a fantastic time in this young man's life.

He was flown to different locations across the world to engage in boxing competitions, all of which took him away from the life of an ordinary seaman. While it was exciting, Wayne had to remember his primary role in the military and in being a part of the defence of the nation. It was quite a challenge keeping that balance.

He achieved a huge amount of success and much publicity, including when he and his Royal Navy Squad beat the Royal Air Force on HMS Nelson in February 1982. It was quite a victory.

Around the same time, Wayne was presented with the NATO trophy for being the best Sportsman of the year from the Combined Services. A tremendous accolade.

Wayne decided to leave the Navy in his late 30s, having served for 22 years. He retained his rank of Able Seaman, but had achieved some stardom in the boxing field, both within and outside the Royal Navy.

When he was in his mid-30s, Wayne went to live in Germany. Eventually, at the age of 40, he decided to take the step to become a professional boxer. His professional boxing career was, however, short-lived, so he retired and took a series of jobs back home in England.

He spent the first years out in civilian life, working mainly on the doors in clubs in Portsmouth and doing aerobics' classes privately. He had made Portsmouth his home. It was a place he was familiar with and where he had always returned, whether from his months onboard ship, or from the various boxing matches for which he was well known.

Wayne then returned to Trinidad, for family reasons and stayed there working as a PT Instructor to the rich and to the Island's politicians. He stayed on the Island for the next few decades until 2022, when he came back to the UK.

Although Wayne speaks well of his Royal Navy service and certainly of the exposure he received for his boxing talent, he does have some regret about not being promoted up the ranks. He realises that the sporting talent he had, was important to the naval establishment. However, his Royal Navy service was more than being entertainment within the boxing ring. He was first and foremost a military seaman, who would be ready to answer the call were there to be any danger to Britain, such as in time of war. He knew he was ready and was willing to stand and defend the freedoms of everyone in the country. His loyalty and commitment, shown over more than two decades, is testament to that.

Team Building in the Royal Navy

Team building and leadership skills are essential to the Royal Navy's training programmes. During the post-world-war period, the Navy developed a range of team-building arrangements, some of which include:

The Navy used traditional military training techniques, such as drill and physical training, to build team cohesion and discipline. Commanding Officers were responsible for promoting teamwork and leadership skills within their units. Unit-based sports teams were often used as a way to build camaraderie and teamwork. However, there was less formal training in team building and leadership skills compared to what is available today.

Around thirty years ago, the Navy introduced more formal team-building programmes, including courses and exercises designed to develop leadership, communication, and wider skills. They also introduced outdoor activities such as mountaineering, skiing, and kayaking to strengthen teamwork and leadership skills. These programmes were often conducted away from the normal work environment to encourage staff to think creatively and develop new problem-solving strategies.

In its work nowadays, it has continued its emphasis on these areas. There are formal leadership and management courses, team-building exercises and simulations, and adventure training opportunities. The Navy also provides mentoring and coaching to develop leadership skills at all levels of the organisation. Unfortunately, this was not always the case. For some of the early Caribbean recruits, especially those recruited in the 1960s and 1970s, there was a sense of opportunities missed at best or unavailable, which reflected their experiences in reality.

Basic Training in the Royal Navy

The Royal Navy's basic training during the 1960s to 2000 evolved to meet the changing needs of service life. Here is a brief overview of the key developments during this period:

Basic training for new recruits was conducted at shore-based training establishments such as HMS Ganges and HMS Raleigh. The training was physically demanding and discipline was enforced through traditional military methods such as drills and physical training. Recruits learned seamanship, gunnery, navigation, naval history, customs and traditions.

As time passed, the Navy began modernising its training methods to reflect changing technologies and tactics. Basic training was still conducted at shore-based training establishments, but the emphasis shifted to developing practical skills and knowledge that could be applied on board ships. The Navy introduced new training facilities, such as simulators and computer-based training programmes to help recruits develop their skills and knowledge. People such as Zac Robinson and Lionel Winston benefitted from some of the opportunities.

The Navy continued to modernise by introducing new technologies and approaches to learning. New recruits still focus on developing practical skills and knowledge, but the Navy uses more interactive and multimedia-based training methods to engage and help recruits learn more effectively. There seems to be greater emphasis on leadership and team-building skills, designed to help recruits develop these skills early in their careers. The Caribbean recruits cited in this book would have welcomed all of these opportunities. Their hope is that the new Caribbean heritage recruits will be able to access these new opportunities, including leadership and mentoring, to help them progress and achieve higher ranks. The data available about the number of officers from ethnic minority groups indicate a promotion plateau for this group over the past few decades. It is an area worth watching.

Recruitment to the Royal Navy

The Royal Navy's recruitment was largely focused on young men leaving school who were often encouraged to join the Navy as a career option. Recruitment was conducted through advertising campaigns, job fairs, and by word-of-mouth. The Navy also organised visits to schools and colleges, with recruitment officers speaking to students about the benefits of a naval career. In the past, most recruits found out about a naval career from a careers teacher in their school or the local Careers' Office.

The Navy realised that it needed to shift its recruitment focus to a broader demographic, including women and individuals from diverse backgrounds and with specific skills or qualifications.

It introduced new programmes such as the Officer Cadetship scheme, which offered a pathway for individuals with a degree or equivalent qualification to become officers. It also recruits some individuals from the Caribbean and other Commonwealth countries. However, using existing data, it appears that the numbers from those backgrounds are still relatively low compared to their white colleagues. When recruited, these individuals, who were often referred to as "West Indians", made significant contributions to the British military. They played a key role in several conflicts and operations, including the Falklands War and the Gulf Wars.

Promotion up the Naval Ranks

There are no current targets for recruiting women and ethnic minorities in the British Armed Forces. Where those targets existed, they came to an end in 2020.

The Ministry of Defence does, however, declare that it is dedicated to achieving a more diverse workforce, which reflects the society it serves. Between 2013 and 2022, the number of ethnic minorities in the Armed, as a whole, ranged from 5.7% to 8.6%.

However, there has been a recent decrease in those numbers caused by a government policy change. This, in part, was related to the MOD re-imposing, in 2013, a five-year UK residency criteria for Commonwealth citizens wishing to join the Armed; having previously waived the criteria in 1998.

There is no available data on the promotion of individuals of Caribbean heritage up the Royal Navy ranks up to and including 2000. However, it is known that the Royal Navy, like other branches of the British Armed Forces, has faced criticism over the years for a lack of diversity within its ranks, particularly at senior levels.

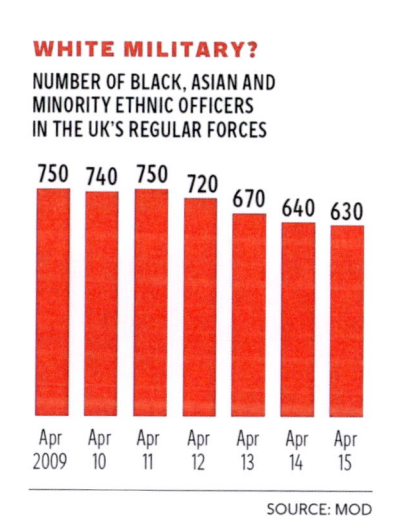

WHITE MILITARY?
NUMBER OF BLACK, ASIAN AND MINORITY ETHNIC OFFICERS IN THE UK'S REGULAR FORCES

Apr 2009	Apr 10	Apr 11	Apr 12	Apr 13	Apr 14	Apr 15
750	740	750	720	670	640	630

SOURCE: MOD

Between 2009 and 2016, the picture was gloomy, with reductions in BAME promotion.

Despite this, there have been a very small number of individuals of Caribbean heritage who have achieved relatively high ranks within the Royal Navy.

In recent years, the Royal Navy has made a more concerted effort to increase diversity and inclusivity within its ranks and has implemented a range of initiatives to support this. For example, in 2018, the Navy launched its "Pathfinder" programme, which aims to support the career progression of women and individuals from diverse backgrounds within the Navy.

According to the Independent newspaper, in 2016, it is understood there was not a single BAME candidate among the Royal Marine officers passing out in 2021 – while just 20 black and 25 Asian officers serve in the Royal Navy, out of a total of around 7,000.

Official data shows that the number of non-white officers has fallen by 16% since 2009 from 750 to 630. In 2021, there were no high-level black officers in the Royal Navy.

When Commodore Steve Prest, Deputy Director Acquisition (Equipment and Systems) at the Royal Navy and Advocate for Gender in Defence spoke, in July 2012, to Madeline Bennett from Diginomica about women's experience in the Navy, his words could easily relate to the BAME group also. He said:

"There's a basic point of fairness. If you subscribe to the view that your organisation is a meritocracy, that can only be true if you've got a level playing field and if everybody can compete on an equitable basis. The second point is as a leader, if you don't understand how the people in your team and your organisation experience things differently from you, then you can't lead them properly."

There were, however, a few Caribbean men who achieved high ranks in the Royal Navy between 1960 and 2000.   Two such examples are Lionel Winston and Fred Coke, whose stories follow later.

Women Serving in the Royal Navy

The sea was, historically, the domain of men. It was not until as late as 1993 that women were integrated into the Royal Navy as fully fledged sailors.

Interestingly, as reported by 'The Historic Dockyard', Chatham, a black female who dressed as a man assumed a man's name, William Brown, served in the Royal Navy in 1804. She spent 12 years on British warships, including the Queen Charlotte, the flagship of the Channel Fleet. She rose up the ranks, eventually becoming captain of the Foretop. Her true name is still unknown.

Given that history, it is rather surprising that in more modern times, including within the Windrush Generation (1948-1971 period especially), few women of colour served in the Royal Navy and none have achieved high ranks.

From the 1970s, there were shortages in the Navy, so there was active recruitment of Caribbean women. A small number were in the Women's Royal Navy Service (WRNS). There was some increase in 1993 when women's position as ordinary navy personnel was normalised. Nevertheless, at that 1993 point, no BAME women were to be seen in the first 20 who were initially allowed to go to sea with their male colleagues.

There are currently around 3.8 per cent BAME personnel altogether in the Royal Navy/Royal Marines, with only around 19 of them being women. It is clearly a tiny percentage, which obviously impacts opportunities to gain the relevant skills and experience to rise up the ranks.

In the 12 months ending 30 September 2022, the proportion of ethnic minorities (excluding white minorities) personnel of a Non-UK Nationality joining the UK Regular Forces had decreased from 38.5 per cent to around 31.4 per cent against the same period the year before. This is in the face of an obvious increase in ethnic minorities living in the UK.

Writer Logistician Nicole Atwell-Mansingh

Nicole was born in Port of Spain, Trinidad. She is the middle child of five, with two older sisters and twin younger brothers. She comes from a close-knit family whose roots are firmly grounded in the Church. She always encouraged by the family's matriarch to travel and see the world having spent some time in Italy herself. She explained, *"My Mum would always say, go out there and see the world before you settle and have a family. For her part of traveling, she came to England and she spent time in Italy, in Milan. So you know, I tried to follow her footsteps."*

After secondary school, her closest schoolmates were leaving for America but Nicole's opportunity to migrate came as a young adult, already fully fledged into the Caribbean way of living.

Nicole raised funds from a job at a local resort in Trinidad and secured her ticket to start a new adventure. She told her mother that she was leaving for England in a month. Nicole recalls her family's reaction. *"My Mother was quiet. And then she spoke to my Dad about it. We had a family meeting and they said "I can't believe that you booked your ticket and you're leaving in four weeks"*

It was February 2002 when she boarded the flight from Trinidad to Tobago, with her immediate family there to wish her well. Nicole spent a couple days in Tobago before the flight to London Gatwick was scheduled to leave. When finally airborne, having only ever taken 20-minute flights between her native Trinidad and Tobago, the flight to London felt eternal. Nicole's final destination was Manchester, and on arrival to London Gatwick, she had to navigate an entirely new transportation system and made her way to London Victoria by coach. There she was met by a childhood friend for the journey to Manchester with whom she would board.

Enrolling at a local college to continue her study in Finance, one afternoon while perusing the streets of Manchester, exploring her new environs, Nicole stumbled upon the Armed Forces Recruitment Office. She decided to head in and make an enquiry. The recruitment officers gave her an overview of the services, the British Army, the Royal Navy and the Airforce. It was the Royal Navy that got Nicole's attention. She felt that it would give her the opportunity to travel and see the world.

She completed the required entry assessments and her scores suggested the option of a role at the Able Seaman rating level, as a Writer/Logistics personnel. A Navy Writer/Logistician is someone who is in charge of Human Resources

■ Nicole: Applied to the navy

(HR), handling legal matters, financial admin, and looking after the welfare of their crew mates. They also provide support in office administration functions such as customer service, document management and personnel management procedures. This role seemed very suitable to Nicole, who had already begun some finance study back home in Trinidad. Therefore, she signed up. Within six months of entering the recruitment office, Nicole was on a coach again but this time heading to HMS Raleigh in Plymouth to begin her eight-week basic training and life as a Sailor in the Royal Navy.

When she got to Plymouth, Nicole found herself in a Division of 30 men and women, many of whom were much younger than her, even as young as 16. All but one of the officers were white. She did however hear about one black officer (a Lt. Commander) who was at HMS Raleigh. She was to meet and work with him some time later.

At HMS Raleigh Nicole was the only black person in her division but not the only black person on the base. There were several Vincentians who had been recruited directly from St Vincent, a programme that started at least two years ahead of her signing up. There were also a handful of Jamaicans and Barbadians. Having never really met other islanders, Nicole used the opportunity to discover their similarities in upbringing, food and culture and from there she was able to forge some long-lasting friendships.

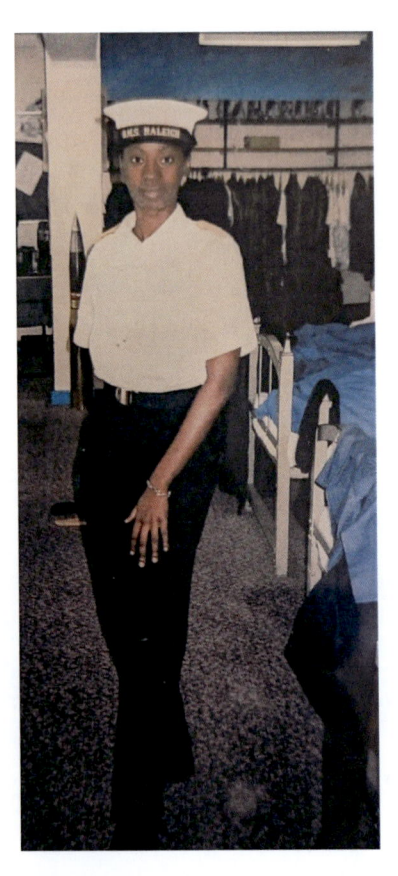

During phase one training, Nicole was introduced to sleeping in a mess of 30 plus females. They shared the same bathroom and toilet facilities, which was part of their many chores and had to be cleaned twice a day. It took a while for her to get used to the food as some of the names were not very appealing. There were dishes such as 'pigs in blanket', 'toad in the hole' and 'spotted dick'! Basic training for Nicole and other new recruits, involved firefighting skills, first aid seamanship, physical fitness and small arms handling. Having always wrapped up warmly when on civilian streets, it was somewhat different in the Navy. During physical fitness exercises meant donning the military issued white t-shirts and dark blue shorts in all weathers. It took some getting used to. Growing up in the Caribbean, although the islands are surrounded by warm waters, back then a lot of people never learnt to swim as swimming pools were limited. So when it came to the swimming test, Nicole struggled and ended up on the 'remedials' programme for four weeks. Despite her innate fear for the water, she managed to succeed in other water-related activities such as the dreaded HAVOC which is a simulation of the ship sinking and requiring damage repair. At this task, and surprisingly to. Her, she surpassed some of her peers. Other than that, Nicole was able to adapt to other physical aspects of the training having being relatively fit prior to migrating to the UK.

Having passed out successfully, Nicole had to 'wait around' a bit due to a delay in admitting the next cohort for the next stage of training. As she waited, she got on with the regular duties expected of her; chores, tidying up the Mess, doing some 'brasso-ing' where needed and generally keeping occupied on HMS Raleigh. Finally, within a couple of months, Nicole was able to start her Writer Training for the next 15 weeks. She knuckled down and again was successful. Those who passed the Course first time (only 3 of them) were invited to the Petty Officer Writer's home for a special dinner. Nicole was so proud of herself. She was however sad that her colleague and new friend she had made, did not pass at the time, although following remedials, did get through. Nicole did especially well and received a plaque for her efforts. She was now ready to start her first draft. This was at the then Royal Hospital Hasler in Gosport, a tri-service base. This was where she got to employ the skills she had developed during her phase two training as a Writer.

HMS Exeter, a type 42 Destroyer was Nicole's first and only ship and second draft to which she was assigned for eighteen months. When she first boarded Exeter, Nicole was struck by the smell of the Ship. It was a distinctive smell that even now, years later, she still wriggles her nose at the memory of it. That smell seemed to permeate everything and everywhere. She was however, excited about all the new countries she was about to visit and to be a part of the Ship's company which could accommodate 250 personnel with females accounting for only 8%. There were also five black men on the ship, making it six of them in the 250-strong company. Nicole and those men became friends, especially as they all shared a common culture, which enabled them to bond quickly. At times, they were able to go out on the short rest and recuperation periods they were allowed, visiting sights and enjoying other social activities.

On arrival on HMS Exeter, Nicole noticed that the living quarters were even smaller than that of the base. She recalls experiencing 'coffin syndrome' during her first couple months onboard ship. This was as a result of sleeping on a bunk bed with the curtains drawn and with limited head space. Early morning 'pipes' which served as the Ship's company alarm clock among other functions, also startled her as they would take place on the upper deck which was right above her mess.

When the ship finally set sail, that's when she discovered that she suffered sea sickness. During exercises onboard which is meant to test the Ship companies' readiness, this was when everyone was expected to get mucked in as it was all hands-on deck. An exhausting but yet adrenaline filled activity while on the waters.

When 'run ashores' were granted as part as rest and recuperation, this meant spending the day with the same people that you work, eat and sleep in the same accommodation with. 'Run ashores' in the Navy, are a night out on land for Navy personnel. Nicole developed positive relationships with her colleagues. They were her family while on board and would mainly be those people with whom she would run ashore for social time.

HMS Exeter docked in Narvik, Cork, Lisbon, Gibraltar, Morocco, Algeria and Malta during her period onboard, an eye opener for a little island girl. She loved these ravel experiences and the opportunity to see different places and experience the varying, fascinating sights, smells and cultures so different from her own.

After sea service, Nicole got drafted to a role in London, at yet another Tri-service base but this time working in the Diversity Awareness Team (DAT). She worked with the black officer she had met earlier on in her career. This new role meant facing the British public on a daily basis, particularly in inner London urban communities, receiving exposure to present to large audiences and hone her interpersonal skills. Nicole did this work for two years. She enjoyed the work as it allowed her to engage with local communities and schools in London and across the country, sharing information and taking questions about careers in the Royal Navy.

Nicole had met her husband-to-be back home in Trinidad some years earlier. He was to join the British Army around the same time as Nicole had joined the Royal Navy. They continued their loving relationship throughout and decided to get married while she was completing her phase two training.

While Nicole was in the midst of her Diversity draft, she decided that it was time to start her family shortly and completed her finance training in preparation for life on the civvy streets. As she had started this training before she joined up and had used some of those skills in her Writer role, the Navy helped her financially, to enhance this training so that she could complete her Association Accountant Technician (AAT) qualification, completing it before she left.

Nicole left the Royal Navy in 2008 as an Able Seaman. She had given six years of service. She recalls looking back at where she came from in Trinidad and what she was able to achieve within a relatively short space of time. Being in the service was difficult at times. Homesickness played a major part in the early days and having to adapt to a completely different culture and climate, but she recommended and continues to recommend the services in particular, the Royal Navy to young Caribbeans, if even as a steppingstone. She is proud of her time spent in the Navy, the camaraderie she experienced with her fellow 'Island Boys' and other cherished memories. One precise memory she will always remember, was a statement from the Ship's Captain while onboard HMS Exeter. He said, *"Nicole will go far"*. She believes that she has done so and is proud of herself. She continued to develop her technical skills, achieving highly in them. They led to her becoming a Chartered Accountant with the Civil Service, doing a job which she enjoys. She lives with her husband and young daughter in Essex.

It was after leaving the Navy, that Nicole learned that she was related to Winfred Atwell, the famous classical and jazz musician. Winifred was Nicole's grandmother's sister. Therefore, she is Nicole's Great Aunt. She is very proud of this connection. In fact, Nicole's teenage daughter, Nile is a budding classical pianist, already in the middle of her Grade 8 exercises. Young Nile also plays the Celtic Harp. Perhaps the talents of her great-great aunt is about to surface and we may well see and hear much about her in the future.

In recommending other Caribbeans to consider joining up, Nicole's advice to them would be different for those coming fresh the Caribbean. She would strongly advise them to do what they can to 'be ahead of the game' by getting relevant qualifications (a degree) in order to apply directly for a commission, if possible. However, she is fully aware that it would all depend on the individual's background. She had gained much from her Naval career and has been able to use those skills, extending them even further in her civilian career.

Looking back to her 24-year-old self, she would look young, bright-eyed Nicole in the eyes and say,

"Based on my background, it was all worthwhile. It was a good move to join the Royal Navy. I had no idea what I wanted to do when I was back home in Trinidad. If better advice had been available to me however, I would have stayed much longer in the Navy and shaped my career differently, trying to get further up the ranks.. I have no regrets and am proud of the service I gave".

Writer Logistician, Nicole Atwell-Mansingh is a thoughtful, skilled veteran, who provided good service to this country in her various roles. She deserves to be recognised and acknowledged for her contribution.

Caribbean Royal Navy Veterans

Hundreds of men and women of Caribbean heritage provided significant service to the Queen and the country throughout the monarch's reign in the 20th and most of the first quarter of the 21st century. Two of these brave Navy Veterans who are representative of this relatively small group are Lionel Winston and Fred Coke.

Lieutenant Commander Lionel Winston, MBE. Lieutenant Commander Lionel Winston was born in Dominica and joined the Royal Navy in 1971, going up the ranks to Warrant Officer 1 until being commissioned by the Queen. Lionel served on various ships, such as HMS Ark Royal. He served in major engineering positions, achieving his HNC and Bachelor's degree, demonstrating his intellectual aptitude in some of the highest scores in tests he had taken throughout his career.

Chief Petty Officer Fred Coke who came from Jamaica at the age of 11 and joined the Royal Navy as a Mid-Shipman at the age of 18. Fred put his whole heart into developing his engineering skills, studied hard and achieved rapid promotion, becoming a CPO, a position he held until leaving the Navy after 22 years of service.

Lieutenant Commander Lionel Winston, MBE

Lionel was born in Dominica and at the young age of nine he travelled to London to join his parents in the early 1960s. He found the new country strange, grey and cold. Nevertheless, he was to enter the local schools to start his education.

Lionel was a bright young boy, but he did not find school allowed him to achieve highly and he left at the age of 16 with few qualifications. He knew he had to find a job and a career and so applied for various jobs. After a short stint as a civil servant, he eventually settled into a trainee position as a welder. He learned to drive, bought a car and was enjoying his social life when he was asked to give his brother a lift to the Naval Recruiting Office in the city.

When they arrived at the careers' office where his brother was to start his tests to join up, Lionel sat back and prepared for the long wait until his brother finished. It was while he was settling down to wait, that the Careers' Officer came out and spoke to him, saying, *"Come on, don't just wait around. Come in and do the tests. There's no commitment and you're just hanging around."* Lionel thought he might as well use up the time and so went in and did the tests. He was not bothered about the results because he was not really interested in going into the Navy.

He was shocked to be asked to go in before the other candidates to get his results, The officer said to him *"Surely you are interested in knowing how you did in the tests?"* Lionel's interest was piqued. He was surprised to learn that he had achieved the highest results and that they wanted him to join up. He was also told that they wanted him to enter the Royal Navy as a Weapons Engineer.

They explained that he would have to sign up for a minimum of 12 years, which he found a little daunting. He was then offered an alternative to join as a Marine Engineering Mechanic (Stoker). By doing this role, he would thus be entering at the very basic entry level, allowing him to be enlisted for a mere four-year period. However, in the Career Officer's view, Lionel's test results showed that he might get bored easily in that position, and it was thus pointed out that there were fast track means of progressing. Lionel became very interested in this idea as it seemed that he would be given every opportunity to succeed.

Lionel had merely gone along that day to support his brother with a lift in his new car. Here he was, doing the tests for entry into the Royal Navy and getting high results which could mean a very new career; one he had never considered. He was 20-years-old, had a girlfriend and was on his way towards becoming a welder. He thought long and hard and finally, made the life-changing decision to take up the offer and join the Royal Navy. His brother, who was already focused on a military career, also joined up.

Lionel was sent his Travel Warrant and set off from Willesden Junction to Paddington Station to take the train to Plymouth. He was met by a duty driver and taken by coach to the Camp at HMS Raleigh to start his six-week training. Lionel joined a class of 13 others for his basic training.

When Lionel arrived at HMS Raleigh on the 11th September 1971, he remembers seeing the wooden huts and the Petty Officer showing him and the other 12 recruits, the dormitory in which they would sleep. There were altogether, at that time, three groups of 13 young men recruits who started at the same time as Lionel.

Lionel was from a Caribbean home in which he had learned everything about self-care. He could do his washing and ironing and knew very well how to take care of his personal space, including its cleaning. He could see that the other recruits were struggling in these areas and he was proud that he was a step ahead of them. However, he had to do his bit, as part of the group to make sure that they all met the rigorous expectations of the senior officer's inspections of their shared areas.

He made some friends while doing his basic training, but lost contact with them. He felt sad about this, but soon realised that this was all part and parcel of naval life. The Royal Navy, unlike the Army, posted their men singularly to other positions, other ships. Postings were not done in groups and therefore you had to act independently as you were on your own in a new place each time, negotiating new friendships in every new location.

Lionel soaked up the information and activities he was involved with in HMS Raleigh. He was woken up and welcomed on his first full day and set off after breakfast to sign up formally to be a part of the Royal Navy. *"Once you sign, you are theirs."* As soon as his signature was obtained, Lionel was led off to get his uniform, overall working clothes, boots and shoes. On the following day, he and the other recruits met with the Petty Officer to be told what they would be expected to do.

In those first weeks of basic training, Lionel would learn a huge amount about the navy, its ships, the types of knots he would have to practice and become proficient in, and also the important military skills such as using a rifle and other defensive, protective skills necessary to a military person.

One of the less exciting and more disturbing things Lionel recalls from the early days of basic training, was the nicknames that ranking personnel seemed to find acceptable to use for black men. That is, to call black navy personnel by the nickname, "Snowy". Lionel was appalled and offended by this. He resented it and was not going to accept it. Thus, he made an announcement that he did not want to be called by that name. He already had a name, - Lionel. He found himself having to be very firm about this, telling people that he would *"deck the next person"* who called him by that [offensive] name. If the tradition was to have a nickname, then he was happy to have one. He decided to adopt the name *"Winnie",* a name he would be called for much of his early career.

Oddly, there seemed to be another accepted tradition, which he discovered much later on in his career while being part of Dartmouth sea training group. He heard about *"The Captain's Doggie"*. This 'Doggie' was a person who shadowed the Captain of a Ship for a day, seeing what he did. Lionel refused to nominate such a person until the role could be renamed *"The Captain's Escort"*.

Lionel completed his basic training successfully and Passed Out after six weeks. After basic training, Lionel was sent to the HMS Sultan, the marine engineering school, which is where his career really took off.

Having achieved an overall 96% during part II training, Lionel was put onto the Specially Selected Marine Engineering Mechanic, (SSMEM) course. During this course, he qualified as a Mechanical Engineer Marine (MEM) at Class 1 and then obtained a Leading MEM qualification.

Lionel's first posting (or Draft) was to HMS Ark Royal. HMS Ark Royal was an aircraft carrier and then flagship of the Royal Navy, until being decommissioned in 1979. This was an impressive aircraft carrier of its time. She was one of the first navy ships to be fitted with an angled flight deck and had all the latest electronic, radar equipment, guns and missiles, necessary to meet the demands of modern warfare. She carried nearly 40 aircraft, including Phantoms, Sea Kings and Buccaneer aircrafts. This ship participated in a variety of exercises as part of the British fleet and NATO squadrons. She was not involved in any major combat duties, but remained ready to do so, if required. She did however, participate in missions in the Central America region, in or near places such as Honduras and Belize. She was subject to some of the Western Atlantic deployment during the 1970s. Ark Royal also led tributes to Queen Elizabeth 11 for her Silver Jubilee in 1977.

Subsequently after a period at sea, again on the HMS Ark Royal, Lionel was sent back to Sultan for the Leading Hand Course. He came top of the class.

Completing this course successfully, qualified him for the Technicians' Course. This would in turn, provide him with administration and leadership skills while also developing his engineering knowledge.

Lionel took full advantage of the opportunities available to him and others in the Navy. The Navy placed great emphasis on education. He remembers Lieutenant White who was his Divisional Officer while serving on HMS Ark Royal, which was his first ship. Lieutenant White who considered Lionel to be one of his bright MEMs was dismayed to discover through an informal chat with Lionel, that the Education Officer refused to put Lionel forward for his 'O' Level mathematics. In Lionel's view, he was, sadly, being blocked by an officer who was clearly prejudiced. Lionel took a maths test separately and achieved the best ever result of anyone. He achieved an A*. The racist officer was therefore forced to allow Lionel to enter for the maths test.

When the results came back, and were posted on the board for all the entrants to see, Lionel's name was missing. The Divisional Officer asked why this was so and was told by the said, racist officer, that he had sent them back to be reviewed as it was impossible that Lionel had achieved an A*. When Lionel's results were returned, they were exactly the same - an A*.

The Navy provided funding for study and therefore Lionel was able to complete his 'O' and 'A' levels and was eventually able to complete his Open University degree in mathematics and computing. He remained grateful for the support he had had from Lieutenant White. Lionel was to benefit from other support throughout his career, but remained vigilant about the incidences of racism he would encounter.

He would serve on Ark Royal for the next two years and made the most of the experience. The job, which Lionel was engaged in on the ship, was in what was called Domestics. In this role, his responsibilities included looking after the air-conditioning and water distillation plants. He would do the higher level, four-hour operator job. If things went wrong, Lionel would refer on to an Artificer who was a highly-skilled naval rating. On Ark Royal, Lionel met and became friends with another black man, who was a Petty Officer. He worked closely with this man, becoming a water tender for him. He learned much in the various roles he carried out on his full Draft on Ark Royal.

Following his second stint on the Ark and having gained the rating of Petty Officer in record time, Lionel got an early slot on the Technicians' course at Sultan where he successfully completed a two-year training programme and was awarded an HNC.

Such a position could also be seen in the army, in Regiments such as the Royal Electrical and Mechanical Engineer (REME), where highly skilled people were needed to keep the armoured equipment working effectively. Unfortunately, this position ceased in 2010, when the Royal Navy's engineering branch was subject to restructuring. An Artificer was however, very much a part of Lionel's navy world when he was doing his military service.

While serving on Ark Royal, Lionel visited several places, even passing on one occasion, his original homeland of Dominica. He was told later, that were he to have mentioned it, he could have been flown to the island for a short leave to see his family and enjoy being back there. He reminisces a bit at this point, when he recalls a later Draft, in which he served on HMS Fife as a Charge Chief and the ship went to Dominica. When he realised that he would actually be stopping there, he was elated. It was much later in his service and he had by this time, received a long service and good conduct award. Receiving this award was one thing, but what was even better, was to be given it by the Island's President and be lauded by his Dominican community, who expressed their pride loudly and energetically, in his achievements.

It was while he was serving on HMS Fife, which was a guided missile destroyer, that Lionel was identified for officer training. Lionel speaks of Fife as one ship which stood out for him. He was a Charge Chief by this time and he really enjoyed his time there.

When he joined Fife for the second time in Scotland, he describes an incident that marked him out as someone who would do well in more senior positions. When Lionel joined Fife, no handover was possible. He joined the ship in Scotland on a Saturday. The senior chiefs on GMDs were usually billeted on the After Chiefs' Mess Deck. As a senior chief then, he was entitled to be billeted there, but somehow, there was no space there for him. The Warrant Officer (WO) who was in charge at the time, decided to fill the Mess so that Lionel could not get a space. Lionel was told later during this draft, that the WO *"didn't want a Ni…r on his Mess"*.

It was not long before Lionel and this WO were at loggerheads, a situation which continued throughout Lionel's time on the ship. Lionel knew his job and was very good at it, but that was not a tension he needed in the two years he served on the Fife. Lionel did come across that WO again, after leaving HMS Fife. Lionel had by then, become Sub-Lieutenant and the WO was still at his WO rank. At first, the WO did not salute Lionel as was expected. Lionel took great pleasure in pulling this Non-Commissioned Officer (NCO) up, insisting that he salute as was required. All NCOs salutes of commissioned officers was not then, and is not now, only expected, it is a duty. The salute was in recognition of the Queen, rather than of any particular individual senior officer. Not to salute was therefore an insult to the monarch and against Naval Law.

Before achieving the commissioned officer status, Lionel was working hard and building up a good reputation and using his skills and energy for the benefit of the ships on which he served. He would soon apply for and gain further promotion. He recalls moving from Leading Hand to the rank of Petty officer and going for the first time, into the Petty Officers' Mess. He wanted to order a beer and was met with some scepticism by the bar staff, who did not know about his early promotion and could not see his Petty Officer (PO) badge. Lionel had become a PO so quickly, that he had not even been given his Stripe to attach to his shirt. He had to go and get the badge so that he could then fit in with the expectation that he was indeed entitled to order that beer in the Mess.

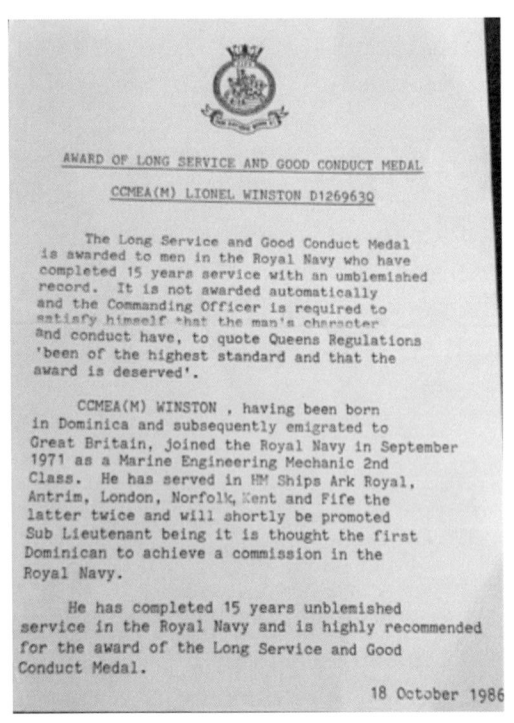

He studied hard on many training courses, coming first or second every time. The tests which followed the studies were tough and often included a verbal grilling known as a Fleet Board, in front of a panel of senior officers. These senior officers took no quarter in respect of the questions they asked and the analyses they employed in respect of his answers. Lionel's ambition was not lessened by these challenges.

He achieved Charge Chief Petty Officer status and this was quickly followed by a Queens Commission in 1987, when he became a Sub-Lieutenant, Royal Navy, on the Special Duties List.

Once promoted Lionel went on to Royal Naval College Greenwich for 6 weeks where he came top of his class. Lionel then went on to HMS Thunderer in Plymouth for 14 months. Here he undertook an HND in engineering. Lionel felt that being an officer and being black, he would need to do more. He decided to do his BSc in mathematics and computing. He was delighted that these qualifications would be financially supported by the Navy. He worked immensely hard in his own time to complete these qualifications successfully. Lionel received first prize at Greenwich Naval College and was presented with his prize by Commodore J J Blackham.

HMS

Sirius was the last ship on which Lionel served. This Draft was to last 20 months ending when Lionel achieved his Marine Engineer Charge Qualification.

On leaving Sirius Lionel was appointed to HMS Sultan where he took the lead of the Gas Turbine and Bulk Fuel Management School. In this role him and his staff of 30 was responsible for the training of Royal Navy, Foreign Navies and Civilian personnel in the operation of Gas Turbines and the management of fuel supplies.

While at Sultan Lionel also fulfilled a teaching role teaching Mathematics, Thermodynamics Mechanics and Engineering to Naval personnel at all levels. He took charge of a SSMEM Course whilst he was at HMS Sultan.

In the middle of all of this work and personal study which led to him achieving his BSc Hons, Lionel was invited to London to meet with a very senior Admiral who needed assistance in answering an off the cuff question which arose when Colin Powell, then USA Secretary of State visited the UK.

The question was, *"Would Colin Powell had achieved the status which he did, had he lived in the UK and subsequently joined the military?"* Because Lionel had experienced the navy as a Mechanic, Technician and now as an officer, Command felt that he was best placed to explain the differing career pathways available in the Royal Navy.

Lionel was therefore asked to take on the job of raising awareness of naval opportunities to the Ethnic Communities' groups. This meeting led to Lionel taking on the role of the Royal Navy's Ethnic Minority Liaison as its EMLO.

It was while he was in the Navy's EMLO, that his achievements were recognised by the Queen through an award of the MBE.

Following the EMLO role he went on to work with the Ministry of Defence as a Software Development Manager, on a new maintenance initiative called Reliability Centred Maintenance (RCM). Lionel was chosen for this role because he was a Marine Engineer with computer degree. By this time, Lionel had achieved his Lieutenant Commander rank.

Lionel had now served 39 years in the Royal Navy. He had served in a variety of ranks and on a number of ships. He was on HMS London when it was sent to repatriate citizens from Malta at a time when there was the possibility of conflict. He was serving on HMS Fife when it was deployed to the Falklands. He served on ships when various incidents happened, including patrolling the Northern Seas during the Cold War. He remembers being on high alert, making sure that as an engineer his department could give command the assurance that the ship could float, move and fight effectively. Failure to do this was not ever an option. Lionel is proud of his service in this regard.

He recalls one of his biggest adventures on HMS Sirius when she was docked in Banbury Australia in 1988. Lionel served on this ship for nearly two years as a Deputy Marine Engineer. He was called upon as a junior officer to deal with what was a serious fuel leak due to a damaged fuel tank in the boiler room. No other senior officer was on board at the time as it was a time for personnel to take a break. The potential fuel leak had to be dealt with as it could compromise the ship's ability to go to sea. Such an issue would be classed as an operational defect. As Lionel was the only officer on board, he decided to take action, to get this defect fixed. Lionel had to get the appropriate signals off to command in London as well as find an appropriate company to perform the task and order fuel to replace that which was lost.

He was now ready to prepare for retirement and so, did a course to secure a smooth transition into civilian life. He was pleased to have the opportunity to plan and prepare for a life beyond this successful career he could not have imagined all those years ago when he had accidentally, entered the Careers' Office with his brother.

As an officer in the Royal Navy, when you reached the age of 50 and had not achieved the rank of Commander, you had to leave. This was the policy when Lionel was a serving officer. Therefore, at the age of 50 and having served for 30 years, Lionel left the Royal Navy.

Approximately 14 months later, he was invited to re-join as a Full Time Reserve Service (FTRS) officer. In this role he completed a further 10 years' service. AS an FTRS officer he was involved in several different roles which included taking part in training rationalising across the three branches of the armed forces. Lionel was involved directly in looking at risks and assumptions, visiting the various bases and developing a database to support this project. His final role was working as a staff officer heading the Fleet Security Warning, Alert and Reporting Point. This role lasted three years.

Looking back on his long naval career, there are some issues that he still mulls over. For example, the issues relating to race and bigotry. When these happened, Lionel often had to rely on, mostly, a common-sense approach to the treatment he received or comments made to him about his colour. One incident came to mind in the remembering. It related to his promotion in 1987, to the rank of Sub-Lieutenant, at Greenwich. He had done very well on the course. Unusually, he had been called in to a one-to-one meeting with the Commodore. Junior officers would not normally have such an opportunity to be in a meeting with such a senior person. The Commodore explained that Lionel had done so well that he would be awarded first place and would be awarded a prize in a ceremony in the Hall. An award of this distinction would be made at a time when the armed forces were being criticised for the amount of racism which seemed to be in evidence.

The Commodore continued to discuss with Lionel, how being presented with first prize might be seen as a tokenism, *"We are giving it to him because he is black."*. He told Lionel that he was getting first place because he was the best and therefore deserving of it. Lionel was asked whether, given the weighted environment at the time, he wanted to take second prize and avoid the potential comments. Lionel was very clear in his mind. He had achieved the best results. He was not going to back off because of other people's nastiness. He was going to take his first and well-deserved prize. The Commodore was being sensitive to the atmosphere of the time, but accepted Lionel's decision and the prize was awarded. Unsurprisingly, there were comments overheard which suggested that very thing the Commodore had feared. Lionel merely raised his head, collected his prize and moved on with his career.

That approach served him well and he was able to survive and thrive in his career. It was not easy, but he was assertive in moving forward with his coping mechanism. In his various roles, he line managed civilian personnel, prepared relevant reports, including some which supported more senior officers to answer parliamentary questions at short notice. Lionel has contributed massively in his various levels of service to the Royal Navy and therefore to the Monarch and to the country.

Lionel's first year of full retirement was very good. He found himself far too busy enjoying his freedom, to miss the Navy. He had served his time. He decided that he did not have to work. He still continues to have some relationship with other navy officers through his attendance at the local Wardroom at HMS Sultan.

Lionel Winston is a man of intellect, skill and resilience; someone who exudes confidence and gravitas. His service to the Royal Navy and to the Queen and country cannot be questioned; nor can his loyalty and commitment to their defence.

He has served with honour, courage and with a level of expertise which has benefitted the technical teams he has led or with whom he has shared his expertise during their training.

He is a serious man with a great sense of humour. He has wonderful support from his devoted wife Vanessa, and the rest of his family and friends. He remains living close to the sea, viewing and enjoying its might on a daily basis.

Lionel is not finished yet. He contributes to his local community through his charity work. He has more stories to share. We hope to hear about and read them over the coming years.

We salute you Lieutenant Commander Lionel Winston, MBE.

Photo by Gill Shaw

Chief Petty Officer Fred Coke

Fred came from Jamaica at age 11, to join his family in London. He attended school in Willesden, North West London. He was one of only five Black children in that school. Fred was good at art and wood carving. He entered an art competition which was being run by the London School of Art and Carving. They accepted his work and with the encouragement of his art teacher, he was keen to attend the prestigious college. However, his father was not keen on the idea, fearing that he would be unable to make a living from it, so that potential career was stopped in its tracks.

Fred left school at age 15 to take up an apprenticeship in electrical and mechanical work. His brother was already working in the electrical company, which serviced laboratory equipment across London.

Whilst at school, he showed a great talent in boxing and was selected to be in the team that went to box in Berlin, Germany. The Berlin experience took place during work-time. Fred was not given time-off to compete in this special event. He decided however, that he would take the week-off to in order to compete. Fred's decision did not go down well with his employers and as a result, they cancelled his day-release and terminated his apprenticeship. It was then too late to undertake another apprenticeship.

During his apprenticeship, Fred used to visit a local café and as he was no longer training his visits ceased, which left him understandably, feeling down. The café he used to visit was owned by a man who had previously served as a Chief Officer in the Navy. He sat with Fred and went through information about the Navy and encouraged him to join-up.

Fred thought long and hard about a career in the Navy and he decided eventually, that he would go ahead and apply. His application was successful and at age 18 he set off to Portsmouth to begin his basic training which took place at shore-based HMS Raleigh.

He started his Navy career as a mid-shipman. He was one of only three young Black men when he joined up. He found himself with only one other Black person on his first ship and only five of them on his second ship, HMS Hermes, an aircraft carrier. As there were so few of them, these young Black men tended to gravitate towards each other and developed a positive relationship during their time on the ship.

The average age of the men in Fred's first year was only 18 years. Fred worked towards becoming a Marine engineer. He was subject to individual performance reviews every six-months. Promotion was based on examinations, written and oral, as well as physical fitness. The exams would usually include a timed exercise to resolve defined but complex problems which was designed to test the skills of the candidates.

There were two branches of engineering career in the Navy and Fred decided to follow a Marine engineering path. He did very well in his exams and was successful in getting through the rigorous Board scrutiny. He became Chief Petty Officer Marine Engineering Artificer, the top non-commissioned officer rank in the Royal Navy. In that position, Fred supervised nine-men and was in charge of a broad range of equipment. When he was on Watch duty, during his time on board ship as the Chief, he reported directly to the Captain.

Although Fred achieved the top rank of a non-Commissioned Officer by the age of 40, he recalls thinking that the salary was not particularly good and had considered applying to become a Commissioned Officer but later decided not to pursue this.

Fred had been a talented boxer before he joined the Navy. He had the opportunity to box for the Navy but in his mind, focusing on boxing would limit him from being involved in other activities. He was clear that being an engineer would be where his focus should be. That was the area in which he spent his time studying and increasing his skills and experience.

Fred's focus was on developing his engineering skills and he studied hard. In this way, he achieved rapid promotion. He read extensively to learn what he needed to, in order to achieve promotion and progress in his career. In this regard, Fred achieved success and was noticed by his superiors. He served at all three Naval Bases - Chatham, Plymouth and Portsmouth.

He served approximately two-and-a-half years on board ship at a time and similar amount of time on shore. He would normally complete a course first on shore, followed by time on a ship. Each ship was different and the engineering demands varied. Therefore, a six-week training period was required, to be competent and confident to undertake what was necessary to ensure that the ship was in a ready state to sail and to take part in action as required.

When Fred was close to ending a period of service with a particular ship, he would ensure there was an effective and efficient hand-over period of at least one week, before the outgoing officer was relieved. That was a critical process to enable a smooth transfer and continuity of engineering support for each ship and fleet. In

Fred's mind and in the diligent way he carried out his duties, this standard of handover, was vital and non-negotiable.

While on board or in onshore positions, Fred would keep fit and engage in reading and studying. He was very focused on keeping himself abreast of and updating himself on the latest technical developments and paying great attention in respect of his skills and ability to support the Navy's engineering expectations.

During Fred's Navy service, he visited several countries. He went to many parts of the African continent. He was in Malta, Turkey, Kenya, Egypt, the Gulf States, Singapore, Hong Kong, the Philippines, Japan, New Zealand and the Falklands. Sometimes, a ship Fred served on might need a day, a week or six-to nine-weeks in port, for maintenance purposes. Fred would also be exposed to various military exercises, living in an area for weeks, or, as was the case in Singapore, for months. He went on exercises where there were simulations which included submarines, various ships and aircraft carriers. In a conflict situation, these activities would naturally form a part of what he could expect, such was the case when in April 1982, Fred saw action in the Falklands war when the Navy was dispatched to engage the Argentine Navy.

Chief Petty Officer Fred Coke was a loyal and committed serviceman. When he was age thirty-five, he briefly considered leaving the Navy but realised that he would need to have completed 22 years before he would be able to secure a satisfactory pension. Wisely, he reconsidered and proceeded to complete 22 years of service.

Fred's studying continued after leaving the Navy and he later successfully achieved a Bachelor's degree (B.Eng.) in Engineering.

Fred, as a British Caribbean man, delivered exemplary service on behalf of his country, the UK. Throughout his naval career, he focused on being a highly skilled professional and emphasised effective, efficient engineering support for all the ships on which he served. He ensured that each ship was prepared for all eventualities, during peacetime or otherwise. In his diligent manner, he left nothing to chance. In doing so, he always expected that high level of excellence throughout his management of every team for which he was responsible. His leadership was therefore of the highest standard.

This former Chief Petty Officer, Marine Engineering Artificer and Falklands War Veteran served in the Royal Navy from 1966 to 1988. He is described by a fellow Naval officer, Lionel Winston, as a *"giant of a man to me"*. Everyone who hears his name affirms this view of him, both as a person and as a retired officer of the British Armed Forces.

Chief Petty Officer Fred Coke could not have done more for the Navy, the country and the Queen. A truly remarkable and modest man.

Very sadly, we now mourn the loss, in September 2023, of this "Giant" of the Royal Navy and of the Veterans' organisation, the British Caribbean Veterans' Association, which he chaired.

As we extend our appreciation and recognition, we know that Fred will rest in peace as he is *"piped on board"* the Ship to take his final journey.

9. The Royal Air Force

The Royal Air Force (RAF) is the aerial warfare branch of the British Armed Forces. Formed on April 1 1918, during World War I, the RAF has played a significant role in many military conflicts and operations since then, including World War II, the Falklands War, the Gulf Wars and, more recently, the war in Afghanistan.

The mission of the RAF is to provide agile, adaptable, and capable air power, both in defence of the United Kingdom and its interests, and in support of national and international security objectives. The RAF operates a wide range of aircraft, including fighter jets, transport planes, helicopters, and unmanned aerial vehicles.

The RAF's capabilities are organised into several operational commands, including the Air Command, which oversees all air operations; the Joint Forces Command, which provides support to all branches of the British Armed Forces; and the Strategic Command, which is responsible for cyber and space operations.

The RAF also works closely with other national and international military organisations, including NATO, to support common defence and security objectives.

During the Cold War, the RAF's main focus was on defending the UK and Western Europe from the threat of Soviet aggression. Since the end of the Cold War, the RAF's role has shifted to a more global focus, with an emphasis on supporting international peacekeeping and humanitarian operations.

The RAF's range of aircraft has changed significantly over the last 60 years. During the Cold War, the RAF's main fighter aircraft were the English Electric Lightning and the McDonnell Douglas Phantom. Today, the RAF's primary fighter aircraft are the Eurofighter Typhoon and the Lockheed Martin F-35 Lightning II. The RAF has also acquired a range of new transport and surveillance aircraft, including the Airbus A400M Atlas and the Boeing E-7 Wedgetail.

The Caribbean aircraft engineers who served during the Cold War and for years afterwards were trained to provide high-level technical support across the range of aircraft, securing safe systems for the pilots going out on operations. Their lives depended on these skilled Caribbean men.

The RAF's organisational structure has undergone several changes since the 1960s. In the early 1990s, the RAF was restructured into a smaller, more agile force with a greater focus on expeditionary operations. In 2007, the RAF's major commands were reorganised into a single Air Command, which oversees all RAF operations. Some of the men interviewed would have experienced some of the early changes over their time in service.

The RAF has also benefited from significant advances in technology. Today, the RAF uses a range of advanced technologies, including satellite communications, unmanned aerial vehicles, and advanced sensors and targeting systems, to support its operations.

The Royal Air Force (RAF) is organised into several major commands, each with specific responsibilities and specialisms. Many of these specialisms attracted the interest of new Caribbean recruits into the RAF. Unfortunately, for many of them, their options appeared limited, often by the lack of information about these different but fascinating career pathways that could have been pursued in the RAF.

Air Command is the primary command of the RAF, responsible for all air operations, including defence of UK airspace, international peacekeeping and humanitarian operations, and expeditionary air operations. Air Command is also responsible for the RAF's training and education programmes, as well as its research and development activities.

The RAF's Support Command is responsible for providing support services to the rest of the RAF, including logistics, communications, medical services, and personnel support. Many Caribbean airmen contributed within the remit of these services.

Joint Helicopter Command is responsible for all of the RAF's helicopter operations, including support to ground forces, medical evacuation, search and rescue, and other missions. Again, Caribbean men and women contributed to this overall umbrella service.

RAF Intelligence, Surveillance, Target Acquisition and Reconnaissance (ISTAR) Force is the RAF's specialist unit for intelligence, surveillance, and reconnaissance missions. It operates various aircraft and other platforms, including unmanned aerial vehicles, to collect and analyse information for military and civilian purposes.

RAF Strike Command is responsible for the RAF's strike operations, including operating the F-35 Lightning II fighter aircraft and developing advanced weapons systems.

RAF Space Command is a new command, established in 2021, responsible for the RAF's space operations, including satellite communications, space-based reconnaissance and other missions.

Like the Army and Navy, the Royal Air Force (RAF) has a hierarchical rank structure, with officers and other ranks organised into different grades or levels.

The foremost commissioned ranks of the RAF, in descending order of seniority, include:
Air Chief Marshal
Air Marshal
Air Vice-Marshal
Air Commodore
Group Captain
Wing Commander
Squadron Leader
Flight Lieutenant
Flying Officer
Pilot Officer

In addition to these ranks, the RAF also has several non-commissioned officer (NCO) ranks, which show the seniority and experience of enlisted personnel. The main NCO ranks of the RAF, in descending order of seniority, are:
Warrant Officer

Flight Sergeant
Sergeant
Corporal
Leading Aircraftman / Leading Aircraftwoman
Senior Aircraftman / Senior Aircraftwoman
Aircraftman / Aircraftwoman

RAF officers are commissioned into the service and hold a commission from the Queen, while other ranks are enlisted personnel who serve under the command of officers. Officers are typically responsible for the leadership, management, and technical expertise required to operate and maintain RAF capabilities, while other ranks are responsible for carrying out the day-to-day tasks and operations required to support the RAF's mission.

Rest and Recuperation (R&R) in the Royal Air Force

The Royal Air Force (RAF) offers a variety of rest and recuperation (R&R) opportunities for its serving personnel, designed to provide a break from the demands of military service. It also helps to maintain morale and well-being.

People serving in the RAF are entitled to a certain amount of annual leave, which varies depending on their rank and length of service. Leave can be taken in blocks of several days or weeks, and can be used for a wide range of activities, from spending time with family and friends to pursuing hobbies or travel.

As part of rest and recuperation, service men and women also have opportunities to engage in a broad range of activities, such as sailing, mountaineering, rock climbing, sports and fitness. These activities help to maintain physical and mental health and promote teamwork and camaraderie.

The RAF provides its personnel with various welfare and support services, including counselling, financial advice, and family support. These services are designed to help personnel manage the stresses and challenges of military life and maintain their well-being. These welfare supports have been strengthened since many of the Caribbean interviewees left the Royal Navy.

Education and training opportunities have always been an important part of the Royal Navy's 'offer' to its recruits and service people. A number of Caribbean personnel took full advantage of those opportunities and studied hard, usually through long-distance learning programmes and achieved higher qualifications as a result.

It would be fair to say that, in recent years, there has been a greater emphasis on promoting the well-being of RAF personnel, recognising that maintaining mental and physical health is crucial for military effectiveness. This has led to a greater emphasis on activities like counselling, fitness, and education that support its staff's overall well-being.

Sport in the Royal Air Force

The sporting opportunities available to Royal Air Force (RAF) personnel have been quite diverse, often reflecting the sports that were popular in British culture over the years.

The RAF has a long tradition of holding inter-station competitions in different sports, including football, rugby, hockey, athletics, and boxing. These competitions were fiercely contested and offered service personnel the chance to represent their base or station in a competitive environment.

RAF personnel were often selected to represent their service in national and international sporting events. This included the Military World Games, the Commonwealth Games and the Olympic Games. These events allowed people with the opportunity to compete against some of the best athletes in the world.

The RAF had a number of sports associations that were designed to promote specific sports and support personnel who participated in them. These associations provided coaching, equipment, and funding for competitions.

The RAF also participated in inter-service competitions against the other branches of the British Armed Forces, including the Army and the Royal Navy. These competitions were highly competitive and offered personnel the chance to represent their service against their rivals.

Many Caribbean service personnel took full advantage of these opportunities, fulfilling their ambitions as well as those expected from the RAF's senior officers. One particularly fine example of a talented Caribbean is Roy Hunte, whose achievements across different sporting disciplines have been outstanding and, therefore, noteworthy.

Sergeant Roy Hunte (The Healer)

Roy Hunte was born in Guyana and came to join his mother and father in the UK at the age of nine. His parents had come to the UK in the late 1950s to make a new life for the family.

Roy and his brother Richard were left with their grandma. His sister Loraine and other brother Roger stayed with their other grandparents. They did a wonderful job during the years of his parents' absence.

Roy recalls the flight from Guyana, when he and his brother were making so much noise that someone said to them, *"If you don't stop making all that noise, we'll give you a parachute and you can jump off the plane."*

When Roy arrived in the UK, the family first lived in Tottenham, before moving to Edmonton in London in the early 1960s. He remembers the cold and snow in his new country. He joined the local primary school, being one of only two black children in the school at the time. A memory which still persists after all this time is being part of the school play. Roy was cast as a slave, singing, 'Nobody knows the trouble I've seen'. That memory remains vivid in his mind.

Roy recalls wanting to be a policeman. He was told that, *"In a line of police officers if you're the only black one, they would be throwing eggs at you."* This put him off that particular career. He then decided that he wanted to be a PE teacher but being more interested in sports than academics, ruled that particular option out.

Roy was in the Boys' Brigade and also joined Enfield Harriers Athletics Club as a teenager. Here he was successful in a number of events - pole vaulting, hurdling, and the high jump. He became the high jump champion for Middlesex Schools and was captain of gymnastics and athletics. He represented Middlesex in the English Schools Championships. Roy was an exceptional hurdler and in 1970, broke the Middlesex Schools 3'6", 110m hurdles record. As hurdles no longer include that particular height, having moved down from 3'6" to 3'3", Roy still holds that record.

On leaving school Roy had not attained the academic qualifications required to gain access to college in which to study PE. Roy started the Lucas Tooth Gymnasium Instructors' course, which took 2 years to qualify. During this time Roy took on other employment in order to gain life experience and survive! These jobs ranged from driving, building, factory worker and postman!

Roy's friend, Steve Clark, told him that he was planning to join the Royal Air Force as a Physical Training (PTI) instructor. To Roy's mind, that sounded like a great idea.

Aged 18, Roy went to live with his uncle, Sammy, who had been a Medic in the RAF.

Roy now decided to join the RAF as a PT instructor, a career he had always wanted to pursue. Around this time a knee injury, surgery, and the subsequent recovery and rehabilitation sparked Roy's interest in becoming a remedial gymnast, working with people returning from injury. At the same time, he was introduced to boxing by his friend Delvin Whyte.

When Roy applied to the RAF Careers' Office, they explained that to be a PT Instructor, it was important to be proficient in a number of sports. By now, aged 20, Roy was a very good boxer and was the North West London Heavyweight Champion, representing North West London against the RAF. Roy knocked out his RAF opponent and afterwards, he spoke to Delroy Parkes, one of the RAF boxers. Delroy introduced Roy to the RAF Manager, who asked for Roy's details as well. He also asked for the address of the careers' office he had been applying to. That conversation was the catalyst to Roy joining the RAF, because two weeks later Roy was on his way to RAF St Athan to be assessed.

Roy's career in the RAF then began with basic training at Swinderby, where he successfully concluded his training with a Passing Out Parade attended by his mother. During his training, he spent 3 weeks at RAF Abingdon, for parachute jumping.

After completing basic training and parachute jumping, Roy went to St. Athan for six months of PT Instructor's training. In December 1974, he was excelling during the gymnastics phase of his training, but he was unfortunately involved in an accident while somersaulting over a piece of equipment called the Six-foot Box.

However, during one of the somersaults, he landed badly and injured his neck.

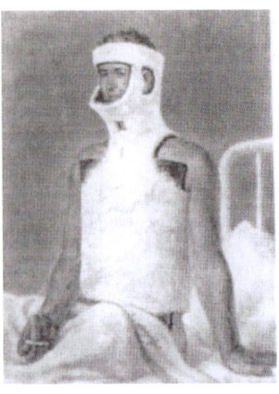

Initially, the injury did not seem serious, but a few days later, an X-ray revealed that he had fractured bones in his neck. He had to wear a collar and a full-length plaster cast down to his waist. As a result, he was unable to participate in the outdoor activity phase of his PTI training course and was left in a 20-man dormitory on his own.

The injury left Roy feeling depressed, and at his lowest point, he even briefly considered taking his own life. However, he ultimately decided to get himself as fit as possible. He was determined to recover and was grateful for the support of Chief Instructor Danny Williams, who persuaded the authorities to make sure that, despite Roy's unexpected injury, but because of his undoubted talent, he should remain on the PTI course and achieve his full qualification. Danny Williams was a former Mr Wales Body Building Champion and the PTI Course's chief instructor. Looking back, Roy realises how close he came to becoming paralysed from his neck injury and losing his military career. He will always be thankful for the support he received from Danny, that gave him the opportunity to achieve his goals.

After graduation, Roy was posted to RAF Brize Norton, where he continued to work on his physical fitness despite wearing a neck collar. He led and participated in weight training and circuit training classes, and led physical fitness/conditioning training for the rugby and football teams, and lunchtime sessions all in addition to his regular military duties.

After 18 months at Brize Norton, now with the rank of Corporal, Roy had a number of postings, firstly to RAF Innsworth, then to Chessington the Joint Services Remedial Unit, and later to the Queen Elizabeth Military Hospital in Woolwich, before going back to Chessington as a Remedial Gymnast in 1980. In all these posts, Roy worked as a PTI, helping other service personnel recover from their injuries and get back to peak physical condition. He was awarded several commendations for the excellence of his work.

Prior to his neck injury, Roy was an accomplished boxer and had already made a name for himself in the RAF Lord Wakefield Championship. He won several titles and competed for the England national boxing team. Roy was the RAF boxing champion in 1975, and went on to win the Combined Services boxing championship in 1976. His skills earned him a place on the England boxing team, where he defeated his opponent from Ireland in 1976. Roy won the fight on points.

Cpl Royston Hunte RAF Heavyweight Champion and Great Britian Representative, a devasting puncher in his time 1976. He missed his ABA final because he was stuck in a London traffic jam!

English heavyweight, Ralston Hunt, scores with a left on his way to a points win over John McLoughlin.

He made the Olympic selection squad in 1976, fighting a man who was much heavier and taller - being 16 stone and 6'6" tall. At this time, there was also another boxer named George Gilbody. Roy and George were the fittest in the squad and got selected to fight in a GB versus USA competition at the Wembley Arena. Roy lost his fight to Jimmy Clark of the USA. Roy never made it to the Olympics. Nonetheless, Roy's accomplishments as an amateur boxer are notable, and he is recognised as one of the best amateur boxers and hardest hitting punchers to come out of the UK in the 1970s.

Roy later became a bobsledder. He was in Winterburg, Germany, when the RAF bobsleigh team broke the British record going so fast that they hit the sides and he ended up with concussion. The following year, he was appointed as trainer and physical therapist to the British bobsleigh team.

In the 1984 Winter Olympics in Sarajevo, Roy was a remedial gymnast for the GB bobsleigh team, when his services were called for by the gold medal winning ice dancers Torvill and Dean! He was fortunate to have met so many talented and interested people, including Royalty.

In 1985, Roy qualified as a physiotherapist. A few years later, Roy was physiotherapist for the British Bobsleigh Team at the Calgary Winter Olympics in 1988.

He was also the Jamaican bobsleigh team's physiotherapist, a role he performed two years before the Olympics. The picture on the left shows Roy (in red and blue) standing behind the Jamaican Team in the 1988 Olympics. The team's story was later adapted into the popular movie "Cool Runnings," which helped to popularise the sport of bobsleigh and raise awareness about the Jamaican team's accomplishments.

He was privileged to be asked to provide physiotherapy to Prince Albert of Monaco, who was also competing.

Roy was also proud to have had agreement from the RAF, to provide support to several other important elite sports people, including the English ski jumper and Olympian, Michael David Edwards, otherwise known as 'Eddie the Eagle'.

While working with the RAF Ski Team, a chance encounter with rower and Olympic medallist who was later Knighted by the Queen, Steve Redgrave, led to Roy becoming a physiotherapist for the GB Olympic Rowing Team for a 5-year period.

Roy was involved in supporting the London Marathon as the Physio for the elite athletes from 1988 to 2019. This was a position he treasured and remembers with pride, treating some of the fastest marathon runners in the world. Roy's contributions to the London Marathon and his work with the elite athletes have been widely recognised and praised.

As he reflects on his time in the RAF, Roy particularly wants to mention Flight Lieutenant Frank Strang, who told him on arrival at RAF Lossiemouth, to go and set up the base physiotherapy department. It was one of the most enjoyable times in his entire career.

Over the course of his career, Roy is proud to have received several RAF commendations and mentions for his work in various sports.

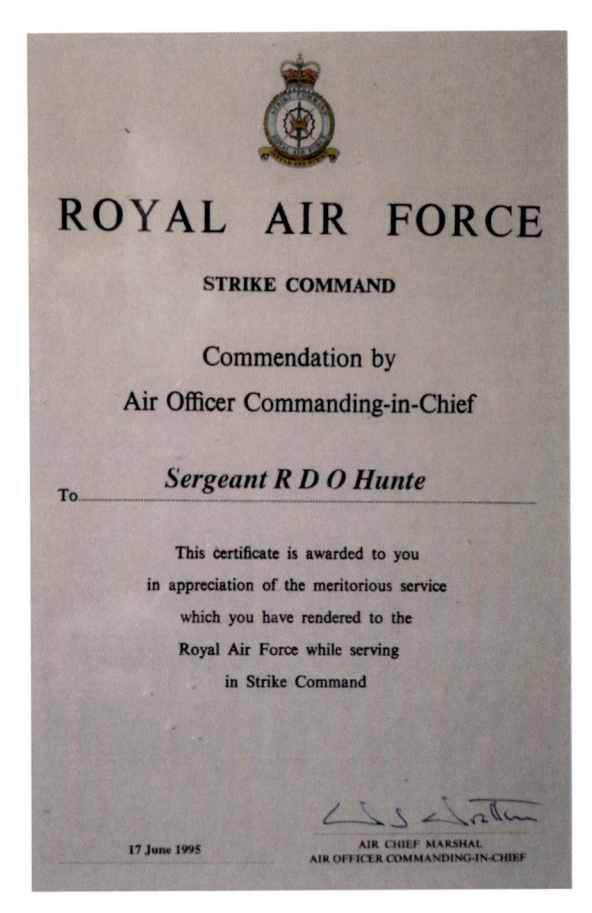

ROYAL AIR FORCE

STRIKE COMMAND

Commendation by
Air Officer Commanding-in-Chief

To Sergeant R D O Hunte

This certificate is awarded to you in appreciation of the meritorious service which you have rendered to the Royal Air Force while serving in Strike Command

17 June 1995

AIR CHIEF MARSHAL
AIR OFFICER COMMANDING-IN-CHIEF

In addition, Roy has been featured in various media outlets and publications, including newspapers and sports magazines. His work and contributions to sports have been praised and acknowledged.

Roy's sporting achievements were facilitated by being a member of the Armed Forces.

He was an airman first, with all the appropriate skills and aptitude that involved.

His sporting prowess was obvious before he joined the RAF and was certainly recognised by his peers and senior officers, and utilised within and outside the forces. He remains immensely proud of his achievements across the full spectrum of his work.

He was given an impressive leaving present, which included words which touched him, *"Mr Roy 'The Boy' Hunte, Thank you for your hard work, dedication and loyalty to physical training and rehabilitation at RAF Lossiemouth 1992 - 2018. We're only a phone call away."*

After serving his country for nearly 26 years (25 years and 200 days), Roy left the RAF in February 2000, at the age of 47. He continued to work for the RAF as a civilian physiotherapist and was commended for his work for them. Roy set up his own private practice, helping people from all walks of life to overcome their physical injuries and challenges. The work that Roy did to support others, both in the RAF and after he left, led to a wonderful nickname, 'The Healer'.

A portrait of him entitled *'The Healer'*, was completed in 2018, by a well-known artist, Graham Pook.

Throughout his life, Roy has contributed greatly to various charitable endeavours including the Princes Trust and Cancer Research and was pleased to meet, when he was Prince Charles, King Charles III.

He has raised nearly £100,000 over the years for the Children in Need appeals, and also fundraised for a number of other charities.

Roy was recognised for his charity work when he was honoured to meet Her Majesty, The Queen.

Roy is very much involved in his local community, including being the Chairman of his County's Swing Band. He is also well-known locally as their alto saxophonist.

Despite facing numerous obstacles throughout his career, Roy has never lost sight of his passion for helping others. He remains a respected figure in the sphere of UK physical therapy to this day. Looking back to his youth, he would advise that young man to:

"Do everything! Remember however, that you're not invincible. You have to be better than everyone else. Work hard and dance to the RAF tune, let them see you doing this and you will succeed."

He was delighted to be asked to carry the Baton for the Commonwealth Games, the memory of which he will always keep in his heart. It was a wonderful experience.

He feels blessed by the connections he has made, both in his military life and outside it. He knows that he has been fortunate. He was in the right place at the right time, has seen and done a lot, and for that he is enormously grateful. But he does not feel that the service and loyalty of the Caribbean men and women who joined the UK Armed Forces has been sufficiently acknowledged.

"It's a travesty. However, it is what it is", he said.

Sergeant Roy Hunte has provided exceptional service throughout and beyond his time in the Royal Air Force and should be commended for all that he has done.

Team Building in the Royal Air Force

Team building has always been an essential part of Royal Air Force (RAF) culture. As with other branches of the Armed Forces, the RAF has a long tradition of emphasising teamwork and camaraderie to achieve common goals, whether on the ground or in the air.

All RAF personnel underwent basic training, which emphasised teamwork, discipline, and physical fitness. Basic training was designed to instil the values and ethos of the RAF and prepare recruits for the demands of military life.

As the RAF is organised into squadrons, typically composed of a mix of non-commissioned officers and other ranks, it encourages teamwork and camaraderie to achieve common goals.

Operational deployments provided its staff with the opportunity to work together in high-pressure environments. This included deployments to conflict zones such as the Falklands, Iraq, and Afghanistan. These deployments emphasised teamwork, communication, and the importance of looking out for one another.

As mentioned earlier, the RAF encouraged personnel to participate in sports and adventure training activities. These activities gave them opportunities to work together towards a common goal and to develop trust and respect for one another.

Leadership training emphasised the importance of effective communication, delegation, and team building. This training was designed to help staff at all officer levels, in particular, to become better leaders and team players.

Basic Training in the Royal Air Force

The Royal Air Force (RAF) has a rigorous training programme, which is designed to prepare recruits for the demands of military service. The training is divided into four phases.

In the first phase of training, recruits learn basic military skills, such as drill, weapons handling, fitness, and fieldcraft. They also receive instruction on RAF values, ethics, and the law of armed conflict. By the 1990s, this part of the training was refined to include more specialist training, which was intended to prepare the recruits for their specific roles within the RAF. The basic training was reduced to around nine weeks. There were further changes in the 2000s. A new recruit training programme called the Initial Force Protection Training (IFPT), aimed to teach those fresh-faced young men and women the skills they would need to protect themselves and their colleagues. This programme focused on weapons handling, self-defence and first aid. The length of the training went back up to 10 weeks.

After completing recruit training, recruits went on to do specialist training in their chosen trade. This training lasted anywhere from several weeks to several months, depending on the trade. Some of the trades included aircraft maintenance, logistics, air traffic control, intelligence, and others.

Once recruits completed their specialist training, they would undergo operational training, which prepares them for their specific role within the RAF. This training was usually conducted on the job and would last for several months to a year.

Throughout their RAF career, they continued to receive ongoing training and development to ensure they remained current and proficient in their role. These trainees would be subjected to examinations, which they would be required to pass in order to progress further. In addition to those completing these training phases successfully, all RAF service personnel are expected to maintain a high level of physical fitness and military discipline throughout their service. The basic training process in the RAF has undergone some changes over the years. During the Windrush generation's time, the general training process was focused on developing military discipline and basic skills such as drill, weapons handling, fitness, and survival skills. The length of basic training was around 12 weeks.

While there may have been some cases of discrimination or bias in the recruitment process in the past, the RAF has reportedly made some efforts in more recent times to promote equal opportunities and diversity in its workforce. Additionally, there have been various policies and legislation over the years designed to promote diversity and equality of opportunity in the Armed, including the Race Relations Act of 1976 and the Equality Act of 2010.

Caribbean heritage recruits should have had access to the same range of trades and opportunities as all other recruits in the RAF during the period these men and women served. RAF recruitment policies and practices were usually based on merit. Therefore, candidates were supposed to be selected based on their abilities, qualifications, and interests. The men whose stories are included here do not accept that this access was always fully equal and fully open to them at the time they served in the RAF.

Over the years, the RAF has had many senior officers of different backgrounds, but very few are people of Caribbean heritage who were various trades and roles. Most people from that background who served tended to be seen in more minor roles. Few achieved higher ranks. None of them were at the highest levels; more were to be seen in the more junior officer roles. This is especially concerning when you look back to Caribbean men's contribution as pilots in WWII. It is as if it was difficult, impossible even, to recognise that these people were perfectly capable and could indeed provide 'normal' high-skilled service equal to that of their white colleagues.

Looking back in history, however, to WWII, there was Ulric Cross, a Trinidadian lawyer, judge, diplomat, and RAF officer who played a significant role during the war and in the period following it. Cross was born in Port of Spain, Trinidad, in 1917 and studied law at Oxford University in the UK. In 1941, he joined the RAF as a navigator and flew missions in Europe and Africa during World War II. He was awarded the Distinguished Flying Cross for his service. After the war, Cross was admitted to the bar in England and worked as a barrister. He then returned to Trinidad and Tobago, where he became one of the first black lawyers in the country. He was also appointed to the High Court of Justice and served as a judge in several Caribbean countries.

In the 1960s, Cross became involved in diplomatic service and was appointed Trinidad and Tobago's High Commissioner to the UK, and later Ghana. He also played a key role in the establishment of the Caribbean Community (CARICOM).

Cross continued to be involved in various social and political causes throughout his life. He was a founding member of the Trinidad and Tobago Human Rights Association and was involved in the anti-apartheid movement in South Africa.

In 2013, a documentary film called "An Uncommon Soldier" was made about Cross's life and achievements. Ulric Cross passed away in 2019 at the age of 96.

There were a number of Caribbean heritage RAF personnel who served between 1960 and the millennium, and some have made notable contributions to the RAF and to British society more broadly.   A tiny minority did break through. Examples of some who pushed their way through the various ranks include the following:

Flight Lieutenant Wayne Howell - born in Barbados and came to the UK at the age of 8 to join his family. He was to achieve the RAF's highest NCO rank of WO before being commissioned as an officer. He provided one of the longest, if not the longest number of years' service (48 years) to the RAF. An impressive achievement.

Squadron Warrant Officer Winston Alleyne - arrived in the UK from Barbados in 1958. He was only 17 years old and travelled on his own. He became the first black man in history to reach the rank of Warrant Officer in the RAF Regiment. Alleyne retired from active service in 1996. Unfortunately, this brave, highly competent leader in the RAF was only to live as a civilian for a further four years as he sadly died three years ago, in October, 2020.

Warrant Officer Donald Campbell - born in Jamaica and provided significant service to the RAF over 36 years.

Sergeant Noel Brathwaite, MBE - came from Barbados at the age of 16 and served in the RAF, boy and man, for 23 years.

Flight Lieutenant Arthur Wint was born in Plowden, Jamaica. He joined the RAF during World War II and served as a navigator in bomber planes. He was later awarded an MBE for his service to athletics and was the first Jamaican to win an Olympic gold medal in the 400 meters at the 1948 London Olympics. He was also awarded the Jamaican Order of Distinction for his service to charities and schools. He became Jamaica's High Commissioner to London in 1974 and served for four years. He then returned to his homeland to continue his work as a doctor at Linstead Hospital. He passed away in 1992 at the age of 72.

Flight Sergeant Peter Brown - born in Jamaica and following his admittance at age 17 to the Air Force, served in WWII. He died in London in December 2022 at the age of 96.

These are just a few excellent examples of the many Caribbean heritage personnel who significantly contributed to the RAF and to British society. Here are a few, in more detail.

Flight Lieutenant Wayne Howell

Wayne Howell was born in Barbados and raised by his grandmother and extended family. Wayne's father had left for England in 1956, when Wayne was just three months old. His mother had followed two years later.

Wayne's parents had settled in and around Wednesbury, West Midlands. His mother had trained to be a nurse in Shrewsbury whilst his father did his motor mechanic training in Wolverhampton.

It was common practice for Windrush parents, once settled in the UK, to send for their children in the Caribbean and so Wayne and his older brother were *"called for"* in the autumn of 1964. Wayne, his parents and brother were born British and remained so, as Barbados did not achieve independence until November,1966. However, due to emerging issues in the United Kingdom surrounding status of Caribbeans like them, his parents had taken action to reaffirm that status via citizenship applications. Wayne was second generation 'Windrush' and was therefore not affected by the changes in government immigration rules in the early 1970s. His family had by then obtained British Citizenship and each of them had their own respective UK passports.

For many reasons, eight-year-old Wayne initially found life in the UK very challenging. Racial tension in the West Midlands and the cold UK climate made life demanding for a newly arrived immigrant from the tropical West Indies. For Wayne, *"That first UK winter was extremely cold, but getting to school in England was an obstacle in itself."*

Life in those early years in the West Midlands was not what he expected. He often wished he was back in Barbados. Being called racist names, being spat at on the way to school by both adults and other children in the Wednesbury area. He would often have to cross the road earlier to avoid trouble. It was a daily challenge in the mid-sixties. *"These experiences left indelible memories"*, he said.

Inside the home, additionally, Wayne and his brother were growing and developing their own personalities. This made life difficult living with parents for the first time; parents one of whom they had not seen since Wayne was a baby, the other since he was a toddler. His parents were not used to having children *"with a voice"*, around the home. There were inevitably some tensions which were not easily resolved. Things came to a head and this led to a significant change in this young man's life. *"I didn't really get on with my parents. Eventually, I was taken into care with the Barnardo's home 'Corris House' in Much Wenlock, Shropshire."*

The Corris House Barnado's Home at Southfield Road, Much Wenlock, opened in 1929. It provided long-term accommodation for 50 boys up to the age of 14. The Barnado's charity changed its focus from direct care of children to fostering and adoption, renaming itself Dr Barnado's in 1965, before simplifying the name even further in 1988, to Barnardo's.

This life-changing move for Wayne also meant moving to a school in Shropshire in 1968. It marked a massive turning point in his life. There were very few black or Asian people in Much Wenlock, outside of the Barnardo's home, so nobody had any sort of pre- conceived opinions. In Wayne's mind therefore, it was a really great place to be. He really loved and appreciated much of that time in his young life. So much of what was organised for him as well as the structure and care he received in the House had a life-changing and long-lasting effect on him. It is likely that the life Wayne enjoyed in Corris House, set the scene for a future in the military.

Wayne recalls that whilst he still faced challenges at the secondary school with his initial bad behaviour, he eventually "came good". He was awarded the Form Prize in his third year (Year 9). He was so happy. Wayne went on to become House Captain (Year 10) and in his final year, was elected Head Boy by students and staff. Wayne was justly proud of his achievements. This was also a positive reflection on the William Brookes Comprehensive school, the students and the people of Much Wenlock. *"I guess, that's what got me in the mood for taking responsibility – when joining the Armed Forces. Within eight years I was promoted to Sergeant."*

Barnardo's had provided Wayne with a more caring, disciplined and structured upbringing, for which he later became a role model. *"I attended the Buckingham Palace Royal Garden Party in 2016 with many other Barnardo children from across the world, celebrating the 150th birthday of Barnardo's."*

At school Wayne realised his passion for sport. He played football for Shropshire Under-19 Schoolboys. He also played on pitches at various Royal Air Force (RAF) stations. Meeting RAF personnel made him consider a Service career. He left Corris house in 1972 and returned home to Wednesbury, and then went to Bilston College with the intention of becoming a school teacher. After a year, Wayne decided to pursue a career in the military, specifically the RAF. He went to the Careers' Office in Wolverhampton. Despite his apparent 'over- qualifications', he pursued his application and was successful in enlisting for the RAF in July 1973, as a potential new member of the RAF Regiment. Travel Warrant in hand, and £2 in his pocket, young Wayne set off from Wolverhampton Station to Newark-on-Trent Station, where he was met by Corporal Allsop and Sergeant Bastable. From the train station, he travelled on a coach full of the new recruits, all men, to RAF Swinderby. In those days, the women trained at RAF Hereford. On the coach there were two black recruits, Wayne and one other. Because Wayne had been used to the discipline and guidelines at Barnardo's, he was quite settled in adapting to the military lifestyle. The six-weeks went very well. Some recruits unfortunately, did not make the grade or have the determination to succeed and requested their Premature Voluntary Release (PVR).

Wayne graduated from RAF Catterick Depot in November 1973 with the "Best Student" award for his intake. Having successfully completed recruit training and passed out from RAF Swinderby. Wayne was firmly and proudly now a part of the Royal Air Force, albeit still a Trainee. He was now ready to begin his Trade Training to become a Gunner, at Catterick. This experience was completely different from those first six-week basic. It was primarily the physical, robustness and camaraderie, with over 50% of the entry opting for PVR within four weeks. It was tough.

The RAF Regiment is part of the Royal Air Force and it operates as a specialist Corps. It was founded in 1942 carrying out soldiering functions related to the delivery of air power. Some examples of its work include non-combatant evacuation, recovery of downed aircrew and defence of airfields. Some of their functions may include aggressive patrolling and defending areas around airfields and working jointly with the Army where required. The Regiment, through its Gunners' arm are trained in infantry tactics, force protection, fieldcraft, sniper and Special Forces Support Group operations. Nowadays, RAF Regiment personnel undertake recruit training at RAF Halton before a 20-week gunner course at RAF Honington. In the 1970s when Wayne was undertaking his training, the training was done at Catterick. It is the RAF Regiment instructors who provide training for all Royal Air Force personnel in basic force protection. Such training would include first aid, weapon handling and other vital defence skills needed in modern military operations.

Members of the RAF Regiment within the RAF, used to be known as "The Regiment", "Rock Apes" (from the Rock of Gibraltar connection) or "Rocks". The RAF Regiment is a vital part of the Armed Forces' response not only for the prevention of enemy attack but also their speedy response in securing continuity of operations after an attack has taken place.

As a member of the RAF Regiment, the Squadrons Wayne served on were responsible for ground and low-level air defence of RAF bases around the world. Wayne became a highly competent operative with the Rapier missile Low-Level Air Defence system, which was first introduced to the RAF Regiment in 1973 - 2004. As a Sergeant, he had a very significant role in respect of deployment of this specialist system within the RAF's area of responsibility. Wayne took his responsibilities very seriously and was effective in their implementation.

His first operational tour was to RAF Aldergrove, Northern Ireland, in 1974. Over the next 26 years, Wayne served on numerous RAF Regiment Squadrons across the UK. He was promoted to Corporal whilst on his first German tour in March 1979. He then achieved the rank of Sergeant on his return to RAF Swinderby, and then to Flight Sergeant in 1989, with a posting to RAF Greenham Common. He achieved the rank of WO whilst he was serving employed at RAF Halton on the Training Development and Support Unit (TDSU) which was based at RAF Halton.

Wayne served at several overseas' locations, including in three different RAF bases in Germany over a 15 year period. He was first deployed to the Falkland Islands in August 1982, with subsequent tours in February 1984, May 1992 and June 2010. He was with 37 Squadron, RAF Regiment, who were relieving 63 Squadron

RAF Regiment who had fought in the Falklands. As they were an air defence element of the Force Protection, the squadron were flown in a Hercules Transport aircraft, which had to be refuelled twice mid-air, travelling the 4,000 miles to RAF Port Stanley. As soon as the Hercules landed, it became very clear to him that he was very definitely in a war zone environment.

During Wayne's time of service, he was subject to some undesirable, discriminatory comments, including ones the perpetrators often described as *"a joke"* or *"banter"*. Wayne made it clear that he did not do banter, especially where race or religion was concerned. On a couple of occasions during his extended military career, he had to challenge the system, particularly given that he was a Sergeant, and other ethnic minority personnel looked to him for guidance and leading by example. Wayne believes that racial conduct and behaviour have improved immensely over the last 20 years, and continues to do so.

There were a number of black role models known to Wayne who had already achieved the rank of Warrant Officer in the RAF Regiment in this challenging period. Some of these men included Winston Alleyne, Kingsley Campbell and Chris Blackman. He served with Mr Campbell for over two years on 26 Squadron RAF Regiment, and met Flight Sergeant Alleyne in 1981 at RAF Catterick, and more regularly beyond 1983 when he became a member of the Rapier Force in Germany.

Other Afro-Caribbean personnel from the wider RAF such as Cliff Walker, had also achieved their Royal Warrant. Many more have since achieved their Royal Warrant. Wayne is full of admiration for all these competent, highly regarded Caribbean men.

However, despite this list of achievers, it must be noted that black officers were a rarity. It had been suggested to Wayne in the early 1980s that he should consider applying for a Commission. Given the RAF officer selection process, the prevailing racial climate and lack of transparency in the selection process, Wayne felt it prudent to continue moving through the non-commission officer ranks. Having achieved the rank of Warrant Officer he subsequently progressed to obtaining his Royal Warrant, in July 1999. A great achievement for this impressive, competent British Caribbean man.

In July 2000 Wayne completed the six-months of the Initial Officer Training (IOT) Course 184, graduating in the rank of Flying Officer.

He was awarded the D Squadron Commander's Prize; with his name 'Officer Cadet Howell' on the prize winner's board at Whittle Hall, RAF College Cranwell.

"I broke many barriers on the way up through the ranks, including being the first black Warrant Officer to complete IOT. Many black people had passed IOT and became officers in the RAF before me, but not someone who had already served 27 years and had their Royal Warrant."

Over the next 15 years as an officer, Wayne completed operational tours in Kuwait, Iraq and Afghanistan as a Force Protection Officer.

He also completed a six-month tour to Sierra-Leone as a UN Military Observer on Peacekeeping duties. He did this in the rank of Acting Squadron Leader.

In 2015, Wayne left the Regular RAF Service, re-joining the next day as a full-time Reservist focussing on Sport Safety. He accepted a staff post at the Directorate RAF Sport (DRS), RAF Halton. Here the focus was on sports' safety for over 50 sporting activities.

During his tenure at DRS, despite being over 60 years of age, Wayne took part in the Cresta Run in St Moritz. He also took part in Bobsleigh, Para-gliding, alpine ski racing, mountaineering and many more challenging sports, including Luge. Luge is one of the oldest winter sports. It involves competitors lying on their backs on a tiny sled, feet outstretched, racing down an icy track at high speeds and without brakes. Wonderful experiences for this highly active military man.

He retired from service life in 2021, but is still very active. Wayne loves sports. He has played almost every sport at some point in his career. Specifically, he played competitive football for over 25 years; cricket for 30 years, ran 16 marathons including in London, Nottingham, Berlin and Hong Kong.

Wayne met Violet, his wife of nearly 44 years in October 1977, whilst both were serving at RAF Gutersloh, an airbase located 60 miles North-East of Dortmund, Germany. Violet was a member of the Medical Admin Branch, serving for seven years. They married in October 1979, and are the proud parents of two grown-up sons Robert and Dean and grandparents to Mayson, their grandson.

Wayne is not a man who has stood still. He always sought opportunities to do more, to *"give back"*. He completed the Nijmegen Marches' event in the Netherlands (walking 25 miles each day for 4 days) for the 25th time earlier this year.

This international four-day march is the largest multiple day marching event in the world. The March always starts on the 3rd Tuesday of July, every year in Nijmegen, Netherlands. It is a means of promoting exercise and sport. The participants walk between 30 and 50 kilometres each day depending on their age and gender. On completion, they receive a royally approved medal. Most participants are civilians, but there are also a few thousand military personnel involved each year. Wayne's first 20 years of participation was as a member of the British Military Contingent (BMC), commencing the walk from Huemensoord Camp, located 5 kilometres south of Nijmegen. Huemensoord is the temporary military base and starting point for the military contingents from more than 25 countries. This year 47,000 registered for the start.

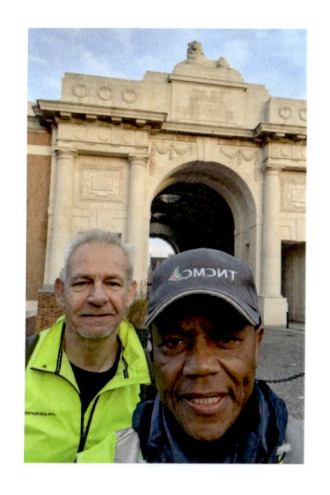

Wayne participated in 'The Long Walk Home', a 100-mile fundraising walk in November 2018, when 100 Veterans and serving personnel (all voluntary) walked from the infamous Menin Gate, Ypres, Belgium which in WWI was a horrific location of three great, bloody battles.

The 100-mile walk ended at the Cenotaph, London on the 2018 Armistice Day, commemorating 100 years since the WWI ended. Wayne's fundraising was in aid of Haig Housing. Haig Housing does some very important work helping British Veterans who have housing needs for over 100 years. This help is often provided to Veterans when they are preparing to transition into civilian life. While the organisation has over 1,500 properties across the country, there is still insufficient housing to meet the growing demands of this Veterans' group.

241

Fundraising such as that done by Wayne and the others who took part in the 'Long Walk Home', is vital to the work done by Haig Housing and other similar charities.

In October 2020, Wayne completed a 350-mile (25 miles per 12 days) Charity Walk with his friend Steven 'Walt' Disney. This charity walk, on behalf of The National Caribbean Monument Charity (TNCMC), raised money for a Caribbean monument at the National Memorial Arboretum (NMA). The walk was entitled 'From Ayr to Eternity'. 'Ayr' was significant as it was the place where Captain Walter Tull, the first black military Officer was trained in WWI and the 'NMA' being 'eternity'.

In October 2021, Wayne undertook a second 350-mile walk to raise money for the same cause. This walk entitled 'From Arras to Eternity', took place from Arras (France) back to the NMA The Arras reference was a reminder of the soldiers of the British West India Regiment who served during some of WWI's most hard-fought battles, including in Arras in 1917.

Altogether, across the three major battles, Somme, Arras and Passchendaele, nearly 1,500 men of the BWIR were killed during the conflict.

Fundraising for the National Caribbean Monument Charity was therefore very important to Wayne and his friend.

So, what did it feel like to leave the RAF after nearly 48 years?

"In truth, Covid played a role. I left the Regular RAF in March 2015 and was properly dined out at RAF Honington, the Home of the RAF Regiment." This was a significant event, which Wayne thoroughly enjoyed.

Wayne's six years as a Full-Time Reservist Serviceperson (FTRS) commenced the day after he left the RAF. He had submitted his notice a year early to take up his new FTRS employment. This job would enable him to gradually adapt to his forthcoming role as a civilian, in 2021.

"With the Covid-19 quarantine kicking in from March 2020, work was never the same and so I crept up to my final departure date in March, 2021 as night follows day, without a sound."

There were no Nijmegen events in 2020 and 2021 due to Covid. Despite what Wayne describes as a 'silent' retirement, he was still fully active, completing his latest post -Covid 100-mile Nijmegen walks in July 2022 and 2023.

Once Wayne retired from the RAF in 2015, and alongside his sporting activities, he decided to seek volunteering opportunities within his local community. He became a school governor at the local secondary school (attended by his sons at some point in their education, 15 years earlier) in November 2016, undertaking various roles within the Board. His governor role has kept him suitably occupied, without being onerous. In December 2022, Wayne was elected as Chair of the Full Governing Body.

"I have also continued my links with RAF Halton, the local base, visiting various parts two or three times a year, but deliberately limit my involvement on Base."

It remains to be seen whether another British Caribbean service person will get the opportunity to complete 48 years of full-time service with the British Armed Services.

Wayne believes that what has proven important and highly significant, are the Veteran organisations such as the British and Caribbean Veterans' Association (BCVA). The BCVA is based in Birmingham and there are other Veterans' associations elsewhere in the country. Wayne is a member of the BCVA. He strongly supports the work of this organisation, especially as it maintains contact with many Veterans who have served over the past 40 years or more. They organise social events and provide other opportunities for people to meet old and new friends who enlisted in the 1960s and 1970s. Most of those Veterans are those who were born in the Caribbean.

"The irony is that very few of the current service personnel of Afro-Caribbean background, but mainly born in the UK, seem reluctant to seek to understand the history of the work done to give them the opportunities they now have in the Armed Forces"

It is important therefore to do much more to communicate the stories of those who have served. We need to write about it, speak about it and generally make sure that this important history is not lost to us, whether we are in the Caribbean community or in broader society.

Wayne is very clear that it is important to acknowledge, but not to forget your past.

"After my 48 years of Service, as per the lyrics from the song Hotel California by The Eagles 'You can check-out anytime you like, but you can never leave!!'"

'Per Ardua', the motto of the RAF Regiment, meaning *"Through difficulties"*. This motto has very strong resonance and deep meaning for Wayne and the way his life has developed. He is a man who, throughout his life and his Service, has faced and overcome many *"difficulties"*. He has met them head on, leaping forward, making progress and achieving highly in the effort. He has paid sound attention to developing his knowledge and skills as an airman and officer in the RAF Regiment. He has also tended to his intellectual development, achieving a BSc (Hons) degree.

Wayne would advise other British Caribbean young people to join the Armed Forces. However, he would caution them to work hard and to make sure that they are 'seen' to do so. He would hope that they would be ambitious and move towards the upper NCO ranks and beyond into a Commission. He believes that it is possible for them to make a good career in the system.

Looking back to his teenage self, he would say to young Wayne,

"I would do nothing differently. I was told that I should go for commission in my early 20s. I made the right decision not to do so as by going through the ranks and showing everyone what I am capable of, nobody could complain that I've got there just

because I'm black. So be ambitious. You can get there. Keep at it and don't forget your past. I'm proud of what I did. I think you would be too!"

Throughout his lengthy military career, Flight Lieutenant Wayne Howell showed immense courage and provided competent, effective and highly regarded service to the British Armed Forces, Her Late Majesty the Queen, and to our country.
He is worthy of our recognition, acknowledgement and appreciation.

Photo by Gill Shaw

Warrant Officer Donald Campbell

Donald was 13 years old when he left his homeland to join his parents in the UK. His father had left for the UK, three years before his mother then joined him in Birmingham. Their children, including Donald, were left with their godparents. It would be five years before most of the children would be able to reunite with them. The reunion was an incredible time for them all.

The experience of Donald's family was very similar to that of other immigrant families at that time. Parents were attracted by the call to come to England to help with the post-war rebuilding efforts. They "gathered some money together", with hope in their hearts that they had made the right decision to answer the call from the Mother Country.

It was tough here in the UK for these new arrivals. They often encountered racism and discrimination in their everyday dealings, around housing and work especially. They had to navigate unfamiliar food and getting access to social settings and even churches, where they were often made to feel unwelcome.

The Campbells reunited however, and young Donald was able to attend school and begin to settle in his new country.

When he was 15, Donald had a conversation with his teacher about career pathways. That conversation confirmed for him that a career in the Royal Air Force would suit him very well. So, Donald joined up at age 18. He was subject to the usual tests, which were graded to clarify which trades new recruits would be allocated to. If a recruit achieved high grades, they were allocated to a technical trade. Donald results enabled him to choose an aircraft trade, as a Survival Equipment Technician.

He set off to start his basic training in Lincolnshire. Here, he learned what the RAF was all about. He undertook 'Square bashing' activities and made sure he was ready for all the room inspections, including for the regulation bed packs the new recruits were all required to do. He had to complete and succeed in all aspects of the basic training.

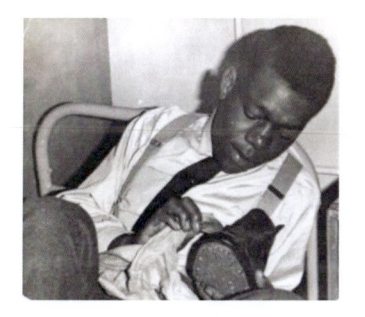

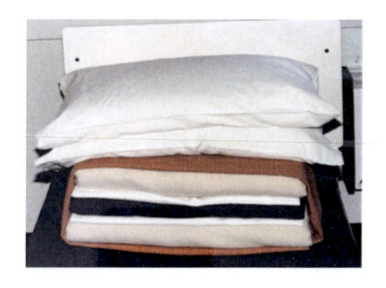

Donald worked very hard, completing the tough challenges he faced, with enthusiasm and determination. This attitude paid off. He got through with flying colours, passing out on time. He was delighted to have his mother to see him at the final Parade. He was enormously proud.

Once basic training was finished, Donald went on to do his Trade Training at St Athans, in Wales. Trade Training lasted for around five months. Again, this young man focused and went on to complete this phase successfully.

There were moments during basic and other training, when Donald would experience treatment, which was 'different' to that meted out to his white counterparts.

He felt that the senior officers did not always *"Look at your worth"*, but rather, judged him merely by his colour. It felt quite disconcerting and frankly, upsetting for this young Airman. Nevertheless, he got on with things, working hard, studying and developing his skills. This included, maintaining elements of the airplane's ejector seat, including Life Support, Assisted Escape and Survival Equipments, to secure the safety of each aircrew. It was an incredibly critical, technical role.

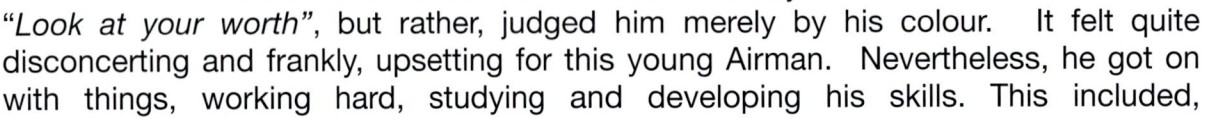

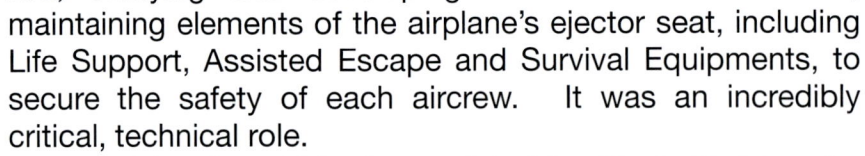

After Donald had completed his Trade Training, he recalls being given a 'Dream Sheet' of places he would love to be posted to. Naturally, he was dreaming of amazing tropical places. Failing that, he would have been happy to go to somewhere like Lincolnshire or Staffordshire. Not so. He was sent to Ballykelly, Limavady, Northern Ireland.

When this young 18-year-old, landed in Belfast, he was not in uniform, but was clearly exposed in the community of white people. He was the only black person around. Other people were invisible to each other, whichever sides they were on. For Donald, here he was, one of only a few RAF personnel in blue, 'swimming' in a sea of army green. It was clear that he had to grow up quickly. The scales had to come off his eyes quickly. He got on with the job. He helped to guard the base, often being on duty at two o'clock in the morning, armed with his rifle. *"Being in Northern Ireland, as a black serviceman, was different."* He was looked at, but not in scorn. Comments would be made, such as, *"We don't have a fight with you...... It's the others."* It was all very strange and the tension was palpable.

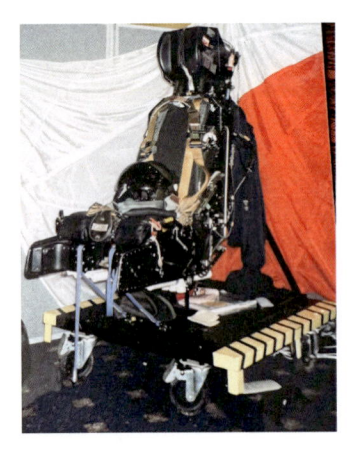

Donald made some friends during that NI tour, including with someone called Ron, from Sierra Leone, whom Donald was to meet again later in another posting. The two men liked each other and remained friends throughout and beyond their military careers. Donald and Ron have joined in various Parades around the country, including at the National Memorial Arboretum. There was also a very senior officer, someone who was second from the top of the RAF, who, when he saw Donald, said to him, *"I remember you. You used to organise a Symposium for your Trade participants. You also welcomed me as the new Station Commander."* Donald was pleased to be remembered. Ron and Donald were also in attendance at a special event held in the Hall of Memory, Birmingham, ahead of Remembrance Sunday, 2022.

One great memory, which Donald shared about his time during his first tour, was when he saw a black man climbing up the aircraft into the cockpit. He was surprised and enthused by the sight, especially as it was unusual. He was the only one, a black pilot, that Donald had ever seen.

During his first tour, Donald was then despatched to Madagascar to use his technical skills in support of RAF aircraft; at least two of them. He had a 20-hour flight, but in a Hercules aircraft. This was an exciting experience for him. The Hercules only refuelled once. There was one toilet in the back of the aircraft, he recalls. That flight was one of the best experiences ever, for this young Airman.

When Donald got to the island and was about to climb into bed, there was a shout outside his door. *"We need you!"* It showed the importance of Donald's job then - even at the tender age of only 19! *"It was great! I felt like a King! I was seen as one of the group there, in Madagascar."*

After recovering properly from his lengthy journey to that tropical and unique Island, Donald got on with the technical tasks in hand. He was also able to enjoy terrific opportunities to fly around the skies in a Shackleton (sister to a Lancaster Bomber), helping to monitor the region. It was a wonderful experience for him. He made great use of his binoculars, trying to identify the various aircraft traversing the skies and unauthorised ships crossing the ocean. Donald learned a huge amount during that posting. He smiles at those memories, which still brings pleasure to him in his mature years.

After being in the RAF for about two and a half years, Donald was posted to Germany. He had a great time there. He learned to drive and bought his first car, a bright red Renault 12. He set off to drive, on leave, to return to the UK. He drove through Belgium and France but got lost when he got to Birmingham. He pauses and smiles at the memory. Donald loved being back home, meeting family and friends. They were amazed to see how much he had changed. In turn, he was surprised to see how little they had changed. He felt it was quite noticeable; they seemed just the same as he remembered them before he joined up.

When he was 23, Donald got married to a woman he had met in Birmingham. The couple lived in married quarters in Lincolnshire and went on to have two children. He continued to travel to different locations to see what the flight crew were experiencing and to solve problems as they occurred.

It was quite difficult for Donald to move up the ranks. He felt that the opportunity to do this seemed slower for people like him, as a non-white person, in comparison to others. In his job, it was vital that he was technically perfect. There was no room for error. Other people's lives depended upon it. Naturally, as his skills and experience grew, so did his confidence. He believed however, that he was judged more harshly and to his mind, this judgement related to his colour rather than to his competence. He merely wanted to be judged fairly, nothing more.

By the time Donald had completed 15 years in the RAF, he had become a Sergeant. Getting to this rank was not smooth sailing, nor was it when following rigorous assessments, he went on to obtain the position of Flight Sergeant. In this latter role, he took over the Survival Equipment Trade Training School as its Manager. In this management position he had responsibility for all the Trainees and everything that surrounded that role. Under his leadership of the Trade Training School, he increased the numbers of trainees; with both additional military and civilian instructors. Donald was responsible for managing a variety of people as well as for the training programme. He became responsible for engineering and weaponry and therefore had to increase personnel accordingly.

Donald was a good leader of personnel and a highly competent expert in his field. So many people depended on him. It was vital to secure safe, efficient and effective systems which would enable RAF aircrew to deliver excellent manoeuvres. He had to make sure that the equipment was working perfectly, with the relevant checks and confirming this before each and every flight. The relief when the aircrew came back (and when they did not) kept Donald's mind sharply focused. His job was never taken lightly, or for granted. Too much and too many people's lives depended on it, on him. Donald would often be one of the last faces the aircrew saw before they left on their missions, and the first on their return.

Donald's immense technical skills and strong leadership skills were being recognised. He was encouraged to apply these further within the top-ranking role of Warrant Officer. This promotion, directly appointed by the Queen, was thoroughly deserved and welcomed by him. He was now responsible for junior NCOs within his Squadron. He acted as a mentor and role model for those around him, including junior commissioned officers.

He was soon posted to the Logistics' Base, which had responsibility for emergency escape systems for all RAF Fast Jets around the world. He was the 'go to' senior person for delivery of safe systems for fast jets and other similar crafts. This was a serious role for a very serious senior officer in the RAF. Donald was certainly up to the job, delivering safe, secure and life-saving systems throughout. He had experience of flights in different conditions to help to build his experience and expertise, learning responses to the aircraft. It was not solely about attaching one bit of kit to another. It was about whether it all worked, its performance and the holistic, efficient nature of the performance in flight.

Donald found the experience of going flying, *"awesome"*. Getting dressed, even with the kit - from underwear to outer clothing and the relevant equipment, depending on the terrain in which the aircraft is flying, mattered. It was crucial to review the clothing, the helmet and boots, alongside the briefing beforehand about all eventualities. Donald and his team were there to ensure that all necessary equipment was systematically maintained and ready on time for each Aviator.

It was also important to make sure the aircrew was ok. Everybody needed to have a good experience, working together for the benefit of the whole. Working as a team was fundamental to Donald's work. He and others were sent away for team building activities, which lasted up to a week or longer each time.

An allocation of 30 days annually, was made for holidays and these could be used in any way by Donald and other service people. They were also given public holidays and weekends off, if that is, they were not on standby duties, with its required 24-hour readiness.

Donald has some wonderful, memorable moments from his time in the Royal Air Force. He loved the travelling opportunities, seeing some amazing places and meeting very interesting people. He was able to learn about the people and enjoy their culture and cuisine. He was struck by those times when he was actually appreciated for *"who I am, especially when it was obvious that those people actually saw me - the black officer, the expert"*. His face warms at the memories of those special times.

He received commendation for his work. There were other special moments too. While managing the Trade Training School, the rate of attrition was low; a statistic which related to his personal leadership and management of each of the trainees at the school. He was able to identify particular talent in young personnel.

He loved working in a Squadron and delighted in flying in jets and helicopters. He was glad of the chance to continue his working life, with support from his wife and the knowledge that his children's education would not be interrupted by his moving to different service locations. With the RAF's support, his children were sent to boarding schools.

In the seven years that Donald was at the Training School, he realised that there was a need to capture the knowledge they were developing through the composition of a video. The content of the video was constructed in such a way that it would clarify and support the four different stages of Trade Training. It would therefore help potential trainees to make an informed choice of profession, prior to selecting this trade. Thus, it could ultimately lead to reducing the attrition rate during training. Trainees would work systematically and onwards to completing their training more efficiently and successfully. This video would also ensure that precious knowledge would not be lost.

Constructing this video took around nine months. The Wing Commander saw it. Unfortunately, someone else tried to 'steal' his idea and leapt forward to register it as his. Donald is still smarting at this injustice. Fortunately, he had all the records of each stage of the development of this special work. It was however, ultimately registered in his name. It is not something he will ever forget. The Recruiting Leader for the Air Force saw the video with Donald and his Team.

Donald was mentioned and commended in the Queen's Honours' List in 2004. That led to him being presented with a congratulatory Certificate.

While Donald had some wonderful times in his military career, there were also some difficult, disturbing and even painful moments, which still trouble this remarkable RAF Veteran. It became noticeable to him that as a black person, with the potential to go up the ranks, there was a distinct lack of mentorship. Few people from an ethnic minority background therefore reached those higher ranks, not through lack of skills and competence, but rather, through lack of support, and worse.

"People could not accept that you were in charge. They would walk past me, even with the ranks obvious on my shoulder. They would pass by me and go on to the next white face, to ask for the person in charge."

He goes on to say, *"They would refuse to acknowledge my presence. Those experiences of them not seeing you in charge, don't go away. They are indelibly set in your mind."*

After Donald had completed 36 years of service, he decided to make plans to bring his career in the RAF to a close. He therefore undertook the transition course to support his relocation into civilian life. He also built a business plan, which included getting a special license for transporting people in executive, luxury vehicles.

That first year outside the military was very different, but still exciting in relation to growing his executive chauffeuring business. Within 16 years, he had around 12 companies depending on him for personal, secure chauffeur services.

Transition into his new life was made a little easier because of the pattern of postings into the various locations whilst he was a serving Airman. In each case, his postings were done as an individual, rather than with a group. It was his specialist technical expertise, which the military utilised and so he was used to acting more independently across and throughout his career in the RAF. He had made good preparations beforehand, buying a house 20 miles from the RAF Base and lived there, commuting each day, in the last three years before he left. He commented that it was therefore easier for RAF people to make this transition than for others who served in the army, for example.

Donald has been able to maintain ties with former colleagues, through attendance at talks, conferences, Veteran organisations and through his voluntary work. He attends events, complete with Standards, which he presents with pride to honour those who have served and in memory of those service personnel who have passed away.

He feels strongly about researching the stories of past service people of African and Caribbean heritage - and honouring them. He is a founder of "The Forgotten Generations" and a contributor to the "Logbook Project", which sought to collect signatures of WWII Veterans around the world.

He speaks with pride about the formation of the British West India Regiment (BWIR), the history of which is full of stories of brave Caribbeans. His face showed some sadness, however, about an unknown but significant young Caribbean teenage WWI soldier, Herbert Morris. Herbert was aged 17 years when he was traumatised by the experiences of war. He was court-martialled, blind-folded and shot at dawn on the 20 September, 1917, by his fellow West Indians who were a part of the BWIR. Donald is one of a number of people who have worked hard to continue to recognise this teenage soldier, who may have been suffering from PTSD before he was court-martialled. There is a 'Shot at Dawn Memorial', at the National Memorial Arboretum that includes young Herbert. Donald and others are trying to keep his memory alive by having an annual remembrance wreath laying event. Donald is a man who will never forget what people like Herbert and others have done for this country.

Over more than three decades of service, Donald developed a breadth of experience and specialist expertise, including with particular aircraft used in the RAF. He feels very fortunate to have done such a lot in his RAF career.

He had great opportunities to travel, including to places such as Belize, Sardinia, France, USA, Denmark, Norway and many more. He has met some fascinating people, gained valuable skills and benefited enormously from leading and developing people. All of this allowed him to grow as a person, to become more confident. He is a man whose professionalism and obvious reliability in his RAF career, shines through.

When he considers the sort of advice he would give to others thinking about a career, similar to his own, he says, *"Keep your eye on the target and go for it."* He believes that life would be fantastic but challenging for them. They would have to be persistent, but resilient, often in the face of discrimination and worse.

His eyes light up as he describes a Black, Asian and Minority Ethnic Annual Conference he participated in a few months ago, where *"the number of black people there was staggering to see."* Recently, he was at an event when he was surprised to see a black Station Commander who was in charge of a large operational unit and who was also a pilot. It was a real pleasure for him to see this change in the RAF.

There is more still to be done, however. *"The service provided by Caribbeans to the UK in the Armed Forces is not well known, or acknowledged"*, he says. He pauses momentarily as he wonders whether, some of that lack of knowledge is the fault of the community itself. *"We have a responsibility to tell others, but especially to make sure our youngsters know about what we have done. We want them to climb on our shoulders."*

In his view, these young people should research the different options - air, ground or water - and be informed about what each offers as the best route towards a qualification, which will enable them to make progress up the ranks and beyond back into civilian life.

There is a feeling from him, that he and the thousands of others did an awful lot, but the youth of today could use their Elders' examples and do even more, go even further.

Donald has always loved writing. He has already written the first part of his story, in "My Path of Life". There is more to come, in parts two and three. He continues to contribute much to the different groups and organisations across the African and Caribbean community. He also attends remembrance events to show respect and honouring of people in the military, often going with his lifelong friend, Ron and with other Veterans.

He joins in talks and discussions to increase and enhance the knowledge base of children, young people and adults.

Meeting this serious Veteran who demonstrates obvious commitment to his community, gives one the impression of a life well-lived and a career fulfilled. His pride in his contribution to this country is obvious and deserved.

He is determined to broaden and deepen the understanding of peoples up and down the country, about what *"we Veterans, have done for the country - we the Caribbeans, in the UK."* He is beginning to make a big difference in this regard.

Warrant Officer, Donald Campbell is satisfied about the work he was able to do in the RAF, the successes he achieved. He did so much better than he expected. To do this, he learned to *"go over the hurdles, under them and occasionally, to knock them down"*. This is an ex-serviceman whose head is held high, his shoulders are back and his whole stature is one of confident authority. He is sure about his worth and his place in society and of the contribution he has made to its security and freedom. We all owe him and others like him, a great debt of gratitude.

Corporal Keith Crichlow

Keith was born in Paddington, London and then lived in Kentish Town. His parents came from Barbados. His Mother, older sister and younger brother, along with Keith then moved to Luton.

Keith went to primary and secondary schools in Luton before deciding at age 16 and a half to join the Boys' Section of the Royal Air Force.

Keith explains that one of the reasons he decided to join the RAF, related to issues with family in particular - especially to those in his environment, who *"talked with their hands"*. Keith was also clear that he did not want to be *"running around the streets"*, with all that entailed for many young black boys in the area. That was not for him. He felt he had to get away and the RAF proved to be an attractive proposition.

Keith was already attending the Air Training Corp as a youth, so he was encouraged to go further and move into the formal organisation. He made up his mind and decided to stop off at a military Careers' Office on the high street. He completed an aptitude test, achieving good results, enabling him to progress into the RAF.

At first, his mother was not in agreement with him joining up. She refused to sign for young Keith. Eventually, she caved in and Keith was able to enter the Boys' Service of the RAF. At that time, Keith had spoken to a number of black boys and girls, who seem to have similar stories to share about the environment they were experiencing in and around their homes and community. Keith realised that in taking the decision he had, about this type of career away from all the limitations there might be in his surroundings, it was in fact, the best thing he had ever done.

Keith went off to Lincolnshire to start his basic training. There was one other person of colour in his intake. There was a lot of racism directed at this young man; *"after all it was in the mid 70's."*, Keith says. Keith decided that as he had lived in London with both black and white people, *"I could manage all of that"*.

Lincolnshire was very strange to Keith. When he arrived at the station, complete with his suitcase of required items, he was met by someone he describes as a Sergeant Major-type individual. This individual's first words to Keith were, *'Right Shaft, where are you from?"'* He directed his other comment to another youngster, saying, *"Hey fa..ie, we're gonna get that weight off you"*. When the bus stopped, the new recruits found themselves outside the barbers, where the Sergeant said, *"Shaft is first!"* They all had their hair shaved off military style. Then the new recruits were despatched to collect their kit and marched off to their dormitories.

Keith managed somehow. It was difficult, however. He recalls, disturbingly, the others wanting to see him naked to see if the stereotypes about black men were true. He was one of 50 other recruits. He remembers Quigley, an 18-year-old from Northern Ireland who befriended and tried to reassure him, saying, *"Don't worry about them."* He tried very hard to heed that advice. Keith went on to build some camaraderie with many he served with then. All of the recruits had to learn to wash, iron, make their beds and spit and polish - 'bull - their shoes to a mirror shine. *"No-one could mess up."*

During the initial weeks, not all 50 of them made the Team, for various reasons. When Keith went on his first parade, he heard the Drill Sergeant call out *"Very good. Look at Crichlow - and he's not used to wearing clothes or shoes."* There were several examples of this sort of casual racism, which this young black man had to contend with.

There were initiation ceremonies, including having black polish smeared all over their private parts. *"With me, it was difficult to do this"*, says Keith as he frowned in the retelling. He ruminates quietly about the '"Trigger" born from the institutional racism experienced by black men and women. These experiences are real and have long-lasting effects. They are seemingly, hidden deep within the minds and souls of many black people. However, they are often triggered by the memories which surface when these black people face one more moment of so-called "banter".

During basic training, Keith carried out drills, learned how to clean and fire guns and to march and salute. The recruits were taught Morse Code, the phonetic alphabet and had to learn about different types of aircraft as well as all about the role and purpose of the RAF.

Keith was a very good cricketer. He loved the sport, especially knowing at the time that it was "Our" - West Indians' main sport. He played cricket for the Air Force, including against Oxford and Cambridge. He believes at that time that he was used as part of the recruitment tool to attract both black and white young men into the forces. He went on to play cricket in a number of countries, including Italy, Germany, Cyprus, Gibraltar and Hong Kong. He thoroughly enjoyed these experiences.

He was also a talented middle-distance runner. He became popular, almost famous amongst the RAF personnel. He remembers being pulled out by the Station Commander, who called him in *"as an "Ethnic", "He was asking me what's going on? How are you getting on with people? Any problems?"*

Some of Keith's colleagues were jealous about the attention he was getting from officers. This jealousy did not get any better, when Keith was selected as the winner of the best parade, receiving a cup in the process. It was a prestigious occasion, viewed publicly by hundreds of people, including very important visitors and top commissioned officers. Keith felt very proud to be identified and selected for the role. There were however, comments, such as *"My father and grandfather were in the RAF. How can you be the person they selected? Why you?"*

Keith just had to be strong in his resolve to just get on with things. He was a resilient young man. This attitude served him well; got him through those moments and other periods of his service in the RAF.

In the Boys' service, each young person was paid weekly, in cash. Their wages were in a brown envelope. At the end of the month, Keith remembers that three of his envelopes remained unopened. He had made a good friend with a Welsh person he had met. It was this Welsh friend who said to Keith, *"Spend less on clothes and shoes and you could buy a house, or shares for your future."* Keith took this advice and so began his savings regime.

He decided to develop a little business, offering to do other people's shirts and shoes. *"I'll do it for you!'"* Soon word got around and Keith was doing business for ten other guys in his Unit. His Unit Sergeant also allocated six other men for Keith to manage their finances in particular. These were young men who could not cook nor wash and who too, got a weekly wage. Keith managed their brown envelopes for them, doling out what they really needed, helping them to save a little themselves.

Keith became quite an entrepreneur and was able to make a significant amount of money. His Welsh friend's advice was invaluable in him being able to start, at the age of 22, his property investment as a young airman. He was well ahead of most young men of a similar age. The financial and economic lessons he learned at that time, has continued to influence him throughout his life.

When Keith had passed the aptitude tests, the results he had achieved pointed to the types of Trades open to him. He selected to become a Logistician.

At that time, black people were guided into less technical trades, irrespective of their test results. The more technical ones tended to go to the white recruits. Keith only realised this apparent discriminatory practice, when he had the opportunity to talk with other black recruits. They were being guided towards more limiting, menial jobs, such as catering. Many of these black recruits, accepted this as *"how it is"*.

One good thing, however, was that by being in the RAF, it was possible to engage in studying, going to night school, taking Open University courses. Keith was able to take advantage of these opportunities.

Keith describes what happened to some of the black men he encountered, and of the opportunities they went on to benefit from. He tells of five of them: three are now Barristers, one is an IT Director and himself, now an Aircraft Engineer with British Aerospace.

These are examples of people who, despite their being engineered into low positions, showed determination and resolve to lift themselves out of the stereotypical circles, to become, *"More than"*. They and many others like them, showed what they were really capable of. There are still questions to be asked and answers sought, about what those early aptitude tests were really about. There are question marks about the extent to which, in today's climate, some of those discriminatory, life changing behaviours from people with power and influence are still being practiced in recruitment into the British Armed Forces.

Keith's trade training was done in Herefordshire and lasted around six months. Once this had been completed successfully, Keith went on to an Operational Unit in High Wycombe, HQ Strike Command. He was in his first unit for two years, during which he was signed to the RAF's Man Service and could register to do overseas' service. He was then posted to Mönchengladbach, West Germany.

Keith completed two tours in Germany, firstly for nearly three years, with an 18-month posting back home in the UK, then a second despatch back to Germany for a further three years.

In the 18-month period Keith was back in the UK, he lived in Walthamstow, London, travelling to Hendon each day for work. Keith had in fact bought his first house in that area. He had to travel through the Tottenham area. It was while he was doing so, that on one particular day, he was to have an interaction with the local police. He was in uniform, driving a sports car and he was pulled over by them. Keith could hear his name being called over the radio as they checked his car. It was clear that they had sufficient details from their radio conversation, but they still decided to question him again about the car and sought other information about him. At no time, did either police officer comment on him being in his RAF uniform. One of the officers, the younger of the two, commented, *"He must be a Pimp"*. The older, more experienced officer tried to diffuse the situation. People began to gather as they saw Keith in his service uniform. Keith asked the officers for their details. It was all very tense, especially as Keith recalls it being around the time of the Blakelock event.

PC Keith Blakelock was murdered during the riots which took place on the Broadwater Farm Estate in Tottenham in 1985. The riot broke out after Mrs Cynthia Jarrett died of heart failure during a police search of her home. The particular event took place against a backdrop of unrest in several English cities and a breakdown of relations between the police and some people in the Black community. Three adults, known as the "Tottenham Three" and some youths, were arrested, and the adults charged with PC Blakelock's murder. Their convictions were later quashed in 1991 after that is, they had already served four years in prison. Sadly, despite further investigations over many years, no one has been prosecuted for this awful murder.

When Keith was posted to Germany, he went as an individual, not with a group of others. In each of his postings, he would turn up to the Base, get his room allocation and bedding and get on with the job he was dispatched to do. He became a Senior Aircraftsman.

The usual procedure was that the morning after he arrived in his new posting, after the parade, he would meet his new boss. He therefore just got on with things each time and in each location.

It was while he was in Germany, that he met other black people. He was at that time, the first black person actually born in the UK, to be posted there. He was also the youngest. He admitted that he had a great time, going clubbing and so on.

During his second tour in Germany, Keith met and married a woman who was also in the Armed Forces. Unfortunately, his marriage was to end in divorce. He was then back and forth in various postings between the UK and Germany. It was while he was involved in these journeys, that he met his current wife. She was also an ex-Armed Forces person who was working for the British Aerospace (BAe aka BAE) Systems organisation. BAE paid for their relocation to Guildford.

Within a year, the company decided to move its business to Humberside and Lancashire. Keith was based in Preston, Lancashire. He was despatched from there to a posting in Kuwait during the particular conflict in which the UK Armed Forces, played a part.

Keith worked with 19 Squadron and with 92 Squadron. He supported Phantoms, Harriers and Jaguars around the world, defending whichever parts of the world he was called to. He met other colleagues who were his equivalent from the USA, Belgium, Spain and Italy. In these war-like arenas, Keith and others would be expected to ensure the efficiency and flight worthiness of particular aircraft. Keith showed great competence and effectiveness in this undertaking.

Keith's personal life continued to flourish. He was blessed to have a daughter from another solid relationship after he had divorced his first wife.

Keith had signed up in the Boys' Service and then went on to a career with the Men's section of the RAF. He had been posted to a number of countries, delivering efficient and effective service each time. While he was in the RAF, he saved up and was able to purchase a house in Walthamstow.

He decided to leave the RAF, after completing, including within the Boys' Service, 13.5 years of service. Keith was only 30 years old, still a young man.

As part of his preparation to leave, he was reminded that the Ministry of Defence was already connected to BAE Systems. As an aviator, Keith was familiar with the aircraft used in 'Civvy Street.' At that time, around 40% of BAE Systems' staff were ex-servicemen and women. Keith decided to apply to join that organisation.

The person who recruited Keith was also ex-RAF. Keith was successful in his application and soon joined the company. It was a smooth transition for Keith, into civilian life.

Keith stayed with BAE Systems for 25 years. He was then offered a job with them in Kuwait, but as a civilian, who while carrying out Kuwaiti work, would be paid *"danger money"*. When Saddam Hussein first invaded Kuwait, Keith was with BAE Systems. He clearly remembers that mines had been planted in the area and he would often hear the loud explosions. Some of those explosions were set off by camels, sheep and the local wildlife he recalls. It was an incredibly intense, stressful time.

It was Keith's job to help to get the customers' planes flying, this being the Kuwaiti Air Force at that time. He was in this job for two years. He went back to the Middle East after a short journey back to the UK. This time, he lived in Dubai and Sharjah, travelling to the United Arab Emirates for work. He also worked in Abu Dhabi for a further year. And Indonesia for three years.

Keith really enjoyed his time working with BAE Systems. He was at his happiest then.

He later, got a job in Munich, Germany, where he stayed for several years. His second daughter grew up there. He loved living in Germany, describing it as *"a wonderful time"*. He was able to live in a village, famously known for its infamous, previous habitant - a Mr A Hitler. All very strange, but fascinating.

Keith is enjoying his life with his family and a good circle of friends, some of whom he has known since his time in the military. He continues to travel with his family, enjoying the chance to develop his knowledge of other places and cultures, whilst also visiting his parents' homeland whenever he can.

Keith has no regrets about his time in the military. *"If I could do it all again, I would do it in a heartbeat!"*

He believes that there is little actual knowledge about, or appreciation for the contribution made by Caribbeans who served in the British Armed Forces.

Despite this view, he would still advise other young people to consider joining it as a career. He would however, remind them that there is a big wide world out there, where *"You have to accept the complexion you have and just live it"*.

Corporal Keith Crichlow is proud of his achievements in the RAF.

He feels that it was a bit of a lightbulb moment when the RAF was mentioned as a career when he was 16 years old. He would love to go back and say to that bright-eyed 16-year-old Keith, *"You done well. The boy done well. You done your family proud."*

This is a man whose pride in his achievements is well-deserved. All of us should appreciate what he has done and recognise and acknowledge his contributions towards keeping us safe and free.

Sergeant Malcolm Smith

Malcolm was born in British Guiana, (now Guyana). He came to the UK at the age of nine, unaccompanied, clad in his smart blue suit and polished brown shoes. He travelled on one of the early BOAC airplanes.

His mother was already in the UK, working hard to save enough money to bring her family over to join her. She had a room in Mortimer Road, in the Kensal Rise area of London. It was a popular area for many Caribbean immigrant families to live in those days. There were large ceilinged rooms available to rent from the few landlords who accepted black people.

Malcolm attended the local primary school before going on to Aylestone School, under the headship of a classics-trained headmaster. Malcolm went to Aylestone School at a time when a sizeable wave of Caribbean young people came to the UK to join their parents. It was also the time when the post-war baby boom, the raising of the school leaving age (ROSLA) and the move from Grammar schools to the new Comprehensive schools, saw some 'churn' in the education system. Several London authorities and schools had to make significant changes to the way they were managed, to their school and class sizes and to the manner of their welcome of the new arrivals from the Caribbean and elsewhere.

Malcolm was very good at sport, especially football, cricket and athletics, which he enjoyed very much. He left school with minimum qualifications. Fortunately, following a successful interview, he obtained a position as a shipping clerk. He did this job for a few months, during which he moved to Willesden, near the Bus Garage. While in Willesden, he met a man who was in the Royal Air Force. This man encouraged Malcolm to consider a career in the RAF. Malcolm decided to do just that, and his stepfather took him to the careers' office in Archway to start the application process. Following success in the interviews and the tests, Malcolm was able to join up.

Malcolm was sent a Travel Warrant and soon set off by train, to start his basic training in Swinderby, Lincolnshire. When he arrived at the station, he was met and taken by coach to the camp. He saw only one other black person there – Joe. Joe was a little ahead of Malcolm in basic training.

When Malcolm arrived at the Camp, he was sporting a pretty sharp Afro. That hairstyle lasted moments, as he was sent straight off to get a haircut. He remembers the cut as being more or less a Number 1, which meant that there was not a lot of hair left on his head.

The accommodation was as expected. Malcolm was in a dormitory with 19 other young recruits. They all experienced the usual activities that all recruits were put through when they first entered the Armed Forces. They did drills, self-care, rifle training and saluting to name just a few of the activities. It was tough, but Malcolm got through it all successfully.

His Passing Out Parade was attended by his mother and stepfather. Malcolm felt very proud. This pride became a little tarnished after the Parade, when he was exposed to what he believed to be some racist comment. When he went into the Hall and as he met the Reviewing Officer, he was told, *"Aircraftman, because of your colour, you're going to have to work twice as hard to get on."* Malcolm was taken aback, as he felt it was unusual to have such a senior person saying this. Malcolm was aware that the reality for him may well be that, but wondered whether this officer was predicting what his experience would be. He assumed that this was therefore, *"how it would be and how it had been, for all black airmen"*. If that was the case he wondered, how was it that this senior officer had not acted to redress this obvious discrimination towards all people of colour in the RAF? He did not speak these thoughts out aloud; and thus, the senior officer had no idea what this young man was feeling at the time.

The officer's comment dampened Malcolm's spirit. He began to wonder whether the enthusiasm he had been feeling, the pride in this early basic training success, would lead to him always having to prove himself additionally, and unreasonably, to his white colleagues. Nevertheless, he was still determined to carry on with his RAF career.

Malcolm was then posted to RAF St Athan, in South Wales. This became his permanent station for the next two years. St Athan taught Malcolm an awful lot about human nature, especially with regard to difference, ethnically. The racism really struck him. He had to toughen up, despite the hurt these behaviours caused him deep inside.

Malcolm was not the only black person there. There were at least ten others. He was not yet 18 years old. Malcolm worked directly with other white colleagues and so naturally, he ate his meals with them. He saw other black men at the base and eventually went over to them. He tried to maintain a presence with both groups - white and black. There were comments from some of the white colleagues about *"Why are you sitting with us, when there are other black guys over there?"* It was not easy for young Malcolm to navigate these situations, these relationships.

He got on with life however, building into his work, some social and very enjoyable times. He partied hard; so much so, that he had a tough lesson to learn, after he was fined at one time for being late for work. Nevertheless, he was often to be found dancing away and drinking, in places such as the "Beer Keller", on Barry Island, "Drones Club" in Bridgend and at discos in Tiger Bay. He was never fined again, managing his social and work life better, while retaining the fun elements.

Malcolm had some of the most memorable times at St Athans. It was there that he met a hugely influential senior non-commissioned officer, FS Dady. FS Dady gave this young man, some life-changing advice. He encouraged Malcolm to consider a West German posting. He told Malcolm, *"There's a notification that you're being posted to Rheindahlen. Are you going to accept the posting? It's the best one you'll ever have"*. Malcolm took FS Dady's advice and accepted the German posting. Once his two years in Wales were completed, Malcolm was therefore posted to Germany, to work with the army and other RAF personnel, who were also there. Once he was in the midst of his German posting, he soon found that the FS's words proved to be absolutely right. It was proving to be the best posting.

In Germany, Malcolm met quite a few people from other units and countries. He was delighted to meet some of the women from the Women's Royal Army Corps. He also met a number of other black people. Together, these young people from different units and Regiments from the land and air forces, joined in the socialising. They partied as much as possible, tasted a great variety of wines and enjoyed cooking and eating 'curry chicken' and rice n peas and other delicious Caribbean food. *"We brought the West Indies to Germany"*, remarks Malcolm. Malcolm had a wonderful time during that tour.

When Malcolm arrived in Germany, he could not speak a word of the language but found that most of the local civilians were keen to practice their English, so he got by easily. Rheindahlen was quite detached from German civilian life, so it was not difficult for Malcolm to settle there. For the first month, he did not go anywhere outside the Base. He just went to work and to the Mess and back to his accommodation. He was beginning to make friends. One of them asked Malcolm to go with him to a local bar for a drink. It was at this bar that Malcolm met his first love. His eyes lit up, but it was not until a couple of months later that he saw her again and asked her out. She was 17 years old. The two young people were together for the next 18 - 20 months. The relationship did not then move forward, but their story would result in another positive connection, much later in their lives.

While he was in this first Rheindahlan tour in 1974, Malcolm was part of the first RAF Ground Crew to visit the USAF Base at Rammstein. He still remembers the Burger King, with its burger, fries and drink, as well as Dunkin' Donuts, where he could get 50 donuts for a mere $3. He remembers hearing that the Camp was expecting a visit from a top entertainer, he thinks it was Frank Sinatra, to entertain the US troops. He laughs with pleasure at the difference between what the USA personnel had access to on their Base, and those available to the British. Such differences were quite amazing to him at the time.

After the Rheindahlen tour, Malcolm was posted to RAF Northolt, where he stayed for some time. At Northolt, he was fortunate to meet FS Mick Wyms. This was a man who Malcolm describes as *"a brilliant Flight Sergeant. He treated me with respect and was influential in getting me promoted"*.

Malcolm was told he would be posted to West Raynham, RAF in Fakenham, but he volunteered to help the government's requirement for military support during a National Emergency. He and many others from the Armed Forces were sent to Govan, Scotland to help during the Firemen Strike.

The National Emergency into which the country was plunged, meant that critical support had to be provided by more than 10,00 members of the Army, Navy and RAF. These men were drafted in, to work alongside the part-time firefighters who were not involved in the strike.

It was a tough time for the country, especially because there had never been a national dispute like it before. The national preparations were not as robust as they could have been. People providing firefighting support had to make use of outdated Green Goddess vehicles, which had been called back into service. Sadly, several civilians and servicemen lost their lives during that state of emergency, which lasted several weeks.

At that time, Malcolm found Govan was one of the roughest places he had seen. As usual, he *"was the only black guy there"*. He got on with the work however, doing all he could as part of the emergency team. He remembers going into a particular place in Govan, where he was told, *"Because you're here serving the Queen and doing the Strike, you can go in"*.

After being a part of the services' efforts during the firemen's strike, Malcolm was then posted to RAF Hendon, where he gained promotion as a Corporal.

He was then posted to RAF Halton for two and a half years. Malcolm describes his time at RAF Halton, as one of the worst times in his career. It was here that he experienced racism like no other, from a Squadron Leader and a Flight Lieutenant. Malcolm is scarred by the viciousness of the behaviours he encountered. Two examples of these behaviours relate to a skin problem and to release to get married.

The first awful incident Malcolm references was in respect to his ingrowing hairs, which made it painful for him to shave until the infection had receded. Instead of being supportive, the Squadron Leader, who had taken a particular dislike to Malcolm, forced him to shave, causing him further pain and distress.

On another occasion, a particular Flight Lieutenant, who was following the Squadron Leader's example, deliberately, ordered Malcolm to turn up to a Parade practice just after being given release to attend his wedding ceremony. Malcolm had gotten married on the Friday and yet he was ordered to return to Camp the following morning for the Practice. It was a Saturday, he recalls. He found this demand both unreasonable and discriminatory.

The sorts of intentional act to which this young black man was subjected, were unknown in terms of comparison to the treatment given to other people, white people. Therefore, he believed that it was clearly targeted towards him as a black man. There was nothing that Malcolm could do about these examples of direct racism. He had no other senior officer to complain to. In fact, at that time and in that particular place, Malcolm felt that the Warrant Officer also seemed to be part of a joint effort to make his life unpleasant, almost unbearable. He will never forget this racist environment. He is pleased however, that he found something deep inside himself, which allowed him to survive.

Fortunately, Malcolm was then posted to Laarbruch, Germany. This tour had followed his posting at RAF Halton, where in Malcolm's view, the three senior officers had tried to ruin his career. The Laarbruch Flight Lieutenant, who read his assessment he had received from Malcolm's previous posting, commented that he really did not recognise what had been written about Malcolm. The written assessment he had received, bore no resemblance to the person in front of him. Malcolm felt vindicated. He begun to relax into his new posting, carrying out his duties to good effect and with the competence and confidence of someone who was being now judged fairly and equitably.

In his Laarbruch posting, Malcolm was able to work well with colleagues who treated him equally and without resorting to racist banter or racist abuse. In fact, he found those people extremely supportive, and he was able therefore, to build positive relationships in his workplace and elsewhere.

Malcolm's day-to-day work was mainly in Logistics. He worked with a group of servicemen who treated him equally. *"It would be fair to say that these colleagues were colour blind, in terms of race and even today, we still meet up, even though we are all retired from the services."*

Laarbruch was one of the best tours for Malcolm. Being on that tour was one of the happiest times in Malcolm's military career. Malcolm loved the camaraderie among the men and the women he met at Laarbruch. While there were only three persons of colour within the Supply unit, everyone, including the white men, got on well together. Many of them, blacks and whites remain friends throughout. There was never a hint of racism amongst them. In Mal's view, these men *"considered themselves as a Band of Brothers". "It did not matter of where each person was from, army or RAF; as a black person who is already in a minority, you got together in Germany and socialised."* Malcolm really enjoyed that time in his life.

He cites an example of a memorable person, from Laarbruch, *"My mate, Spike"*, with whom he served for three years. Malcolm and Spike have retained a lifetime of friendship, which Malcolm treasures.

Many of the black people whom Malcolm met, mainly from his Laarbruch posting, in Germany, still meet up once a year since leaving that posting. Malcolm and several others are now a part of a close West Indian Black British Military Veterans' Group. He enjoys this group and the opportunity to connect with like-minded people, who have common experiences and histories.

He describes the diverse groups at RAF Laarbruch with whom he worked - whether West Indians from the different islands or Welsh, Scots, English, Mauritians, they all got on well. They would play football regularly, often competing against each other in the different country groups. He smiles as he recalls the Scots coming out in their kilts and bagpipes, before playing football.

He also remembers the monthly Beer Calls, which, along with his particular friends, Winston and Tony and others from RAF 1 Squadron Regiment, he enjoyed thoroughly.

When Malcolm was in Germany, he had the opportunity to visit other countries, such as Holland, France and Belgium. He was also really pleased to go back to his island home of Guyana. Malcolm achieved further promotion during his second tour of Germany. He became a Sergeant and was then involved in mostly administrative work at Command headquarters.

Malcolm had met and married, on posting from RAF Halton. After RAF Halton, he was posted to Laarbruch before going back to RAF Stafford. From RAF Stafford, he obtained an exchange posting to Northolt. After this, in 1987, he was promoted to Sergeant and posted to RAF Lyneham. He was delighted to welcome his first child, Natasha before being posted back to Rheindahlen. While he was at Rheindahlen, working at Command headquarters, Germany, he met two brilliant officers, who he rated as some of the best he had worked with during his RAF career: a Flight Lieutenant and a Squadron Leader. These two men treated Malcolm with respect throughout his time in that posting.

Whilst at Rheindahlen, he was detached to the Falkland Islands to serve a 4-month tour. He then returned to Rheindahlen for the remainder of his 3-year tour. He then was posted back to Lyneham where his lovely son, Jordan was born. Malcom was then posted to Decimomannu, Sardinia with his family, who loved it there.

The children, who were by then three and seven years old, had a wonderful time. They attended school in the cooler mornings and set off to spend the rest of their time on the beach, afterwards. Malcolm found the Sardinia tour, a *"brilliant one"*. He had a villa which was 100-yards from the beach, which suited his family perfectly. He went on to serve in Sardinia for two and a half years, as the Unit was closing down.

Malcolm was the Barrack Warden in Decimomannu when he appeared in an article in the RAF News, which reported the drawdown of the RAF Base there.

After completing 26 years in the RAF, Malcolm decided that it was time to leave. He had completed approximately 14 tours of duty in several locations, both in the UK and abroad. He had achieved the rank of Sergeant. However, it was clear that despite his work record, loyalty and commitment, opportunities for promotion were limited. This made him angry and resentful. He was losing faith in the organisation. He wondered if perhaps, he was not quite *"the right sort of black person"*, the RAF was prepared to consider for promotion to the higher ranks.

He was aware that there were not many black men who carried on into the commissioned ranks. There were very few, even at the highest NCO, Warrant Officer rank. He found out later, that there was a black Group Captain, retired. That Group Captain's son was the only black pilot that Malcolm ever met during his 26 years in the RAF. Clearly, in Malcolm's view, there was a "type" of black person whom the RAF perceived to be promotion material. It appeared that it would not be someone like

Malcolm. However, Malcolm still hoped to see other promoted black people but did not do so in his near three decades in the RAF.

Towards the end of his service, the RAF used Malcolm to shut down camps in different locations. He wanted more for himself. He wanted to travel more. He therefore looked for postings to enable him to achieve that objective, including to places such as Cyprus or Hong Kong, but there was a 5-year waiting list. Malcolm became disenchanted with those limitations, both in types of postings and in relation to opportunities for moving up the ranks. He had reached the age of 44 and had to consider where the next stage of life and career would take him. He decided to take premature, voluntary release from the RAF. He wanted to have a life outside.

Malcolm felt scared when he left the RAF. Civilian life was very different. *"There was no order to each day."* He found civilians difficult to get used to. He experienced racism, sometimes from more elderly people, but he had made his decision and had to move forward with his chosen path, in his new environment.

Above – J/T Woody Woodward of General Engineering.

Right – Sgt Mal Smith of Supply checks the station's stock of heaters often required by the permanent staff during the surprisingly cold Italian winters.

Left – Flt Lt Mark Chinery with the under-pylon pods fitted to aircraft using the Air Combat Manoeuvring Instrumentation range. Such pods help keep an accurate electronic record of how the aircraft perform in combat training and are vital to the aircrew de-brief.

When Malcolm was leaving the RAF, they gave him the princely sum of £500 towards resettlement. He used that money to do a health and safety (H&S) course at the Tidworth Army Base. An acquaintance he met on the health and safety course encouraged him to get some further qualifications.

The H&S qualification was never used. Instead, Malcolm set out to sign up for some higher qualification and focused on studying hard. He achieved a Level 4 NVQ, in Logistics. He applied for and was successful in getting a post with Panasonic, as a Logistics' Supervisor, earning then, a good salary of £30,000. Thus began his new civilian life.

Over the past dozen years, Malcolm has continued on his career pathway, going into roles which have enabled him to provide over many years, targeted support to vulnerable adults.

Malcolm has no regrets about his service in the RAF. Undoubtedly, there were some concerns about his promotion journey through his military career. Nevertheless, he had much to be proud of, to be very pleased about. He had enjoyed the great majority of those 26 years. *"The good outweighed the bad"*, he says.

Malcolm feels very disappointed by the lack of support from the RAF, especially as a Veteran. *"No-one has come and asked me if I am alright."* He commented that, *"The people in the service, from the Caribbean, were so totally committed, all the time. They gave unquestionable loyalty. The country has never acknowledged the sacrifices that West Indians have made for the people of Britain."*

If Malcolm had the chance to speak to his 16-year-old teenage self, he would say to him, *"I'm so glad you were brave and sensible enough to join. You will end up with qualifications you did not achieve at Aylestone School. You did a good job."*

He would ask new Caribbean recruits to the Armed Forces to think carefully about what they want out of a military life. He believes that there are significant changes to the training process and to the opportunities for travel. He believes that recruits are more likely to be sent to conflicts around the world.

Sergeant Malcolm Smith accepts that a career in the RAF, gave him discipline, purpose, a sense of duty, loyalty to the country and to the Late Queen. It also provided him with a great chance to build and appreciate the camaraderie, which he continues to value in the friends he was able to make. He is proud of his contribution to the defence of his country and to supporting the continuation of the freedoms we all treasure. There is very little he would do differently.

Sergeant Noel Brathwaite

Noel, who was born in Barbados and his younger brother were left on the Island to be cared for by their grandmother, Winifred and great-grandmother Soley. At the time, Noel was only three years old.

His strong, confident mother Eugene, had been part of the Windrush recruitment, attracted to Britain's rebuilding efforts after WWII.

Eugene travelled to the UK alone and spent some years working and saving so that she could be reunited with her beloved sons. Noel considers that he had the benefit of living with two strong women in the years before he became a teenager and also having a resilient, adventurous woman in the form of his mother.

By the time Noel came to the UK aged 16, his mother had met a fellow Barbadian whom she married and borne three more children. It was a challenging time for this young man. He had to get used to a new family, including new siblings. He had a difficult relationship with his stepfather.

He had joined the local secondary school, Christopher Wren School in White City. There, he was put into the lower CSE stream. This was despite having been in the 'A' stream in his native Barbados, where he was achieving highly. He tried very hard to catch up with learning he had missed in his new school, staying up at night in the room he shared with his younger brother. There were regular complaints and remonstrations from his stepfather about *"keeping his brother up"* by revising late into the evening.

Noel became very unhappy. He felt stifled in the home, despite trying to focus on a hobby he loved; electronics.

Noel tried to keep himself busy, by participating in summer training courses, including tennis in the local park and by starting his Duke of Edinburgh Award training, where he later achieved The Gold Standard of the Duke of Edinburgh's Award.

The situation at home was not getting better, however. So much so, that Noel soon realised, a year after his arrival, that he had to get away from home. One day, Noel saw an advert on the television. This was for recruitment into the armed services. He decided to apply and did the aptitude tests which would determine which career pathway would best suit him. He did very well and chose nursing, to do his State Enrolled Nursing (SEN) qualification. He prepared himself for his new career, away from home and after a few weeks, he went off by train to start his RAF training.

The basic training, lasting six weeks, took place in RAF Swinderby. This Station was located near the village of Swinderby, Lincolnshire. It was the main place for the training of male recruits to the RAF. This base was responsible for the six-week basic training of all male enlisted personnel prior to their trade training.

Noel was the only black person in his intake. Initially, there were 30 recruits, but this was to reduce, by the end of the training. All the recruits needed to be fit, have a good mental attitude and a strength of character to tackle and succeed in their basic training. The new recruits were involved in intensive drilling, running, marching and related military activities. He was housed in a dormitory with around 25 other recruits. The recruits had to make sure their beds were carefully and properly made, with their blankets and other bedding folded to an exact 'bed-pack' size at the ends of their beds. They were subjected to rigorous daily inspections, which they had to pass. Noel got a lot from these robust procedures and with his fellow recruits, responded well, each day. The whole dormitory of recruits had to work as a team to get through these processes effectively.

Noel made friends in this first stage of his career. People were generally friendly towards each other. In Noel's case, there was a bit of a fly in the ointment, as one person, a chap from Yorkshire, when he asked Noel his name, having told him, he insisted on calling him, *'Snowey'*. So, *'Snowey'* became one of Noel's nickname. He was also called *'Winnie'*, by his pals. This was a shortened version of his first name Winfield and the nickname of his grandmother, Winifred.

Following a successful and enjoyable Passing Out Parade, Noel was sent off to RAF Halton near Aylesbury, to do a 4-week first aid training, before starting his nursing training.

Noel undertook his SEN training, which was scheduled to be completed within two years.

It was while he was doing this nursing training that Noel took up boxing. He became part of the RAF Germany Boxing Team. Unfortunately, he suffered a brain haemorrhage, which rendered him medically unfit and he was therefore downgraded for a period of 12 months.

His nursing qualification period was extended by six months after his brain haemorrhage. After his recovery, he decided to train as a boxing coach to help others to develop their skills in that sport. Noel lost a bit of his confidence after his medical issue, but he managed to move on and take up and strengthen his talents in other sporting activities. During this time, he was able to do quite a lot of parachuting and also developed his tennis. Tennis became his main sport, but he was also involved in playing Rugby Sevens, which he also enjoyed

After achieving his State Enrolled Nursing qualification, Noel was employed at the RAF Halton Renal Unit where he was also able to purchase his first car, from a Welsh Sergeant working on the unit. The Sergeant, Bob Williams, was to

271

become a mentor and advocate for Noel throughout his RAF Nursing journey.

After his period on the Renal Unit, Noel was posted to Germany for the next two and a half years. He really enjoyed his time in this posting, especially as he was able to meet other black people. One person in particular, Keith Crichlow, also of Bajan heritage, is someone with whom he still remains friends. There were however, few black people overall, but where Noel met them, whether RAF or army personnel, they all got together. They were a small but significant black community and were able to socialise in clubs and in other gatherings which they organised.

Whilst in Germany, Noel did a tour of the famous Wall, which separated East and West Germany. He was also involved in a Frontier Tour, an important part of the defensive processes at the time. After completing his first German tour, Noel was posted to a hospital in Cambridge (Ely) for the next 18 months, before being posted back to Germany for a further two and a half years. It was on this second tour that Noel reunited with Sergeant Bob Williams, who had in the interim period, been commissioned as a Nursing Officer. He was now Noel's direct manger and a Squadron Leader. Noel's nursing skills along with his extracurricular activities, were being identified as exceptional. So much so that with the support of the now Squadron Leader Bob Williams, he was nominated and won The Corner Memorial Trophy, an award for Nurse of the Year. Noel not only won that prestigious award once. He went on to win it twice. The memory of these successes still pleases him. He was at the time, the only person in the RAF to have won this award twice. He was runner-up at a third nomination, having lost out to his long-time friend and colleague, Tony Nichol.

Throughout his time in the RAF, Noel was involved in various conflict areas including the liberation of Kuwait during the first Gulf War. During the Gulf War, his role was working as part of a team to evacuate allied and enemy combatants, according to the rules set out in the United Nations Convention. Noel received a number of medals for his significant efforts during these tense, difficult events. Noel has been awarded the Gulf War Medal with Clasp for active service in the Gulf War.

He holds the RAF Long Service Good Conduct Medal (LSCGM), which was presented formally to him.

He is also the holder of The Liberation of Kuwait Medal from the Kuwait Government and the Kuwait Liberation Medal, issued by the Kingdom of Saudi Arabia.

Prior to his participation in the Gulf War, Noel was annually dispatched, on loan to a NATO Winter Survival School in the mountains of Bavaria, Southern Germany.

Noel was able to participate in the RAF skiing competitions, which he enjoyed enormously. He provided important medical support to NATO Aircrew in their Training School, especially regarding survival activities and escape and evasion exercises as well as post-crash survival in cold environments. He was able to work with people from other military forces, including French, Dutch and American. Noel also responded positively to requests for volunteers to go to Brunei for two months, undertaking and supporting jungle survival training. He undertook this role annually for three years. He found all these events, both fascinating and exciting, especially as he was sure his contributions were making a difference to overall military knowledge and the survival of their personnel, like himself.

After his promotion to Corporal and following a posting to the Falklands, Noel was later seconded from the RAF to Addenbrookes' Hospital in Cambridge to

274

undertake Registered Nurse Training. Following his qualification as a Registered Nurse, Noel later had a further secondment to Charing Cross Hospital in London to undertake Intensive Care Nurse Specialist Training. At the age of 39, Noel had by now achieved the rank of Sergeant. He applied to become a Commissioned Nursing Officer. He had previously applied for this role on a number of occasions but was never selected. On this application, he was approved for Officer selection at the Royal Air Force Officer training College at Cranwell. Whilst not selected on this intake, his results and feedback were very positive. The former Sergeant Williams was at this time promoted to Group Captain and the Director of Nursing Services. The Group Captain, through Noel's nursing manager, advised that it was likely Noel would be offered an Officer Training Course the following year.

It was 1996 and Noel was now nearly 40 years of old, with a wife and daughter. He had to consider whether to continue with his military career, or prepare to move into a new one as a civilian. A restructuring of the Armed Forces under Options for Change was by now in full swing and Noel had to decide whether to stay and hope to become a Commissioned Officer, or apply for the available option of redundancy from the Royal Air Force.

He decided it was time to move on. Having previously been involved in some work in the hospital's Information Systems and building personal computers for colleagues and patients, he felt this was a pathway he should follow. He decided to take redundancy from the RAF and begin resettlement interviews in readiness for his proposed new life. He recalls a conversation he had then, with a Lieutenant Colonel, who told him, *"You're a qualified nurse. You'll never make it in IT."* Noel took his redundancy money, which he then used to support him to retrain. He also took out a bank loan and commenced training to be a Microsoft Engineer.

Weeks after leaving the RAF, Noel got a job with an American company in Swindon, as an associate engineer. He took a reduction in salary of around £7,000 and survived on his redundancy funds. He progressed very well within the Company. Before long, he had doubled his salary and undertook numerous customer-facing technical roles and pre-sales activities on behalf of the organisation. The company, as part of its technical development framework, frequently sent Noel to the Company's headquarters in the United States for technical training and development. As part of the same framework, it also repaid Noel's bank loan. As an RAF Sergeant, he had been earning, around £25,000. In his new job, he was able to earn at least twice that amount in just one year, including performance bonuses.

He had made the right decision to change his career. He had contributed very well to the country, as a military man. It was now time to develop other skills and work towards more successes in his life. He worked on development programmes, where he went out with field engineers to learn from the bottom up. Thus, he was able to begin his own projects and also pre-sale consultancy. He was in people-facing roles for seven years, before he decided to move into his own freelance company working with the Home and Foreign Offices and other major Civil Service organisations.

Sergeant Noel Brathwaite has no regrets about his career in the RAF. *"I would do it all again in a heartbeat"*, he says. He especially, loved the trust, camaraderie, the feeling of belonging and of people *"having your back"*; all of which, have been invaluable to him. He was able to meet great people. He would later, in recognition of his recovery from a previous brain injury while he was in the military, been given the honour of attending one of Her Majesty, the Queen's famous Garden Parties.

He continues to have a close relationship with a lifelong friend Robert Fleming whom he met when he was around 21. They still have a very strong relationship. Robert has been very supportive of Noel following his departure from the RAF. He is godfather to Noel's older daughter and was at his wedding. Robert even stepped in to escort Noel's bride down the aisle after, alleges Noel, *"her racist parents refused to attend the wedding"*.

Noel also continues to maintain close contact with former servicemen both black and white. He believes their shared experiences have created an unbreakable bond.

He feels somewhat disappointed that outside the confines of the Service, little is known about the service and contribution given by Caribbean Veterans, to the UK. He recalls having conversations at the funeral of Flight Sergeant Peter Brown (A WWII veteran from the Windrush Generation). These conversations were had with a number

276

of elderly black people who expressed surprise that there were so many black servicemen in uniform.

Meeting Noel at the FS' funeral was a privilege. His aura of confident authority was clear to see, as was his pride in his long service in the RAF. He would certainly encourage young Caribbeans to consider a career in the RAF as well as the Navy. The only concern he has about this encouragement, is in relation to the recruitment stage. Here, he would argue, is where these new recruits could be persuaded to accept a trade into a military career pathway, which is not suitable for them. They would need to have better-informed choices, he believes. Otherwise, they could be limited to staying not only in careers they do not particularly love, but their promotion prospects might well be then depressed.

Were he to be able to go back and speak to his 17-year-old self, all those years ago, he would still say, *"Go for it! You will encounter individuals with racist attitudes, but do not assume everyone you meet will be a racist. Racism still exists as it does in our wider society. Rise above it. Challenge it, and maintain your self-respect. Make sure you build skills. You can do well."*

Noel is satisfied with his life and enjoys time with a loving family, including with his mother, Eugene. He was delighted to be able to honour her recently, during the Windrush Day celebrations, drawing together a rather impressive collage for her. He is very proud of the opportunity to show how she too has contributed to the UK over time.

Photo by Gill Shaw

Sergeant Noel Brathwaite is a talented, thoughtful man, whose life experiences within the military have been invaluable to him both personally and professionally. His contribution to our defence and freedom as a country, and his service to the Queen, is beyond question.

Senior Aircraftman Tony Brown

Born in Huddersfield in 1961, Tony is an African-Caribbean British citizen who grew up in Huddersfield, West Yorkshire. He left his hometown in June 1980 to join the Royal Air Force Regiment. His father, a Windrush pioneer, arrived in the UK in 1958; his mother followed in the 1960s, accompanied by a three-year-old daughter. His father, mother and sister are pioneers of the Windrush generation. The last of Tony's siblings, a brother, was born in 1962, making a family of five.

Tony recalls feeling the tension in his home from the age of seven. He reflects on that time in his life and especially to his father. Tony believes that his father was emasculated by racism, by the treatment he received outside the home: in his local community, by police, in housing, and especially at work. Racism and discrimination fuelled his father and produced undiluted anger in the family home after he finished work.

Tony's father was a hard-working man whose way of tackling his feelings about this treatment was head-on. Tony vividly remembers his father coming home one evening, beaten up from a racist encounter outside. Later that evening, his father and friends discussed what had happened and decided they had had enough. They had to retaliate, or things could escalate even further to possibly a loss of life, including their own. It was an awful, dangerous time for black people living in racist Britain between the late 1940s and the early 1990s. That evening, the men strengthened their resolve and decided that they would take no more from these racists. There would be *"No retreat. No surrender"*. Tony's father was the most vocal in the group.

So, Tony grew up in a challenging household where he and his siblings had to dodge as much as they could as kids to avoid a Jamaican discipline fuelled by colonialism and internalised discrimination. That discipline was sometimes harsh. Some of this avoidance by Tony and his siblings was not always possible. These experiences, which Tony observed, were pretty tough. He knew his father loved his family despite the "heavy handedness". His mother and father always worked hard to ensure their children ate three meals daily and were always smartly dressed. Tony has since been able to rationalise his childhood and fully understand the social and economic pressures his mother and father faced during those early years in Britain. All of these memories sadden him.

Tragically, Tony's mother died when he was only 14 years of age. Her death had a devastating effect on this young man. He was emotionally scarred and now began to internalise the discrimination his mother and father faced. He became very angry. Some of that anger then spilt onto the streets when he faced white Skinheads, Teddy Boys, and football hooligans who would project racist insults at him, his family or his friends. Without appropriate support following the tragic loss of his mother and with his evident immaturity, Tony's behaviour went downhill. Like his father, Tony met the racism and the racists head-on, even to the extent of getting into trouble several times with the local constabulary.

The only place where Tony would get some respite and some freedom was when he participated in sports: cross-country running, cricket, basketball and football. He excelled in football and was ambitious in his desire to be the best, representing the school, playing at County level and one day playing professionally.

Tony, aged 16 and armed with English and Geography qualifications, went straight into the Youth Training Scheme (YTS) for 12 weeks to learn basic construction trade skills. Over the next two years, he tried plumbing welding and worked as a labourer in a cotton mill. He was still getting into trouble for fighting against prejudice and racism and continued brushes with the police. Realising that the only places he could end up was either in prison or death, Tony decided to take matters into his own hands.

He visited the local Careers' Office to join one of the branches of the Armed Forces. The Royal Air Force (RAF) office was upstairs, and the Army office was downstairs. Tony went upstairs and took the RAF tests, hoping he could train as a physical training instructor. After receiving his test results, Tony was offered a place in the RAF Regiment, which he accepted.

Tony joined the RAF at 18 and seven months old in 1980. He started his training at RAF Swinderby in the County of Lincolnshire. At Swinderby, there were ten different barracks. Each barrack consisted of 30 young men from all over the country. There were only three black men in each Flight. Tony experienced language that he had never heard before, attitudes and culture that seemed alien to him. Excited and unsure, he wanted to give the opportunity of being an RAF Regiment Gunner a chance. First, he had to get through the next six weeks of basic training.

Unfortunately, it was not long before Tony came into conflict with others around racism. Young men from different parts of the country made prejudiced and stereotypical references to him and the other black Airmen. They used racist names. The other two black Airmen somehow shrugged it off and got on with their duties. Not Tony! He called the racists out and told them he *"wasn't having it"*. When Corporals and Sergeants were referring to black Airmen with racist names, this infuriated Tony. Once, he was having a severe argument with a Corporal and had to be restrained by other new recruits.

A particular black officer seemed to delight in "having a go" at this young man. The Officer would ransack Tony's bed space every other morning when on inspection. White recruits were shocked when they saw this. They could not understand the abuse Tony was being subjected to. For two weeks, Tony would cry under the covers every night, contemplating if he had made the right choice. As a civilian, he could vent his anger in the only way he knew, and that was to fight! He knew however, that he could not physically fight the racists inside the Armed Forces. That would be a one-way ticket back to Huddersfield. Faced with nowhere to run or hide, except at night when he was in bed, Tony sought advice from his father about how best to deal with this black Officer and the racism he was experiencing in the RAF. His father said, *"Stick with it, Son"*. Tony took that advice. It was really tough. Tony stuck with it all and completed RAF Swinderby, his first stage of training. He was then posted to RAF Catterick North Yorkshire for the next phase of his military career.

Tony recalls the day before the course started at RAF Catterick. He went straight from the guardroom to pick up his bedding and stood outside a barrack with twenty-five young airmen. *"We were all waiting to be told where we would be sleeping and what time we needed to be on parade."* Four men, two Corporals, one Sergeant, and one Flight Sergeant turned up. One of the Corporals started counting. He counted only the six black Airmen in the group and then said, *"Only one of you will complete the 13-week course"*. Tony could not believe it. He was shocked that it was only the day before the course started and already the Corporal was saying that only one black Airman would succeed! It seemed extraordinary to the young man.

Nevertheless, he and the rest of the group of young men got on with what they were expected to do. The group was instructed to clean the barracks, which would then be inspected at eight o'clock the following morning.

The racism started in the barracks, and again Tony had to make it clear that he *"wasn't having it"*. Each of the barracks had a designated senior man and deputy who were 'in charge'. On one occasion, the Barrack's deputy senior man called Tony a racist name. Tony retaliated, and the two men started fighting. The following day, Tony was made deputy senior man. Everyone knew Tony could look after himself, and the regime exploited Tony's strength of character to keep the rest of the troops in line. Tony felt they also did not like him because he was a black airman who refused to be bullied or racially abused.

He and the others engaged in various activities and study and went through 4-weekly tests, which they had to pass. They had to be able to identify the different aeroplanes, take turns in the gas chamber and outdoor survival training, and participate in simulations on the battlefield. By the end of the first eight weeks of training, the recruits had gone through their test, and only two black men were left in the whole group. Tony was one of them. The last test was Omega, a physical endurance field training lasting four days. Finishing the physical demands of the course and applying your training that you had received, would he believed, successfully see Tony through the course.

Tony completed the course successfully and arrived back on the Base. He was called into the Sergeant's office and told he had failed the course. He could not believe it. Tony argued, said it was impossible, and explained how the instructors had passed him on every field test. The Sergeant told him to *"Shut up"*, and sent Tony back to repeat day one of the course. Any recruit who fails any aspect of the course goes back four weeks to retake the training phase they failed. Tony was sent back to day one. What the Corporal said the day before the course had come to pass. Only one Black airman and 15 other soldiers qualified as an RAF Regiment Gunner. Tony retook the 13-week course and thus completed 26 weeks of training at RAF Catterick.

Tony's next posting was to RAF Laarbruch, Germany. He believed that with a fresh start in another country, if he kept his head down, he could succeed. His feelings about the RAF were optimistic despite the institutional racism he had experienced. However, being part of a team and also being responsible for others still came hard to him. Yet the RAF gave him fun, respect for orders which he found challenging, stability, a home, and safety.

Tony enjoyed the diversity in the RAF and made some long-lasting friendships. He still could not trust himself enough to trust people. Tony did not like orders shouted at him. The angry raised voices triggered something in him when he lived at home and he was not afraid to let anyone in the RAF know, despite their rank. Tony's entire history was shaped by fights with white people who did not like black people.

He met 16 black men at RAF Laarbruch. After asking several questions over time, Tony was aware that more white airmen had been promoted to the rank of Corporal than the several black airmen who had been in the service much longer and had several active-duty tours under their belt. He was, however, only too aware that he was "lucky" to have even made it to Germany, given his attitude to orders and stance on racism.

Tony was in Germany for three years. While there, he was asked if he would play football for his Squadron's second team. When Tony turned up to play for the second team, he scored six goals. News of his success spread around the Squadron and the Station. By the second week, he played for the Squadron's first team. He played for the Station's first team

282

again the third week. His footballing success was even profiled on the British Forces Broadcasting Service (BFBS) Radio.

Within three months, Tony played in one of the RAF's biggest cup competitions, the Presidential Cup. He represented RAF Germany and won the Cup.

A year later, Tony's RAF Germany Team would win the Cup again, and Tony was also awarded 'Player of the Tournament'.

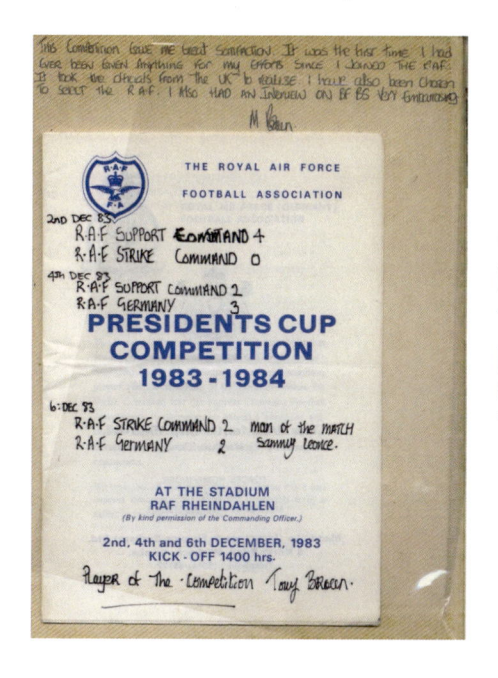

He was doing so well in his chosen sport that he was called to play for the Combined Services Team.

While at Laarbruch, he was presented with 'Colours' for sport. Colours were awarded to those who have achieved personal excellence, or who have made significant contribution. Tony had succeeded in doing both. These were proud and enjoyable moments for him.

Because of his sporting skills, especially with football, Tony was welcomed into the RAF.

Sports were significant in every part of the Armed Services. They saw this as supporting and strengthening team building amongst the men and women in the services. To a great extent, this idea worked well, as it bonded people well and enriched their dependency on each other.

"My name was everywhere. However, this recognition didn't play out well for me. On my squadron, there was resentment from my Squadron's superiors and there were threats to beat me up, which I had to deal with."

Despite his successes on the football field, it seemed to be an awful time for Tony. He had some very positive memories of his time in Germany, but unfortunately, there were several incidents of *"explicit racism, discrimination and threats of violence", he recalls.* When he had to defend himself from the threats and discrimination directed at him, he was reprimanded by his Warrant Officer, *"for fighting"*.

Looking back, he does not believe however, that he was innocent of using racist language himself. At that time, he felt he was unconsciously complicit in contributing to the institutional culture of the RAF, using language he was not proud of. For example, for Welsh Airmen, it was T..F. For Scottish Airmen, it was J..K; and for the Irish, it was P...Y. He was complicit. Regarding racial names, he rebelled, argued with his superiors and found himself reprimanded. He lost privileges many times while serving in Germany. He disobeyed orders because of the tone and way the orders were given. He was seen by most of his superiors as the *"gobby sprog"*, someone who has not been in the military service long or ever seen any action. He regularly lost privileges because he disagreed with the principle of what he was asked to complete. Tony openly admits he did not know where he was or appreciate what it meant to be a soldier then. The connection *"do as you are told in the military, or else"* was not made for him. He did not like the institutional culture but in the end, agreed it was better than leaving and returning to civilian life.

Tony and several other black men he met in Germany formed their own football team. Tony and another black Airman, Charlie Booker, were the only black Airmen who could get into the representative RAF Germany Team. There were however, several talented black footballers around to make up a strong team. This newly formed black group of footballers called themselves 'The Caribs'. Tony recalls Nigel Gilbert, Keith Crichlow, and Colin Broom were instrumental in establishing the team. The Caribs caused an uproar across RAF Germany. There were even less than positive comments about them at very senior levels of the RAF. The powers that be seemed to be against an all-black team. Nevertheless, the Caribs got on with playing their football, including having matches with some local German football teams in the nearby towns.

Tony's German experience was a mixture of highs and many lows. He got on with the military training exercises which all the men were expected to do and did well in them.

However, he had difficulty resisting the urge to *"give as good as he got"* to others, even those at a very senior level.

Tony will always be grateful for two particular Airmen. The first is Al Brown, whom he met at Laarbruch. He and Al were both from the North of England and jelled quickly. Al was always there to cover Tony's back, or to talk to him when things were not going well for Tony. He also has much to thank Keith Crichlow for. Keith was always the voice of reason. He trusted Keith. Keith, also known as 'Sparrow', helped Tony during some of the worst times in his German posting. *"He looked after me in a way that made me realise how angry I was."* Tony will never forget that support and will be forever grateful to Keith.

Now a Senior Aircraftsman. (SAC), Tony was quite happy to put the German experience behind him and accept his posting back to the UK. He was posted to RAF Hullavington, near Chippenham, Wiltshire. RAF Hullavington had been an essential RAF Station during WWII and continued to support its work in training and other operational activities until the station was decommissioned in 1992.

At 22, Tony was sent to Hullavington to work with another Tank Regiment. When he got there, on his induction, he met his boss, a Flying Officer, who spoke with him, saying, *"I have heard about the treatment you have received in Germany, which has not been fair. No one here will mistreat you"*. This man, it turned out, was a man of his word. Tony was treated respectfully, and for the first time in four years of service, his work was positively judged, and the racism was significantly reduced.

Tony spent two years at RAF Hullavington and two tours of active service abroad. He had by now, completed six years in the RAF. He decided it was now time to leave the RAF and go back into civilian life.

Tony's only regret concerning his time in the RAF is his service record. He realises that he was a bit of a maverick in the service and did not understand the environment he had signed up for. He found it hard to obey orders, and the service did not have the appropriate mentorship and support for him. Tony had to fight racism all his life and was an angry, immature young recruit. He regrets that he did not utilise the RAF's complaints' process. He should have been able to hold the officers, Sergeants, and the institution accountable. He reflects and wisely, says, *"Age teaches wisdom. It's not the other way around"*.

It has taken this man over 20 years to truly understand and explain why he should not have felt as angry as he had been. He has had years of traumatic stress about what he went through and spent years in the healing process. It has not been easy. He would have liked to advise his young teenage self about life journeys by saying, *"It's not where you start, it's where you finish. It's lifelong learning. Take your time. Be patient."* He references a psychoanalyst and former WWI Tank Regiment soldier, Wilfred Bion, who said, *"Patience is the gateway to reality".* Profound and prophetic words which clearly describe a point in Tony's history.

It has been 37 years since Tony left the RAF. His time out in civilian life has been marked with both challenges and successes over the years. He has experienced depression and has spent years reflecting on who he is and what he can do to tackle personal issues in his life. When he left the RAF, he initially found it challenging to get a job. When he turned up for interviews, he would regularly receive comments such as *"The job is gone"*, or be subject to the 'double look' from the interviewer, surprised to see a name like Brown, actually being the black man in front of them.

In 1989, Tony decided to study a City & Guilds bricklaying course. Following some experience on building sites, he was able to set up his own successful construction business. In 1997, he founded the Space Football Academy in his local community. This Academy linked ten football clubs from the Premier League to League One and semi-professional football teams. The SPACE Football Academy linked health and well-being, civic responsibility and education to young people, and developed parents to be certified football coaches.

In 1995, Tony went on a *"rites of passage"* journey to Uganda, a beautiful experience that enabled him to recover a sense of pride and *"centredness"* in himself. In 1997, working in partnership with a local sports' club, he established a football development school in Harare, Zimbabwe. He returned to Uganda in 2000 to share his skills and knowledge, contributing to a multi-agency partnership in Kampala, Uganda. The multi-agency collaboration focussed on providing help and support to street kids, women and children, fostering better relationships with the police, municipal council, and various community stakeholders.

Tony has paid sound attention to his intellectual growth. He started selling Black History books in 1992 to pay for his studies. In 2011, he was awarded a Fellowship at the United Nations, Geneva for people of African Descent. The fellowship focused on Human Rights, Minority Rights, Cultural Rights and indigenous rights for people of African descent.

After 33 years of study, completing various diplomas and a Masters in 2023, he has now completed his Ph.D.

Tony is a man who, from a very young age, was seen in the military and outside, as intense, challenging, and at times potentially violent due to explicit racism directed at him, to others as well as to his parents. Those experiences left him with a deep anger that fuelled some of his responses to strict discipline and unjust treatment in his chosen career.

He lives a rich and productive life, contributing to a range of events and organisations, leading discussions and delivering keynote speeches on topics he feels passionately about. His contributions are very much appreciated by those around him.

It is admirable that he is now in a stronger, more resilient place in his life. He contributed to the military over many years and made every effort to make that contribution count. Tony attributes his pride and determination to his mother and father.

Once he returned to civilian life. *"The focus, dogged determination and going beyond what I thought I could achieve, is all down to the RAF and some good people who never stopped believing in me."*

Promotion of Women in the RAF

The number of women serving in the RAF was relatively small during the post-war and late period. They were primarily employed in support roles, such as administrative, technical, medical, and logistical positions. Women of Caribbean heritage serving in the RAF during this period served in similar support roles, although the specific roles they held varied according to their interests, skills and aptitudes.

Some of the roles that women of Caribbean heritage held in the RAF included nursing, administrative officers, logistics officers and technical officers.

In the 1990s, women were allowed to serve in operational flying roles for the first time. However, women of Caribbean heritage serving in the RAF between 1960 and 2000 primarily held support roles.

It is worth noting that the number of women of Caribbean heritage serving in the RAF during this period was relatively small, as the RAF did not begin admitting women into operational flying roles until the 1990s. However, there were more women of Caribbean heritage who served in various support roles and made valuable contributions to the RAF's operations.

10. Conflicts, Peacekeeping and Armed Support

The British Army was involved in several conflicts between the 1960s and 1980s and the 1990s and 2000s in conflicts such as the Bosnian, Serbian and Kosovan conflicts and the Gulf Wars in Iraq and Afghanistan. Windrush Veterans played their part in all of these war arenas, contributing fully to the defence efforts provided by the British. Some of the major conflicts included:
1. The Aden Emergency (1960-1967)
2. The Nigerian Civil War (1967-1970)
3. The Dhofar Rebellion (1965-1975)
4. The Northern Ireland Troubles (1969-1998)
5. The Greek/Turkish Cypriot conflict (1974 -)
6. Operation Banner in Northern Ireland (1969–2007)
7. The Falklands War (1982)
8. Gulf War (1990-1991)
9. Balkans War (1991-1999), including the Kosovan War (1998-1999), the Bosnian War (1992-1995)
10. Iraq War (2003-2011)
11. The War in Afghanistan (2001-2021)

Northern Ireland "Troubles"

The British Army was deployed to Northern Ireland in 1969 as part of Operation Banner. Its role was initially to protect the population from sectarian violence between Catholics and Protestants, but it soon became involved in counter-insurgency operations. The Army remained in Northern Ireland until 2007 when its mission formally ended. At its peak in the early 1970s, more than 20,000 British soldiers were posted to Northern Ireland. By 2007, this number had decreased to around 5,000 as the security situation improved and Operation Banner came to an end.

The Good Friday Agreement, also known as the Belfast Agreement, was a peace agreement signed in 1998 that ended the Northern Ireland Troubles. It established a power-sharing government between unionists and nationalists in Northern Ireland and provided for North-South cooperation on matters of mutual interest and British–Irish relations. The Good Friday Agreement is widely regarded as one of the most significant political agreements of modern times.

According to an MOD report entitled "Caribbean Heritage in the British Army: An Assessment of Ethnicity and Representation" from 2017, around 8 per cent of British Army personnel in Northern Ireland were from Caribbean backgrounds at the peak of Operation Banner in 1978. This figure was higher than that for other deployments, such as Afghanistan and Iraq. According to the 2017 report, around 4 per cent of British Army personnel in Afghanistan and Iraq were from Caribbean backgrounds.

The Falklands War

The British Army was heavily involved in the Falklands War, which took place between April and June 1982. The conflict began when Argentinian forces invaded the British-controlled Falkland Islands in the South Atlantic. In response, Britain sent a large naval task force to retake the islands, backed up by an amphibious assault force of Royal Marines and Paratroopers from 3 Commando Brigade. After several weeks of intense fighting, British forces were able to reclaim control of the islands, and Argentine forces surrendered on 14 June 1982.

There is information about the number of Caribbean heritage personnel involved in the Falklands War. According to a 2017 report from the Ministry of Defence, around 6 per cent of British Army personnel and 2 per cent of Royal Navy and RAF personnel who deployed to the Falkland Islands were from Caribbean backgrounds. Some of the men interviewed in this book include Owen Bernard, RSM and Fred Coke, Chief Petty Officer.

Some Caribbean personnel received medals for their service during the Falklands War. According to a 2017 report from the Ministry of Defence, around 70 Caribbean personnel were awarded medals for their service in the conflict.

Other Conflicts and Peacekeeping Activities

There were also numerous other smaller-scale conflicts and peacekeeping missions, as well as ongoing deployments to a number of regions across the world. The UK has been one of the largest contributors to UN peacekeeping missions over the years. Some of the other peacekeeping missions that British soldiers were involved in during this period include:

The UN Operation in the Congo (1960-1964): British troops were deployed as part of a larger UN force in the Congo (now the Democratic Republic of Congo) to help maintain order and stability following the country's independence from Belgium.

The UN Transitional Authority in Cambodia (1992-1993): British soldiers were part of a UN peacekeeping force in Cambodia to help monitor and implement the peace agreement that ended the country's civil war.

The UN Assistance Mission for Rwanda (1993-1996): British soldiers were part of a UN peacekeeping force in Rwanda to help maintain peace and security following the country's civil war and genocide.

The Royal Navy was involved in many of the notable conflicts described earlier, including:

The Falklands War (1982): This conflict between the UK and Argentina over the Falkland Islands and South Georgia lasted 10 weeks in 1982. The Royal Navy played a significant role in the war with ships and submarines deployed to the South Atlantic to recapture the islands.

The Gulf War (1990-1991): The Royal Navy was part of a coalition force that fought against Iraq during the Gulf War. The Navy's primary role was to enforce the UN-imposed embargo on Iraq and protect shipping in the Persian Gulf.

The Bosnian War (1992-1995): The Royal Navy was involved in the conflict in Bosnia and Herzegovina as part of a NATO-led peacekeeping mission. The Navy's main role was to enforce an embargo on arms shipments to the warring factions and to provide naval gunfire support.

The Gulf Conflict (2003): The Royal Navy was part of a coalition force that invaded Iraq in 2003 as part of Operation Telic. The Navy's primary role was to support the ground forces and provide naval gunfire support.

The Sierra Leone Civil War (1991-2002): The Royal Navy was involved in the conflict in Sierra Leone, primarily in a humanitarian role, providing support to the government forces and delivering aid to those affected by the conflict.

The Royal Air Force (RAF) was also involved in several of the major conflicts described below.

It was involved in a number of operations during the Cold War, including the air defence of the UK and NATO countries and intelligence gathering missions. The RAF also participated in the Gulf War in 1991, which was a conflict between Iraq and a coalition of countries led by the United States.

Aden Emergency: The Aden Emergency was a conflict in South Yemen between 1963 and 1967, during which the RAF provided air support to British forces on the ground.

Falklands War: In 1982, the RAF was involved in the Falklands War, a conflict between Argentina and the UK over the Falkland Islands. The RAF provided air support to ground forces and also carried out bombing missions against Argentine positions.

Gulf War: In 1991, the RAF participated in the Gulf War, a conflict between Iraq and a coalition of countries led by the United States. The RAF provided air support, including bombing missions against Iraqi targets.

Kosovo War: In 1999, the RAF participated in the NATO-led intervention in Kosovo, providing air support to ground forces and carrying out bombing missions against Serbian targets.

Overall, the RAF played a significant role in a number of conflicts between 1960 and 2000, both in support of UK military operations and as part of international coalition forces.

The Royal Air Force (RAF) was also involved in various United Nations peacekeeping operations. They supported the UN peacekeeping operation in Cyprus, which began in 1964 and continues to this day. The RAF has provided transport and surveillance capabilities to the UN mission in Cyprus.

In the early 1990s, the RAF was involved in the UN peacekeeping operation in Somalia, known as UNOSOM. The RAF provided transport and logistical support to UN forces on the ground.

In the mid-1990s, the RAF participated in the UN peacekeeping operation in Bosnia and Herzegovina. The RAF provided transport capabilities to the UN mission and carried out air strikes against targets in the region as part of NATO's Operation

Deliberate Force. In the late 1990s, the RAF was involved in the UN peacekeeping operation in Sierra Leone. The RAF provided transport and logistical support to UN forces on the ground.

The RAF's involvement in UN peacekeeping operations during this period was not as extensive as its involvement in other conflicts. It did, however, play a role in supporting UN efforts to maintain peace and stability in conflict-affected regions.

11. Tours of Germany

Tours in Germany were significant for both the British Army and the Royal Air Force (RAF). During this period, Germany was a key location for British military forces in Europe, and many soldiers and airmen served tours of duty there.

For the British Army, tours in Germany were an important part of their service during the Cold War period. The presence of British forces in Germany was a key component of NATO's strategy for deterring Soviet aggression in Europe. The Army maintained a significant presence in the country throughout this period. Soldiers from the British Army served tours in Germany as part of several units, including infantry, armoured, and support units.

For the RAF, Germany was also an important location for operations during this period. The RAF maintained a number of bases in Germany, including in West Germany during the Cold War period, and played a key role in supporting NATO operations in Europe. The RAF deployed a range of aircraft to Germany during this period, including fighters, bombers, and transport planes.

Tours in Germany were significant for both the Army and the RAF for a number of reasons. First, the presence of British forces in Germany was an important part of NATO's strategy for deterring Soviet aggression in Europe. Second, the experience gained by soldiers and airmen during tours in Germany was valuable for maintaining a strong defensive position against potential threats from the Soviet Union. It also supported each service person's future military career. Finally, the presence of British forces in Germany helped to build strong relationships between the UK and Germany, which remain important to this day.

It would be fair to say that for most veterans, their German deployments were largely positive, especially in relation to the social opportunities available or were created by them. They were able to meet other Caribbeans from the various Islands and to see black personnel from other countries, including the United States and France. There were however, instances of less positive experiences, some of which are described in their various stories.

12. Some Key Regiments in which British Caribbeans have Served

The regimental system is thought to be one of the Armed Forces' major strength. From all the conversations held with the Veterans interviewed, it was clear that each person from the different regiments considered themselves much more than a collection of soldiers gathering together to perform specific military tasks. Within their regiments, they saw themselves almost as 'families' with a strong sense of belonging, of being part of a group that is bigger and better than any single individual within each regiment. It became like a brotherhood, sisterhood. It is those close relationships which allowed each person to give their utmost in extreme situations and conflicts. While they served and even beyond that time, they forged bonds of friendships within the particular regiments which were long-lasting and emotionally powerful. Many continued their friendships well into their lives as veterans.

There has been a strong British Caribbean presence in a several armed services' regiments over several decades. A regiment would normally contain around 650 soldiers depending on its role. Sometimes infantry regiments have more than one unit of this size and are referred to as a battalion. A battalion unit comprises of three or more companies of similar size. A regiment is headed by a colonel and is organised into companies, battalions, or squadrons.

Some key regiments include the Royal Artillery, The Royal Green Jackets, The Royal Army Medical Services, especially the Queen Alexandra's Royal Army Nursing Corps, the Royal Marines' Commandos, the Royal Electrical and Mechanical Engineers, the Royal Signals, the Paras, the RAF Regiment, the Royal Air Force Aircraft Technicians and the Armed Services Postal System. This last one is a key Unit providing vital support to service personnel in overseas postings especially. One such person supporting these particular efforts includes Lance Corporal Annette Erskine (nee Johns).

While there have been Caribbeans in many other regiments, their number has tended to be fewer. This is particularly so, interestingly, in Regiments such as The Coldstream Guards, the Blues and Royals, the Grenadiers, the Irish Guards, the Welsh Guards, the Scots Guards and the Lifeguards. There seem to be few, or in fact often no black people observed in the make-up of these troops until relatively recently.

Lance Corporal Annette Erskine (Nee Johns)

At the age of nine, Annette, along with her brother and sister, left the Island of Jamaica, to join her family in North West London. Annette attended school in North London, from Junior to Secondary, leaving at age 16, having achieved six CSEs at varying grades.

When Annette left school, she saw an advert in one of the tabloid newspapers, seeking recruits for the Women's Royal Army Corp. She completed and sent off the form and received a glossy folder. This showed the various Army bases located around the world, where you could be posted, if you chose to join.

It all sounded very exciting and so she completed the application form. She was invited to interview and for tests in the Army's Career Office in Shooters' Hill. Following receipt of her results, she was told what options were open to her in the military. Armed with this information, Annette decided to join the Women's Royal Army Corp (WRAC).

She then received her Travel Warrant and in January 1973, Annette arrived in the Guildford Army Camp to start her basic training. It was all very strange, drastically different from anything she had ever known. She knew no-one. She was also one of only two black women there.

The new recruits lived in a dormitory with up to 10 other young women.

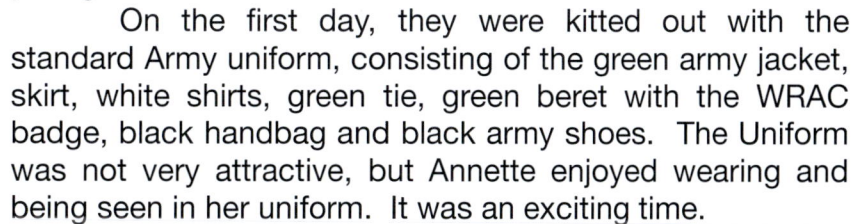

On the first day, they were kitted out with the standard Army uniform, consisting of the green army jacket, skirt, white shirts, green tie, green beret with the WRAC badge, black handbag and black army shoes. The Uniform was not very attractive, but Annette enjoyed wearing and being seen in her uniform. It was an exciting time.

Annette saw differences between herself, her black colleague, and the other women, in the way they conducted themselves. She recalls how open the white recruits were in speaking about intimate things. This type of 'sharing' was uncomfortable for her. She also remembers how many probing, quite revoltingly rude questions they would ask us about the black women's hair and skin. *"It was as if they felt these two non-white*

295

women were not human. It was quite horrible, but being young and a bit naive, I didn't know how to respond, so largely ignored or just avoided them."

However, Annette got on with the training; learning to march, how and when to salute an Officer, and all that was required to pass the test, to "Pass Out" successfully, within the required six-week training period.

She enjoyed much of her basic training and had opportunities to return home at weekends, to see her sisters and rest of the family.

At the women's army training camp at Guildford, each Squadron competed for the Drilling Trophy. Annette's Squadron won this most coveted trophy, which all trainees aspired to win. At the time, because of her height, Annette was the Squadron's Right Marker. Taking on the position of Right Marker is crucial for any Squadron to win that trophy. It was therefore, a very proud moment and achievement for her.

Annette, the proud Soldier, passed the required test to work in the Army Post Office, based at Mill Hill. The Postal Service was attached to the Royal Engineers which became her Regiment.

She found the work interesting; the postal workers were a tight-knit supportive group, so Mill Hill was also an enjoyable place in which to work. It was satisfying work, supporting the communication system for soldiers posted out either in the UK, or to various bases around the world. Annette remained at this first posting for a year, learning all the British Forces Post Office (BFPO) numbers, a unique system recognising the locations using numbers rather than location names, for security purposes.

During this period, women in the Army worked in administrative roles only and were not posted to war zones as they are now. Annette was however, one of the first women to be involved in the first military exercise to determine whether it would be possible for women to become active soldiers. These early exercises did lead to changes in the military, and today, women joining the military are able to fight alongside their male counterparts.

From Mill Hill, Annette was posted to Dusseldorf in Germany, a posting she did not enjoy. It was a small base and she discovered quite quickly that she had no future there. She therefore requested to move to Rheindahlan, a NATO Base with soldiers from other NATO countries, and one of the largest military bases in Europe.

The base was racially mixed and included white and black soldiers in what was a more open environment. One drawback for Annette, was the aloofness and racism, which seemed evident in the German civilian staff, who worked on the Base. She was disappointed by this, especially as there was so much to learn and enjoy from the diverse and skilled military personnel she met on the Base.

However, she soon noticed that promotion prospects were better for new white recruits who, despite being younger and less experienced, would be promoted above her very quickly. Nevertheless, despite her observations and sense of not "fitting in", she was able to involve herself in some of the social life.

The soldiers from the Caribbean (male and female), formed a close-knit group who supported and looked out for each other. She was delighted to meet the black soldiers and airmen, including those from other parts of the Armed Services. It was during one of these events that Annette would meet her future husband, who was in the RAF.

When Annette was in her third year of army life, she got engaged and thought carefully about the next stage of her life. It was a tough time for her in relation to these considerations. Finally, and with a heavy heart, but some anticipation and excitement, she gave notice of her intention to leave.

Shortly after this decision was made and rather unexpectedly, Annette was asked to see her Commanding Officer (CO). She was offered a promotion to the rank of Lance Corporal. Initially, Annette refused to accept this promotion. Her reasoning was that she had just submitted notice to end her service. Thus, she could see no point in accepting a promotion, which had not been forthcoming much earlier, despite her having an exemplary work record. She had the distinct impression that this promotion offer was due to an oversight, and should have been made earlier. She also felt it was due to the racism she had observed during her time on the Base. However, she did not articulate this to the CO at the time.

Annette was called back a few days later by her CO, who apologised that she had not been offered a promotion much earlier in her service. The CO persuaded her to accept the promotion, which he felt Annette deserved. He also told her that he would assist her in her job search as she moved into civilian life. Despite the way it was given, she was immensely proud to wear her Lance Corporal stripe. She knew that she had worked hard to achieve it.

Annette got married shortly after leaving the army and moved to Kent. She found civilian life very strange at first, being outside the strict, disciplined environment of military life, which she did miss initially.

As part of the Army Resettlement programme, Annette attended Sight and Sound College in West London to learn typing and office administration. She went on to become a Legal Secretary, progressing, over time to become a Personal Legal Assistant. She worked in numerous roles with some of the UK's largest law firms in the UK and abroad. She really enjoyed her career and continued to do so, right through to the end of her full-time working life. She continues to work, part-time, in her chosen area of work, enjoying the opportunity to meet a varied group of professionals in different, but interesting locations.

Looking back on her life in the army, she feels it was, after all, a very positive and rewarding experience. She has no regrets at all as she had developed a range of skills and had learned so much about herself and the world in general. She was a shy child and being in the army had made her much more confident and able to face things head on.

She is aware that the military service within the British Armed Forces of people like her, from her heritage, remains largely unknown and thus unrecognised and unacknowledged. *"It is only in the last few years that I have seen a bit of a change."*

She goes on to describe an exhibition organised by the RAF, focused on contributions made by Caribbeans. She was surprised, but pleased by this. She spoke further about the contributions made by the black WRAC Veterans, to have them be a part of the Remembrance Day Parade. The fact that organisers had not considered these Veterans also central to, or even worthy of being included in the first place, is a question she tries not to think about anymore.

Reflecting on her decision all those years ago, Annette would still advise her 17-year-old teenage self, to join up.

"It was the best move I've ever made. This was especially so, given that I had only been in the UK for seven years at that time. I wanted to do something more with my life, and this seemed a worthwhile road to take to achieve that."

She would still advise other Caribbean young people to consider a career in the army. She would however, caution them to investigate everything beforehand, to make sure they really know what to expect. She believes they would benefit greatly from the discipline, travel and opportunity to study and gain a profession within and beyond their service.

Lance Corporal Annette (Johns) Erskine is a woman of integrity and strength of character. She retains a positive relationship with other Veterans, some of whom are great friends.

She often joins in events and ceremonies, which are concerned with honouring those who have served. We should applaud her service and her continuing commitment to the Army and its purpose in defence of our country.

13. Promotions Across the Armed Forces

There is information about how Caribbean men and women were treated in the British Armed Forces regarding promotion up the ranks. In 2017, the Ministry of Defence (The UK Armed Biannual Diversity Statistics) published statistics relating to the gender, ethnicity, nationality, religion, and age of the Armed Forces. It found that while Caribbean personnel made up 8 per cent of Army personnel in Northern Ireland during Operation Banner, they only accounted for 2 per cent of senior non-commissioned officers (NCOs). Additionally, while 6 per cent of all Army officers deployed to the Falkland Islands were from a Caribbean background, this figure was just 1.5 per cent for those holding higher ranks such as Major and above. It is clear, therefore, that Caribbean personnel were consistently under-represented in terms of promotion up the ranks in all three services (Army, Navy and RAF). This data is reflected in the individual stories represented in this book.

It is difficult to speculate as to why Caribbean personnel were under-represented in terms of promotion up the ranks, but it may be due to a combination of factors such as institutional racism and cultural bias. Additionally, there may have been a lack of awareness or understanding within the Armed Forces about the potential for Caribbean personnel to excel. It is unclear as to why this could possibly be the case.

The MoD produced its Strategy for achieving change, in 2018 and it sets out its ambition.

"The challenging vision, goals, objectives and commitments in this strategy clearly set out where we want to see change: building a more inclusive workplace for all; increasing diverse representation at all levels…".

It recognised that *"we still have a lot of scope for improving our..performance. For example: In the military, BAME and female representation is still very low (particularly at senior levels).*

There are personal stories contained in the various sections of this book, as well as others which may confirm these views. The situation therefore, when the Ministry of Defence published the 2017 report, was that there were no Caribbean heritage personnel in the highest ranks of any of the British Armed Forces Services up to and during the period. However, there was a very small minority of Caribbean personnel holding higher ranks, such as Major or Lieutenant Commander. The first black Colonel, Andy Allen MBE, achieved that rank in 2008. There is currently one Caribbean heritage Brigadier, Karl Harris, serving in the British Army.

Interestingly, the RAF's top officer, Air Chief Marshall Sir Mike Wigston, told Sky News on 6 April 2023, that he was ready to do everything possible to improve diversity, despite the clear and apparent opposition from some of his top team. Indeed, it is alleged that one of that team resigned because of the Air Marshall's direction relating to ethnic minority recruitment. When the Air Marshall appeared before Members of Parliament in February 2023, he admitted that his *"aspirational goal"* to improve diversity cascaded down to become an *"unattainable"* target for his recruitment officers. How disappointing.

If this approach addresses an obvious problem but is being opposed, allegedly, by senior and powerful officers, how can ethnic minority personnel gain access to senior ranks? It is not just a glass ceiling; it is therefore a ceiling made of steel. The Veterans whose stories are in this book testify to these sorts of behaviours. They reflect serious obstacles to them gaining promotion to upper ranks which seemed to be in play then and which appear to be still of concern. So, *"When is change gonna come?"*

14. Medals and Awards

There were many Caribbean Army personnel who served in the British Armed Forces in and beyond the 1960s, and many of them were recognised for their service with medals and awards.

One of the most common medals awarded during this period was the General Service Medal (GSM), which was awarded for operational service in various campaigns and home and foreign conflicts, including the Falklands War, the Gulf War, and the Bosnian War. Many Caribbean personnel were involved in these campaigns and were awarded the GSM for their service.

Another common award was the Long Service and Good Conduct Medal, which was awarded to personnel who had served for at least 15 years with good conduct. This medal recognised the dedication and commitment of Caribbean personnel who had served in the British Armed Forces for many years.

In addition to these medals, some Caribbean personnel were also awarded medals for their service in specific campaigns. For example, personnel who served in the Gulf War may have been awarded the Gulf War Medal, while those who served in Bosnia may have received the Bosnia Medal.

Finally, some Caribbean personnel were recognised for their bravery and courage, with awards such as the Military Cross or the Conspicuous Gallantry Cross. These awards were given to personnel who had demonstrated exceptional bravery and leadership in the face of danger.

Overall, Caribbean Army personnel who served in the British Armed Forces between 1960 and 2000 were eligible for a range of medals and awards depending on their service and achievements. These awards recognised their contributions to the British Armed Forces and demonstrated the important role they played in the defense of the United Kingdom and its allies.

However, this has not always been the case. Caribbean personnel have not always been recognised for their service and achievements in the British Armed Forces throughout history. For example, in World War II, despite over 16,000 Caribbean personnel serving in the British Armed Forces, they were rarely, publicly, recognised for their contributions. Only a few received the range of medals and honours which others seemed to have more easily done. They seemed absent, until very recently, in the public honouring and significant parades and displays.

It is worth noting, however, that during the Falklands War in 1982, a number of Caribbean and other Commonwealth personnel served alongside British forces and were recognised for their contributions with medals and honours. Not enough is known about them.

In recent years, the British Armed Forces have made more of an effort to recognise the contributions of personnel from ethnic minority backgrounds in the more recent conflicts, such as those in the Middle East - the Gulf Wars and the war in Bosnia and Kosovo.

In 2019, the British Army announced that it would award the Elizabeth Cross to the families of soldiers who died in service and were from ethnic minority backgrounds.

Some Caribbean personnel were recognised for their bravery and courage with awards such as the Military Cross or the Conspicuous Gallantry Cross. These awards were given to personnel who demonstrated exceptional bravery and leadership in the face of danger.

15. Family Support in the Armed Services

The British Armed Forces provided basic support to the families of soldiers. Some of the support that was in place included the provision of Service Families' Accommodation (SFA) and accommodation for service personnel and their families. Children of service personnel were entitled to receive education in British Forces schools located on or near Army, RAF and Navy bases and Camps. These schools were staffed by qualified teachers and offered a full range of academic and extracurricular activities. Personnel and their families were entitled to receive healthcare through the National Health Service (NHS) or through the MOD's own medical services. The Army also provided medical and dental care on base.

There was a range of welfare services to support service personnel and their families. This included support for mental health, financial advice, childcare support, and pastoral care. These supports were in addition to annual leave entitlement, which allowed them to visit family and friends or take holidays. There were also social and recreational opportunities for service personnel and their families, including sports clubs, community centres, and social events.

In reality, this support did not always reach the people concerned. In fact, many of the people who were interviewed do not feel that the support has continued beyond their immediate discharge. Many report that once they left, that was it. No contact. No support. Nobody cared about the service they had given. This is despite the existence of the Armed Services Covenant, which, unfortunately, has no legal, enforceable 'teeth'.

16. Arrangements for Transition to Civilian Life

The British Army, RAF and Royal Navy provided various transition arrangements to support Caribbean heritage men and women who were leaving. Some of these arrangements included resettlement training; employment services including CV writing and interview coaching; financial support in the form of a tax-free resettlement grant; housing assistance consisting mainly of advice about affordable housing and assistance with applications for social housing; and medical support to assist with medical and dental care for up to six months after leaving the service. Some of these arrangements were provided through government programmes that were available to all individuals leaving the military, while others were specific to the Army, RAF and Navy. Not all of the Caribbean Veterans received considered and consistent support to enable them to effectively transition into civilian life. Most felt abandoned.

Pension Arrangements

For many Veterans, the issue of pension remains a contentious issue. There were significant changes made over the last 40 years of the 20th century. These changes affected, sometimes very negatively, the future income of a significant number of Caribbean Veterans. Service personnel who joined the Army before 6 April 1975 were enrolled in a non-contributory pension scheme, which provided a pension of up to 75% of their final pensionable pay after 22 years of service. They were not able to claim a pension if they served fewer years. Those who joined the Army after this date were enrolled in a new pension scheme, which was a career-average pension scheme.

Those who served less than 22 years were adversely affected by this policy. This has affected both black and white Veterans. Many still feel resentful that there was no recognition, through a designated military pension, of their years of service. After all, and in the Veterans' view, if you worked in a factory for even two years, you had a small pension, *"Even if it is only a few pence,"* says two of them. Many are still smarting at this perceived injustice which has left them less well-off than many others. There may have been some variation in pension arrangements depending on the rank, length of service, and specific circumstances of each individual service personnel. A number of Veterans who left the forces before 1990 are still trying to sort out their pensions, which they believe are lower than they should be, given their length of service in the forces. Some of the Veterans represented in this book have been affected and have been *"fighting"* for years to achieve what they believe they should be entitled to, that is, more fairness in pensions. For these particular Veterans, now in their late 60s, 70s and even into their 80s, they feel they do not have much more time on their side to continue that fight. They want to redress a perceived wrong before their life is over. They believe they deserve it.

17. The Armed Forces Covenant

The Armed Forces Covenant is a pledge made by the UK government and society as a whole to ensure that members of the British Armed Forces, Veterans, and their families are treated fairly and not disadvantaged as a result of their service to the nation.

The Covenant recognises the unique sacrifices and challenges faced by military personnel, including frequent deployments, long periods of separation from family, and exposure to dangerous and stressful situations.

The Covenant was developed in order to ensure that these amazing individuals receive the support and recognition they deserve, including access to healthcare, education, employment, and housing.

The Covenant also promotes the principles of mutual respect, understanding, and integration between the military and civilian communities. It encourages businesses and organisations to pledge their support for the Armed Services community.

The Armed Forces Covenant was enshrined in law in the Armed

The Armed Forces Covenant

An Enduring Covenant Between
The People of the United Kingdom
Her Majesty's Government
-and-
All those who serve or have served in
the Armed Forces of the Crown
And their Families

The first duty of Government is the defence of the realm. Our Armed Forces fulfils that responsibility on behalf of the Government, sacrificing some civilian freedoms, facing danger and sometimes suffering serious injury or death as a result of their duty. Families also play a vital role in supporting the operational effectiveness of our Armed Forces.
In return, the whole nation has a moral obligation to the members of the Naval Service, the Army and the Royal Air Force, together with their families.
They deserve our respect and support, and fair treatment.

Those who serve in the Armed Forces, whether regular or Reserves, those who have served in the past, and their families, should face no disadvantage compared to other citizens in the provision of public and commercial services. Special consideration is appropriate in some cases, especially for those who have given most, such as the injured and the bereaved.

This obligation involves the whole of society: it includes voluntary and charitable bodies, private organisations, and the actions of individuals in supporting the Armed Forces. Recognising those who have performed military duty unites the country and demonstrates the value of their contribution. This has no greater expression than in upholding this Covenant.

Forces Act 2011, and is supported by a network of organisations, including the Armed Forces Covenant Fund Trust, which provides funding for projects that support the Armed Forces community.

By the designated cut-off date of September 2021, all local authorities in the UK had signed the Armed Forces Covenant, along with many other organisations, charities, and businesses. In Northern Ireland, the Covenant is supported by the Northern Ireland Executive and a wide range of organisations.

However, it is important to note that signing the Covenant is a voluntary commitment. While many Councils and organisations have pledged their support, not all have done so. Additionally, signing the Covenant is just the first step. Organisations are expected to take concrete actions to support the Armed community, such as offering employment opportunities, providing housing support, and improving access to healthcare and education.

Local Councils in the UK may have information about the number of Veterans living in their area, as well as their needs and priorities. This information is often obtained through surveys and consultations with Veterans and their families, as well as through data-sharing agreements with government agencies and organisations that support the Armed community.

The UK government has also established a Veterans' Gateway service, which should provide a central point of contact for Veterans seeking advice and support. Local councils are able to use this service to refer Veterans to the appropriate organisations and services in their area.

The Armed Forces Covenant sets out a number of commitments for local authorities, including the obligation to gather information on the needs of the local Armed community and to use this information to inform policy and service provision. Therefore, local councils are expected to have a good understanding of the needs of their local Veteran population in order to provide appropriate support and assistance. Sadly, this support is not always forthcoming and is often absent.

There are a variety of factors that can contribute to Veterans, including those from black communities, *"falling through the net"* when it comes to accessing support and services. This could be because of a lack of awareness of the support services available to them. This can be due to a lack of information or outreach by local authorities or service providers.

They may feel stigma and shame. Some Veterans may feel reluctant to seek help or admit that they are struggling due to the stigma surrounding mental health or a perception that asking for help is a sign of weakness.

Black Veterans may face additional challenges, such as discrimination or racism, that can exacerbate mental health problems or other issues.

Additionally, some Veterans may have complex needs, such as homelessness or substance abuse, that require a more holistic and coordinated approach to support.

Some Veterans may face practical barriers to accessing support and services, such as transportation or childcare issues, that can make it difficult for them to attend appointments or access treatment.

These are challenges that really need to be tackled. It is important for local authorities and service providers to take a culturally sensitive and inclusive approach to supporting Veterans from black communities. They need to work closely with community organisations and other stakeholders to ensure that support is accessible and effective. This may involve targeted outreach and awareness-raising campaigns, as well as efforts to remove practical barriers to accessing services.

As this Armed Services Covenant is voluntary, it is clear that in an unsatisfactory number of cases, Veterans are not being well-served once they have transitioned out of the services.

There is, or should be, information available about the number of Veterans in each local authority, but many Veterans report that once they leave the forces, no contact is made with them. They feel abandoned and unappreciated by society. A number of charities try to help, but again, these charities depend on referrals. There are many examples of ex-servicemen being homeless or having mental health issues. Some are left to die alone. One such example, as mentioned earlier, is of Flight Sergeant Peter Brown, who died alone in the City of Westminster. Others have died alone, their needs unrecognised.

18. Post-traumatic Stress Disorder (PTSD)

It is very likely that people serving in the military may be exposed to different traumatic events than those in which civilians might be involved. In addition, the conflicts or wars in which military personnel will have served may also affect their risk of post traumatic stress disorder. Therefore, combat zone deployment, training accidents or other traumatic events may lead to PTSD.

The results, published in the British Journal of Psychiatry (8 October 2018), estimates the rate of PTSD among UK veterans of all conflicts to be 7.4%. The rate of PTSD among the public is 4%. The rate of PTSD is apparently, even higher for veterans who served in Iraq or Afghanistan.

A report from the British Medical Journal, in 2022, claims that around 40% of British Army Veterans have suffered depression, anxiety, alcoholism or post-traumatic stress. The report, in the British Medical Journal and based on records of 2,500 ex-personnel, warned that those who see combat are most likely to be affected, with Veterans being twice as likely to develop mental health problems compared to people on civvy street. Someone with PTSD often relives the traumatic event through nightmares, intrusive memories and flashbacks. They may experience feelings of isolation, irritability and guilt. Many of them may also have problems sleeping or may find it difficult to concentrate.

According to an article published in the Mirror online in 2022, since 2017 more than 350 Veterans and service personnel are feared to have killed themselves. In that same article, the MoD responded by saying that *"Wellbeing is a top priority. Former service personnel can access specialist care from the NHS, including via the Veterans' Gateway and every part of the UK now has a dedicated mental health service for Veterans."*

In a report from Combat Stress for Veterans' Mental Health, their Medical Director said *"Of the veterans we treat, 92% have two or more mental health conditions and almost 80% have served in a combat role".*

Several ex-members of the Armed Forces who were interviewed for this book, assert that they feel that generally, the support for them once they left the service, was patchy at best, but was mostly non-existent. Since most of them had served several years ago, they can only hope that things have changed and better support is now available to current service personnel and for those more recent leavers.

19. Charities Supporting Veterans

Many charities in the UK that provide help and support to Veterans from all branches of the Armed. These charities offer different services, including financial assistance, housing support, mental health support, and employment opportunities. Some of the most prominent charities providing support to Veterans in the UK include:

- **Royal British Legion** - This charity, one of the most well-known, supports all Veterans and their families, regardless of which branch of the Armed they served in. The Royal British Legion provides assistance with housing, employment, and financial support, as well as operating several care homes for Veterans. It also does much to publicise the stories of the service of many who have served. From its publication, it states, *"The story of Black British and Black African and Caribbean service and sacrifice is one that we are keen to share, a story of men and women who have done so much in defence of Britain and in protecting all our citizens."*
- **Help for Heroes** - This charity supports wounded, injured, and sick Veterans from all branches of the Armed. Help for Heroes provides support with housing, mental health, and employment, as well as funding a range of sports and activity programmes for Veterans.
- **Soldiers', Sailors' & Airmen's Families Association (SSAFA)** - This charity supports serving personnel, Veterans, and their families from all branches of the Armed. SSAFA provides assistance with housing, financial support, and welfare services, as well as operating several care homes for Veterans.
- **RAF Benevolent Fund** - This charity supports serving and former members of the Royal Air Force and their families. The RAF Benevolent Fund provides financial assistance, housing support, and welfare services, as well as funding several projects aimed at improving the well-being of serving personnel and Veterans.
- **Army Benevolent Fund** - This charity supports serving and former members of the British Army and their families. The Army Benevolent Fund provides financial assistance, housing support, and welfare services, as well as funding several projects aimed at improving the wellbeing of serving personnel and Veterans.
- **Naval Children's Charity** - This charity supports children of serving and former members of the Royal Navy and Royal Marines. The Naval Children's Charity provides financial assistance, educational support, and welfare services to children whose parents have served in the Royal Navy or Royal Marines.

These are just a few examples of the many charities providing help and support to Veterans in the UK. While some charities focus specifically on one branch of the Armed, most provide support to all Veterans and their families, regardless of which branch they served in. Other charities in the UK specifically focus on providing support to Caribbean Veterans. Some of these charities include:

- **Windrush Caribbean Veterans** - This charity was established to support Caribbean Veterans who served in the British Armed Forces during World War II and subsequent conflicts. The charity provides financial assistance and healthcare support, and helps to connect Veterans with relevant services and support networks.
- **Caribbean & African Veterans' Resettlement & Support (CAVRS)** – This charity supports Caribbean and African Veterans who have resettled in the UK. CAVRS offers financial assistance and housing support, and helps Veterans to access relevant services and support networks.
- **British West Indies Veterans Association (BWIVA)** - This charity supports Veterans of the British West Indies who served in the British Armed Forces during World War II and subsequent conflicts. BWIVA offers financial assistance, healthcare support, and helps Veterans to access relevant services and support networks.
- **The West Indian Ex-servicemen and women Association (UK**) was formed in 1970 by a group of Ex-servicemen and women based in the London area. These were mostly volunteers who came to England during and just after WWII. The West Midlands branch was formed in 1995, as a self-financing registered charity parented by the West Indian Ex-servicemen and women Association in London. In subsequent years, membership of the Birmingham Branch grew to over 80 members but, unfortunately membership gradually declined.

  In 2010, the organisation underwent restructuring with the Birmingham branch adopting a new constitution and the name **'British and Caribbean Veterans Association' (BCVA)**, thus becoming a totally independent self-financing charity. They hoped that, with a new constitution, the British and Caribbean Veterans Association would appeal to Veterans, regardless of location. They were hopeful that they would then recruit and retain a significant membership. The Charity's Objects are To provide relief for serving and former members of Her Majesty's Armed Forces or Forces of the Commonwealth and their dependants who may be in condition of need, hardship or distress, by advancing any lawful charitable purpose, at the discretion of the Trustees. Sadly, the organisation mourns the loss on 30 August, 2023, of their Chairman, Fred Coke, a former Chief Petty Officer who had given 22 years of service to the Royal Navy.
- **The West Indian Association for Service Personnel (WASP)** This is a UK-based charity that supports Commonwealth Veterans and their families, including those from the Caribbean. The charity was founded in 2000 by a group of Caribbean ex-service personnel who recognised the need to support their fellow Veterans in the UK. WASP offers a range of services to Veterans and their families, including financial assistance, housing support, and access to healthcare services. The charity also provides social activities and events to help Veterans and their families connect with each other and build support networks. One of the main focuses of the West Indian Association of Service Personnel (WASP) is to help Veterans

navigate the complex process of applying for UK residency and citizenship. Many Commonwealth Veterans who served in the British Armed Forces are eligible to apply for residency and citizenship in the UK, but the application process can be challenging and confusing. WASP provides assistance and support to help Veterans complete the application process and secure their status in the UK.

- In 2010, Selena Carey, a Londoner and historian, decided to launch the Black Poppy Rose in remembrance of those black, African, Caribbean and Pacific Islanders who lost their lives at war. She also decided to give the profits to WASP to help them with their work. Poppies, red ones, were already being used to remember the loss of lives in the major world wars and since. They were chosen because poppies sprung up in the ravaged battlefields of Northern France and Belgium and had, therefore, become symbolic and iconic. WASP play an important role in supporting Caribbean Veterans and their families in the UK, helping to ensure that they receive the recognition, support, and assistance that they deserve. They welcome any support from others, including financial and pro bono, to enable them to continue with their work. These last two charities recognise the unique challenges faced by Caribbean Veterans and their families and work to provide tailored support and assistance to address these challenges.

Homelessness Amongst Veterans

Homelessness is a significant issue in the UK, and Veterans, whether black. Or white, are among the populations most at risk. According to a 2021 report by the UK Ministry of Defence, there were an estimated 3,500 homeless Veterans in the UK in 2020. The report also noted that Veterans from black and minority ethnic backgrounds may face additional challenges accessing support and services. There are organisations in the UK that provide support and services to homeless Veterans, including those from Caribbean backgrounds. For example, the Veterans Aid organisation offers services to homeless and at-risk Veterans in the UK, including emergency housing, health care, and employment support. Another helpful organisation is the Forces in Mind Trust, which conducts research and advocacy related to the well-being of Veterans. In addition, there are organisations such as the West Indian Association of Service Personnel (WASP) and the British Caribbean Veterans' Association (BCVA), mentioned earlier, which continue to provide direct support to Caribbean Veterans in need.

20. Current Recruitment of Caribbean Personnel to the Armed Forces

The UK Armed continue to recruit men and women from a range of backgrounds, including those from the Caribbean and other ethnic minority backgrounds. In recent years, they have made efforts to increase the diversity of their personnel to better reflect the society they serve.

They have developed programmes and initiatives aimed at encouraging more people from diverse backgrounds to consider a career in the Armed. For example, the Armed Forces Covenant was supposed to help potential recruits see the benefits of such a career and that they would know that society would recognise and even appreciate their contributions beyond that career.

Frankly, there have been mixed responses to the implementation of this Covenant in the different local authorities and across the various branches of the Armed Forces. A particularly well-publicised example of the poor execution of this Covenant, as described earlier, is that of Flight-Sergeant Peter Brown, who was an RAF Veteran. In 2021, at the age of 95, his neighbour in the City of Westminster reported to the RAF that he needed help. This help was not forthcoming, as apparently, he had to directly request that help himself despite his frailness. It appears that no one visited Mr Brown to check the extent of his need. He died alone in his flat the following year, in December 2022. It was at this stage that, in January and February 2023, there were numerous media reports about his life and death. No help in life, but plaudits and acknowledgements in death. There is a great and overwhelming tragic irony in this.

Additionally, the Army's "Step Up" programme is aimed at encouraging more young people from ethnic minority backgrounds to consider a career in the military. The programme offers mentorship, training, and support to help candidates prepare for the rigours of military life. It is difficult to evaluate the effectiveness of this programme in enhancing the number of people choosing to join up. There would need to be more work done in this area.

The UK Armed Forces have high standards for physical fitness, mental resilience, and professional conduct, and the recruitment process is competitive and rigorous. Many Caribbean heritage people are continuing to meet those expectations, both Black British, born and living in the UK and a few hundred who apply successfully from Islands in the Caribbean. There is still not a significant increase to the numbers, however, when compared to previous years.

Caribbeans are still joining the Armed Forces, however. The 'Old Guard', in the form of the Veterans who have been described throughout, would want to see these new recruits take full advantage of all the opportunities, which all the branches undoubtedly have. They would ask however, that these young, talented and keen young people are afforded just and fair treatment along with sound mentoring support to enable them to rise up the ranks in exactly the way their white counterparts do.

That would be a wonderful legacy for their hundreds of years of service to British society and the Crown.

Two of the more recent recruit Caribbean recruits, not technically a part of the Windrush Generation, include Nekesha Thompson and Nicolette Skyers. These women demonstrate the ongoing service provided by Caribbean personnel to the British Armed Forces. They made successful applications from their native homelands and served in the British Army for several years.

Sergeant Nicolette Skyers

Nicolette was born in St Catherine, Jamaica and came to the UK when she was 23 years old. She was already a mother to a son who was being cared for by an older friend, as she pursued her career. It had been very painful to leave him at that time, but she knew that a long-term career in the forces would enable her to provide better for him in the long run. She therefore took the advice of a former Caribbean Regimental Sergeant Major who had served in the UK, and set off to pursue her ambition with the Army.

She had also applied to join the Jamaica Constabulary Force but as a female and as a single parent with a very young child, this proved impossible for her in her home country. She therefore applied for and was provisionally accepted, into the British Army.

At the age of 24, she joined the British Army and set off to England, firstly to find somewhere to live and then once her tests were passed, to begin her initial training.

When Nicolette arrived in the UK, she lived with her sponsor, who had been introduced to her through the ex-RSM who had encouraged her in Jamaica. She reported for a 2-day training in Pirbright. Unfortunately, there was a medical issue, which caused her to delay her training.

Nicolette was able to begin her Phase 1 training in Winchester, in the Adjutant General Corps (Staff and Personnel Support) AGC (SPS) to undertake a career providing Staff and Personnel support to soldiers.

The Adjutant General's Corps (AGC) is a corps of the British Army responsible for the personnel, training, and administration of soldiers in the Army. The AGC has a vital role in supporting the Army's operational effectiveness by providing essential services, including human resources, education and training, and legal and financial support.

The AGC has a diverse range of responsibilities, with each of its six branches specialising in specific areas. The branches include the Provost Branch which includes the Royal Military Police (RMP), the Military Provost Staff, and the Military Provost Guard Services (MPGS). The Army Legal Services (ALS), the Educational and Training Services (ETS, and the Staff and Personnel Support (SPS).

Nicolette recalls those first few days and months very well. She questioned herself at times, *"What am I doing coming here? Being shouted at!"* However, she wanted to take a good run at her new career and therefore soon developed that necessary thick skin, needed for survival. She knew that she had a competitive streak and was keen to be first in everything. She was fit and able to tackle all the physical exercises with vigour, succeeding every time. She admits that she struggled a bit with the rifle skills, but eventually got through these as well.

She made a few friends in the Phase 1 training and there is one with whom she still remains in touch. There were very few other black women around her; not many *'looking like me'*, even amongst the trainers leading sessions. Mostly, she was one of very few black people. She would sometimes hear comments from more senior personnel. Sometimes the *"If Jamaica is so beautiful, why are you here?"* And, she recalls, other condescending comments which peppered general conversations. She learned fast. She adjusted well, including eating at speed, as they all had to, in order to meet the demanding schedules, set out for them.

She was a part of the 1st Battalion, The Royal Anglian Regiment, serving initially as a Private. It was not too long before Nicolette was promoted to Lance Corporal. She was posted out to North Luffingham as part of the 104 Military Working Dog Regiment. In this Regiment, Nicolette was in a position to offer advice and support to soldiers. Her main focus was in relation to ensuring operational effectiveness, including providing appropriate human resources support to her army colleagues, as appropriate.

Within two years of being in the Army, Nicolette was deployed abroad to do her part in the defence of the country. She recalls the serious briefings they all received to secure each other in the difficult environments.

She pictures arriving at airports, putting on her helmet and the tension she felt when being briefed about mines and movements around civilian roads, as well as working in darkness. At those times, she truly appreciated the important part she played in that common military effort. She donned her armour, accepted the need for lockdowns, wore her rifle 24/7 and was driven hard by adrenalin throughout those six-monthly tours.

It was important to be firm about the discipline required in the forces, but in her view, it was also important to retain a sense of humanity in the work. Sometimes, that sense of humanity seemed a little hard to find. There were tough challenges to overcome, but Nicolette was a part of a bigger group, who drew together and made sure their common purposes within the armed forces, were efficiently carried out. She was close to her comrades and this comforted her in the face of the known aggressors. She had of course, moments, down times, where she was able to enjoy some short breaks for rest and recreation in a country nearby. These moments were very necessary for her and for her colleagues, who were bombarded, daily, by the stresses of impending and real, combat.

Nicolette achieved a further promotion, to the rank of Corporal, a position she held for nearly three years.

She was fortunate to have served in a number of Regiments. She was moved across to the 1st Battalion Coldstream Guards, where, as one of the few black people in the Regiment, she served for a further three years. She was honoured to have met Her Majesty, The Queen and her husband, the Duke of Edinburgh, during this period in her service.

Nicolette showed obvious skill and talent in her various roles. So much so, that she was able to achieve further promotion, to the role of Sergeant. She was very proud of this promotion. She was now responsible for soldiers' disciplinary matters, supporting senior commissioned officers by preparing appropriate documentation. This was a significant role as it ensured that appropriate paperwork for those procedures related to conduct, was available to secure its effectiveness. She was additionally, in her role as sergeant, responsible for a team of soldiers; a role she took very seriously.

Meanwhile, she was still a mother, with a wonderful son who needed to have a good education. His schooling was being supported by the military and this proved a comfort to Nicolette, as she carried out her service in the army. She was deeply grateful for this support and is especially proud that her son did very well, going on to complete university successfully.

Nicolette met and married her husband while she was still in service. She became pregnant and following maternity leave, had to make big decisions about her life. With her new status as a married soldier, there would be consequences to the school fees for her son and for where she and her family would live. Her preference would have been for a career break to stabilise her situation, and for her then to continue with the army. In the end, her decision to leave seemed the only way to manage her family life; to be *'present'* with them.

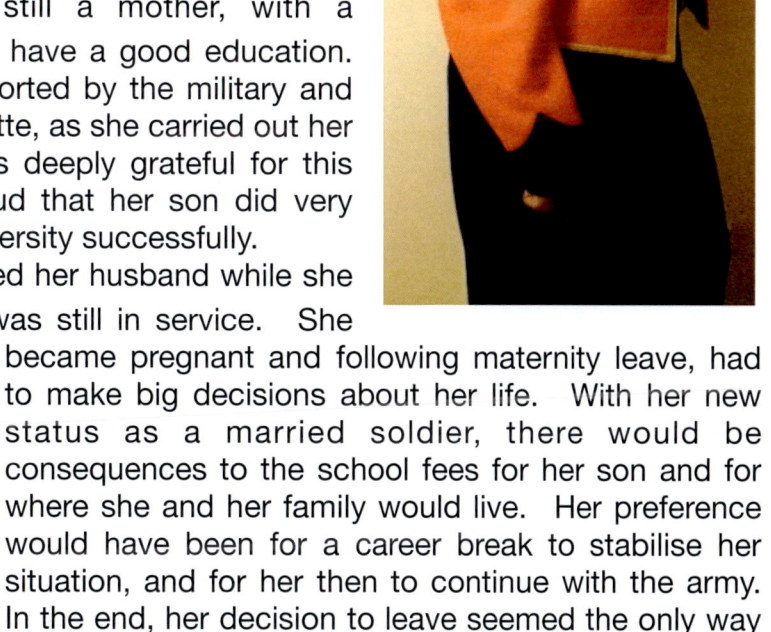

Her husband and son were in South Korea and her daughter was with her. Following her resignation and completion of a year's notice, she was able to join her family in South Korea. They stayed there for several years, travelling and exploring many countries in that time.

Nicolette found herself missing the army very much in that initial period. She believed she could have achieved so much more, including further promotion. These feelings became stronger, the more discussions she had in the various ex-pat groups she met in this new country, South Korea. There she was, without a degree and with feelings of inadequacy that she was not really qualified for anything. She had much more to offer and thus set about tackling the perceived gaps in her knowledge.

She therefore decided to identify ways in which she could gain further qualifications. She took the Association for Accounting Technicians (AAT) exams in Hong Kong to enable her to enter the accountancy field. She is currently in the middle of her higher-level Association of Chartered Certified Accountants (ACCA) studies in the hope of achieving chartered accountant status. With her accountancy studies and initial qualifications, she is very well employed; popular and busy all the time.

Meeting her in her current workplace was a real privilege. Here was a strong, confident woman whose rich, powerful history shone brightly in her eyes. Nicolette knows her worth and is clear about how her contribution helped to make a difference in the work she did in the military.

Sergeant Nicolette Skyers looks back on her time in the Armed Forces, with pride and very few regrets. She knew that she had *"stepped up"* throughout this service, doing everything expected of her; the drills, the skills training, the support to soldiers and the tense, but important involvement in conflict as required.

Overall, being in the army was a positive time in her life. She realises that few people actually know about the service provided by people from her background. This knowledge is often reinforced in conversations she has, in things she reads, as the annual Remembrance Days come around. *"No"*, she says, *"We are not acknowledged"*. That is a great shame.

Corporal Nekesha Thompson

Nekesha grew up in St Catherine, Jamaica. She had joined the Jamaica Defence Force as a medic, serving with them for almost 4 years. She was a 'first responder', an Emergency Medical Technician, providing services similar to a Combat Medical Technician here in the British Army.

While in Jamaica, she knew she wanted more in life and had ambitions to join the British Army. She had met someone who remains an inspiration to her. He is ex-RSM, Owen Bernard. Owen was a huge influence in Nekesha's decision to join the British Army. He really encouraged and supported her and is someone she admires. Indeed, he encouraged her to train in Podiatry, a profession she enjoys today.

Nekesha applied for a British Army place a number of times and was soon successful with her application. She was sent a letter inviting her to come to the UK.

She travelled to the UK and was soon able to take the test in the army's careers' office in Charing Cross. Nekesha passed the required tests and was then able to commence her basic training. Following successful completion of her basic training, she was considered for Phase 2 Trade Training. Her original request was to train either as a nurse or as an Environmental Technician (ET). Interestingly, she was told that she would have to wait for five years before she could train in either of those careers in the army. She was very disappointed as she had been told at the application stage, while she was in Jamaica, that she could do that training. Nevertheless, now she was in the UK, it appears that the five years applied. Instead, she was told that she could train as a Medic and transfer to one of the other career options later on. So, she went forward to train as a Medic.

When Nekesha arrived in the UK and joined the British Army, she found the new country unfamiliar and unwelcoming. Being a stranger in a foreign land, she felt anxious about passing the rigorous tests she was expected to undertake. Although she had some prior experience in the Jamaica Defence Force, she was aware that the British Army was a different ball game. Her determination to succeed and avoid returning home as a failure, pushed her to channel all her energies into excelling at her work. And she succeeded in doing just that.

As a new recruit, she was assigned to a dormitory with other soldiers, with whom she had to establish positive relationships. Being the only black person in her section, she initially felt isolated. However, she soon befriended two other Caribbeans, one from Grenada and the other a Jamaican. She also connected with a Ghanaian colleague from a sub-group during lunchtimes. Nekesha could not help but compare her experiences in the British Army to those she had while in the Jamaica Defence Force. In that force, she had previously been a part of a close-knit community where she enjoyed banter with her Jamaican colleagues. However, in the UK, people were more reserved and distant. She often noticed people's surprise when they met her after only seeing her name, Thompson, in writing, as they typically expected a white person.

She joined the Royal Army Medical Corps (RAMC) firstly at Pirbright for basic training, then on to Phase 2 Trade Training at the Keogh Barracks in Aldershot, as a Private. In her case therefore, the Phase 2 training was the medical training.

The Royal Army Medical Corps (RAMC) is the specialist Corps of the British Army responsible for providing medical services to soldiers and officers in the field, as well as in barracks and hospitals. The Corps has a long and distinguished history, dating back to the late 19th century. It has played a key role in the provision of medical care in all of the major conflicts in which the British Army has been involved.

The RAMC provides a wide range of medical services, including medical and surgical treatment, dental services, veterinary, and mental health support. The Corps also plays a key role in the training of soldiers and officers in medical skills, and has a number of specialist training schools and centres.

The RAMC is made up of a range of different units, including field ambulances, medical Regiments, and specialist medical units. These units are staffed by a combination of regular and reserve soldiers, and are often deployed alongside combat units on operations.

The Corps also has a number of specialist units, including the Defence Medical Services Training Centre, which provides training in medical skills to soldiers and officers; and the Army Medical Services Museum, which tells the story of the Corps and its role in military history.

The RAMC is known for its high standards of medical care and professionalism, and is held in high regard by soldiers and officers across the British Army. Its motto, "In Arduis Fidelis" ("Faithful in Adversity"), reflects the Corps' commitment to providing medical care to soldiers in even the most challenging of circumstances.

When Nekesha joined the British Army, it was as part of the Combat Medical Technicians (CMTs). Her training was similar to that of her male counterparts. CMT training included both military and medical aspects, with an emphasis on providing first aid and medical support in a combat environment.

The training programme lasted around 14 weeks and included both classroom instruction and practical exercises. Nekesha learned about anatomy and physiology, as well as basic and advanced medical procedures such as taking vital signs, administering medications, providing wound care, chest drainage and emergency cricothyroidotomy.

In addition to medical training, Nekesha also received basic infantry training, such as weapons' handling and fieldcraft. She learned how to operate in a combat environment, including how to move and communicate as part of a military unit. She already had some experience in these areas, when she was in Jamaica. Her basic training in the Jamaica Defence Force was six months long. Nekesha describes that training as *"intense, non-sympathetic"*, in the hills of Newcastle and Moneague, at the Military Training ground there. Newcastle is a settlement in the Blue Mountains of Jamaica. It was formerly a military hill station for the British Army and is now a training centre for the Jamaica Defence Force. *"Both males and females had the same training, so no room for the instructors to compromise or feel sympathetic towards the female recruits."*

Back in her new military force in the UK, the aim of her Combat Military Technician (CMT) training was to provide her and her peers with the skills and knowledge they needed to provide medical support in a variety of challenging situations, both on and off the battlefield. When women joined as CMTs, they were expected to meet the same standards of proficiency and fitness as their male colleagues.

After successfully completing her basic six months' Trade Training, Nekesha was fit enough to be selected (one of two females and overall, one of only 5 people) for a first posting to Colchester in a high readiness, fast-paced Regiment. *"You had to be extra fit to support the Paratroopers there"*, she said.

This first posting in Colchester was in the medical unit (16 Medical Regiment), supporting the Paras. All of the soldiers, including Nekesha, were on high readiness, being fit and ready for any eventuality. They drilled, exercised, honed their skills and ensured they were on top form to defend and represent the British Army in the UK and abroad. *"The Colchester Paratrooper Regiment is one of the elite Regiments in the British military hence you have to be fit, confident and competent to join them even if it is to give support as a combat medic."*

While based in Colchester, Nekesha was surprised and delighted to meet a senior NCO, a RSM, Roger Dussard, on an exercise in which her unit and soldiers from other Regiments were participating. To see a black person leading a Regiment was inspirational for this young Medic.

Nekesha's work included participation in public duties such as the Olympic Games in London in 2012. Nekesha and the other military personnel were continually alert, ensuring the safety of members of the public, the Olympians and staff, as well as the thousands of spectators and visitors to the country.

Overall, the breadth and range of her duties contributed to Nekesha's enthusiasm for her work and helped her to feel motivated to learn more, and to see a good future in the army.

In Colchester, Nekesha's talents were recognised by senior officers, including a commander and a sergeant there. Both these men were concerned that she had yet to be promoted, especially as her level of skill was patently high. Nekesha therefore, received her first promotion to Lance Corporal while she was at Colchester. That qualified her for a foreign posting to Germany.

When Nekesha left Colchester, she was posted to Hohne, Germany to provide medical support to a Royal Engineers' Regiment. The Engineers provide military, technical engineering and support with specialisms such as in buildings, building bridges, roads, providing water availability and purification in the fields. Nekesha's role was similar to that she had undertaken as part of the Colchester Medical Regiment, but different, in that at this point, she was one of only three medics responsible for over 400 plus soldiers.

While she was carrying out her work in Germany, Nekesha met two black soldiers from the Lancers. They were sergeants. She did not see any other black people in more senior positions and none at the Regimental Sergeant Major ranks. She was rather surprised and even disappointed by this.

She went to work with the Royal Engineers with the intention for her to join them on tour to a conflict in another country. She did not know anyone in Germany but spent a good deal of time teaching other soldiers about battlefield first aid and making sure each person was medically fit and well prepared before their deployment.

She also ensured she kept up with her fitness and participated fully in all the exercises to keep her soldier skills sharp and always at the ready. In preparation for deployment, Nekesha, as well as other soldiers, were issued with new kits, suitable for their new deployment.

With just weeks before deployment, she was taken off the list to be deployed. She was replaced by another medic (a Caucasian male) who was not in her unit, but was more popularly known. Nekesha was confused and queried the matter at the highest level, but no success.
 She was told that *"during the Medic's skill's assessment on an extremely - minus degree- cold day, one of the assessors was not completely pleased with one of my skills."*

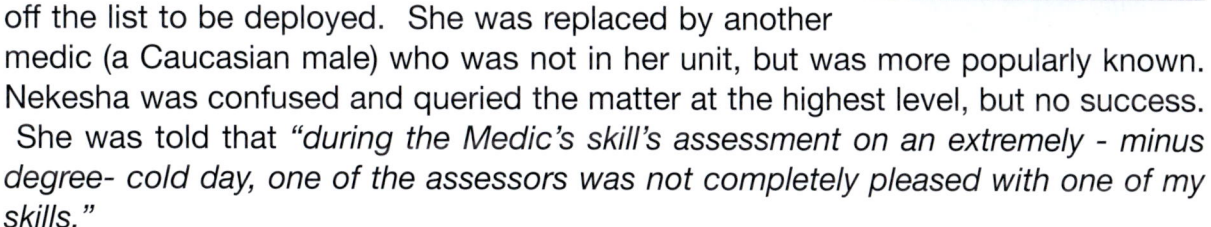

Prior to the assessment, orders had been given by the Officer Commanding that it was not a pass or fail assessment, but more of a skills' refresher day. At the end of the assessment, all soldiers were briefed that they did well and if anyone did not do well, they would have been told already.

Nekesha felt happy therefore, that she had done well. However, a few days later, while conducting her usual morning clinic, she was told by a medical senior that she did not pass the day's assessment and was therefore not able to be deployed. Nekesha pleaded with this medical senior, but the senior was deaf to all her pleas. Nekesha also recalls that her immediate reporting officer tried in many different ways, to get the decision changed; to no avail.

Nekesha felt even worse. She was heartbroken. She felt that she had good relationships with the people with whom she worked. She was surprised in two ways. Firstly, that apparently she had failed the assessment, when it was supposedly a refresher activity and secondly, that she was unable to progress to the deployment. She was the only black Medic in the group and the only person who did the assessment and was not deployed. She still recalls this incident clearly. She has questions that cannot be answered about what she believes to be unjust treatment. *"If my skills were not good enough, how come I was the main Medic teaching and assessing theory and practical (pass or fail) with the soldiers in relation to battlefield first aid before they were deployed on such a tour? How come I am the Medic taking charge of sick parades and other medical duties each day?"*

From that moment, Nekesha felt that this sort of alleged discriminatory treatment towards her, became "normalised", especially so when she joined a new group, such as when on a promotional course or other group activity. In her view, this was even if she had done everything that was expected of her. She still feels aggrieved about these matters.

Nekesha was a good sportswoman. She competed in track events for the army and AMS, getting a bit of a 'name' for herself in relation to wins achieved on the track. She had also achieved Army colours for outstanding achievement in athletics not long after attending the Colchester Regiment.

All Medics, including Nekesha, were subject to annual assessment to ensure that they were in top shape. After completion of these rigorous physical assessments, she still managed to keep positive, smiling even when she was absolutely exhausted.

As a Medic used to more tropical climates, Nekesha was well-placed to provide appropriate support, especially in similar hot climates where she and her colleagues were deployed. She believed that assessments would take her additional experience into account and hopefully the tests would also align to that dimension. Unfortunately, this was not always possible and occasionally, tests were skewed to cold conditions without, in Nekesha's view, allowance for an individual's strengths, climate-wise. As a soldier however, she was aware that conflicts would happen in different locations and climates and so got on with job.

Nekesha was able to support other soldiers in preparing for the hotter areas in which conflicts were taking place at that time. She continued to believe that her work, her level of skill, would still be seen and she would be able to maintain her contribution in the Armed Forces. She provided targeted training and support to others in their readiness regime. She is pleased that those efforts seemed to make a difference to the men and women prior to their deployment to conflicts elsewhere. She felt confident that it helped them in their objective to sustain life and adapt to their challenging, tough, sweaty, dangerous, cold or hot environments. She felt their nervousness, despite the brave faces they adopted. She also prepared herself to be ready if needed, as she too was on notice.

When Nekesha was in Germany, she was sent on duty to Cyprus before returning to Germany. When the soldiers were withdrawn from Germany, Nekesha and the unit then went back to the Catterick Base in the UK.

There were, unfortunately, some issues which were not positive in relationship terms for Nekesha. These soured her time in one particular posting, later on. The issues felt insurmountable at the time, especially as they involved senior people who were in more powerful, influential positions. She felt that there was little that she could do personally, to overcome much of these, as she saw it, *"trials, discrimination and tribulations"*.

Nekesha describes an incident, which troubles her still and where she describes becoming a clear victim of racism. She was called a "black c...t" by a senior who, she alleges, also became physical with her. An altercation developed between herself and the senior. Unfortunately, it all resulted in angry, nasty, racist comments being directed towards Nekesha. That was not the last of it. The whole situation sadly, led to what Nekesha describes as being unjustly charged and fined. She had to take steps, later on, to have the charge reviewed. Fortunately, she was successful in getting the charge overturned and her good name restored, on paper. Nekesha was grateful that this whole matter was cleared from her record. *"I could now apply for an advanced DBS check."* This was a significant action on Nekesha's part. Such a charge would have had long-lasting, career-blocking consequences to her future profession. However, she still feels aggrieved that nothing was said about the alleged assault perpetrated upon her, nor about the racist comments to which she was subjected.

Nekesha reports that soon after the incident, the particular senior with whom she had had the altercation was now posted to Nekesha's Regiment's administrative office. Nekesha was uncomfortable about all of this, especially as she began to feel that she was being segregated and treated differently. It reached a stage where Nekesha felt she had no option but to send a message to the Commanding Officer (CO) about the poor treatment she was experiencing. The CO responded well and a meeting was called to discuss the matter. Sadly, in Nekesha's view, the poor treatment continued, including it seems, when Nekesha applied for DOMCOL, for which she was qualified.

Domiciled Collective Leave (DOMCOL) allows people to visit their country of origin for an extended period of leave, of up to 45 working days (instead of 30 days annual leave allowance) every five years.

Nekesha knew that according to the policy, she qualified for DOMCOL. She wanted to visit Jamaica with the leave to spend time with and care for her sick father. She applied to the administrative office several times over several months and was turned down. Nekesha strongly believed then and still believes, that it was likely that someone in the administrative office may have influenced the decision not to grant her the DOMCOL. Clearly, she has no evidence to that effect, just a strong belief. Nevertheless, having her DOMCOL application turned down stopped her from being able to see and care for her sick father. She did not get the DOMCOL. Months later, she heard that her father was in hospital in Jamaica and she now needed to get there quickly. Sadly, it was while Nekesha was on her flight back to Jamaica, that her dad passed away.

Nekesha is still scarred by what had happened originally, with the senior person. She finds it difficult to forget and to really move on from these events. She knows she has to, however.

Nekesha's Catterick posting was otherwise positive. It was whilst there that Nekesha was promoted, as part of recommendations and reports about her hard work and competence, to the rank of Corporal.

It was not long before she was sent for cold weather exercises and training in Scotland in advance of deployment to a major conflict. She and other soldiers would form part of strategic and defensive work in a key area of conflict.

This first foreign tour lasted the usual six months. Nekesha also provided medical support and training to soldiers and local people in a region of Africa. *"Whilst in Colchester, I was deployed to Afghanistan for six months. I also went to Kenya. When in Germany, I went to Kenya twice with the Royal Engineers."* Nekesha saw this work as significant, especially as it was *"All a part of the military effort to defend my new country in ways that were required of me"*. She was proud to be a part of this national defence organisation – the Army - and felt she could and did represent it well over a decade of service.

Nekesha enjoyed the great majority of her time in the military. She had gained a huge number of skills. She also made great friends. She was a part of a massive army 'family' of soldiers, all involved in a common purpose to which she was also committed. It became increasingly clear that she might have to make a change to her career. She had to forge a different pathway for herself.

Nekesha had at first seen herself completing the full 22 years of army service. However, with countless times of living and working in extremely open, cold conditions, she considered how that might affect her health and military future.

In her first year out, she felt isolated. She did not know any civilians. She had no family in the UK. The army had been like her family. Finding herself on her own was a bit of a culture shock. She was living in a new place and studying to be a Podiatrist. The military was helping her with a part of the costs of her first degree. She was able to secure somewhere to live and worked part-time to cover her living costs. She focused on getting her qualification. She continued with her studying during the Covid Pandemic. She was however, isolated and very lonely; no one to talk to. She found it very difficult to cope.

Nekesha is, fortunately, someone who found the strength to 'dig deep' inside herself and push hard to tackle the darkness of isolation, compounded by the Lockdown and related issues. She has now moved to a different location and is more comfortable. She is in a better place.

A few years ago, she decided to apply for a job in the south of the country. She is now managing jointly her own practice, working predominantly with older people, all of whom are white. She has lovely clients and is enjoying her work. She is somewhat satisfied with her life, but hopes things will improve even further in the future.

Nekesha does miss the camaraderie of army life. She has some regrets. She wishes that she had been a bit more vocal in her own defence at times; speaking up more for herself. She wished she had not been so quiet and reserved all the time. On the other hand, even though she gets frequent flashbacks because of being treated differently in her last years of military life, she would not have missed her military experiences for all the world.

Recently, in 2019, she had the chance to join, at the Cenotaph, other Veterans, a few of whom were black. She really enjoyed the opportunity to be alongside other colleagues and to be recognised as having contributed to Britain's defence. She is immensely proud of her work on our behalf.

Meeting Nekesha in person, during a visit to Jamaica, in April 2023, I observed a person who was remarkable in her humility as a Veteran who had provided good military service to the UK's Armed Forces.

She remains very positive about her military service. She realises that very few people actually know about the service she and many, many others of her heritage had given to the British Army. She feels a bit cheated by this, especially when she hears people, mainly Caucasians, talking about their family serving, exclusive of other Commonwealth people, including those from the Caribbean.

"We have been there! We too have served," she reminds us.

21. The Term 'West Indian'

The term "West Indian" can also be used to refer to individuals from a range of countries and territories in the Caribbean region, including Jamaica, Guyana, Trinidad and Tobago, Barbados, Grenada, St. Vincent, St Kitts, Dominica and others. It is more usual nowadays to refer to West Indians as Caribbeans. As such, there will be other commissioned men and women officers in the UK Armed Forces who are referred to as West Indians, but the point is that their service still often goes unrecognised within our society.

The Term 'Windrush Generation'

While West Indian, Caribbean and Windrush Generation has been used interchangeably, it is important to be clear about the use of the last label that was assigned to thousands of Caribbeans around 2016/17. At that time, there was an outcry about the apparent discrimination towards those people from the Caribbean Islands who believed themselves to be British and therefore entitled to live and work in the United Kingdom. These people were being told that their citizenship was being called into question. Some of them were deported and were unable to access healthcare and pensions, despite having lived in the UK since they were children or had lived here for decades. There were even questions about those who were born here in the UK, to those early settlers.

Several people whose stories are included here, felt disturbed and unsettled by the questioning of their British citizenship, despite being able to prove that they were born under the British Flag during the period before their home Island/colony achieved independence.

Generally speaking, the term 'Windrush Generation' is used to describe those who arrived in 1948 aboard the ship, HMT Empire Windrush. However, it has gone beyond the specifics of that time, to include thousands of men, women and children who left the Caribbean for Britain from the late 1940s to the early 1970s. These Caribbean peoples were motivated by the 1948 British Nationality Act which granted citizenship and right of abode in the UK to all members of the British Empire. The scandal which broke out in 2017 when many had their citizenship status questioned, is not fully settled as there remains cases of disputed citizenship, deportations and failed compensation awards for those who challenged the allegation that they were not entitled to be in the UK. Some of these individuals have even served in the Armed Forces.

There remains an 'air of them being different', perpetuated by reports in the media, which imply and reinforce the view that Caribbeans do not belong in the society in which they have made their homes. The history of their earlier presence here in the UK is largely forgotten or worse, not known.   There were black Roman soldiers, black Tudors, black Jamaicans, such as Francis Williams, who was a scholar and wealthy landowner and whose portrait from 1745, hangs in the Victoria and Albert Museum.

There are many other more recent examples (pre-Windrush), such as Trinidadians, Hazel Scott and the amazing Winifred Atwell, musician, who achieved the first number 1 single "Let's Have Another Party". Winifred's life story was heard on Desert Island Discs in 1952. Who remembers or even knows about these people? There are many others too. Alongside these Veterans, we must take a bit more time to strengthen our knowledge and enrich our understanding of the real history of a diverse United Kingdom, where everyone would feel very much a part and whose contributions are properly valued.

22. Ongoing Risks for Caribbean Veterans

There are particular issues faced by Caribbean personnel who served in the British Armed Forces. These include difficulties accessing services due to perceived language barriers, or a lack of understanding by those providing the services about the Veterans' cultural backgrounds and experiences. Additionally, Caribbean Veterans may face discrimination when seeking employment due to racial prejudice.

There are, however, many support services available to Caribbean ex-servicemen and ex-servicewomen. These include the British Legion, Combat Stress and Help for Heroes, all of which would provide financial assistance, counselling and advice on employment opportunities. Unfortunately, many Veterans feel unable to seek that assistance, often because of embarrassment about 'begging'. Additionally, many local authorities should also provide specific services tailored towards the needs of Veterans from minority backgrounds. Veterans do not believe that support is explicit or communicated effectively, so they feel unsupported and abandoned.

There are many small but concrete examples which demonstrate the potential effectiveness of some of these support services. A few Veterans have been able to access counselling assistance, which has helped them to cope with post-traumatic stress disorder. Additionally, in recent years, Help for Heroes has provided employment opportunities for Veterans from minority backgrounds through its 'Hidden Wounds' project. More needs to be done. Better and more effective support is required to help these ex-servicemen and women whose service was freely and loyally given and utilised in times of conflict. It is clear that both white and black Veterans have been failed in receiving this support.

Serving in the British Armed Forces and Application for British Citizenship

Ex-servicemen and women from the Caribbean can get British citizenship after they end their service with the British Armed Forces. Under current UK immigration rules, those who have served in the Armed for at least three years are now eligible to apply for Indefinite Leave to Remain (ILR), which will allow them to live and work in the UK on a permanent basis. After 12 months of holding ILR status, individuals may then be eligible to apply for naturalisation as British citizens. However, according to a 2017 report from the Ministry of Defence, only around 10% of Caribbean personnel who served in the Armed between 1965 and 1990 were granted British citizenship.

23. Recognition and Honouring

The thousands of men and women who hail from the Caribbean, either by heritage or birth, have provided between them thousands of years of military service in many conflicts, wars and within British peacekeeping efforts across many countries. They have had that service go unrecognised and seemingly unappreciated.

It is wonderful to see programmes such as 'Fresh Cuts' being televised on the ITV1 Channel late on a Sunday night in October, 2023, covering the story of Ex-Marine, Ben McBean. He describes his experience of being in the British Armed Forces and finding out more about the service and sacrifice of other black soldiers and male and female veterans past and present, who he knew little or nothing about.

They are decent, loyal subjects whose fierce defence of the Crown and Country is deserving of equal praise. That expectation is one we should all fulfil, individually and as a society.

These brave men and women do not expect more than being shown the respect and recognition given to their white colleagues who also served. Caribbeans have been here all along, have served the nation. They have known each day that they could be making the ultimate sacrifice and yet most of them have been forgotten. It is all about a just and equal treatment. Nothing more.

We honour and thank these British Caribbean Veterans, each and every one of them.

Photo by Gill Shaw

ABOUT THE AUTHOR

Rose Johnson is a proud British Caribbean woman with a passion for collecting the stories of the people from the Islands.

She was an educator and charity leader, working at all levels of the system including headship, inspection, chief officer and chief executive. She provides coaching, mentoring and consultant support to senior managers. She is sister and cousin to Veterans from the British Armed Forces.

This is her third book. The first two, **"Breaking Through Racist Clouds"** and **"Windrush Women of Courage"** records the experiences of a range of Caribbean people, young and old as they tell their stories as they experienced them, warts and all.

Rose loves the beautiful words and pulsing rhythms of Caribbean people. She is committed to sharing their voices with others. She hopes that by you taking this third Book journey with her, you will be able to see what these amazing ex-servicemen and women have done on behalf of **all** of us.